# DEVON AND CORNWALL RECORD SOCIETY

New Series, Vol. 30

*Frontispiece:* Seal of Launceston priory attached to Prior Robert Fissacre's charter to the lepers of Gillemartin. For details of this grant see Introduction, note 52.

DEVON & CORNWALL RECORD SOCIETY

New Series, Vol. 30

# THE CARTULARY
# OF LAUNCESTON
# PRIORY

(Lambeth Palace MS. 719)

*A Calendar*

Edited with an Introduction by

## P. L. HULL

1987

ISBN O 901853 30 5

*Printed for the Society by*
THE DEVONSHIRE PRESS LTD.
TORQUAY
ENGLAND

# CONTENTS

# ABBREVIATIONS

Blake   D. W. Blake, 'The Church of Exeter in the Norman Period'. (Unpublished MA thesis, University of Exeter, 1970)
*Book of Fees   The Book of Fees*, 3 vols., PRO, 1920–31
Cartulary   The cartulary of Launceston priory, Lambeth Palace MS. 719
*Cornwall FF.i   Cornwall Feet of Fines* (Devon and Cornwall Record Society) vol. i, 1195–1377, ed. J. H. Rowe 1914
*CPR   Calendars of Patent Rolls*
Delisle, *Recueil*   Delisle, Léopold and Berger, Elie (eds.), *Recueil des actes de Henri II* . . . 4 vols. (Paris 1909–27)
DB.   Domesday Book, vol. iv (Exeter Domesday) Record Commission edition, 1816
*D & C N & Q   Devon and Cornwall Notes and Queries*
D C R S   Devon and Cornwall Record Society
*Devon FF. i and ii   Devon Feet of Fines* (Devon and Cornwall Record Society), vol. i, 1196–1272, ed. O. J. Reichel 1912; vol. ii, 1272–1369, ed. O. J. Reichel, F. B. Prideaux and H. Tapley-Soper 1939
*EHR   English Historical Review*
EPNS   English Place-Name Society
Eyre of 1201   D. M. Stenton (ed.) *Pleas before the King or his Justices*, vol. ii (1952) (Selden Society vol. LXVIII, 'The Cornish Eyre 1201', pp. 30–225).
*Heads of Religious Houses*   Dom David Knowles, C.N.L. Brooke and Vera London (eds.), *The Heads of Religious Houses: England and Wales 940–1216* (Cambridge 1972)
Henderson   MS. transcript of the cartulary of Launceston priory by Charles Henderson: Henderson MSS. vol. 32, Royal Institution of Cornwall, Truro
*HMC Report   Historical Manuscripts Commission Report*
*JRIC   Journal of the Royal Institution of Cornwall*
Maclean, *Trigg Minor*   Sir John Maclean, *Parochial and Family History of the Deanery of Trigg Minor*, 3 vols, 1868, 1876, 1879
*Mon. Dioc. Exon.*   G. Oliver, *Monasticon Diocesis Exoniensis*, 1846 (supplement 1854)
Morey   Adrian Morey, *Bartholomew of Exeter, Bishop and Canonist* (Cambridge 1937)
Oliver, *Lives*   G. Oliver, *Lives of the Bishops of Exeter* (Exeter 1861)
PRO   Public Record Office
*Red Book (of the Exchequer)*   Ed. H. Hall, Rolls Series, 3 vols., 1897
*Regesta (ii & iii)   Regesta Regum Anglo-Normannorum 1066–1154.* Vol. ii, 1100–35, *Regesta Henrici Primi*, ed. C. Johnson and H. A. Cronne, Oxford 1956. Vol. iii, 1136–54, *Regesta Stephani* . . ., ed. H. A. Cronne and R. H. C. Davis, Oxford 1968
*Rot. Litt. Claus.   Rotuli Litterarum Clausarum in Turri Londinensi asservati*, ed. T. D. Hardy, 2 vols., Record Commission, 1833 and 1844
Round, *CDF   Calendar of Documents Preserved in France, 918–1206*, ed. J. H. Round, 1899
Sincock   William Sincock, 'Principal Landowners in Cornwall . . . 1165' and 'Cornish Landowners *circa* 1200', pp. 150–75, *JRIC* vol. x, pt. 1 (1890)
Soulsby   I. N. Soulsby, 'The Fiefs in England of the Counts of Mortain, 1066–1106'. (Unpublished MA thesis, University of Wales, 1974)
*Trans. Devon. Assoc.   Transactions of the Devonshire Association*
*TRHS   Transactions of the Royal Historical Society*
*VCH   Victoria County History*
Watkin   Hugh R. Watkin, *The History of Totnes Priory & Medieval Town, Devonshire, together with the sister priory of Tywardreath, Cornwall.* 2 vols., Torquay 1914 and 1917, + index vol., 1917

# INTRODUCTION

## THE MANUSCRIPT

The cartulary of Launceston priory went to Lambeth Palace Library when Thomas Tennison was archbishop (1695–1715) and was given the reference Cod. Tennison 719, or as it is now known, Lambeth Palace MS. 719. A preliminary page of the MS. records[1] that one William Griffith[2] bought the cartulary in London, *nec pretio minimo* in 1678.[3]

William Griffith was not the first owner. The words *liber Johannis Legh* occur on the inside of the last leaf of the cartulary, a name not otherwise known. Thomas Tanner[4] states that it was in the possession of Richard Escott of Launceston and Lincoln's Inn and M. R. James thought that this was possible. According to Mr R. Walker, the librarian of Lincoln's Inn, two men of that name were admitted to Lincoln's Inn in the seventeenth century. Richard Escott, son of a gentleman of Launceston of the same name, was admitted 6 November 1613 and called to the Bar on 14 November 1640.[5] On 23 February 1640 Richard Escott, son and heir of Richard, late of Launceston, deceased, was admitted.

It is clear that the Escotts (or Estcotts as they are called in the registers of St Mary Magdalene, Launceston) were settled in Devon in medieval times and were armigerous. In Launceston they were a family of substance. A Richard Escott was a member of Parliament for Newport in 1624 and 1625, and for Launceston in 1626 and 1628.[6] Unfortunately, the two Richard Escotts cannot be identified in a printed pedigree[7] nor with the registers,[8] though one of them was the son of Richard Escott (of Launceston's) second marriage on 5 August 1593. This son Richard was baptised 8 July 1596 and Vivian gives his wife's name as Alice Brett. Richard had a nephew called Richard who was born in 1614 and had died by 28 October 1656. He was the grandson of Richard Escott (senior's) first marriage. As Richard Escott senior was probably too old to have been a lawyer *c*.1620, the owner of the cartulary was possibly his son Richard who may also have been the M.P. He could have had a son Richard, the second Escott mentioned in the (?confused) record at Lincoln's Inn, who was not born, or rather baptised, at Launceston.

---

[1](Preliminary) folio 1. (Modern folio numbers are cited throughout).

[2]For whom see Venn's *Alumni Cantabrigienses* sub verbo.

[3]Mr E. G. W. Bill, the present librarian at Lambeth, informed me that a number of Griffith's MSS. went to that library, citing the catalogues of Todd (1812) and M. R. James (1932).

[4]*Notitia Monastica* (1744), 68n.

[5]Mr Walker thought he 'may have been the Richard Escourt who was elected a Bencher on 16 November 1648 and held office as Keeper of the Black Book in 1659'.

[6]W. P. Courtney, *The Parliamentary Representation of Cornwall to 1832*, 364. Richard Estcott's colleague at Newport in 1625 was Sir John Eliot.

[7]J. L. Vivian, *Visitations of Cornwall* (1887), 158–9.

[8]Register of St Mary Magdalene, Launceston, Cornwall County Record Office DDP. 118/1/1.

The cartulary has been described and collated by M. R. James[9] and noted by Dr Godfrey Davies.[10] It is written entirely on paper in one fifteenth-century hand, and a few grants squeezed in at the foot of two folios in a later fifteenth-century hand which also appears (carelessly written) on seven other folios. The latest dated grant in the cartulary is dated 3 March 1441.[11] A few later documents have been included but all of these are in the careless and later hand already noted.[12] The scribe of the cartulary, as Charles Henderson noticed, may have been one Thomas Bank whose name appears in the scroll decoration of an initial letter.[13] Some 40 per cent of the documents in the cartulary are of fourteenth-century date, only about 10 per cent belonging to the fifteenth-century;[14] approximately 38 per cent are dated or (mostly) undated documents of the thirteenth century, with dated and undated twelfth-century charters and the two of 1050 and 1076 making the remaining 12 per cent.

In the same hand which records William Griffith's purchase of the cartulary[15] there are some preliminary pages of miscellaneous notes on the priory including the name of the first prior, Theoricus, *natione Normannus*.[16] This name occurs on the reverse side of what appears to be the original vellum cover of the cartulary: the front of this cover bears the words, *Regestrum Munimentorum*. After three blank leaves following the end of the cartulary on f.236, there are directions in a seventeenth-century hand, 'I praye you place the loose sheets where you would have them & send y[tt] to morrow if you can or I will call Thursday morninge for this booke is very unperfytt.' This would appear to be a direction to the binder and seems to mean that the original binding had become imperfect with folios which had become detached, unless it means that not all of the cartulary was bound.

The vellum cover now included in the preliminary pages of the binding was probably the original cover of some or all of the quires which constitute the cartulary. The cartulary was re-bound in the seventeenth century, most likely for William Griffith and the old boards were then covered. The spine was re-backed at Lambeth Palace library in the 1960s.[17] The late seventeenth-century binder cropped or cut off some of the original numbering of the folios. The bound manuscript is large quarto in size, measuring 29.9 cm. by 21 cm., with the paper folios a little smaller.[18] Dr Davis gives the total number of folios as 236+vii, though

[9]*Catalogue of MSS. at Lambeth Palace* (1932), 797–9.

[10]*Medieval Cartularies of Great Britain* (1958), 6.

[11]Cartulary no. 328. (Hereafter nos. 1–600 always refer to the numbers given to the documents in the cartulary. For the later hand squeezed at foot of pages, see ff.182r. and 198v. See also ff.132v., 133r., 176v., 232r.–236r.

[12]e.g. nos. 595–6 (1491 and 1494) and nos. 599–600 (1495 and 1477). No. 492 (1451–2).

[13]For Thomas Bank see also no. 118. He also appears on f.137 of the Register of Launceston Priory, Bodl. MS. Tanner 196, cited on p. 37 of Henderson's calendar no. 38 at the Royal Institution of Cornwall, Truro.

[14]Cf. Davis, *Medieval Cartularies*, 6.

[15]Above, p. vii.

[16]Griffith's notes on the cartulary also occur in British Library, Lansdowne MS. 939, ff.20b–21. Theoricus does not occur in the cartulary itself. Presumably he could have been the first prior of the regular canons *c*.1127.

[17]Ex. inf. the librarian.

[18]E.g. f.39 is 28.3 by 20 cm., but the latter is approximate because of the paper taken up in the binding.

some are blank.[19] Documents are given in full for the most part with a heading in black letter script.

The first folio of the cartulary is missing and it begins on the second[20] in the middle of Edward the Confessor's charter uniting the sees of Devon and Cornwall. Thereafter follow the foundation charters and grants etc. relating to the *matrix ecclesia*, then documents about the *capella Magdalena*, followed by some of the charters of the priory's manor of Launceston Land.[21] After that the documents follow in topographical blocks to each of which a separate black letter title is given.[22]

The modern folios (in pencil) 7 to 35 are numbered in roman figures iii to xxxi.[23] From folio 36 the original foliation is in arabic numerals.[24] As far as modern f.75 the original folio numbers continue (from 36) to 72 (arabic). Henderson thought folios 76 and 78 out of place, assigning f.76 to 'nearer f.123'[25] and he stated that f.78 should be placed between folios 229–30.[26] He also thought that folios 123–132 – grants etc. relating to properties in St Stephens by Launceston and Newport – originally formed a separate book. The foliation is further complicated by the fact that at (modern) folio 77 an extra series of modern arabic numerals begins. For example, folios 77–9 are numbered 5–7 on the corners of the folios. In places all three numbers appear together, e.g. folio 86 is ancient f.81 plus a new arabic number 14. Sometimes the new arabic numbers do not appear; occasionally the medieval folio number is missing. The extra modern arabic numbers which occur are 5–11, 14, 17–20, 22–3, 25–33, covering folios 77–106 and the original folios numbered 80 to 101, the latter with some omissions. New arabic folios 34–7 correspond with modern folios 124–6. From folio 127 to the end of the cartulary there are no medieval numbers. A solitary arabic number 38 appears on modern folio 135, and thereafter to folio 236 (the end of the cartulary) the numbers are modern and (as throughout) in pencil.

No definite conclusions can be reached from this. It is known that the binding was 'very imperfect' when the cartulary was bound. The extra numbers in arabic may have been intended as a help to the binder. Part of the cartulary may have been in loose separate books or quires, though there is no sure evidence. The disappearance of the older foliations after modern f.135 is no argument for separate books before that folio nor necessarily their cessation after it. The evidence of the old oak boards suggests a medieval (fifteenth or early sixteenth-century) binding, and, as has been mentioned, these boards were used again for the later seventeenth-century rebinding.

[19]i.e. ff.68v., 134 (followed by 7 blank leaves), 152, 164r. A folio after 178v. is missing. 2½ inches of the text (from *demanda seculari . . . videlicet*) have been cut out of f.156r. (no. 396).

[20]Modern folio 6. This 'second' folio bears an arabic numeral 2.

[21]There is a useful list of contents with folio references in Henderson's transcript, see note 33.

[22]e.g. *incipit registrum de Biestwey.*

[23]Henderson reported ancient f.xxviii missing but this is not so.

[24]See C. Johnson and H. Jenkinson, *English Court Hand . . .* Part I (Oxford 1915), 73–4, especially the printed table of arabic numerals which are fourteenth-century examples.

[25]See nos. 172–6 and 302–4.

[26]See nos. 179–181 and 584–9. Some of Henderson's statements comparing modern and medieval foliation are only approximately correct because of missing medieval folio numbers. But the sequence and concurrence of the two sets of numbers is generally clear.

Most folios have a reference on the top right hand corner of the page, e.g. *De Dudston* on f.97r., to provide a ready reference to a charter relating to Dutson in St Stephens by Launceston.[27] There are some thirty marginal notes in the cartulary in the hand of the main scribe. For example, a marginal note on f.16r. reads *M.ᵈ quod exemplum istarum libertatum scribitur in 100 folio a capite istius registri.* This links f.16r. with f.105r.–v. and provides a useful cross-reference from cartulary no. 24 to no. 264. Sometimes a more elaborate reference occurs as on f.34v.: *M.ᵈ quod placita de Twichen scribuntur in primo folio quinti quaterni istius regestri et in sequent' in 98 folio capite.* This links nos. 74 and 261 of the cartulary. Occasionally a marginal note adds a statement of fact as on f.35v.: *Memorandum quod ad peticionem Johel Dawbene domini de Faweton de terra de Trebennek videlicet consilio prioris et conventus quod tenetur in pura et perpetua elemosina extra feodum predicti domini Johel.*[28] It must be admitted that the arithmetic of cross-referencing does not always work out, though a marginal note about two grants concerning Tresmeer gives a folio reference for the first, as well as the number of folios ahead where the second charter is to be found, and this note makes sense.[29] On f.180r. (cartulary no. 456) there is a reference that the end of a plea concerning the advowson of Talland *est in vij folio precedente*, but no further reference to this plea can be found.[30] A note on f.141v. refers to the pyx or deed-box where grants relating to Treworgie in St Gennys were kept.[31]

In 1875 Sir John Maclean issued a printed prospectus for his projected publication of his *Registrum Munimentorum Prioratus Launcestonensis*, an edition which was to be limited to 250 ordinary and 25 large-paper copies. At least one copy of the prospectus survives[32] which shows that publication depended on a sufficient number of subscriptions. Obviously there were not enough. Charles Henderson made a transcript of the cartulary in June 1926 in the record time of 59 hours. His transcript is a mixture of abbreviated and full texts, at times in English, at others in Latin (or a mixture of both). Although it was more of a calendar than a full text, it was not transcribed with publication in view. Henderson's transcript has been extremely useful for this edition of the cartulary. His transcript of the Register of the priory has also been helpful.[33]

---

[27]No. 237.

[28]See no. 78. Cf. no. 315, *deficit hic relaxacio Jo. Mason de eodem tenemento.* A note in latin in what appears to be a seventeenth-century hand on the fairs of the borough of Newport which is contained on a small square of paper bound in between ff.43 and 44 has no relevance to its position.

[29]Nos. 201 and 225. No. 225 is on original folio 88, the folio number cited in the note to no. 201 (which is on ancient folio 80). As no. 225 extends to ancient f.89, the note, *in 88 folio istius registri a capite viz. in ix f. sequente*, makes a reasonably good reference. Note the similar cross-reference by marginal note between no. 225 and no. 289.

[30]The marginal note, of course, refers to the original foliation.

[31]No. 352: *quod dampnum iacet in pixide de Treworgy.*

[32]Royal Institution of Cornwall, Gatley MS., f.37. See also Boase and Courtney, *Bibliotheca Cornubiensis* iii (1882), 973. In 1909 Otho Peter advocated the Royal Institution of Cornwall raising 'a sufficient sum' for a more complete abstract of the cartulary than he had made. See *JRIC* xvii, pt. 3 (1909), 372. See also Alfred F. Robbins, 'The Muniments of Launceston Priory' in *Devon and Cornwall Notes and Gleanings*, iii (32) (1890), 125.

[33]Henderson MSS., R.I.C., vol. 32. For Henderson's notes on the Register of Launceston Priory, see note 13, above.

## THE CASTLE AND THE PRIORY (A SUMMARY)

Sometime after *c*.1075/6, when Count Robert of Mortain was granted the 'earldom'of Cornwall, he constructed, or continued the construction of,[34] a castle on the hill-top of Dunheved, 'across the river Kensey from the Saxon town of Launceston St Stephen'.[35] Domesday Book records that he moved the market on Sundays from the old town to his new castle. The new castle must have compelled most of the inhabitants of St Stephens to move to the protection of Dunheved, the 'new Launceston'.[36] Professor Beresford shows that a third borough developed on the north bank of the river Kensey between the old and new towns in the suburb of Newport.[37] Dunheved or 'new' Launceston town 'was walled from the early thirteenth century and gated to form a common defence with the castle to which it formed an outer bailey and from which it takes its shape'.[38]

There was a college of secular priests at St Stephens before the Conquest and in the 1120s Bishop William Warelwast of Exeter converted this into a foundation for regular (or Augustinian) canons, culminating in the foundation charter of 1127. In 1140 the priory, then at St Stephens church, suffered the destruction of the tower of the priory church by Reginald de Dunstanville, earl of Cornwall and his father-in-law, for which Reginald was excommunicated and for which both Reginald and William made amends: an almost forgotten episode of the civil war in King Stephen's reign.[39] A new priory was built at the ford over the river Kensey, close to the chapel (now the church) of St Thomas by Launceston, and the move to the new site was most probably made on 7 February 1155.[40] The castle had its own chapel – the *capella castelli* – a moiety of which was granted to the priory. There is a reference to it as 'the parish of the chapel' in 1291 and in the following century the *capella Magdalena* had moved away from the castle into the town.[41]

Count Robert's seizure of the canons' market and the dominance of the castle was a hard blow to the dean and canons, even if they received a compensation of twenty shillings yearly from the reeve of the castle,[42] the empty promise of the 'privilege' of a 'free borough', and (eventually) the moiety of the *capella castelli*.[43] Domesday book bears other evidence of Robert Mortain's despoliation: the same thing happened, for example, at St Germans where the (secular) canons' market was moved to Robert's castle of Trematon.[44] Launceston castle dominated the priory as it still towers above the scanty remains today.

[34]For Robert of Mortain's exchange of two Devonshire manors with the Bishop of Exeter for Dunheved castle, see Finberg, *D. & C. N. & Q* xxiii, 123.
[35]M. Beresford, *New Towns of the Middle Ages* (1967), 405.
[36]Loc. cit. See also Henderson, *Cornish Church Guide*, 180.
[37]Beresford, loc. cit.
[38]Ibid. The best account of Launceston castle (following the author's excavations of recent years) is contained in A.D. Saunders, *Launceston Castle* (Historic Buildings and Monuments Commission, 1984).
[39]See below, pp. xvii–xx.
[40]See below, p. xvi, n. 84. Henderson, *Cornish Church Guide*, 113, wrongly dates the move to 1136.
[41]See below, p. xxi.
[42]See no. 11, a charter of Earl Reginald which refers back to Robert of Mortain's time.
[43]No. 27, a charter of Earl Reginald.
[44]DB. Exon. (1816), f.200.

Count Robert of Mortain's charter of 1076 to the dean and canons of St Stephens by Launceston was partly, if not wholly, a confirmation of existing endowments.[45] The charter seems to be genuine: the indiction is correct and the Count's first wife (Matilda) is mentioned. It is not witnessed, but nearly all the place-names can be identified as land possessed at a later date by the priory. The date is correct and supports the probability that Count Robert did not succeed Count Brian of Brittany in Cornwall until *c*.1075–6, because of Count Brian's likely involvement in the Breton (or earls') rebellion against King William in 1075).[46] There is no agreement between the size of the priory's holdings in the Exeter Domesday book and the evidence of the charter of Count Robert in 1076.[47] As will be seen,[48] lands were taken from the canons and the question has been asked, had Lawhitton been taken from the canons before the Conquest? [49] Launceston was only one of the parishes given by King Egbert to the see of Sherborne in 838. The others were South Petherwin with its dependancy of Trewen and the parishes of Lezant and Lawhitton, which, with St Stephens by Launceston, constituted the later episcopal peculiar of Lawhitton. This was established by H. P. R. Finberg,[50] who later showed that the episcopal estate of Lawhitton passed to the sees of Sherborne, Crediton and St Germans in turn, but by 1066 Launceston (i.e. St Stephens) had become detached from the episcopal manor of Lawhitton, for the Exeter Domesday refers to the manor of Launceston being held by Earl Harold T.R.E.[51]

Exeter Domesday shows that the lands of the canons of St Stephens totalled four hides and that the manor was worth £4 yearly, and £8 yearly

---

[45]The charter of 1076 (no. 3) mentions *octo mansas terre et dimidiam et v acras . . . quas prius habuerat*, followed soon afterwards by a list of place-names. Here the main total of lands are considered. For the places where the properties lay, see below, pp. xxiv–xxvii.

[46]For the rebellion of 1075 and Count Robert's investment with Earl Brian's lands, see Soulsby, 61–2. In view of this evidence and that the Norman colonisation of England took several years to complete (Soulsby, 56–7), I accept the fact that *c*.1070 is too early for Count Robert's grant of St Michel's Mount to the Norman abbey of Mont St Michel (see my edition of the *Cartulary of St Michael's Mount* no. 1 and Soulsby, 41, note). In that charter the dating elements support a date of 1076 which is too late for some of the witnesses: see Hull, op. cit. xiii–xvi. The words *postea autem* of *Cart. St M.M.* nos. 1 and 2 make an earlier and later date possible for the grant to Mont St Michel, i.e. *c*.1070 and 1076, though Count Robert cannot have been able to implement the grant before 1076.

[47]The charter shows approximately 6½ hides in the Launceston area, whereas DB. Exon. shows that the canons had 4 hides in and near Launceston. See below, pp. xii–xiii n.

[48]Below, p. xiii.

[49]See Canon Thomas Taylor, *The Celtic Christianity of Cornwall* (1916), 153, where it is stated that Lawhitton had been given to the new see of Crediton in 909.

[50]In. *D. & C. N. & Q.*, xxiii, pt. iv (1947), 123.

[51]H. P. R. Finberg, 'Sherborne, Glastonbury and the Expansion of Wessex' in *TRHS*, 5th ser. iii (1953), passim. Canon Doble's plea (*St Patern* (1940), 42) that Launceston 'seems to have been a fortified residence of the kings of Dumnonia' on the evidence of St Constantine and his father St Patern (patron of N. and S. Petherwin) cannot be accepted. There is nothing to connect Constantine with St Stephens by Launceston. There is no evidence of a 'fortified residence' at St Stephens and if Dunheved began as an Anglo-Saxon fortification for which there is no real evidence, the derivation of the word is only the English word 'Downhead', see Oliver Padel in *Old Cornwall* viii, no. 10, 482–4. Count Robert obtained 'the Castle of Cornwall' from the Bishop of Exeter, but though this was Dunheved castle, Robert may have constructed it anew. See note 34.

when Count Robert received it.[52] This reduction of the value of the canons' lands could mean an abstraction of land, like the three manors which belonged to their manor of Pendrym (1 hide) T.R.E., but which had been taken away from them.[53]

The evidence of the charter of 1076 shows that 8½ *mansiones* (manors) and 5 acres was the canons' endowment which Count Robert confirmed.[54] The secular college had 4 hides and 3 acres; 26 free men had 21 acres, and the *cervesarii* (who presumably paid ale-rents) and the serfs had 2¾ and 2 acres which they cultivated with the ploughs of the community of the college. These figures make a total of 6¾ hides and 26 acres. Adding up the sizes of lands named and detailed in the text of the charter only amounts to 6¼ hides and 25 acres.[55] The canons are stated to have eight burgesses whose Saxon names are given. The name of the dean of the college was Robert: he had six manors (*mansiones*). His successors (? and he himself) were given for their prebend the tithes of grain rents, cheese, lambs, deer calves, foals, pigs and gabelle, 'except for two parts of the grain rents, cheeses and pigs of Liskeard and a third part of grain rents and cheeses'. The five secular canons had as their prebends the five *mansiones* of Rillaton in Linkinhorne, Fawton in St Neot, *Tiguarnel* (manor of Tywarnhayle),[56] Helston (presumably Helston in Trigg) and Treglastan (probably the manor of Treglasta in Altarnun and Davidstow).

## THE FOUNDATION OF THE AUGUSTINIAN PRIORY OF LAUNCESTON

When were canons regular introduced at Launceston? The foundation

---

[52]F.206(b). (*VCH . . . Cornwall Domesday*, 72(b)). For Count Robert's predecessor as 'earl of Cornwall' (in fact, if not in title), see D. C. Douglas, *William the Conqueror* (1964), 267. See also James Tait in *EHR* xlix (January 1929), 86, citing Prior Robert Fissacre's charter to the lepers of Gillemartin from R. and O. B. Peter, *History of Launceston*, 39. The text of this charter is printed from the original (a fine charter with the priory seal which survives among the Launceston borough MSS.) by Oliver, *Mon. Dioc. Exon.*, 25. The witnesses show that it may be dated between 22 October 1245 (election of Bishop Richard Blund) and before 13 January 1257 when Earl Richard was elected King of the Romans: N. Denholm-Young, *Richard of Cornwall* (1947), 89. Tait did not cite the relevant part of the text: the old tenement which the lepers had in Launceston before they moved to Gillemartin is said to have been enfeoffed to them by Earl Brian of Cornwall, *de quo comes Brian Corn(ubie) ipsos quondam feoffavit.*

[53]The three manors taken from Pendrym are given in the Exchequer Domesday as Bonyalva, Bucklawren and Bodigga. See *Domesday Book: Cornwall* (ed. C. and T. Thorn from the translation of Oliver Padel, 1979), p. 120(b) and they occur in their 'Domesday' forms in DB. (Exon) (1816), f.101(b), p. 93. The derivations given of the three manors in *VCH: Cornwall Domesday*, 65(b) are incorrect. The *Inquisitio Geldi* (*VCH: Cornwall Domesday*, 62) shows that 'St Stephen' had 2½ hides in the hundred of Rillaton. The sense of DB. Exon (1816), f.73 (p. 66) shows that these 2½ hides were in demesne. This land may have constituted part of the prebends of the secular canons, see below, p. xxi.

[54]No. 3. A moiety of the 8½ *mansiones* and 5 acres were said to be *vestita*, the other moiety was waste (*vasta*).

[55]There are some obscurities, cf. *et harum terrarum iiij hydas et acri* (sic) *iacent in omnium fratrum communitate* with *et iiij hydas et iij acros habent ipsi canonici in sua proprietate sicut in subsequentibus dividam* (sic). I have not counted the 4 hides twice but only used the 4 hides and 3 acres once.

[56]In the parishes of Perranzabuloe and St Agnes.

charter of Bishop William Warelwast[57] bears the date of 1127.[58] King Henry I's confirmation of Bishop William's introduction of regular canons is dated by the editors of the second volume of the *Regesta* as 'between April and May, 1121 at Winchester'.[59] This could mean that the introduction of regular canons at Launceston could have been as early as 1121, a point stressed by C. Johnson and H. A. Cronne, though they admit that Henry I's charter could be the same date as *Regesta* (ii), no. 1486, i.e. 1127 (May 22?) Winchester. This charter[60] refers to the canons regular already constituted at Launceston and the gift to them by King Henry I of the portion and alms of his chapel in the castle there which Bernard and Hamelin the priest held.[61] The introduction of regular canons may well have taken a few years to complete, culminating in the foundation charter of 1127.

The text of Henry I's first charter confirming the foundation of a priory of canons regular (cartulary no. 4), addressed to Bishop Warelwast and Dean Ralph, states that the prebends of deceased canons and the goods of the church in the Bishop's hand were to be applied to the commons of the canons regular. Canons who wished to become regular canons might hold their prebends for life and no one was to molest them. Johnson and Cronne give an entirely opposite reason: any of the former canons who do not accept the new rule may retain their prebends for life.[62] The full text reads:[63]

> Ego eciam volo et concedo ut canonicos eiusdem ecclesie qui ad ordinem regulare converti voluerint, prebendas suas et quod ad eas pertinet habere in pace quamdiu vixerint.

At first sight the reading *noluerint* might appear to make better sense: Dean Ralph was granted his prebend and certain lands for life for his commons when he resigned his deanery on account of age at some time between 1128 and 1131.[64] His case was special, however, and the wording of the text is clear: *voluerint*. Canons who wished to become regular canons might hold their prebends for life.

Bishop Warelwast's charter gives no solid information about the foundation except to state that he had constituted canons regular of the rule of St Augustine in the church of St Stephen of Launceston and endowed them with the lands and rents of St Stephens.[65] William Warelwast founded Augustinian priories at Launceston, Plympton and

---

[57] No. 5.

[58] The date of 1127 is in the text of the charter. See J. C. Dickinson, *The Origins of the Austin Canons* (1950), 113 note 7.

[59] No. 4; *Regesta* ii, no. 1281.

[60] No. 28 in the cartulary.

[61] *Regesta* ii, no. 1486. (Note the editors' amendment of *Bern(ardus) et presbiter Hamelinus*. Bernard the Scribe (below, p. xv) held land *in castello* and land between the well and the chapel of the castle before 1123 and earlier than 1130: see Round, *EHR* lv, 418, 420.

[62] *Regesta* ii, no. 1281 and full text (n. cxxxvi) on page 341.

[63] i.e. of no. 4.

[64] No. 17.

[65] The new canons were to 'render due thanks to God there and to intercede without ceasing for the sins of the people and themselves'. The preamble gives reasons for his charter: the sons of Belial had multiplied on earth to subvert the church, the bride of Christ.

Bodmin.[66] The secular college at St Stephens at Launceston was colonised by the canons of Holy Trinity Aldgate, in London, a house itself probably begun by canons from St Botolph's Colchester.[67] Aldgate had several daughter houses including Plympton founded in 1121.[68] A late eleventh century foundation of St Mary's Huntingdon was of importance because one of its daughter houses was Merton priory in Surrey (founded in 1114) from which the priories of Taunton (*c*.1120) and Bodmin (*c*.1124–5) were founded.[69]

The connection of Launceston priory with Aldgate was of prime importance. Norman, the first prior of Holy Trinity, had studied in France with Anselm, and it was Prior Norman who was the first to introduce regular canonical life into England.[70] The *Historia* of Holy Trinity, Aldgate, writes of him as:

> Vir Dei Normannus . . . fratrem suum videlicet Bernardum mittens ad ecclesiam Sancti Petri de Dunstaple et alium ad Lanston in Cornubiam [*sic*] ad Plympton eciam in Devonia . . .[71]

The connection of Aldgate and Launceston priories continued. The fourth prior of Aldgate was called both Peter of Cornwall and Peter of London. He was a Cornishman and was born in or near Launceston *c*.1140, becoming a canon of Holy Trinity Aldgate no earlier than 1170. Peter was prior of Aldgate from 9 May 1197 to his death on 7 July 1221.[72] He was a famous scholar [73] and in 1200, when he was 60 years old, he wrote an account of his family in a few of the early folios of his monumental work *De Visionibus*.[74] His grandfather was Ailsi and Ailsi's eldest son was Bernard.[75] He and his brother Nicholas (Ailsi's second son) were said by Peter of Cornwall to have earned the familiarity and affection of King Henry I at his court.[76] It has been seen that Bernard (with a priest called Hamelin) held a moiety of the chapel of the castle of Dunheved

[66]St Germans was a later Augustinian priory. It seems that Leofric introduced secular canons there *c*.1050 and regular canons were introduced late in the episcopate (1161–84) of Bishop Bartholomew of Exeter. See D. Knowles and R. Neville Hadcock, *Medieval Religious Houses* (1971), 172.
[67]Dickinson, *Austin Canons*, 109–10, 113.
[68]Ibid., 112–14.
[69]Op. cit., 117–18 and note. For Taunton and Bodmin see further M. L. Colker, 'The Life of Guy of Merton by Rainald of Merton' in *Medieval Studies*, vol. 31 (1975). Colker gives dates of *c*.1110 and *c*.1120 for the foundation of Taunton and Bodmin priories (pp. 257, 259).
[70]Dickinson, op. cit., 99–100. Probably St Anselm.
[71]The first modern text of the *Historia* appeared in Gerald A. J. Hodgett (ed.), *The Cartulary of Holy Trinity Priory, Aldgate* (London Record Society 1971). For the quotation, see Hodgett, pp. 227–8. Dunstable priory was founded *c*.1131–2, see Dickinson, op. cit., 115.
[72]Hodgett, *Cartulary*, Chronicle no. 16, p. 3. See *Cornish Studies*, 13 (1985), 5–53.
[73]R. W. Hunt, 'The disputation of Peter of Cornwall against Symon the Jew' in *Studies presented to F. M. Powicke* (Oxford 1948), 143–56.
[74]Lambeth Palace Library MS. 51, ff.23r. and 26r.: *iam nunc fere sexegenarius . . . scripsit anno . . . m°cc°*.
[75]The best short account of Ailsi and his family is R. W. Southern, *Medieval Humanism and Other Studies* (1970), 225–8. Southern connected the evidence provided by Ailsi's visions in his grandson's (Peter) MS. with other evidence from Merton priory described by J. H. Round, 'Bernard, the King's Scribe' in *EHR* lv (July 1899), 417–30.
[76]Lambeth MS. 51, f.25r. (B), chapter 10. (Each folio of the MS. is divided into two columns designated 'A' and 'B').

before 1127.[77] Both Bernard and his brother Nicholas made gifts to
Launceston priory, including a banner and a writing casket which the
canons used as a reliquary.[78] Bernard was certainly a clerk in Henry I's
chancery, though his brother Nicholas left the royal service to become a
canon at Merton priory.[79] It seems that Bernard had died by 1148.[80] By
then he had retrieved by lawsuits the lands of his grandfather Theodulf,
an owner of land in the Launceston area before the Conquest, and lands
lost by his father Ailsi and his uncle Brictric, and he had consolidated his
estates in Cornwall and in other counties and in Normandy.[81]

Ailsi was more than the master mason which R. W. Southern called
him. He worked for the prior and canons and it is clear from his *visiones*
that he was custodian of the fund for building the tower of the secular
canons' church at St Stephens. The *De Visionibus* of Ailsi's grandson Peter
shows considerable building work was going on: there are references to
waggon-loads of stone and a lime kiln near the houses of the secular
canons for finishing the tower. Another vision shows St Stephen blessing
the work Ailsi was supervising on the erection of the tower.[82]

King Stephen's confirmation charter of 1136[83] to the priory gave
authority to the regular canons to move themselves and their houses to a
better site on their own lands. In strict logic this need not have meant the
move to a new priory, but there was a move to new buildings and a new
priory at the ford over the river Kensey, and the most likely date for this
move was 7 February 1155.[84]

Reginald de Dunstanville, created earl of Cornwall by the Empress

[77]See note 61 above.
[78]Lambeth MS. 51, f.25v. (B).
[79]Ibid. and Round, *EHR* lv, 429. Southern's genealogical table, op. cit., note 75, 226, is in
the wrong order. The sons of Ailsi were (1) Bernard, (2) Nicholas, (3) Jordan, (4) Pagan.
[80]Round, art. cit., 418. Bernard may have been born in the eleventh century. He was with
King Henry I on one of his Welsh campaigns (see Lambeth MS. 51, f.25v.(A).) These
campaigns took place in May to June 1114 and in June 1121: see W. Farrer, *An Outline
Itinerary of King Henry I* (Oxford 1919), 65, 95, 97. Bernard had three sons, Luke, Peter and
John, see cartulary, nos. 192, 227.
[81]Round, loc. cit., *Regesta* ii, nos. 1363, 1366, 1486 etc., Southern, op. cit., 226–7. Theodulf
does not appear as a landowner in Domesday Book, nor Ailsi for lands in the Launceston
district (*pace* Soulsby, 122). Brichtric was a tenant of Count Robert of Mortain but not in the
Launceston area. For Bernard's lands etc. in Launceston see note 61. He also held the
church of Lawhitton, Trecarrel in Lezant, Menwenick in Trewen, the church of Liskeard,
Trekelland in Lezant, South Carne in Altarnun, Trethew and Bodway in Menheniot,
Tregastick in Morval and Trevarledge in Advent. See Round, art. cit., 418. I am indebted to
the Revd W. M. M. Picken for the identification of most of these places printed in Round's
charter from the cartulary of Merton priory.
[82]Lambeth MS. 51, ff.23v.–24r.(A).
[83]No. 9.
[84]No. 12 would suggest that land given symbolically on the altar by Earl Reginald before
his destruction of the tower, and (?) as a site for the new priory had not been given c.1146.
No. 428 shows it was Robert I, bishop of Exeter, who died on 28 March 1155 who transferred
the relics to the new priory. Nos. 493 and 525 show that the canons moved to the new
building at the ford on the same occasion and a comparison of the witnesses of these two
charters with no. 11 would suggest after the accession of Henry II on 29 December 1154. But
the precise date would seem to be 7 February (i.e. in 1155) as the *Translatio Reliquiarum* is
marked in the thirteenth-century calendar of Launceston priory as a feast of the first class on
7 February. See F. Wormald in *Journal of Theological Studies* xxxix, no. 153 (January 1938),
1–21.

Matilda in 1140, destroyed the tower of the canons' church.[85] Was this the tower of the new priory or of the priory church of St Stephens by Launceston? If Stephen's charter of 1136 gave formal consent for a new priory by the ford this might be taken as a compelling reason for Reginald, King Stephen's enemy, to destroy it. It is quite possible that the new priory was being built in 1140. But the answer must be that it was the tower of St Stephen's church that was destroyed – the *ecclesia Sancti Stephani* of charters nos 12 and 13 in the cartulary. Throughout the cartulary a clear distinction is made between St Stephens priory and the new priory 'at the ford'.[86]

Why did not Peter of Cornwall refer to the destruction of the tower of St Stephen's church? He knew Earl Reginald and states that he was related to him.[87] Earl Reginald, as will be seen,[88] was a man of great power and importance. A possible answer to the question is that, in view of Earl Reginald's benefactions to the priory, it would have been embarassing to mention his destruction of the tower and Reginald's role when Stephen and Matilda's civil war came to the west country,[89] even though Reginald had been dead for twenty-five years when Peter wrote the account of his family in the *De Visionibus*.

Reginald de Dunstanville's name occurs not infrequently in the cartulary. As an illegitimate son of King Henry I[90] and brother of Earl Robert of Gloucester (another bastard of the same king), he was of high importance.[91] Reginald was probably born in the first decade of the twelfth century.[92] By 1130 he was a landowner in Wiltshire.[93] He married Beatrice, a daughter of William fitz Richard in 1140 or just before. This was a powerful alliance with the foremost baron of Cornwall, William fitz Richard, who by marrying his son Robert to Agnes Hay at some time before 1166 united the feudal honours of Cardinan (51 knights' fees) and Bodardle (20 knights' fees).[94] In April 1140, about the same time or just after his marriage, Reginald was made earl of Cornwall by the Empress

[85]Nos. 12 and 13. The title to no. 12 includes the words *pro turre ecclesie Sancti Stephani prosternenda.* For Reginald's creation as earl in the Spring of 1140, see R. H. C. Davis, *King Stephen* (1967, reprinted 1980, 139–140). See also H. A. Cronne, *The reign of King Stephen* (1970), 145.
[86]See index under 'ford'.
[87]Lambeth MS. 51, f.24v.(A). Southern is probably correct in seeing the relationship with Earl Reginald through Peter's sister, his father Jordan's married daughter living in Launceston (Lambeth MS. 51, f.26r.(A)), but I cannot discover the evidence for Southern's assertion that Jordan's married daughter was related to Earl Reginald's wife (Southern, *Medieval Humanism*, 226.) Jordan had another son as well as Peter, see Lambeth MS. 51, f.24v.(B).
[88]Below, p. xx.
[89]Below, p. xx.
[90]By Sybil, alias Adela, alias Lucy, daughter of Sir Robert Corbet of Alcester, co. Warwick, see *Complete Peerage* (2nd. ed.) xi, 107, appendix D.
[91]Below, p. xx.
[92]The editor of the *Complete Peerage* (2nd. ed.) xi, 108 cites Eyton's opinion that Reginald was born *c.*1110–15 but he thinks this date is too late.
[93]Loc. cit. (last note) citing the Pipe Roll of 1130. For the Dunstanville connection with Wilts., see Oswald Barron's article in *The Ancestor* xi (October 1904), p. 56.
[94]Charles Henderson, *Essays in Cornish History* (Oxford 1935), 50; H. R. Watkin, *History of Totnes Priory* (1917), ii, 1014; P. L. Hull, *Caption of Seisin of the Duchy of Cornwall 1337* (DCRS 1971), xii, note 7.

Matilda.[95] The sequel is best told in the words of the chronicler of the
*Gesta Stephani*:[96]

> William fitz Richard, a man of very distinguished family who held
> wide sway over the earldom,[97] treacherously broke the faith that he
> had promised on oath to the King and admitting Reginald, a son of
> King Henry, into a castle that had always been in the King's power
> and jurisdiction and, marrying his daughter to him, he put in his
> hands the earldom of Cornwall. And Reginald for his part on
> becoming lord of so great an earldom, began to behave with much
> more vigour than discretion to bend all to his will by force of arms, to
> strengthen any castle that existed and put garrisons of his own men
> into them and most grievously to oppress all supporters of the King
> that were in the neighbourhood. And the mad rashness of his reckless
> proceedings went so far that he neither spared churches nor in any
> degree kept his plunderers from the Church's property. Wherefore we
> saw him, not long afterwards, caught by the deserved lash of divine
> vengeance, because the Bishop of Exeter[98] struck him with the sword
> of excommunication and removed him from the threshold of the
> church and his wife, driven to a frenzy, offered to his embrace no
> ordinary woman but a frightful and terrible demon, and the land he
> had received from the traitor, his father-in-law, was taken from him
> by the King and he lost it for a great space of time,[99] keeping only the
> castle he lived in with much difficulty, since his enemies were too
> strong for him. For the King, fearing that a rebellion had been stirred
> up against him in Cornwall too, as I have related, arrived there
> rapidly and unexpectedly and after recovering the castles of which
> Reginald had taken possession put the county into the hands of Earl
> Alan,[100] a man of the greatest cruelty and craft, and leaving him
> there with a body of soldiers very ready for action, ordered him to
> wage continual warfare against Reginald until he was driven out of it.

Chapter 49 of the *Gesta Stephani* relates how Robert, earl of Gloucester,
and a very strong force of King Stephen's enemies stationed at Gloucester,
hearing that King Stephen was in Cornwall, rejoiced because they
thought he would be an easy target as he was separated from his army. So
they gathered a large host and hastened to Cornwall, only to discover that
the King had been successful and had gathered a large army around him.

[95]R. H. C. Davis, *King Stephen 1135–54* (1967), 62, 139, correcting J. H. Round's date of
1141, the date which also appears in *Complete Peerage* (2nd. ed.) iii, 428–9 and elsewhere.
[96]Edited by K. R. Potter in a new edition with R. H. C. Davis, *Gesta Stephani* (Oxford
Medieval Texts 1976), pp. 101 et seq., chapters 48 and 49.
[97]'of Cornwall' is intended. As the editors of the *Gesta Stephani* state, William fitz Richard
was a tenant-in-chief of King Stephen, but not earl of Cornwall.
[98]Robert I, bishop of Exeter, 1138–55.
[99]The editors note that this was an exaggeration as Reginald regained the earldom in the
next year.
[100]See P. L. Hull (ed.), *Cartulary of St Michael's Mount* (DCRS 1962), no. 5, a charter of
Alan III, count of Britanny and earl of Cornwall, dated at Bodmin 1140. The charter was for
the redemption of the soul of Earl Brian his uncle and *pro stabilitate domini mei regis Stephani*. It
is likely that King Stephen appointed Count Alan to oppose Matilda's appointment of Earl
Reginald and therefore that Alan was appointed earl of Cornwall after Reginald's creation as
earl *c.* April in 1140. But cf. note 102.

King Stephen had been secretly warned of Earl Robert's arrival and had skilfully prepared for battle, summoning 'all the barons of Devon to his aid'. The result was that Earl Robert and his army retreated hastily to Bristol. King Stephen proceeded to demolish 'a great many unlicensed castles' and received the surrender of other castles and also captured some by force of arms,[101] thus restoring tranquillity to those regions. The civil war of King Stephen's reign includes a forgotten episode of Cornish history about which one would like to know more.[102] What is clear is that Reginald and William fitz Richard held Launceston castle and 'wrought such havoc that the bishop of Exeter put them under the ban of the church. King Stephen led an army to Cornwall, captured the castles which Reginald had taken, and entrusted Cornwall to Count Alan, leaving him a body of troops with whose aid he eventually expelled Reginald.'[103] Although Earl Reginald was restored and temporarily won lands and castles from King Stephen, he was not in a position to keep them permanently.[104] His conduct is reflected in the cartulary: he made ten grants to the priory to atone for the destroyed tower and whatever other losses he inflicted on churches. As one of them (no. 428) concerned the transfer of the relics and canons to the new priory by the ford (by Bishop Robert I, bishop of Exeter), who excommunicated him, it is quite possible that part of Reginald's penance was to provide Launceston priory with a new site as well as other grants, notably of the churches of Liskeard and Linkinhorne. Also in one of Ailsi's visions Earl Reginald is seen accepting Peter's father Jordan's advice about tithes in dispute between the priory and the vicar of South Petherwin.[105] There is some evidence also of the reparation made by William fitz Richard to the priory.[106] William's father, Richard fitz Turold, occurs in Count Robert of Mortain's charter of 1076[107] as a tenant of the Count for 1½ acres in Goodmansleigh in St Stephen by Launceston. Richard was a major sub-tenant of Count Robert in 1085 and before his death (c.1120) he had become a tenant in chief by

[101]Chapter 57 of the *Gesta Stephani* relates King Stephen's imprisonment in Bristol by Earl Robert. The *Gesta* show Earl Alan's loss of the earldom of Cornwall after a plot of Earl Alan against the earl of Chester to avenge the imprisonment of King Stephen, by which time Reginald had gained the upper hand in Cornwall.
[102]See the brief comment in H. A. Cronne, *The Reign of Stephen* (1970), 40 where William fitz Richard is wrongly called Richard fitz Turold. R. H. C. Davis, *King Stephen* (1967) has a little more to say: William fitz Richard's rebellion was in February 1140. King Stephen 'marched against him, installed Alan of Brittany as earl of Cornwall, and on his return through Devon did his utmost to force the earl of Gloucester to give battle . . .' (Davis, op. cit., 43–4).
[103]Charles Henderson, *Essays in Cornish History*, 6. Henderson pointed out that Richard de Lucy came to Cornwall with Earl Alan and that the 'Cornish rebellion of 1140 was probably followed by extensive confiscations'.
[104]R. H. C. Davis, *King Stephen*, 124.
[105]Lambeth MS. 51, f.24v.(B). For Reginald's grants to the priory, see nos. 11–13, 27, 115, 415, 493, 525, 537–8.
[106]See no. 244 and the grant by William fitz Richard's son to the priory, no. 246. Both relate to Goodmansleigh in St Stephens by Launceston. Both mention Earl Reginald. In all the Cardinan family made four grants to the priory: nos. 244, 246, 251–2.
[107]No. 3. For Richard fitz Turold, see Soulsby, 210–11, 249.

the forfeiture of William of Mortain's lands in 1106 after the battle of Tinchebrai.

One begins to see more forcibly why Peter of Cornwall did not record Earl Reginald's conduct in 1140, the year of the birth of Peter, who wrote his *Visiones* when an Angevin king was on the throne. It would have been too embarrassing to criticise a great benefactor of the priory and a very powerful man. Reginald played a major part in affairs not only in Stephen's reign but also from 1154 to his death in 1175, as a glance at the witnesses of King Henry II's *acta* shows.[108] When Duke Henry sailed from England in March 1154, the man *qui in . . . negotiis meis locum meum tenet in Anglia* was Earl Reginald.[109] In one text of a confirmation charter of Duke Henry to the Norman abbey of Troarn, Reginald is described in the list of witnesses as *cancellario regis comitis Cornubie*,[110] an odd description, but which suggests he was thought of as chancellor when Duke Henry became King Henry II at the end of December 1154. The earldom of Cornwall from 1140 to 1175 was a palatinate, exempted from the ordinary administrative system of a county: until Reginald's death in July 1175 no accounts from Cornwall were rendered into the Exchequer.[111] Earl Reginald had a barony of 215⅓ knights' fees in Cornwall and Devon in 1166 and the honours of Trematon (59 fees) and Cardinan (71 fees) were held of his barony.[112] His family relationships were strong: he was a half-brother of the Empress Matilda and a cousin both of Earl Robert of Gloucester and of William (II) de ̈otreaux. He married his daughter Denise to Richard de Reviers, the second earl of Devon (1155–April 1162). Reginald's other daughter Matilda married (*c*.1165) Robert, count of Meulan and earl of Leicester.[113]

The church of St Stephen (whose tower was destroyed in 1140) was cruciform in shape (with north and south transepts) in the twelfth century.[114] It was re-consecrated by Bishop Bronescombe on 25 October 1259, doubtless a stage in the church becoming wholly parochial after the departure of the prior and canons to the new priory on 7 February 1155.[115] Apart from drastic alterations in the nineteenth century, the medieval church had major alterations when a south aisle was added in the latter half of the fourteenth century.[116] A fine new tower was added

[108]See L. Delisle and E. Berger, *Recueil des Actes de Henri II* (4 vols. Paris 1909–27), especially vols. 1 and 2.
[109]*Regesta* iii, no. xxxix. For a mission of Earl Reginald to Anjou in March 1152, see W. L. Warren, *Henry II* (1977), 42.
[110]Delisle and Berger, *Recueil*, vol. 1 (1916), no. lxv, p. 73, from an inspeximus of Richard II of 9 November 1387.
[111]See the description of Earl Reginald's powers in D. M. Stenton, *Pleas before the King or his Justices* (Selden Society vol. 68) (1949) ii, 118.
[112]F. M. Stenton, *The First Century of English Feudalism* (Oxford 1932), 228. *Red Book of the Exchequer* i, 261–2. For Earl Reginald's possession of the manor and hundred of Kingskerswell in Devon and the manor of Diptford in the same county granted to him by King Henry II, see *Book of Fees* ii, 97; *Red Book* ii, 678.
[113]*Complete Peerage* (2nd. ed.) iii, 428–9 and xi, appendix D and vii, 740 (Meulan). For Reginald's status as son of King Henry I before he became earl in 1140, see J. H. Round's reconstruction of Stephen's court at Easter 1136 in *Geoffrey de Mandeville* (1892), 263–4. For the marriage of Denise, see *Complete Peerage* (2nd ed.) iv, 312–13.
[114]See *JRIC* xvii, 364 note 5 (1909).     [115]Above, p. xvi.
[116]Edmund H. Sedding, *Norman Architecture in Cornwall* (1909), 365. M. Fisher, 'Launceston's Ancient Churches', *Old Cornwall* ix, no. 7 (1982), 315, suggests that the work was done when Stafford was bishop (1395–1419).

early in the sixteenth century.[117] St Stephen was the *matrix ecclesia* of such chapels as Tremaine, Egloskerry, Tresmeer, Werrington, St Giles, Laneast, St Thomas and St Mary Magdalene.[118]

As for the new priory at the ford occupied in February 1155, only a few ruins at ground level adjacent to the church of St Thomas by Launceston are to be seen today. The North Cornwall railway cut through the site of the priory in 1886 and 1891, and in 1888 the Launceston Gas Company demolished such old walls as there were above ground level to build a wall round the gasholders. As Michael Fisher has written, the priory was 'a noble building . . . over 230 feet long and 50 feet across at the widest part'.[119]

After the *matrix ecclesia* (including the new priory), the next section of the cartulary[120] is concerned with the *capella Magdalena*, the chapel of the castle. A moiety of this chapel worth four marks yearly belonged to the dean of the secular college of St Stephens as his prebend.[121] When regular canons had been installed at St Stephens by 1127 this prebend of a moiety of the chapel of the castle was in the hands of Bernard (Ailsi's eldest son) and Hamelin the priest.[122] In 1127 Earl Reginald gave the prebend to the regular canons[123] who were to serve the chapel with one priest.[124] After some disputes about the advowson of the moiety of the *capella castelli* King John confirmed Reginald's grant.[125]

A charter dated 1291 in the cartulary, settling a dispute between the priories of Launceston and St Germans about tithes within the bounds of the *capella Magdalena*, refers to the surrender by the prior and convent of St German's 'within the true and ancient limits of the parish of the said chapel'. It is quite possible that in 1291 the bounds of the later parish of St Mary Magdalene were there, but it is too early, as later evidence shows,[126] to state that a parish of St Mary Magdalene then existed. No. 37 in the cartulary (dated 14 May 1395) refers to the repair and maintenance of the Chapel of Blessed Mary Magdalene in the high street of Launceston. It was the thesis of the Peter brothers[127] that the *capella castelli* which stood at the foot of the castle mound fell into decay in the fourteenth century and was replaced by a new chapel in the town. Charles Henderson thought that the settlement of 1291, together with a similar settlement of 16 July 1293, paved the way for 'the building of a public Chapel of St Mary in the

[117]Sedding thought the tower was fifteenth-century. But Dame Thomasine Percival left a legacy in her will proved 31 July 1513 (copy at Cornwall County Record Office, FS/3/784) specifically for the building of the tower of St Stephens church.

[118]Henderson, *Cornish Church Guide* (reprinted 1964), 180.

[119]Art. cit., 316. Fisher compares the measurements of St Mary Magdalene, 100 × 50 feet. The definitive article (with plan) is Otho Peter, 'Excavations on the site of Launceston Priory', *JRIC* ix (1891–3), 91–6 and 249–509.

[120]Mainly nos. 26–40.

[121]No. 31.

[122]No. 28.

[123]Nos. 26–7 where only Hamelin the priest of the chapel is stated to have held it.

[124]No. 29.

[125]See no. 33. He had already confirmed the priory's possession of the moiety of the chapel as earl of Mortain, see no. 545.

[126]Below, p. xxii, notes 128–9.

[127]R. and O. B. Peter, *Histories of Launceston and Dunheved* (1885), 297 et. seq.

town'. This new chapel did not replace the *capella castelli*.[128] Henderson
states that the burgesses of Launceston had built St Mary Magdalene as a
chapelry to St Stephens before 1319 and that the high altar of the church
of St Mary Magdalene was dedicated by a suffragan of Bishop Grandisson
in 1338. This parochial chapelry was rebuilt in 1511 by Henry Trecarrel
and consecrated in 1524. Trecarrel's church was probably the first
parish church of St Mary Magdalene: as late as 1428 St Stephen
was the only parish church. Churches within the borough were only
chapels.[129]

Launceston priory's encroachment on lands originally in the parish of
South Petherwin began quite early in the twelfth century. The encroach-
ment is first mentioned in Ailsi's visions in Peter of Cornwall's *De
Visionibus* (written *c*.1200). Ailsi, his grandson wrote,[130] had lands outside
Dunheved in the parish of St Paer or Paternus (i.e. South Petherwin), and
the priest of that parish complained that Ailsi was paying tithes on his
lands in South Petherwin to the *capella castelli*. St Stephen appeared to
Ailsi in a dream and directed him to pay his tithes to the priest of South
Petherwin and Ailsi obeyed willingly. Peter of Cornwall said that the
canons in his own time disputed the tithes of the same lands in South
Petherwin and that they were supported by Earl Reginald.[131] Jordan
(Peter's father), the owner of the lands in question, told the earl about St
Stephen's warning to his father Ailsi and this resulted in the earl and
canons ordering the payment of the disputed tithes to the priest of South
Petherwin. There were thus two disputes about tithes between the priory
and South Petherwin: Ailsi's, probably in the reign of Henry I, and a
subsequent dispute, probably in the reign of Henry II.[132]

The dispute with South Petherwin and its appropriator, the priory of St
Germans, broke out again in the late thirteenth century. No. 34 in the
cartulary is an agreement about the visitation of the sick and the burial of
the dead in Dunheved: in fact in Hay, Hurdon, Badash and Pennygillam.
No. 35, a settlement about tithes at about the same time, concerns the
Hideland, Scarne, Hurdon, Pennygillam and an unidentified place called
Colyngton. All of these places in 1291–3 belonged to 'the parish of the
chapel' but anciently they formed part of the parish of South Petherwin.
This was an encroachment on South Petherwin, if not also an
encroachment on the hypothetical ancient district of *Piderwin*, i.e. North
and South Petherwin. Was *Piderwin* a district like the hundred of Pydar or
an ancient *regio*?[133] It is uncertain, but Charles Henderson and Canon
Doble explained the meaning of *Piderwin* as 'probably . . . the "white" or
blessed Paternus', a conclusion with which Oliver Padel agrees.[134] The

---

[128]'A private establishment continued down to the Reformation'. For all this paragraph,
see *Cornish Church Guide* (reprinted 1964), 114. Henderson's account agrees with that of R.
and O. B. Peter: see last note. The private nature of the *capella castelli* is illustrated in no. 415,
a grant of Earl Reginald to the priory, *salva capelle dignitate mee de castello Lanst'*. For the
settlements of 1291 and 1293, see nos. 34–5.

[129]*Feudal Aids* i (1899), 243.

[130]Lambeth MS. 51, ff.24r.(A)–24v.(B).

[131]Above, p. xix, note 105. Certainly after Peter's birth *c*.1140 and Earl Reginald's death in
the summer of 1175.                                        [132]See last note.

[133]See F. M. Stenton, *Anglo-Saxon England* (2nd. ed. 1947), 290–4.

[134]*Cornish Church Guide*, 196; Doble, *St Patern*, 39.

encroachment of Launceston priory affected North Petherwin as well as
South Petherwin (though as regards North Petherwin almost a century
earlier than South Petherwin): Launceston priory claimed North Petherwin's daughter churches of St Giles and Werrington against Tavistock
abbey.[135]

The entry in the Exeter Domesday for Dunheved reads,

> The Count has 1 manor which is called Dunhevet . . . and it rendered
> geld for 1 virgate. And yet there is 1 hide . . .[136]

The Peters[137] maintained that this other hide persisted as the Hideland or
Hidelond (other recurring forms are Hydlond and Hillond) and comprised part of the later Hay Common,[138] Scarne, Windmill and
Pennygillam. Throughout the Peters' book there are clear indications that
the Hideland persisted through the middle ages, was the property of
Launceston borough, and was (later) let out on lease. The Peters quote
examples from Launceston borough archives from 1319, and in a rental of
1512 the corporation were receiving rents from twenty-six pieces of land in
Hay and thirteen pieces in Hilland.[139]

In the matter of the encroachment of Dunheved and the priory, South
Petherwin suffered worse than North Petherwin. By charter no. 34 in the
cartulary the vicar only received part of the dues for burials at Dunheved
or in his own parish and his dues as vicar. Hay (or Bernhay), Hurdon,
Badash, Pennygillam and Scarne no longer belonged to his parish.
Launceston priory received the third part of the tithe on these lands from
the rector, St Germans priory, by an annual payment of one silver mark to
the prior and convent of St Germans. As for North Petherwin, Launceston
priory was awarded the chapels of Werrington and St Giles 'in the name
of the abbey of Tavistock'.[140] Tavistock abbey kept the Cornish parish of
North Petherwin with the manor of Werrington and its revenues.[141]

---

[135]*St Patern*, 40–1; Finberg 'The Early History of Werrington', *EHR* lix (1944), 251;
Finberg, 'Some Earl Tavistock Charters', *EHR* July 1947, 373 no. 50 and 361 no. xvii;
Finberg, 'The Making of a Boundary' in W. G. Hoskins and H. P. H. Finberg, *Devonshire
Studies*, 38–9; Finberg, *Tavistock Abbey* (1951), 22. See also (cartulary) nos. 291–2, 300 etc. for
Werrington and St Giles.

[136]*VCH, Cornwall Domesday*, 101 from DB. Exon. (1816), f.263(b).

[137]See note 127, *Histories of Launceston* etc., 169.

[138]The priory court (or one of the courts) was at Bernhay (see index) and Bernhay is
identical with the Hay Common marked on the older editions of the Ordnance Survey 6″
map (up to and including 1907).

[139]Which might suggest that Hay or Bernhay was not necessarily part of the Hideland in
1512, see *Histories of Launceston* etc., 167. For the other references see op. cit., 88–9, 94, 104,
128, 135, 145, 162, 184 etc. In the eighteenth century an Act of Parliament of 18 Geo. II cap.
xxxviii (1755) vested the hundred acres of Scarne common (possibly including Hay,
Pennygillam, Windmill and Longland) in the guardians of the poor of Launceston, i.e. the
mayor and corporation. A later statute of 1784 (14 Geo. III cap. xvii) empowered the mayor
and corporation to sell the 'aftermath' or depasturage of these commons for the benefit of
the relief of the poor, i.e. they ceased to be common land. 'Aftermath' accounts continue in
the borough archives well into the nineteenth century. (Most of the borough archives were
deposited at Cornwall County Record Office in 1985.)

[140]The prior and convent had to pay 50s. to Tavistock abbey and the abbey kept the tithes
of the manor of Werrington and of the church of North Petherwin. South Petherwin was
appropriated to the priory of St Germans before 1269. *Cornish Church Guide*, 178.

[141]For a convenient summary see Finberg, 'The Devon–Cornwall Boundary' in *D. & C.
N. & Q.* xxiii, pt. 4 (Oct. 1947), 104–7. A longer account by Finberg is in *Devonshire Studies*

## THE LANDS AND ENDOWMENTS OF LAUNCESTON PRIORY

The manor of Launceston Land comprised the major endowment of the priory. For the most part it was a series of properties adjoining Launceston in the present parishes of St Stephens (including Newport), Lawhitton, St Thomas by Launceston, South Petherwin, Lewannick, Laneast, North Tamerton, Treneglos, Tresmeer and Trewen and, in Devon, Lifton and Luffincott with outlying properties in Bridgerule and Diptford, and, in Cornwall, in St Gennys, Linkinhorne and St Neot. Apart from the outlying properties, the manor of Launceston Land encircled Launceston to the north, south, east and west.[142]

The manor of Launceston Land had a court with free bailiffs and a steward.[143] It was free from view of frankpledge and suits of shire and hundred courts, sheriffs and sheriffs' tourns, pleas, cliff-wards, aids and hue and cry within the manor.[144] Launceston Land was thus a free liberty of the priors. They had their own jurisdiction[145] together with the enforcement of the assize of ale within the manor and a moiety of the same assize in the new vill of Newport.[146]

One charter in the cartulary[147] mentions free conventionary tenants of the manor of Launceston Land. This is also attested in the *sessiones* of the tenants of the manor given in a rental of the priory dated 1474.[148] This rental provides a detailed source of information on the tenements of the manor of Launceston Land and some other manors and estates belonging to the priory.[149] From the cartulary and the rental a gazetteer of the main properties which constituted the manor of Launceston Land can be made. All of these appear either in the charter of 1076 and/or the bull of Pope Alexander III.[150]

(1) Diptford in Devon. Land. Cartulary nos. 6, 93.
(2) Gatherley in Lifton, Devon. Nos. 3, 234–5.

---

(see note 135), 19–39. For Tavistock abbey's economic exploitation of the manor of Werrington, see Finberg, *Tavistock Abbey*, passim. Although the abbey of Tavistock's possession of North Petherwin and its manor of Werrington was disputed in 1086 (and Tavistock disseised of Werrington) by 1096 the matter had been fixed between the abbot and William Rufus (*D. & C. N. & Q.* xxiii, pt. 4, 107). North Petherwin and Werrington remained in Devon for some 970 years. They were returned to Cornwall by *The Cornwall & Devon (Broadwoodwidger) Order (1965)* which came into force on 1 January 1966. (*Statutory Instruments 1965 no. 2087*).

[142] There is a useful map of the parishes where the lands of the priory lay in O. B. Peter's article on Launceston priory in *JRIC* xvii, pt. 3 (1909), facing p. 359.

[143] e.g. no. 328 (court), no. 169 (free bailiffs), no. 352 (Sir Richard de Hywis, kt, steward).

[144] No. 16.

[145] i.e. view of frankpledge, hue and cry with sac and soc, tol, theam and infangenetheof.

[146] Nos. 24 and 57.

[147] No. 228.

[148] The rental was kindly made available by a former Town Clerk of Launceston, Mr W. G. Moffat. It was purchased by Otho B. Peter as secretary of the Launceston Scientific and Historical Society in January 1913 from Mrs F. D. Lawrence of London (the Lawrences were a notable and long established family in Launceston) and added to the Launceston borough muniments. The original is at the Guildhall, Launceston, but there is a copy at Cornwall County Record Office, County Hall, Truro.

[149] The evidence of the rental of 1474 for the economy of the priory is considered below, p. xxxix.

[150] Nos. 3 and 6.

(3) Laneast. Land, common pasture, right in chapel and advowson. Land etc. at Badgall, Lidcott and probably also at Trekenner. Nos. 3, 6, 189–194, 196–200.

(4) North Tamerton. Included chapel and Hornacott and Ditchen. Nos. 6, 74–5, 591, 593.

(5) Land in St Stephens by Launceston:
   (a) Athill. Nos. 3, 6, 239–40, 258.
   (b) Cargentle. Nos. 3, 6, 222.
   (c) Dutson. Nos. 3, 6.
   (d) Goodmansleigh. Nos. 3, 6, 205, 243, 245–6.
   (e) Hendragreen. Nos. 3, 6.
   (f) Kernick. Nos. 3, 6, 241–2.
   (g) Trewithick. Nos. 3, 6.
   (h) Truscott and Over Truscott. Nos. 3, 6, 40, 52, 268–9.

(6) South Petherwin. Burdown, nos. 3, 6. Also Tresmarrow, no. 156.

(7) St Thomas by Launceston:
   (a) Carneadon. Nos. 3, 6.
   (b) Kestle. Nos. 3, 6, 170.
   (c) Landrends. Nos. 3, 54, 62, 121, 126, 131, 137–9, 140, 150–1, 153.
   (d) Trebursy. Nos. 3, 6, 158–60, 164–7, 545.
   (e) Tredidon. Nos. 3, 6, 177.
   (f) Tregadillet. Nos. 3, 6, 159, 168–9.
   (g) Trevallet. Nos. 3, 6.

(8) Treneglos: Kyrse, nos. 3, 6, 218, 220. Also weir and mill-dam (running to priory mill of Treglum in Tresmeer), nos. 214–15.

(9) Tresmeer:
   (a) Land, tithes, chapel of St Nicholas. Nos. 3, 6, 201, 226, 289.
   (b) Treburtle. Nos. 3, 6.
   (c) (North) Tregeare. Nos. 3, 6, 167, 202–5, 223, 251, 382–3.
   (d) Treglum: mill, tithes. Nos. 3, 6, 214, 289.
   (e) Trehummer. No. 6.
   (f) Trew. Nos. 3, 6, 289.

(10) Parish uncertain: Hill near Launceston (probably either St Stephens or St Thomas by Launceston). Nos. 3, 40, 52, 182, 268–9.

There were also a number of properties known to have been in the manor of Launceston Land which do not occur in Count Robert of Mortain's charter nor in the bull of Pope Alexander III. They are

(1) Bamham in Lawhitton. Houses, gardens, lands. Nos. 170, 273, 308–10, 312, 314.

(2) Bridgerule in Devon. Tackbeare. No. 70.

(3) Lewannick. Church and advowson. Nos. 96–9, 101, 105–6, 114–15, 545.

(4) Linkinhorne. Clampit. Nos. 180, 584, 588, 590.

(5) Luffincott in Devon. Chapel and West Peke etc. Nos. 71, 73, 76.

(6) St Neot. Trebinnick, nos. 77–8, 81.

(7) St Stephens by Launceston. Kellygreen, no. 274. Houses and lands in Newport, nos. 53, 151, 196–7, 257, 302, 322–3, 327. Ridgegrove mill at Goodmansleigh, nos. 247–50.

(8) St Thomas by Launceston. Hamlet of Pole Park, outside the gate of the priory, nos. 58–61. *Le Birch Doune*, no. 135. Trecaru or Trecarew, nos. 122, 126.
(9) Tremaine. Castle Milford, including mill. Nos. 251, 253.
(10) Trewen. Gospenheale, no. 187.

A third list is given below of properties included in the charter of 1076 and/or the bull of Pope Alexander III for which there is no evidence that they formed part of the manor of Launceston Land.

(1) Altarnun and Davidstow. Manor of Treglasta. Nos. 3, 95.
(2) Beaworthy in Devon. Church. No. 6.
(3) Bodigga, no. 3.
(4) Boyton. Chapel, nos. 6, 98–9. Bradridge, nos. 3, 6, 40, 52, 66, 68–9, 268–9.
(5) Bratton Clovelly, Devon. Risdon. Nos. 6, 275.
(6) Bridgerule, Devon. Tatson. Nos. 6, 428–31, 440–1, 443.
(7) Egloskerry. Chapel, nos. 6, 98–9, 223, 283. Penheale, nos. 3, 6, 186. The chapel lay in the manor of Penheale. *Trelouthet* (=? Treludick). Nos. 3, 40, 52, 183, 268–9.
(8) St Germans. Bonyalva, nos. 3, 6, 481–92, 592.
(9) St Gennys. Pencuke. Nos. 6, 165–6, 351, 369–71.
(10) Laneast. Trespearne. Nos. 3, 6, 159.
(11) Lanteglos by Camelford. Helston in Trigg. No. 3.
(12) Liskeard. Houses and lands. Glebe (=manor of Hagland). Church. Nos. 3, 54, 150–2, 493–5, 497–8, 500–6, 508, 512–15, 517–21, 524, 544, 600.
(13) St Martin by Looe, Bucklawren. Nos. 3, 461–76.
(14) North Tamerton. Church of Bridge, no. 6. Chapel, nos. 6, 591, 593.
(15) *Rethirhaduc*, no. 6.
(16) *Rettahirin*, no. 3.
(17) St Stephens by Launceston
   (a) Hospital of Gillemartin. No. 6 (*Terra Spitel*).
   (b) Church of Launceston (*sic*), no. 6. This may have included the *capella castelli* (above p. xxi) and places set apart for maintaining a light there and the sustenance of a chaplain. See no. 40: the endowments lay in Bradridge in Boyton, *Trelouthet* in Egloskerry, Truscott in St Stephens by Launceston, Hill near Launceston, Halswille, and Treworgy (= Treworgie in St Gennys). This evidence suggests that the manor of Launceston Land may have included more properties than are given in the first list.
   (c) Menheniot (in SS. by L.) Nos. 3, 6, 119. 229–31, 272.
   (d) New Churches, no. 6.
(18) Stratton. Efford, including chapel. Nos. 6, 202, 205.
(19) St Thomas by Launceston. Trethorn, no. 6.
(20) *Tiquarnel*, no. 3. (Tywarnhayle in Perranzatuloe).
(21) *Trelonet*, no. 6.
(22) Warbstow. Forest and mill of Downinney. (The manor of

Downinney lay in Davidstow, Poundstock, Treneglos and Warbstow). Nos. 6, 205, 252, ...
(23)  Werrington, chapel of (Eggbear), Devon, nos. 6, 291, 293–6, 598.

Counting tenements and properties of various types can only be very
approximate, but it does provide a guide to total numbers and when they
were acquired. The charter of 1076, Pope Alexander III's bull and John's
confirmation charter[151] account for about 136 properties. Grants not in
these documents, nor in the manor of Launceston Land, add up to a
further 76 properties. Tenements etc. in the manor of Launceston Land
total approximately 136, 99 of which are found in the three documents
mentioned above and 37 of which are not found there. So the priory had
some 249 properties or 'blocks' of properties altogether.

Thus out of 249 properties of the priory, about 150 were acquired in
1076 and in the twelfth century,[152] i.e. under two-thirds of the priory's
endowments had been acquired by 1200 (which is what one would
expect). Twelfth-century grants not recorded above include Caradon and
Rillaton in Linkinhorne and the church of Linkinhorne and also the
manors of Climson and Climsland, to name only the largest grants. Many
acquisitions of the thirteenth century or later might have had earlier
origins or additional grants to lands etc. already belonging to the priory.
Possessions probably acquired in the thirteenth century included the mill
of the manor of Bradford in the Devonshire parishes of Pyworthy and
Clawton[153] and tenements in the Cornish parishes of Kilkhampton[154] and
Morwenstow.[155] Earl of Richard of Cornwall granted and confirmed to
the priory the water fair of St James by the river Kensey (*c.*1227–43).[156]

## DISPUTES AND AGREEMENTS

To begin with the priory's liberties in Launceston (relations with the
mayor and burgesses of the borough are described later):[157] the prior and
canons had rights over breaches of the assize of bread and ale. Earl
Reginald had given the prior and canons 65s. 10d. for these fines in the vill
of Launceston, but it seems that by 1302 the prior and canons were taking
them. The prior claimed before the itinerant justices that the king was
seised of a moiety of the fines and the mayor and burgesses had not paid
the sum of 65s. 10d. yearly which was due to the priory.[158] It appears in
1342[159] that the priory had the assize of bread and ale in their manor of

---

[151]No. 545.
[152]Cf. above, p. viii, where it is stated that eleventh and twelfth century grants account for
about 12 per cent of the documents in the cartulary. This is only an approximation and it
should be realised that counting documents and determining when the priory acquired lands
are different: charters later than the twelfth century sometimes contain evidence of twelfth-
century grants and, of course, several properties are often contained in one charter.
[153]Nos. 448, 450–2.
[154]Nos. 396, 401–2, i.e. Elmsworthy, Heatham, Lymsworthy and Spritsland.
[155]Nos. 391, 395–8, i.e. Cleave, Coombe, Harscott, Hollacoombe and Hollygrove.
[156]No. 63.
[157]Below, pp. xxxiii–xxxiv.
[158]Nos. 262–5 dated 1301–2, 1342 and 1284.
[159]Nos. 262–3. P. L. Hull, *The Caption of Seisin of the Duchy of Cornwall (1337)* (DCRS 1971),
xliv.

Launceston Land and a moiety of the same assize in the vill of Newport. An earlier agreement of 24 June 1284[160] with Edmund, earl of Cornwall, and this evidence of 1342 make it clear that the prior was bound through his bailiff to account for a moiety of the fines of the assize of bread and ale with the Earl or his attorney each year at Michaelmas.

Corrodies were frequently disputed.[161] A list of what benefits a corrody conferred is contained in an undated plea of assize.[162] The privileges of John de Skewys were equivalent to those of an esquire of the prior. More interesting than the fact that his corrody (endowed by the de Botreaux family) was in dispute was the strange arrangement made by William de Botreaux (most probably the second of that name)[163] that when he (William) died, an armed man riding before his corpse should be granted the corrody by the prior. (There had been three previous owners of the corrody before it was granted to John Skewys.)

The outcome of the dispute is not known, nor of a later dispute of 1392 concerning a corrody granted to one John Elys for his services to King Edward III.[164] Another corrody at the priory (*c*.1262)[165] states that the holder was to have the equivalent of the corrody for one canon: pannage, wine, ale and a competent room.

A considerable number of the documents in the cartulary relate to disputes with laymen about lay property and their settlement. These are of too many kinds to be described here. They consist of *composiciones*, bonds, chirographs, final concords, grants, documents concerning manor courts, inquisitions, memoranda, pleas and pleas of assize, mesne pleas, wardships and marriages. Settlements were by assizes: mort d'ancestor, novel disseisin[166] (comprising disseisin by priors or of priors). Disputes were settled by pleas before royal justices, by the priors' courts at Bernhay and elsewhere, by hundred and county courts, by sheriffs tourns and ecclesiastical courts (including those of papal delegates). Disputes were mainly about lands and services, properties and rights. So there is mention of advowsons, chantries, common pasture, exchanges of land, tenure by free alms, hundreds,[167] mesne pleas, mills, reversions, relief, services, warranty. Again the subject-index must be used; only a few disputes with lay people which are of special interest can be considered here.

In a royal plea about Roger de Carminow taking four heifers and an ox belonging to the prior at Ditchen and then driving them to Hornacott in North Tamerton it is stated that the prior held land in Ditchen of Roger

[160]No. 265. Rights claimed by the mayor and commonalty in 1337 included the assize of bread and ale within the borough (Hull, op. cit., xliii, 4). It was said (op. cit., 5) that the prior took fines of the assize 'which in former times belonged to the lord of the said castle: by what warrant they know not . . .'.
[161]e.g. nos. 32, 224.
[162]No. 271 (*c*.1328–26 June 1346).
[163]See W. Sincock, '*Principal landowners in Cornwall*, . . . *1165*', *JRIC*, x, pt. 1 (1890), 155–7. William (II) de Botreaux died *c*.1211; his father in the 1130s.
[164]No. 330. Both nos. 271 and 330 were adjourned and no further mention of them is made.
[165]No. 236.
[166]For other assizes of novel disseisin concerning priors of Launceston, see D. M. Stenton, *Pleas before the King or his Justices* (Selden Society 1949, vol. 68) ii, pp. 105, 117, 171.
[167]Including the bailiwick of the hundred of Launceston, no. 194.

de Carminow in return for finding a chaplain to celebrate mass at *Taleburgh* chapel during Christmas, Easter and the whole of Lent.[168] Roger impounded the cattle because the chantry was thirty years in arrears. In the continuation of this plea (the pleas being heard at York and Westminster respectively in 1296), Roger de Carminow sought to recover against Richard de Ditchen a messuage, eighty acres of land and ten acres of wood by royal writ of right.[169] Richard called to warranty the prior who placed himself on the grand assize,[170] i.e. he submitted his case to a jury of knights to try and prove his right to the land in the right of the priory and not as tenant of Roger de Carminow. A jury of four knights gave the verdict the prior wanted:[171] his greater right to the land because of the chantry provided, though he was to continue to hold the lands of Roger de Carminow.

Following the second Statute of Westminster in 1285, actions of mesne became possible and are found in the cartulary.[172] For example, Prior Roger de Horton held land at Pencuke in St Gennys of Philip de Lamettin in pure and perpetual alms for a quarter of a knight's fee, but William de Ferrers was the chief lord. The case began in the county court at Lostwithiel in 1281 and came before the same court in 1322.[173] It was continued before the justices of the King's Bench at York in 1328.[174]

Likewise there are agreements about warranty.[175] The first, c.1242, is an agreement for William de Hethford and Margaret his wife to defend the land of the priory in Bradford in Devon from all suits and services of court due to the chief lords.[176] There was a similar agreement in 1292.[177]

Several documents concern tithings and tithingmen.[178] One has special interest, the presentation of the prior in November 1349 at the tourn of Black Torrington hundred as responsible for the repair of the bridge of Bullapit in the tithing of Werrington. In the following year a jury of the same hundred assembled at Druxton Bridge reversed the presentation of 1349.[179] The document is interesting in relation to the successful attempt in the late eleventh century to transfer Werrington from Stratton hundred in Cornwall to Black Torrington hundred in Devon.[180] Some of the disputes and agreements in the cartulary concerned the

---

[168]No. 259.

[169]No. 260.

[170]For which see D. M. Stenton, *English Justice . . . 1066–1215)* (1965), 49.

[171]No. 261 (Westminster 1296).

[172]Nos. 375, 403–4. For the statute, see T. F. T. Plucknett, *A Concise History of the Common Law* (5th ed. 1956), 31, 678, note 2.

[173]Nos. 371–2.

[174]No. 376.

[175]For the general implications of warranty, see Plucknett, op. cit., 529. For pledges of faith as the precursor of warranty (12th century to c.1230), see David Postles, 'Pledges of faith in transactions of land', *Journal of the Society of Archivists*, vol. 7, no. 5 (April 1984), 295–8.

[176]No. 449.

[177]Nos. 551–2.

[178]For other documents of interest concerning tithings (not dealt with here), see nos. 438, 445, 554 and 557.

[179]No. 446. The heading to this charter shows that it was also judged that the prior of Launceston had not to find a tithingman for Hogslade in Boyton.

[180]Above, p. xxiii and H. P. R. Finberg, 'The Early History of Werrington', *EHR.* lix (1944), especially 244–5. See also Finberg in Hoskins and Finberg, *Devonshire Studies*, 29.

relationship of the priory with parishes. There are only two thirteenth-century documents concerning the priory and the parish of St Stephen by Launceston.[181] The first is the record (May 1271) of a controversy between Prior Richard and 'the parish of Launceston' about mortuaries and other customs affecting the church of St Stephen. The settlement was 'that their parishioners and free tenants by homage' were to have their free customs as in former times. They were to be quit of providing the sub-prior's habit and a heriot of their best beast when they died. The parishioners were to have legacies of parishioners left voluntarily for the work of the church in the view of the guardian of the church. 'Whatever was bequeathed or given for the stock or work of the church (other than of their parish) should be given for the use of the church of "La Forde" for ever'. Finally, the parishioners promised not to introduce unjust or 'contrary' customs.

The second agreement between the prior and the parishioners of St Stephens is more informative about the rights of the latter. Stock given or bequeathed for the fabric of the parish church was to be taken over immediately 'for the use of the parish church and of the conventual church of Blessed Stephen' by the proctors both of the prior and the parishioners. Defects in the fabric of the church were to be reviewed at a meeting of the prior and parishioners and both parties were to elect two men who by sale of the parish stock could pay for the repair of such defects. Parishioners were responsible for the upkeep of the chancel and the body of the church as well as the lights and these were to be paid for from their store or common fund 'by the view and advice of the prior'. No tithes were to be exacted from the parishioners' store by the prior. Books and vestments were to be maintained at the expense of the parishioners.

Other disputes between the priory and parishes concerned South Petherwin, the substance of which has already been discussed in relation to the encroachment of the *capella Magdalena* on the lands of that parish.[182] Mention has also been made of the dispute of the priory with the abbey of Tavistock when the priory acquired the chapels of Werrington and St Giles.[183] Later agreements with these two chapelries established the responsibility of the parishioners of both to repair their chancels and provide service books.[184] One Richard Cole, who had established in the early thirteenth century a chapel at Polapit Tamar (in Werrington), was to bear the whole expense of its upkeep and to remit oblations received to the prior and convent. His chaplain was to be 'of the jurisdiction and fealty' of the priory and to respect the indemnity of the parochial right of the church of Werrington. Richard Cole was not 'to overlook the due and customary suits to the church of Werrington in the principal feasts of the year'.[185] There is a suggestion here of an almost jealous protection of the priory's rights over Werrington.

There were several similar cases of the protection of the priory's rights. In the later twelfth century, one Stephen, the owner of the advowson of

[181]Nos. 22–3.
[182]Above, p. xxii–xxiii.
[183]Above, p. xxiii.
[184]Nos. 293–6 and 301.
[185]No. 297.

the chapel of Luffincott, was told that before his chaplain could be presented to the bishop the man was to swear fealty to the church of Launceston and to pay yearly 2s. 6d. to the prior and canons. Stephen de Luffincott had to bear the entire cost of maintaining the chapel and those who died at Luffincott were to be taken with their possessions to the church of St Stephen (the mother church) for burial.[186]

Incidental information of great value occasionally emerges from such records. An action before the official of the peculiar jurisdiction of the bishop of Exeter at the parish church of South Petherwin on 21 July 1333 refers to a letter received by the rural dean of East Wivelshire stating that the proctor for the priory had asked for the payment of forty shillings (in the official's presence) from Thomas, perpetual vicar of Lewannick. Thomas admitted that he owed this sum to the priory for the costs of rebuilding and construction of the church of Lewannick.[187]

There are records in the cartulary about the repair of chapels and chancels relating to St Nicholas, Tresmeer,[188] and the chapel of St Juliot and the church of St Gennys, though in the latter case the prior and convent were to bear two-thirds of the cost of repairing the chancel of St Gennys, and the vicar was to receive a moiety of the mortuaries from the chapel of St Juliot and 2d. for a mortuary at the burial of parishioners of St Gennys,[189] an agreement made in 1320. The matter came up again in 1380 when Robert Moka, vicar of St Gennys, acknowledged that he was responsible for one third of the cost of repairing the chancel and presented the prior with one noble and a portable breviary (to remain at St Gennys while he was vicar) to atone for a controversy which had continued for a long time.[190]

Other chapels of St Gennys belonging to the priory were at Crackington and St Gregory of Hill.[191] There was a dispute between the parishioners and the priory concerning the lesser tithes of St Gregory of Hill.[192] The settlement in July 1336 revealed that the chapel of St Gregory had been in existence for a hundred years and that from time immemorial there had been a chantry there which ceased at Michaelmas 1335. It is clear from a document of 5 January 1402 that the chantry at the chapel of St Gregory of Hill was continued.[193]

One of the most important settlements of disputes with parishes was by Bishop Oldham in 1506 which regulated the relations of the chaplain and the inhabitants of the Chapel of St Thomas (by Launceston) but this is not in the cartulary.[194]

---

[186]No. 76.
[187]No. 101.
[188]No. 226.
[189]No. 336.
[190]No. 337. In the late twelfth and early thirteenth centuries there were disputes about the ownership of the advowson of the chapel of St Juliot not settled until the episcopate of William Briwere (1224–44), see nos. 342–4, 345–7.
[191]No. 344. The priory had possessed these chapels from the later twelfth century.
[192]No. 386.
[193]No. 387. For an agreement between the rector of St Martin by Looe to pay to the priory oblations from the chapel of St John the Baptist in the manor of Bucklawren, see no. 467.
[194]It is printed in *Mon. Dioc. Exon.*, 26–7. The parishioners of the chapel of St Thomas had, *inter alia*, to repair the chapel and provide and maintain service books and, in general,

There are two interesting agreements of the prior and convent as rectors of the church of Liskeard with the mayor and commonalty of Liskeard for the construction and addition of a south choir aisle and a north choir aisle to the parish church of Liskeard, dated 31 March 1430 and 31 March 1477 respectively.[195] The agreements have similar wording: the wall of the chancel was to be broken and the aisles to be formed with timber and arches. This was the responsibility of the mayor and commonalty, and they and the parishioners of Liskeard agreed to maintain the new aisles. The muniments of the former borough of Liskeard contain copies of the two agreements in the cartulary.[196] They also contain an earlier agreement for the erection of a south choir aisle dated 23 April 1428.[197] The cartulary also contains part of a grant by Prior Thomas de Burdon (1346–61), the title to which suggests an addition of twelve feet in length to the nave and chancel of Liskeard church.[198] The description of Thomas as a former prior probably means that the work was carried out after he was prior: the last mention of him in the cartulary is in 1361. So the work may have been done in the time of his successor, Roger Leye, who occurs in the cartulary between 1370 and 1387.[199] In 1381 the Bishop of Exeter granted permission for the patronal festival to be changed from its former date of the Vigil of St Bartholomew (23 August) to the Translation of St Martin (4 July) and it was therefore from this date that the dedication to St Martin was established. Charles Henderson noted that the chancel formerly extended ten feet further east and that there are slight remains of fourteenth-century work 'doubtless dating from the re-dedication in 1381'. It is difficult to reconstruct from the church of Liskeard today precisely what was done in 1428–30 and 1477, but it would seem that an aisle was added to the south of the chancel, that this aisle became the Lady Chapel and that a north choir aisle was built in 1477.[200]

Some settlements of disputes related to pensions payable to the priory which were in arrears: a pension from the church of Lapford in Devon had not been paid for twenty-six years.[201] In 1308, John, vicar of Liskeard, was in arrears in paying an annual pension of 100s. to the priory which he

were subject to the mother church of St Stephens and even more to the conventual church of the priory.

[195]Nos. 507 and 600.

[196]Cornwall County Record Office, Borough of Liskeard muniments, nos. 79–80.

[197]Borough of Liskeard muniments no. 78.

[198]No. 506.

[199]The word *Rogerum* was first written in the title to no. 506 and then struck through and the word *Thomam* substituted.

[200]*Cornish Church Guide* (reprinted 1964), 123–4. See Hingeston-Randolph, *Reg. Brantingham*, p. 448. The late Sir N. Pevsner in *Cornwall* (1951 ed.), 90 pointed out that the chancel of Liskeard church is lower than the nave. For various interpretations of the grants of 1428 and 1430, see John Allen, *History of Liskeard* (1856), 39. (The 1428 grant was a failure, hence the grant of 1430.) J. C. Cox, *County Churches, Cornwall* (1912) writes of the erection of a south aisle with Lady Chapel annexed in 1428 and of a (presumably) separate south chancel aisle built in 1430, a view also held by R. and O. Peter, *Histories of Launceston*, 16–17. Pevsner (loc. cit.) writes of 'an extra outer S. aisle (Lady Chapel)'. Later restorations do not make the question capable of a definite answer, e.g. see the modern plan of Liskeard church in Edmund Sedding, *Norman Architecture in Cornwall*, facing p. 250.

[201]Nos. 594–5. Nicholas Treryse, parson of Lapford begged pardon of the prior on bended knees and took an oath on the gospels that the pension was due. For the pension of a vicar of Linkinhorne in 1233 see no. 536.

had not paid since his induction. Nearly a century later in June 1403 John Warin, vicar of Liskeard, was £15 in arrears with this same pension of 100s. John asked for forgiveness and promised a yearly pipe of wine to the prior and canons as well as payment of the arrears.[202]

Advowsons were contested. The abbot of Glastonbury and the prior of Launceston argued for ten years about the advowson of the chapel of St Michael of Lamanna, or Looe island. Did it belong to Walter de Treverbyn who had bought it from the abbey of Glastonbury, or to the prior of Launceston who owned the advowson of the parish of Talland in which Lamanna lay? About 1289 the answer was that Walter was the owner with the prior claiming that he ought to have the advowson because he had the tithes of the chapel.[203] In 1235 the advowson of Linkinhorne was said to belong to the priory.[204] Ten years earlier the priors of Bodmin, Tywardreath and St Germans had been appointed judges delegate by Pope Honorius III because the vicar, one Master Hamo, and other clerks of the diocese had injured the priory with regard to tithes, possessions and pensions. Hamo was made to bear the ordinary and extraordinary costs of the church and to pay yearly three marks of silver to the prior and canons from whom he was to hold the church.[205] A few years later the vicar's pension payable to the priory was only two marks.[206]

Evidence about the relations of the priory with the mayor and burgesses is not plentiful.[207] There was an agreement, already noticed, at the priory on 14 May 1395 by which the prior and convent agreed to repair and maintain the chancel of the *capella Magdalena* in the high street of the borough of Dunheved 'in walls and timber as well as glass and covering'. The borough had to maintain the service books and vestments and other ornaments of the chapel.[208]

There was an agreement at Launceston on 4 September 1400 about part of the western boundary of the borough with the priory. It was made between the prior (Stephen de Tredidon) and convent and Richard Cobbethorn, the mayor of Dunheved, and the commonalty of the borough.[209] Evidently this boundary had been in dispute. The main features are well described by R. and O. Peter in their *Histories of Launceston and Dunheved*.[210] The boundary ran northwards up the stream called Harper's lake near St John's chapel,[211] 'to Maiden's Well' (the site

[202]Nos. 503 and 508. The pension of 100s. from the vicar of Liskeard went back at least as far as 1265, see no. 502.

[203]No. 458. See no. 456 for the advowson of Talland.

[204]Nos. 530–1.

[205]No. 533.

[206]No. 536.

[207]See above, pp. xxvii–xxviii for disputes relating to the assize of bread and ale. The first recorded mayor, Hamelin Miles, witnessed Prior Robert de Fissacre's grant to the Lepers of Gillemartin *c*.1245–1257: see note 52 above.

[208]No. 37. John Cokeworthy was to present to the chapel an antiphonary and an invitatory before the following feast of St John the Baptist (24 June).

[209]No. 38 by final concord, another copy of which still survives among the borough muniments bearing part of the seal of the priory. (Cornwall County Record Office, Borough of Launceston, (Hart-Smith) box 2, no. 7).

[210]Pages 13–16 and 355. See also the useful map of the borough facing p. 195.

[211]A private chapel dedicated to St John the Baptist built *c*.1414 (R. and O. Peter, *Histories of Launceston and Dunheved*, 120–1) which has now disappeared, though the site is known.

of which is known) 'near the head of Wooda Lane' by the garden of the
prior to Sextenyshaye (part of the churchyard of St Thomas) and thence
to the west of a fulling mill and so to the river Kensey on the west part of
the chapel of St James [212] The Peter brothers thought that this chapel was
on the eastern or Dunheved side of Harper's Lake, and the priory garden
and the chapel of St Thomas were to the west of the boundary, i.e. outside
part of the western boundary of Dunheved. Except for the Water Fair[213]
belonging to the priory, the mayor and commonalty were to have this
boundary without the interference of the prior, though the mayor and
burgesses ratified 'the state of the prior and convent's steps, porches and
stair erected within the liberty of Bastehay and the lands, rents and
services held by John Tregorrek and others in the same liberty'.[214] The
mayor and burgesses had no right to the way through Sextonshaye to the
chapel of St Thomas.[215]

The agreement of September 1400 raises the question of the status of
the priory (and priors) in Launceston. In the case of Bodmin priory it
seems that Bodmin borough was very much the prior's borough.[216] The
standing of any prior of an Augustinian priory (except perhaps the
smallest) was of importance: this can be seen, if only vaguely, in the
cartulary.[217] The difference between Bodmin and Launceston was that
the new borough and castle of Dunheved had been planted or continued
by King William I's half-brother and the borough was very much in the
hands of the earls (and later dukes) of Cornwall. This factor undoubtedly
strengthened the position of the mayor and burgesses.[218]

More than a third of the total revenues of Launceston priory at the
Dissolution, as the *Valor Ecclesiasticus* shows, derived from sheaf or greater
tithes[219] and these were a fertile source of disputes. In 1238 papal intervention ordered the settlement of differences between Montacute and
Launceston priories about the tithes of the demesne lands of (the manor
of) Fawton and Fowey Moor.[220] As a result of the agreement, the priory of
Launceston received two-thirds of the tithes. In relation to newly
cultivated land, both priories were to receive a moiety of the tithes and

[212]One of the several chapels which clustered round the priory. The others were St
Catherine, St Margaret, St John of Bridlington and St Gabriel. The only chapel which has
survived is the present church of St Thomas: see R. and O. Peter, op. cit., 34.

[213]No. 63.

[214]R. and O. Peter, op. cit., 13 suggests that the prior and canons had encroached on waste
grounds within the borough. They do this by making the word Bastehay into *Vastehaye*, for
which there is no warrant, though there can be no quarrel with their statement (op. cit., 15)
that 'it was part of the compromise that these encroachments should be forgiven, and the
prior's right to retain his steps, porches etc. admitted'.

[215]Otho Peter defined the Sextonhaye, as the cemetery of the laity (the canons being
buried in the cloister square). See his 'Launceston Priory', the substance of a lecture which
he gave to the Launceston Scientific and Historical Society on 7 January 1889, p. 17.

[216]For Bodmin as a town belonging to Bodmin priory, see Charles Henderson, *Essays in
Cornish History* (1935), 223.

[217]e.g. nos. 48–51.

[218]See note 207.

[219]*Valor Ecclesiasticus* (Rec. Comm. edition), 402–3. For the dispute of 1291 with St
Germans priory concerning $\frac{1}{3}$ of the tithes of Dunheved, see above, p. xxi.

[220]Nos. 86–8. In no. 87 there was a subsidiary settlement about St Luke's chapel on
Fowey moor. Both priories were to share the expenses and the profits of the chapel and the
dead were to be buried at St Neot until a cemetery had been built for the chapel.

Launceston priory received in addition 'the tithes of one carrucate of land which they cultivated at their own expense and also the small tithes of their own store'.[221] In 1303 a synodical judgement by the bishop's commissary at St Germans ended by a confirmation of the possession by Launceston priory of two-thirds of the greater and lesser tithes of Fawton in St Neot.[222] One fifteenth of all tithes of the manor of Bucklawren had also to be paid to the rector of St Martin by Looe.

There is a record of a dispute about the tithes of the chapel of Drywork in Altarnun between the farmer, Roger le Rus, and the appropriators, the dean and chapter of Exeter and Launceston priory. It was said that the chapel of Drywork needed repair and rebuilding: the parishioners had been ordered by the bishop of Exeter to go to the parish church of Altarnun. By February 1282, however, the prior was able to show that the chapel had been repaired, so the bishop's official decreed that all the profits of the chapel, including the tithes, should be paid to the prior as they used to be paid.[223]

One agreement concerned all the tithes (greater and lesser) of a mount called *Oddedoune* (not located) between Altarnun and Lewannick. The dean and chapter of Exeter, as appropriators of Altarnun, disputed the tithes with Launceston priory, which possessed the church of Lewannick. Two canons from Exeter and two from Launceston viewed the site and it was agreed at Exeter on 24 July 1328 that the tithes of a moiety of the mount towards the west were to belong to the church of Altarnun, and the tithes of the eastern half were to go to the priory as owners of the church of Lewannick. The boundaries of the two halves were to be marked by a line of stones or brushwood.[224] A mandate of Pope Gregory IX led to the precentor and succentor of Salisbury investigating in 1239 a dispute concerning the tithes of the mount of Brown Willy, following a complaint by Odo, rector of St Breward. The tithes were owned by Montacute and Launceston priories and it was resolved that Odo should pay four shillings yearly to the two priories for the tithes of Brown Willy.[225] Tithes of the chapel of Tresmeer were for long in dispute between Tywardreath and Launceston priories. The settlement was a simple division of the greater tithes of the vills of Tresmeer, Trew, Treglum and *La Dune* between the two priories.[226]

Werrington and St Giles, chapelries belonging to the priory, also gave trouble about tithes. Henry Marshall, bishop of Exeter, judged (*c.*1194–9) that the priory should have these tithes from Tavistock abbey to which the prior and his successors should pay 50s. yearly, saving the tithes of the

[221]An obscure phrase. Does it refer to the store of St Luke's chapel or furnishings (wax etc.) which had to be provided for that chapel?

[222]No. 90. For the whole paragraph see also nos. 468, 470–6. In nos. 470–1 (1384) the rector of St Martin's did not mind 14/15ths of the tithes of Bucklawren going to the priory, but if the manor was leased out, he thought he should be paid all the tithes. The prior eventually agreed to pay the rector a pension of 40s., see nos. 470–5.

[223]No. 89.

[224]No. 100.

[225]No. 92. There is an interesting description of the bounds. Cf. the account of the bounds of Fowey moor in no. 88.

[226]No. 289, witnessed by Auger, abbot of St Sergius of Angers and Geoffrey, prior of the same abbey, the parent house of Tywardreath priory.

produce of the abbey's demesne throughout the manor of Werrington,[227] and the priory was not to have the tithes and obventions of the church of North Petherwin. A few years later, in July 1202, the parishioners of the chapel of St Giles were warned to implement an agreement with the prior and canons concerning the tithe of hay and mortuary fees on pain of being cited before the archdeacon's official or his commissary at Bodmin the following Michaelmas.[228] Another dispute in which St Giles was involved concerned the tithes of the manor of Panson in Devon and the villeinage of Newton. Bishop Walter Bronescombe settled the dispute at Launceston on 7 July 1261: the tithes were halved, the moieties (of Panson and Newton) to go to the prior and canons and the rector of Sydenham Damarel. The rector was given the small tithes and oblations and the small tithes of the villeinage of Newton went to the priory, which also was awarded a moiety of the sheaf tithes of the demesne of Panson and of the villeinage of Newton.[229]

John Pecham, archbishop of Canterbury, on a visitation of the deanery of Trigg Major in 1281, decided that the vicar of Stratton, Andrew de Kayinges's, taxation (made by Bishop Bronescombe) of twenty-five marks to the priory for the privilege of having the greater tithes, altar dues and other obventions was uncanonical. Andrew and the prior appeared before the archbishop at Hartland abbey on 5 April 1281: the priory was awarded the greater tithes and the whole of the glebe. The vicar had to be content with altar dues and offerings, the small tithes and his manse and garden, though the prior and canons were to give him a quarter of wheat in the middle of Lent to make the host for Easter.[230]

On Saturday, 27 May 1279, a dispute between the abbey of Glastonbury and the priory was settled concerning the tithes of the chapel of St Michael at Lamanna, or Looe Island.[231] Lamanna had been granted to Glastonbury by Hastutus, son of John de Subligny,[232] and the grant had been confirmed by a bull of Pope Alexander III of 19 April 1168.[233] By a charter of Richard, earl of Cornwall, the island of Lamanna had to pay ten shillings yearly to the Earl's seneschal or the bailiff of Cornwall at Launceston castle at Michaelmas for (*inter alia*) freedom from customs, manorial courts, hundred and shire courts.[234] A mandate of Pope Gregory IX relating to a dispute between the priory and Glastonbury about tithes of land between the way from Porthbighan (West Looe) to *Ternent* and the water of Looe – i.e. on the demesnes of the land of Odo de Portlooe – led to an agreement of 4 November 1239 by which the prior of Launceston was to pay the abbey of Glastonbury five shillings yearly via the 'prior' of

---

[227]No. 291.
[228]No. 300.
[229]No. 298. An earlier episcopal settlement of 1236 had awarded the sheaf tithes of Panson in demesne and villeinage to both prior and rector. The latter and his successors were to pay the prior 12d. yearly: see no. 299.
[230]No. 422.
[231]No. 457.
[232]Thomas Hearne, *Adami de Domerham Historia de Rebus Gestis Glastoniensibus* (Oxford, 1727), 599–600.
[233]Dom. Aelred Watkin (ed.), *The Great Chartulary of Glastonbury* (Somerset Record Society) i (1947), no. 173.
[234]Hearne, op. cit., 603–4.

Lamanna or a messenger of the abbot sent to Lamanna.[235] In 1279 Launceston priory granted all tithes to the abbey of Glastonbury.[236]

Finally, there is a record of a dispute between the priory and the parishioners of the parochial chapelry of North Tamerton about the tithe of hay.[237] The parishioners had paid a composition of 5s. 6d. yearly to the priory to have this tithe. In 1407 it was agreed that the parishioners should pay the prior and convent 6s. 8d. 'except the tithe of hay of the vill of Tamerton which was glebe land of the demesne of the church of St Stephen Launceston'.

It is not necessary to describe the relation of the priory and other religious houses, but mention should be made of the renunciation by the abbot and convent of the Cistercian abbey of Cleeve in Somerset *c.*1238 of their right in the church of St Olaf of Poughill which they granted to the priory in pure and perpetual alms.[238] About 1223–31 the priory entered into an agreement with the abbot and convent of the Premonstratensian abbey of Torre who promised not to molest the church of Liskeard in return for a payment by the priory of four marks of silver at Easter and Michaelmas, during the lifetime of Master William de Linguire, clerk.[239]

## GRANTS AND LEASES: SOME INDICATIONS OF THE ECONOMY OF THE PRIORY

When considered in conjunction with the rental of the priory of 1474,[240] grants and leases provide some evidence of the economy of Launceston priory. A grant of land in 1404 imposed fealty on the tenant, an annual rent, and suit to the priors' court of Bernhay every three weeks.[241] A former serf of the priory and his wife were regranted in 1419 lands which they formerly held in stock at a rent and by military service, with customary services due to the prior as chief lord of the fee. If there were no legitimate heirs the lands were to revert to the priory.[242] Mention is made of tenants holding by homage, fealty and scutage with a yearly payment for service (12d.) and suit of court to the manor of Launceston Land every three weeks.[243] A mid-thirteenth century grant of land in Pyworthy (in the priory manor of Bradford) was for homage and service and rent, with suit to the mill of the priory at Pinkworthy and, twice yearly, to the prior's court of Bradford. 'If they [Roger Lene and Alice his wife] were to incur a fine they could acquit themselves by four capons for all the pleas of one day'.[244] There were variations: it was stated in a grant of land in Wideslade in Stoke Climsland in 1434, that if the tenant or his heirs 'fell into mercy they would be judged by their peers in the prior's court [at

[235]Op. cit., 602–3.
[236]No. 457.
[237]No. 591.
[238]No. 405.
[239]No. 501, sealed by the priors of Plympton and Totnes.
[240]Above, p. xxiv.
[241]No. 157.
[242]No. 179.
[243]No. 273. See also no. 207 which mentions military service of 'the old enfeoffment' *c.*1414.
[244]No. 447.

Climson] and for a plea of one day they could acquit themselves of the fine for 3d.'[245]

It appears from the memorandum of an agreement of 25 July 1359 that Walter Penhirgard had not paid the full rent for the third part of an acre Cornish and other lands in Badgall in Laneast.[246] (The 'other lands' were claimed by the prior.) Neither had Walter paid reliefs of 25s. 0¼d. on the deaths of two tenants who held land in Crannow in St Gennys, nor had he paid rent or amercements of court for this land. Walter had not performed reaping and ploughing services (one day each) for land he held of the priory in Tresmeer. It was agreed that he should pay the full rent for his land in Badgall and perform a day's reaping service in the autumn. As for the ploughing service for the land he held in Bagdall and Crannow, it was agreed to put this question to a jury of twelve: if the service was not due from these lands they should be quit of all reliefs, rents and amercements. Prior Thomas gave Walter 'up to the sum of forty shillings' to pay his rents and services and to make suit for the two days' work of ploughing the land he held in Tresmeer which six tenants had sworn was due.

Leases did not always state a term, but 20, 40, 45, 50 and 65 years occur.[247] Leases are also found for one, two, or three lives.[248] The payment of rents varied from the usual four terms (Easter, the Nativity of St John the Baptist, Michaelmas and Christmas) to one term, and examples of two or three terms occur.[249] Suit of court was generally at the nearest manor. The courts of Bernhay and Launceston Land were perhaps one and the same. Bradridge was the venue of the court for Boyton, Climson for Stoke Climsland, Eastway for lands in Morwenstow. Suit might be twice yearly[250] or every three weeks.[251]

Reliefs occur[252] and also heriots[253] and suit of mill.[254] Tenants of the priory were sometimes required to perform the office of reeve when elected by the jurors of the manor court,[255] though in the vicar of Stratton's lease for life in 1437,[256] it was specified that he should hold that office for two tenures only. Sometimes a tenant was liable to serve as a tithingman. In a fifteenth-century lease of land at Tregadillett the tenant had to make suit of court every three weeks, perform two days' work yearly and also be bailiff of the manor of Launceston Land when chosen.[258]

[245]No. 578. The grant was for homage and service and was in fee and inheritance with a small yearly rent of 20d. with suit to the priory court twice yearly.
[246]No. 200.
[247]Nos. 228, 305, 143, 328, 577.
[248]Nos. 455, 283, 400, 394.
[249]No. 140 specifies the payment of rent at the Invention of the Holy Cross (3 May) and Michaelmas. Suit of court on 3 May also occurs in nos. 134–6.
[250]Nos. 135–6, 177, 283 etc.
[251]Nos. 207, 228 etc. Courts of the prior were also held for the 'borough' of Newport (no. 328), Hagland in Liskeard (no. 510) and for the manors of Caradon and Climson, (nos. 577–8).
[252]Nos. 135, 328 etc.
[253]Nos. 283, 394, 427, 577.
[254]See note 244.
[255]No. 394.
[256]No. 427.
[257]e.g. no. 577.
[258]No. 169.

Repairs were frequently an obligation of the lessee: a lease of land at Upton in Linkinhorne in the manor of Caradon states that the tenants were to repair all houses, buildings and ditches at their own costs.[259] An agricultural covenant occurs in one lease only, in this case the tenants being required to manure the land, spread sand on it and to burn it.[260] Distraint for arrears of rent, or re-entry by the lessor if there was not enough for distraint, was a frequent provision.[261]

Works are occasionally mentioned: reaping the corn of the priory and ploughing.[262] A lease in St Stephens by Launceston required two days' work at Newhouse in the same parish.[263] A lease of 1441 of property in Newport required a day's reaping in the autumn and the tenant had to make suit of court to the prior's borough of Newport and his court of the manor of Launceston Land.[264] A lease for 65 years to John Henry and his wife Felicia stipulated the service of carrying lime and salt as the other conventionary tenants of the manor of Caradon did.[265] The information provided by the cartulary on such matters is by no means abundant. More is to be learnt from the rental of the priory of 1474.[266] This shows ploughing, reaping and carrying services being performed at Newhouse and there is a bailiff of Newhouse mentioned. Free tenants were required to plough and reap at Newhouse. Conventionaries of the manor of Launceston Land had to plough, reap and carry salt and lime.

The most interesting information from the rental of 1474 is about conventionary tenants who held by assession (the taking of tenements, etc.). John Ford and his wife took a tenement in Lemalla in Lewannick for ten years. They had to pay rent and to attend the manor court at Bernhay every three weeks. They owed suit of mill; they were to carry salt and lime and also to plough reap and carry at Newhouse (or to pay 18d.) and to pay a farleve of 5s. if they left the manor. A heriot of a best beast was required at death. Before they took the land they had to pay a fine of ten shillings. Most conventionary tenants of Launceston Land held for a term of ten years.[267] Sometimes part of the term of the 'taking' at the last assession still remained. Thus John Cottell took a tenement *cum septem annis de prima capcione non determinatis*. At Boyton the assession was generally for twenty years and one of the services was the annual carriage of wood from Bradridge to Launceston. Again part of a term could be carried over: William Crokker took a property for 20 plus 16 years.

Mention is made of an assession at Stratton in 1476,[268] though no

[259]No. 577.
[260]No. 228 (Michaelmas 1335).
[261]e.g. nos. 135, 283, 400 etc.
[262]No. 169.
[263]No. 305.
[264]No. 328.
[265]No. 577.
[266]Above, p. xxiv. Folio numbers, of which there are two series (ancient and modern) have not been quoted. See note 148 above.
[267]Miss L. M. Midgley mentions conventionary tenure for ten or twelve years in her edition of *Ministers Accounts of the Earldom of Cornwall 1296-7* (Royal Historical Society, Camden 3rd series, vols. lxvi and lxvii (1942 and 1945), but this was exceptional: see P. L. Hull, *Caption of Seisin . . . 1337*, xxxi, citing J. Hatcher, 'Non-Manorialism in Medieval Cornwall' in the *Agricultural History Review* vol. 18 (1970) part i, 8, note.
[268]16 Edw. IV.

further details are given. At both the manors of Climsland Prior and Carnedon Prior (Caradon) *sessiones* show conventionaries holding from seven years to seven years, just as on the ancient manors of the duchy of Cornwall.[269] It should be noted, though, that at Stoke Climsland in 1474 there are tenements held by charter (one being for forty years with a customary payment of hens). Holding by charter also occurred in sessions of the manor of Launceston Land.

No picture of the priory's economy can be gained from the cartulary. All there is are rare references: the cultivation of land by the priory on Fowey Moor in the third decade of the thirteenth century;[270] a right of way eighteen feet wide for driving and leading horses and cattle with ditches on either side to prevent the cattle of the tenant straying into the corn or pasture of the glebe land of the priory at Stratton.[271] There are references to the priory demesne at Holeburgh in the manor of Bradford in Devon,[272] also to land being kept in hand and cultivated at Bucklawren in St Martin by Looe, though the prior and convent let it for one year only.[273] Mention is made of the pigs and cattle of the canons[274] and of their timber.[275] They had turves: three hundred cartloads were stolen from their turbary at Newhouse in the Moor (next to Dozmary Pool).[276] The prior and canons had common pasture in Lewannick, Polyphant, Laneast, St Gennys, Kilkhampton, Stratton and at Bonyalva in St Germans and in the manor of Caradon in Linkinhorne.[277] There is a reference to land held by villeins: villein land of the priory in West Bonyalva.[278] A reference to lands at St Gennys where 13 acres made a knight's fee is of exceptional interest.[279]

## NOTES ON CALENDARING AND EDITING

For the most part this edition is a calendar: full texts are given only for the charters of Count Robert of Mortain, Earl Reginald and Earl (later King) John, the foundation charter of the priory, a bull of Pope Alexander III, a charter of Bishop Robert I of Exeter, one charter of King Henry I and a few (mainly confirmations of existing charters) by King Henry II. The main criterion was that these charters had not been published before.

The rules laid down by Dr R. F. Hunnisett, *Editing Records for Publication* (British Records Association, 1977) for transcribing c/t, u/v, i/j and divine names have been followed. Occasionally italics have been used where words, or part of a word, are uncertain. Extensions where they occur have

[269]Hatcher, art. cit., 2, 4. Seven-year takings on the seventeen *antiqua maneria* occur in 1326 and became normal from the assession of 1331 and these were continued after the creation of the duchy in 1337.
[270]Nos. 86–88.
[271]No. 421.
[272]No. 447.
[273]No. 469.
[274]Nos. 81, 259.
[275]No. 443. No. 159 mentions the forester of the priory.
[276]No. 85.
[277]e.g. nos. 103, 111, 190, 217, 338, 401, 420, 485, 498.
[278]No. 592.
[279]No. 333. Cf. Hull, *Caption of Seisin . . . 1337*, ix and notes for references to 4 and 9 Cornish acres making a knight's fee.

been made silently, sometimes in round brackets. Round brackets are also used for editorial interpolations in the calendar. Square brackets have been used only for explanatory notes on dating documents. Capital letters have been modernised and additional punctuation has been added sparingly in the case of the full transcripts. Forenames have been translated in the calendar entries; surnames are given throughout in their original form, prefixed by '*de*', for even if a surname is obviously connected with a particular place-name, it does not necessarily mean that the bearer was living there at the time the document was written. When place-names are given in the calendar in their modern form the original form in italics is added in round brackets, at least on the first occurrence. Every identifiable place appears in the Index under the modern and most widely accepted form of the name, followed by variants. Unidentified place-names appear in their MS forms, within single quotes. Titles or headings to charters have not infrequently been omitted where they offer no additional (or misleading) information and, this edition being a calendar, marginal notes have been curtailed. In calendaring the text long clauses of common form such as 'holding from the chief lords of the fee' have been considerably reduced. Clauses of warranty *contra omnes gentes* merely appear as 'warranty' with any variant forms reproduced in full.

I worked on the text of the manuscript from enlargements from a microfilm of the original, the copies having been kindly made for me by Miss Sarah Pengelly when she was on the staff of the library of the Camborne School of Mines. Recourse was sometimes made to the microfilm and final checks were made with the original MS. at Lambeth Palace Library.

## ACKNOWLEDGEMENTS

First and foremost my thanks go to the members of the Council of the Devon and Cornwall Record Society, in particular to Mrs Audrey Erskine for all her help and guidance over the years. In the final stages of preparation I would like to thank Professor Frank Barlow for reading the typescript and Professor Joyce Youings for supervising the printing of this edition by the Devonshire Press. Mrs Margery Rowe, archivist to Devon County Council, was of great help in relation to certain specific points, as also was Miss Margaret Holmes, the former county archivist of Dorset. Postgraduate theses by Mr D. W. Blake and Mr Ian Soulsby have saved me (I hope) from some mistakes: Mr Blake's work on the Church of Exeter in the Norman period inevitably covered some of the ground.

Throughout the long years of preparation I felt a sense of gratitude to Charles Henderson whose transcript of the cartulary at the Royal Institution of Cornwall was always a *vade mecum* made possible by the copy provided by Leslie Douch (the curator). I would like to thank the county librarian, Mr J. Farmer, and especially his staff in the book loan section, who provided so many of the books I could not otherwise easily have obtained. I also wish to thank the Revd Dr J. C. Dickinson and the Revd Dr Adrian Morey O.S.B. for providing me with copies of their books on the Austin Canons and Bishop Bartholomew of Exeter, both of which had long been out of print.

Detailed help was given to me by discussion with Mr Richard Sharpe of the editorial staff of the *Medieval Latin Dictionary* on Peter of Cornwall (and his occasionally difficult Latin) and his family. The difficulties of identifying Cornish place-names were lightened by the help of Oliver Padel, who also very kindly commented on the text and eliminated many errors. I should also like to thank Mr Simon Bailey, formerly archivist at the Guildhall Library; Mrs P. Basing, research assistant in the department of MSS. at the British Library; Mr R. Walker, librarian at Lincoln's Inn and my daughter, Mrs Susan Palmer, for information not readily available in the deep South West. Mr E. G. W. Bill, librarian of Lambeth Palace Library, gave me every possible assistance, including the benefit of his knowledge of the Lambeth MSS. I received great help in the temporary loan of MSS. from Launceston from two town clerks, Mr W. G. Moffat and Mr P. Freestone.

I should like to end by thanking my wife for her understanding, constant help and (constructive) criticism, for putting up with a large pile of files, books and card-indexes which grew with the work and for her labour on the index. In short, the family were a source of inspiration. My thanks are also owing to Mrs Margaret Bunt of the Institute of Cornish Studies who so ably typed the indexes.

TRURO, PALM SUNDAY 1985                                    P. L. HULL


The Council of the Devon and Cornwall Record Society wishes to express its thanks to Mr Oliver Padel for his help in preparing the text for publication.

# THE CARTULARY

**1.** Part of a diploma of King Edward the Confessor merging the sees of Devon (Crediton) and Cornwall and transferring the seat of the united bishopric to the monastery of St Peter, Exeter. Dated 1050.

MS.: Cartulary, f.6r. For an incomplete list of MS. and printed versions, see P. H. Sawyer, *Anglo-Saxon Charters, an annotated list and bibliography* (Royal Historical Society 1968) no. 1021. The original MS. is D. and C. Exon. no. 2072, printed in W. B. Sanders, *Facsimiles of Anglo-Saxon Manuscripts*, 3 vols. (Ordnance Survey, Southampton, 1878–84) ii (Exeter) xiii. Printed: the Revd F. C. Hingeston-Randolph, *The Registers of Walter Bronescombe . . . and Peter Quivil . . . Bishops of Exeter . . .* (1889), 485–7. The version in the Cartulary begins with the last word (*est*) of line 14 of Hingeston-Randolph's printed version and ends abruptly on the word *manu* of line 60. The variant readings of the Cartulary compared with Hingeston-Randolph's text are listed below.

| Hingeston-Randolph | Cartulary |
|---|---|
| line 18 *Eadgyde* | *Eadgydie* |
| line 23 *eciam* | *autem* |
| line 23 *eundem* | *eum* |
| line 26 *ibi* | *inibi* |
| line 27 *hubertum* | *ubertim* |
| line 28 *ipsiusque* | *ipsumque* |
| line 29 *attestacione* | *attestacionem* |
| line 29 *deincepsque* | *deinceps* |
| line 35 *quoniam* | *que* |
| lines 35–6 *Cridunensem* | *Cridinensem* |
| line 39 *ab uno episcopo* | *ab ipso episcopo* |
| line 40 *Eadweardus* | *Edwardus* |
| line 43 *consanguineis* | *consanguinibus* |
| line 44 *Eadsino et Alerico* | *Eadfyno et Alfrico* |
| line 45 *Enimvero* | *Etenim vero* |
| line 48 *centuplicato* | *centiplicato* |
| line 50 *fautoris* | *fauttoris* |
| line 50 *nevo* | *necnon* |
| line 54 *dissegregacione* | *disgregacione* |
| line 54 *anathematus* | *anathematizatus* |
| line 56 *karecterata* | *carectarata* |
| line 57 *karecteribus* | *carecteribus* |
| line 57 *Eadweardo* | *Edwardo* |
| line 60 *Eadsinus* | *Eadfynus* |

**2.** Charter of King Henry I granting to the church of St Peter, Exeter, the churches in Cornwall of St Petroc, St Stephens by Launceston, St Piran, St Kew and St Probus. Also in Devon the churches of Plympton, Braunton and St Stephen, Exeter, with lands, tithes and appurtenances which his father, King William I, gave to William, bishop of Exeter, when he was King William's chaplain. Also the church of Cullompton which King Henry had given to Bishop William, with lands, tithes and appurtenances. Not dated [?1107].

MS. Cartulary, f.6v. There is a 13th-century copy, pressmark ED/M/2, in Exeter City Archives, Devon Record Office, Exeter, sealed with the seals of Bishop Bytton (1292–1307) and the dean and chapter of Exeter. Only one of the endorsements is legible, *Littera domini Regis H. sub sigill(o) Episcopi et Decani et Capituli Exon.* Printed: C. Johnson and H. A. Cronne, *Regesta* ii, no. 841 (calendared only).
The editors say the style of this charter is unlikely. Yet it is repeated in *Regesta* ii, no. 1391 (calendared entry), the words being the same, except for trifling variants, though Colyton is substituted for Cullompton and there is a witness list. Johnson and Cronne date *Regesta* no. 1391 as 1123, April 15?, Winchester. Both in *Regesta* ii, nos. 841 and 1391 St Kew (Docco=Dohou) needs to be added to the list of Cornish churches. A further confirmation by King Stephen of Henry I's grant (*Regesta*, iii no. 284, April 1136—November 1136) is in the same words (*mutatis mutandis*) as *Regesta* ii, nos. 841 and 1391. *Regesta* ii no. 1391 is derived from later copies, but Blake (p.115) may well be right in seeing this charter of 1123 as King Henry's original grant. He thinks that the ?1107 charter could be a forgery, but, as he says (Blake p.114), there is no apparent reason for a forgery. The reference in the ?1107 charter to Cullompton instead of Colyton is peculiar. None of the texts of the three charters are entirely satisfactory. If it is unlikely that Henry I issued two charters, I would prefer to reject the ?1107 charter. Blake suggests (*Trans. Devon Assoc.* Civ (1972) that this charter 'is an unskilful second copy of the original act' (*Regesta* ii, no. 1391) 'to which has been added a confusing witness list'. See also King Stephen's confirmation, *Regesta* iii, no. 284.

*Copia carte regis Henrici filij Willelmi regis primi*
In nomine Sancte et Individue Trinitatis. Ego Henricus Willelmi Anglorum primi regis filius tocius Anglie rex ac moderator notum facio omnibus clero simul et populo tam presentis seculi quam futuri. Quia Dei misericordia compunctus pro absolucione peccatorum meorum et salute anime mee, reddo et restituo Sancte Marie et Sancti Petri Exoniensis ecclesie has subscriptas ecclesias ita omnibus modis liberas et quietas sicut eas donatas esse a preclaris regibus predecessoribus meis ipsorum carte testantur: ecclesiam videlicet Sancti Petroci, Sancti Stephani, Pirani, Dohou, Probos cum omnibus terris et rebus ad eas pertinentibus ita liberas et quietas ab omnibus geldis querelis et consuetudinibus sicut fuerunt temporibus antecessorum meorum; preter autem has tres ecclesias in Devonia, quas pie memorie[a] Willelmus rex pater meus Willelmo episcopo Exonie dum ad huc capellanus suus esset dedit, ecclesiam de Plympton, de Brauntona, et ecclesiam Sancti Stephani infra ipsam civitatem Exonie ipsas concedo et dono sedi episcopali Exonie iure hereditario imperpetuum obtinendas pro redempcione anime mee et patris mee cum omnibus terris et decimis et rebus ad eas pertinentibus ita liberas et quietas ab omnibus consuetudinibus et querelis sicut pater meus predicto Willelmo eas dederat necnon et ecclesiam de Columptona quam ego prefato Willelmo episcopo dederam. Similiter concedo et dono episcopali sede Exonie pro remissione peccatorum meorum cum terris et decimis et omnibus rebus ad eam iuste pertinentibus. Et ut hec ita data inviolabiliter et inconcusse sub eterno munimento permaneant signo Sancte Crucis consignata dimitto.

[a] a signum cross follows the final sentence in the MS.

**3.**   Charter of Robert, count of Mortain and earl of Cornwall, brother of

William, king of the English, concerning the foundation of the church of secular canons of St Stephen. Dated 1076, fourteenth indiction.

MS.: Cartulary, ff.6v.–7v.

*Carta Roberti comitis Moretonij et Cornubie fratris Willelmi Anglorum regis de fundacione ecclesie Sancti Stephani canonicorum secularium.*

In nomine Patris et Filij et Spiritus Sancti Amen. Quoniam commodum annuente superni iudicis censura sub cirographi testimonio Sancte Dei ecclesie largior hereditatem predictam nobis videtur ut per futurum Sancte Dei ecclesie servientibus usque ad ultimum cursum secularis vite perpetualiter ligaminibus litterarum retentum regali auctoritate firmatum consularique dedicione datum permaneat quamvis a temporibus antiquorum regum ecclesia Sancti Stephani Lanstavetonensis canonice fuisset fundata et terris et alijs honoribus ditata. Tamen ne tempestate secularium cupidatum vel maculis reproborum religio eiusdem ecclesie in subsequentibus temporibus dissipetur ac rumpatur, ego Robertus comes Moretonij et Cornubie, frater Willelmi Anglorum regis, et Matildis uxor mea concessione supradicti regis hoc privilegium in ecclesia prothomartiris Stephani supradicti sub canonica auctoritate pro Willelmo rege et pro nobismet ipsis et pro nostris infantulis eternaliter constituimus. Et eciam octo mansas terre et dimidiam et v acros eidem ecclesie quas prius habuerat concessimus, quarum dimidietas est vestita et alia dimidietas vasta. Tali autem tenore hoc prefate munificencie munus tradendo concessimus ut possideat et firmiter teneat usque ad ultimum diem secularis vite cum omnibus utensilibus que Deus in *ipso* telluris gramine creavit tam ignotis causis quam notis, campis, pascuis, pratis. Et harum terre supradictarum hidarum iacet semis hida inter Lenega' et Melenec et una hida inter Lendren et Trebursy et Tregadylet et dimidia hida inter Chestell et Trenellat et dimidia hyda inter Tredydan et Trelodat. Et duo acri inter Carnaithan et Landpudic et una virgata inter Trespernan et Tregenner et virga in Lanast. Et una virga in Treuf et Tregloman et dimidia hyda in Tregvasmer et una virga in Tregher et ij acri in Trehonnudr et unus acrus in Trebretell et ij acri in Botgallon et unus acrus in Hendriden. Et unus acrus in Carhegintell et ij acri in Attel et unus acrus in Tregemon et unus acrus in Chernoc et ij acri in Treguethuc[a] et una virga in Trescoit et unus acrus *visum*[b] in alio Trescoit et unus acrus et *semis* in Dodestona et dimidia hida inter Bradrige et Birford et Berdun et una virga in Languenec et una virga in Penhel et ii acri et *semis* in Lanstavatona et in Lodcoit unus acrus et unus acrus in Cheuros et tres acri in Ghiderlega et una hyda et dimidia inter Botcoloer et Bodcodigu et Banathelva. Et harum terrarum iiij hyde et acri iacent in omnium fratrum communitate, xxj acrum[c] quarum tenent xxvj franci homines et ij hydas et iij virgatas et ij acros tenent cervesarij et servi et cum proprijs carucis fratrum communitati lucrantur et iiij hydas et iij acros habent ipsi canonici in sua proprietate sicut in subsequentibus *dividam*. Et viij burgenses habent canonici in commune in Lanceavetona quorum nomina hec sunt: Cola Rigensona, Elnot Hat, Adric Ghegia, Goduina, Hocanasune,

Humflet Pila, Edeman, Beates Faber, Jouin Faber. Et eciam ita canonice hanc ecclesiam constituerimus quod Rodbertum gratia Dei sacerdotem decanum in eadem basilica posuimus et decimas de sex nostris propriis mansionibus Sancto Stephano ad proprietatem victus eiusdem decani, et eciam ad prebendam subsequencium decanorum supradicta racione perpetualiter dedimus omnes decimas scilicet annone et caseorum et agnorum et vitulorum et pullinorum et porcorum et gablorum tam denariorum quam pecudum ceterarum-que terre rectitudinum exceptis duabus partibus annone et caseorum et porcorum de Liscaret et excepta tercia parte annone et caseorum ceterarum quinque mansionum quas *partes*<sup>d</sup> sacerdotes qui ecclesijs eorumdem mansionum serviunt habent, quarum nomina hec sunt: Ridlatona, Liscaret, Faitona, Tiguarnel, Henlistona, Treglastan. Et Ricardus filius Turoldi debet de uno acro et dimidio Gudmanneslega xxx denarios ad festum Sancti Michaelis ecclesie Sancti Stephani reddere et tres oves ad Pascha. Si quis autem hoc nostrum decretum privilegij minuerit reus sit ante tribunalem Christi et coram omnibus sanctis. Acta est autem hec prefata carta anno ab incarnacione domini nostri Jhesu Christi millesimo lxxvj<sup>to</sup>. indiccione xiiij<sup>mo</sup>.

<sup>a</sup>*Trewaythek* interlined   <sup>b</sup>*sic.* <sup>c</sup>*sic.* <sup>d</sup>*sic.*

**4.** Charter of King Henry I to William, bishop of Exeter, and to Ralph, dean of the secular canons of the church of St Stephen Launceston, granting confirmation of Bishop William's substitution of canons regular at St Stephen. The prebends of deceased canons and the goods of the church in the bishop's hands were to be applied to the commons of the canons regular. Canons who wished to become regular canons might hold their prebends for life and no one was to molest them. Witd. the bishop of Winchester and B(ernard), bishop of St David's and B.<sup>a</sup> the chancellor, and W. de Tancardvilla and Nigel de Albin(eio). Not dated [1121, April–May?, Winchester. The editors of *Regesta* ii suggest that the institution of canons regular might have been in 1121, not 1127, but they state that *Regesta* ii, no. 1281 could be the same date as no. 1486: '1127, May 22?, Winchester.']

<sup>a</sup>The editors of *Regesta* ii, no. 1281, note, think that 'B' is a mistake for 'R', i.e. Ranulf the Chancellor.

MS.: Cartulary, f.7v. Printed in *Regesta* ii, no. 1281 and also full text, p.341, no. cxxxvi.

**5.** Charter of William Warelwast, bishop of Exeter, about his first foundation of canons regular at the church of St Stephen by Launceston on the advice of the King, William, archbishop of Canterbury, his brother bishops, and the noble men of his province.·The canons were to live according to the Rule of St Augustine and were to have the possessions of the church of St Stephen free from all exactions. Dated 1127.

MS.: Cartulary, f.8r. Blake, appendix of documents, 234–5.

*Carta Willelmi Exoniensis episcopi de prima fundacione ecclesie Sancti Stephani Launceston canonicorum regularium.*
Quoniam multiplicatis malis super terram viri iniqui filij Belial undique ad hoc invigilant, ut nequissimus[a] adiuvencionibus[b] sponsam Christi ecclesiam sanctam et immaculatam vel perturbent vel subvertant. Caventes imposterum, et tam ecclesie quieti quam gregis domini saluti providentes scriptis memorie commendare curavimus que oblivione deleri tempore[c] succedente pertimuimus. Imperante igitur et in eterna beatitudine regnante mundique machinam solo nutu moderante una et individua Trinitate, anno ab incarnacione Domini millesimo c. xxvij°, tocius Britannie monarchiam rege Henrico disponente, sedique Cantuarensis archipresulatis Willelmo presidente, ego Willelmus Exoniensis ecclesie pastor licet indignus servus servorum Dei humillimus dolens temporibus meis tepidius et indecentius solito et iusto in quibusdam ecclesijs regimine[d] meo commissis a clericis eisdem deputatis laudes Dei frequentare et extolli decrevi viros ydoneos et religiose conditos in eis substituere, ut dignas Deo gratias ibidem agant, et tam pro populi quam pro suis excessibus sine intermissione intercedant. Unde factum est ut tam regis predicti quam archipresulis ceterorumque coepiscoporum meorum, et provincie mee optimatum consilio fretus et auxilio pro delictorum meorum remissione in ecclesia Sancti Stephani de Lanzavetona canonicos secundum Sancti Augustini regulam viventes constituerim et confirmaverim. Reddens eis et concedens imperpetuum possidenda omnia que eiusdem ecclesie iuris sunt tam in terris quam in alijs redditibus, ita libera et quieta ab omnibus consuetudinibus et exactionibus, sicut erant dum ego ipse ea tenerem. Si quis autem huius nostre donacionis et confirmacionis contra legum decreta et patrum instituta preter votum violator presumptuosus extiterit, sit pars eius cum Dathan et Abyron, fiant dies eius pauci et episcopatum eius accipiat alter; ceterasque que in eodem psalmo subsequuntur incurrat maledicciones nisi respuerit et digne satisfecerit. Facta est autem hec donacio et huius donacionis confirmacio sub istorum qui subscribuntur testimonio clericorum et laicorum. Odo archidiaconus, Magister Leowinus, Robertus Blundus, qui hanc cartam scripsit et dictavit; Willelmus Lotharingus, Walterus filius Gotsellmi, Willelmus filius Theobaldi, Hugo de Orbec, Herveus clericus episcopi, Godefridus de Mannavilla.

[a]*Sic* for *nequissimis.* [b]*sic.* [c]*sic.* [d]*sic.*

**6.** Bull of Pope Alexander III to Prior Geoffrey and his brethren of the church of St Stephen by Launceston. The pope took the church into his protection and ordered that the Rule of St Augustine be kept inviolably. He confirmed the possessions of the priory. Tithe was not payable on crops or on the food of animals. On the death of a prior, his successor was to be elected by the common consent of the canons, i.e. the wiser part of them. Right of free burial was granted but not for excommunicated or interdicted persons. No one was to disturb, take away, or keep the possessions of the church.ᵃ Not dated. [1159–81, pontificate of Alexander III.]

MS.: Cartulary, ff.8r.–9r. Not in Jaffé-Wattenbach-Loëwenfeld, *Regesta Pontificum Romanorum* ii (Leipzig 1888) nor in W. Holtzmann, *Papsturkunden in England*, 2 vols. in 3 (Berlin 1930, 1935, 1936; reprinted 1970 and 1972).

ᵃFolios 8r. and *verso* and 9r. are both cancelled by crossing out in a later hand.

*Bulla Alexandri papa Gaufrido priori et suis confratribus ecclesie Sancti Stephani de Lanstavetona super confirmacione omnium spiritualium et temporalium eiusdem ecclesie.*
Alexander episcopus servus servorum etc., dilectis filijs Gaufrido priori ecclesie Sancti Stephani de Lanstavetona eiusque fratribus tam presentibus quam futuris regulariter substituendis imperpetuum. Quociens illud a nobis petitur quod religioni et honestati convenire dinoscitur animo nos decet libenti concedere et petencium desiderijs congruum suffragium impartiri. Ea propter dilecti in domino filij vestris iustis postulacionibus clementer annuimus et prefatam ecclesiam in qua divino estis obsequio mancipati sub Beati Petri et nostra proteccione suscipimus et presentis scripti privilegio communimus. In primis siquidem statuentes ut ordo canonicus, qui secundum Deum et Beati Augustini regulam in eadem ecclesia institutus esse dinoscitur, perpetuis ibidem temporibus inviolabiliter observetur. Preterea quascumque possessiones quecumque bona eadem ecclesia in presenciarum iuste et canonice possidet aut infuturum concessione pontificum largicione regum vel principum oblacione fidelium seu alijs iustis modis prestante domino poterit adipisci, firma vobis vestrisque successoribus et illibata permaneant in quibus hec propriis duximus exprimenda vocabulis: locum ipsum in quo prefata ecclesia sita est cum omnibus pertinencijs suis. Capellam de Wlurinton cum appendicijs suis; capellam de Tamertuna cum appendicijs suis; capellam de Boitona cum appendicijs suis; capellam de Eglescheria cum appendicijs suis. Dimidiam capellam de castello cum appendicijs suis; capellam de Lanast cum appendicijs suis; capellam de Threusmur cum appendicijs suis. Ecclesiam de Lawanec cum appendicijs suis; ecclesiam Sancti Genesij cum appendicijs suis; ecclesiam de Stratuna cum appendicijs suis. Capellam unam Hebforde cum dimidia carucata terre. Ecclesiam de Brugge cum appendicijs suis; ecclesiam de Becchwrthi cum appendicijs suis; ecclesiam de Eggebery Lanstavatonaᵃ cum appendicijs suis. Duddestuna, Cudemaneslega, Gyderlega, Rosmarch, Rettahirin, Trebursy, Cestel, Torn, Trolonet, Carnaithan, Penhel, Trevallad, Tredidan, Hilla, Lanwanech, Trewanta, Lutcotte, Lanast, Trehemener, Tresparnan, Tregudilet, Bodgalla, Treusmur, Trebrytel, Tremuer, Treger, Treglumma, Treius, Keuros, terram forestarij et molendinum de Dounech'. Penchenech, Smalehille, Henterdren, Hattel, Chernoch, Treweitoch, Truschothe, Niwachircha, Fulaforda, Charginthel, Mellonoch et aliam Mellonoch, Linelega, Braderiga, Broduna, Birford. Terram Spitel, Twichene, Treger, Hilla. Item alia Truschoth. Tottesduna, Milnetuna, Dupeford, *Penros*, Risduna, Boctholama cum Benalva. Trekeneth, terram Chebel. Dimidiam

acram in Thewen. Ferling de Rethtraduc, Brenchvit. Sane novalium vestrorum que proprijs manibus aut sumptibus colitis sive de nutrimentis vestrorum animalium nullus a vobis decimas exigere presumat. Obeunte vero te nunc eiusdem loci priore vel tuorum quolibet successorum, nullus ibi qualibet subrepeticione astucia seu violencia preponatur nisi quem fratres communi consensu vel fratrum pars consilij sanioris secundum Deum et Beati Augustini regulam providerint eligendum. Sepulturam quoque ipsius loci liberam esse concedimus ut eorum devocioni et extreme voluntati qui se illic sepeliri deliberaverint nisi forte excommunicati vel interdicti sint nullus obsistat salva iusticia illarum ecclesiarum a quibus mortuorum corpora assumuntur. Preterea cum generale interdictum terre fuerit liceat vobis clausis januis non pulsatis tintinabulis exclusis interdictis et excommunicatis suppressa voce divina officia celebrare. Decernimus eciam ut nullo omnino homini fas sit prefatam ecclesiam temere perturbare aut eius possessiones afferre[b] vel ablatas[c] retinere minuere seu quibuslibet vexacionibus fatigare, set omnia integre conserventur eorum pro quorum gubernacione ac sustentacione concessa sunt usibus omnimodis pro futuro, salva sedis apostolice auctoritate et diocesani episcopi canonica iusticia. Si qua igitur in futurum ecclesiastica secularisve[d] persona hanc nostram constitucionis paginam sciens contra eam temere venire temptaverit, secundo tercio ve[d] commonita nisi reatum suum congrua satisfaccione correxerit potestatis honorisque sui dignitate careat reamque se divino iudicio existere de perpetrata iniquitate cognoscat et a sacratissimo corpore ac sanguine Dei et Domini redemptoris nostri Jhesu Christi aliena fiat atque in extremo *examine districte* ulcioni subiaceat. Cunctis autem eidem loco sua iura servantibus sit pax Domini Jhesu Christi quatenus et hic fructum bone accionis percipiant et apud districtum iudicem premia eterne pacis inveniant. Amen.

[a]*sic.* [b]note in right margin, *leg' auferre.* [c]*sic.* [d]*sic* (in two words).

**7.**  Confirmation by Bishop Robert I of Exeter of the institution of canons by his predecessor, Bishop William Warelwast, in the church of St Stephen, Launceston. Not dated. [1131–50. Blake, 139, note 1.]

MS.: Cartulary, f.9r.–9v.

*Carta Roberti Exoniensis episcopi super confirmacione fundacionis predicte.*
Robertus Dei gratia Exoniensis ecclesie indignus episcopus omnibus sancte ecclesie filijs in Christo salutem. Quoniam ex officio servorum Dei quieti et saluti providere debitores sumus dignum duximus tam futurorum sciencie transmittere quam presencium memorie committere, quod ratam habemus, et presentis scripti et sigilli nostri attestacione confirmavimus constitucionem canonicorum regularium a venerabili episcopo Willelmo, predecessore nostro, in ecclesia Sancti Stephani Lanstavaton factam, et omnimodam donacionem et ordinacionem terrarum possessionum et quorumcumque bonorum ad eorum sustentacionem iuxta carte sue testimonium ab eodem episcopo ecclesie illi factam. Providentes ut per hanc concessionem et

confirmacionem nostram imposterum minus inquietati[a] quietius et
liberius Dei servicio vacare studeant. Si quis autem hanc prenominati
domini et predecessoris nostri constitucionem, et nostram concessionem et bona servorum Dei in ecclesia illa Deo servientium
confirmaverit, conservaverit, vel aliquo modo iuste auxerit, cum
servis Dei vitam et requiem eternam possideat. Qui vero infringere,
diripere, vel aliquo modo violare temptaverit, perpetue malediccioni
subiaceat, nisi resipuerit et ad satisfactionem venerit. Huius quidem
concessionis et confirmacionis testes sunt: Galfridus, prior Plympton[b];
Walterus Archer, Willelmus de Augo archidiaconus, Hugo de Auger
archidiaconus, Robertus cantor Exonie, Brictius capellanus meus,
Rogerus de Winchal', Johannes presbiter, Robertus camerarius et
multi alij.

[a]*sic.* [b]*sic.*

**8.** Bull of Pope Eugenius III to Bishop Robert I of Exeter, confirming
the possessions of the cathedral church under papal protection in
Cornwall and Devon and elsewhere. The churches of St Petroc of Bodmin,
St Stephen of Launceston, St Piran, St Crantock, St Probus[a] and St Kew
in Cornwall. In Devonshire the churches of Braunton, Plympton, St
Stephen Exeter and Colyton. The church of Bampton in Oxfordshire. The
Cornish manors of St Germans, Tregear, Treliever, Methleigh, Lanisley,
Burniere, Pawton and Lawhitton. In Devon the manors of Crediton,
Morchard Bishop, Slapton, Dittisham, Bishops Teignton, Lyndridge in
Bishops Teignton, Chudleigh Knighton, Paignton, Bishop's Tawton and
Ashburton. With other properties in Oxfordshire, Sussex, Gloucester-
shire, Surrey, Norfolk and Suffolk. Dated 7 February 1146.

[a]Probus omitted in Launceston cartulary.

MS.: Original bull in MSS. of the late Earl of Ilchester, ref. D 124, now at Dorset Record
Office. Cartulary, ff.9v–10r. Printed: D. W. Blake, 'An original Bull of Pope Eugenius III,
7th February 1146' in *D & CN & Q*, xxxiv (part viii), Autumn 1981, 307–11. Like no. 6,
both folios have been crossed out at a later date.

**9.** Charter of Stephen, king of England,[a] confirming the canons regular
of St Stephen, Launceston, placed there by Bishop William, and the
prebends of deceased canons and the goods of the church which the
Bishop had in his hands. Canons who wished to be converted to the
regular order might hold their prebends and whatever pertained to them
in peace. He commanded that the canons there might not be impleaded
for their lands held of the ancient prebend and that the prebends might be
recognised and safeguarded against any relatives of deceased canons
claiming in heredity. King Stephen also granted by the council of the
bishop and his barons of the neighbourhood that the canons might move
themselves into houses and outbuildings in a more suitable place for
themselves and the service of God in their own land wherever they wished
without loss. The canons were to be left to live in peace and to serve God
without injury or violence as King Henry had ordered by his charter.
Witd. Henry, bishop of Winchester, and A(lgar), bishop of Coutances,

and B(ernard), bishop of St David, and Robert Arundell and Warin the
sheriff, G(eoffrey) de Furnellis. Not dated. [Gillingham, Dorset, 1136,
*Regesta* iii, no. 434.]

ᵃ*Regesta* iii, no. 434: Angl(orum).

MS.: Cartulary, f.10r.–f.10v. Printed in full from the cartulary in *Regesta* iii, no. 434.

**10.** Confirmation by King Henry II to the canons regular at Launceston
introduced by Bishop William Warelwast of Exeter. They were to have
the prebends of deceased secular canons granted by King Henry I and
Bishop William (Cartulary nos. 4 and 5) and no one was to do them injury
or ill-treat them. Not dated [*c.*1155–8, determined by the witness *Warinus
filius Geroldi camerarius*, see Delisle, *Recueil des Actes de Henry II*, introductory
volume, Paris 1909, 468–9.]

MS.: Cartulary, ff.10v.–11r.

*Carta Henrici tercij$^a$ regis Anglie super concessione et Confirmacione carte
Henrici regis primi et Willelmi Exoniensis episcopi facta canonicis regularibus
de Lanstavetona.*
Henricus rex Anglie et dux Normannie et Acquietannie et comes
Andegavie archiepiscopis episcopis abbatibus comitibus justiciis
vicecomitibus ministris et omnibus fidelibus suis Francis et Anglis et
Wallencibus salutem. Sciatis me concessisse quod canonici regulares
sint apud Lanstavetonam quos Willelmus episcopus Exoniensis
ibidem posuit et habeant prebendas secularium canonicorum defunc-
torum et omnes res et possessiones quas rex Henricus avus meus et
idem episcopus Exoniensis eis dederunt et concesserunt. Quare volo
et firmiter precipio quod predicti canonici habeant et teneant
ecclesiam suam de Lanstavetona et omnes predictas prebendas cum
pertinencijs eorum et omnes res et possessiones suas et tenementa sua
ita bene et in pace et honorifice et quiete et libere cum omnibus
libertatibus et liberis consuetudinibus predicte ecclesie et prebendis
et tenementis pertinentibus in boscho et plano in pratis et pascuis in
aquis et molendinis in vijs et semitis infra burgum et extra et in
omnibus locis sicut carta Henrici regis avi mei et carta Willelmi
episcopi Exoniensis eis testantur. Et prohibeo ne quis sibi vel rebus
suis iniuriam vel contumeliam faciat quia ipsi et omnes res et
possessiones eorum sunt in mea propria custodia et protectione.
Testibus Rogero archiepiscopo Eboracensi, Roberto episcopo
Lincolniensi, Waltero episcopo Cestrensi, Thoma Cancellario,
Reginaldo comite Cornubie, Willelmo fratre regis, Ricardo de
Humeto constabulario, Warino filio Geroldi camerario, Manassero
Biset dapifero, Willelmo filio Hamonis. Apud Notyngham.

ᵃ*sic* for *secundi.*

**11.** Charter from Reginald, son of the king, earl of Cornwall, to all his
men French, English and 'Welsh' (Cornish). He had taken into his

protection and the protection of God and King Henry (II) the church of Launceston with all its appurtenances, ecclesiastical and lay, and the canons who ministered there in honour of God and the blessed protomartyr Stephen, for the stability, tranquillity and peace of Henry, king of England (King Henry II) for the salvation of the soul of his (Reginald's) father, the (late) king Henry, and of all his ancestors and successors. Wherefore he wished, granted and confirmed that the canons should have and hold the said church of Launceston and all (its) lands and tenures they had or would acquire freely, quietly, peacefully and honourably as ever they or their ancestors more freely and better held the same. That is to say with soke and sake and toll and theam and infangentheof and with all other liberties to them and their men and freedom from suits of shire courts and hundred pleas and castleguard[a] and all other aids and secular service and exaction and all other occasions and customs. Moreover he wished to bring to their notice that Prior R(obert) in full county court before Reginald at the castle of Dunheved in the presence of the reeve and burgesses of the same vill lawfully and sufficiently proved that when the count of Mortain transferred the market on Sundays from the vill of St Stephens to the new vill of the castle of Dunheved, the canons of Launceston (with the will and assent of the count) retained for themselves and their borough and burgesses of Launceston all the liberties pertaining to a free borough, with the same integrity which they had formerly, except only the Sunday market. For the latter the church and canons had of the reeve of the castle 20s. yearly at the feast of St Martin. And they had and held these liberties fully and quietly during the reign of his father, King Henry (I). He had granted and confirmed all these liberties pertaining to a free borough to the said canons, to the vill of Launceston and to the men who had their hearth and home there with the 20s. of annual rent. Witd. Robert de Dunstanville, Richard de Raddon, Bernard the sheriff of Cornwall, Robert son of Asketil, Hugh de Dunstanville, Jordan de Trecarl, reeve, Mordant Sprakelin. Not dated. [c.1154–65, to adopt the date of A. Ballard and James Tait (ed.) *British Borough Charters, 1216–1307* (C.U.P. 1923, appendix H) modified by dates of Richard de Raddon (1146–65), see note to nos. 12, 13.]

[a]*clyvewardis.*

MS.: Cartulary, f.11r.–f.11v. Printed: *Mon. Dioc. Exon.*, 23 no. 1. F. C. Hingeston-Randolph, *The Registers of Walter Bronescombe* . . . (1889), 199–200. A translation is given in R. Peter and O. B. Peter, *Histories of Launceston and Dunheved* (1885), 4–5. Another copy, *Calendar of Patent Rolls 1377–81*, p. 116 (1378).

**12.**    Grant by Reginald, son of the king, earl of Cornwall, of 40s. from his farm of the castle of Dunheved for the tower of the church of St Stephen which he destroyed until he should give to the church the land which he had given on the altar. Not dated. [c.1146–65, see note to no. 13. Just possibly before 1146, e.g. 1140 when the civil war came to Cornwall.]

MS.: Cartulary, f.11v.

*Carta Raginaldi regis filii consulis Cornubie de xl solidis pro turre ecclesie sancti Stephani prosternenda*
Raginaldus regis filius Cornubie consul. Omnibus baronibus et vicecomitibus et ministris suis salutem. Sciatis me dedisse ecclesie Sancti Stephani de Lanst(aveton) xl solidos per annum ex firma mea de castello Dunheved donec reddam ei secundum voluntatem suam terram quam super altare dedi antequam turrem eiusdem ecclesie prosternerem. Et volo atque precipio ut prepositus castelli illos xl solidos canonicis reddat ipsis terminis quibus firmam meam michi reddit. Testibus Johanne capellano, Hamelino capellano, Roberto de Dunstavilla, Ricardo de Raddona et multis alijs.

**13.** Notice by Reginald, son of King Henry and earl of Cornwall, that he had given in pure and perpetual alms 40s. to the church of St Stephen, Launceston, which he had given on the altar before he destroyed the tower. This gift was from his farm of the castle of Dunheved and the money was to be taken from the reeve of the castle, except the rent of 20s. which the church had for the market of Launceston at the feast of St Martin. Reginald also gave in alms to the same church the mill which he had under the castle with the multure of the said town. Not dated. [After 1140, see nos. 11 and 12. Richard de Raddon occurs *c*.1146–65, see Finberg in *EHR*, July 1947, 356, no. xi. See also no. 251 of the Launceston cartulary for Robert de Dunstanville. The dating limits are therefore *c*.1155–65.]

MS.: Cartularly, ff.11v.–12r. Another copy appears in *Calendar of Patent Rolls 1377–81*, p. 116 (1378).

*Carta Reginaldi H(enrici) regis filij consulis Cornubie de xx solidis pro mercatu et de xl solidis pro turre predicta et de molendino subtus castellum.*
Reginaldus Henrici regis filius consul Cornubie omnibus baronibus et vicecomitibus et ministris suis salutem. Sciatis me dedisse ecclesie Sancti Stephani de Lanst(aveton) in puram et perpetuam elemosinam quadraginta solidos per annum ex firma mea de castello de Dunheved quos super altare dedi antequam turrim eiusdem ecclesie prosternerem, percipiendos a preposito castelli eisdem terminis quibus firmam meam michi reddit salvo redditu xx solidorum quos habent annuatim de prepositura castelli pro mercatu de Lanst(aveton) ad festum Sancti Martini. Sciatis eciam me dedisse in elemosinam et incrementum eidem ecclesie molendinum quod habebam subtus castellum de Dunheved cum molta eiusdem ville et omnibus alijs pertinencijs et consuetudinibus quas habebat dum in manu mea erat. Testibus Johanne capellano et Hamelino capellano, Roberto de Dunstanvilla, Ricardo de Raddona, Willelmo de Boterell, Willelmo fratre meo, Osberto de Bichalega et multis alijs.

**14.** Grant by William, count of Mortain, to Richard fitz Turulf and William Desbiardus about the grant of the lands and customs of the

churches of St Stephen, Launceston, and St Petroc, Bodmin, for the souls
of his mother and father. Not dated. [*c*.1090–1106; perhaps 1103–4.]

MS.: Cartulary, f.12r. See *Regesta* ii, no. 680.

*Carta Willelmi comitis Moretonii de concessione terrarum et consuetudinum
ecclesiarum Sancti Stephani Launc(aveton) et Sancti Petroci Bodm'.*
Willelmus comes Moretonij Ricardo filio Turulfi et Willelmo Desbiardus[a] et omnibus baronibus Cornubie salutem. Sciatis quod concedo
Deo et Sancto Stephano et Sancto Petroco terras suas et consuetudines
suas et clericis ita solidas et quietas sicut melius habuerunt una die
vel una nocte et numquam amplius ponam eas et[a] in manum laicorum
pro anima patris mei et matris mee et mea dedi eis hanc libertatem.
Testibus Willelmo de S(e)biardus[b] et R. monacho et G. capellano.

[a]*sic.* [b]written *Sbiardus.*

**15.** Grant and confirmation by Richard, count of Poitou, earl of
Cornwall, brother of Earl Edmund, for the peace of his brother, King
Henry III, and for the salvation of the soul of his father, King John, to the
church of St Stephen of Launceston of all churches and chapels belonging
to them and all grants of land inside and outside the borough in pure and
perpetual alms, free from all secular and servile service. The canons of the
church were not to be impleaded over any tenement except before Earl
Richard or his ministers. Witd. Andrew de Cheanseaus, Richard de
Turre, Henry Teutonicus, Henry de Franchenne, Richard de Ponchar-
dun, Yvo brother of the earl, Herbert de Novila, Alan Horry, Henry de
Bodrygan, Ralph Bloyo, Nicholas the clerk, Simon de Brekelay. Not
dated. [*c*.1227–41, i.e. between the earliest date of Richard's assumption
of the style 'Earl of Cornwall' and the time he abandoned the style 'Count
of Poitou', see N. Denholm-Young, *Richard of Cornwall* (1947), 9, 51,
i.e.1227–43, but these limits are modified by the death of Ralph Bloyou
(Maclean, *Trigg Minor* iii, 159).]

MS.: Cartulary, f.12r.–f.12v. Printed *Mon. Dioc. Exon.*, 23 no. 2; Hingeston-Randolph,
*Registers of Walter Bronescombe* (1889], 200. Cf. *Calendar of Patent Rolls 1377–81*, p. 115 (1378).

**16.** Confirmation by Edmund, earl of Cornwall, to the church of St
Stephen of Launceston, by inspection of the charters of Reginald, earl of
Cornwall, and Richard, king of Germany and earl of Cornwall, and by his
own inquisition, of the prior and convent's free manor of Launceston
Land (Lanceuelond) and its liberties, including view of frankpledge,
freedom from suits of shire and hundreds, sheriffs and sheriffs' tourns,
pleas, cliff-wards, aids and hue and cry within the bounds of the manor
etc. Witd. the lords William de Boterell, John de Unfranvile, Reginald de
Boterell, Roger de Ingepenne; Thomas de Auners, then steward of
Cornwall; Reginald de Bevyle and William Cole, knights; the lords Roger
de Drayton, Walter de Ayllesbur', Master Hamon Parlebien, Serlo de
Nanslatheron, Stephen de Bello Prato, Richard de Trevaga, John de

Treleuny, Roger de Meles, Robert de Bodmam and others. Dated
Restormel, 4 May 1291.

MS.: Cartularly, ff.12v.–13r. Another copy in *Calendar of Patent Rolls 1377–81*, p. 115 (1378).

**17.** Notification of the resignation by Ralph Pullo, dean of the secular
canons of Launceston, of his deanery, and all rents and lands pertaining,
to William, bishop of Exeter, and the regular canons. Ralph's prebend
and certain lands were granted to him for life for his commons on account
of his old age. Not dated. [*c.*1128 Geoffrey became prior of Plympton
18 January 1128.]

MS.: Cartulary, f.13r.–f.13v.

*Carta resignacionis decanatus Radulphi Pullo decani ecclesie Sancti Stephani
canonicorum secularium de Lansaveton.*
Noscat presentis temporis etas, noscat omnis successiva posteritas
quod Radulphus ecclesie Sancti Stephani de Lanzavetona decanus
coram maxima multitudine clericorum et laicorum voluntarie
decanatum suum et omnes terras et redditus ad decanatum
pertinentes sine aliqua retraccione michi Willelmo episcopo reddidit.
Et ego, quicquid Radulphus michi reddidit, canonicis regularibus
quos in eadem constitui sine aliqua dilacione totum dedi. Radulpho
vero tam pro etate senili quam pro pristino quem possiderat honore
prebendam suam et quasdam terras ad ecclesiam pertinentes ad
victualium usum prestiti dum viveret. Post cuius decessum prebendam
et easdem terras canonicis regularibus in eadem ecclesia Deo
servientibus concedo in eternum possidendas sub istorum testimonis
virorum quorum ista sunt nomina: Osbertus, abbas de Tavistoca;
Gofridus, prior Plymptonie; Walterus de Augo, archidiaconus
Cornubie; Clarenbaldus, capellanus regis; Magister Odo; Thomas de
Linconia; Teodericus canonicus; Radulphus de Luy; Bletheu; Ailricus
Strenn; Algarus de Sancto Motho[a] filij ipsius Radulphi; Bernardus et
Vitellius presentibus parochianis et presente conventu canonicorum
regularium et canonicorum secularium.

[a]Henderson read *Niotho.*

**18.** Licence to elect a prior of Launceston by King Edward I during a
vacancy in the see of Exeter. Warin de St Germans and Stephen de
Alternon, canons of Launceston priory, had brought letters patent of the
chapter notifying him of the need for an election through the death of
Prior Richard. The person elected should be devoted to God, necessary for
the rule of the priory, and useful and faithful to the king and the realm of
England. Dated Dover, 13 January 1273.

MS.: Cartulary, f.13v.

**19.** Writ of King Edward I to his escheator in Cornwall. He understood that since Prior Richard's death the priory was without a prior, and that there was a vacancy in the see of Exeter. He asked him to find out by his liege men of the county what profits of the priory the bishop of Exeter was likely to receive during a vacancy. Dated Dover, 13 January 1273.

MS.: Cartulary, ff.13v.–14r.

**20.** Inquisition made in the presence of the escheator at Launceston on the oaths of Sir Richard de Hywys, kt, Sir Reginald de Bevyle, kt, John de Haldesworth, Roger Cola, Walter de Carnedon, Roger de Tredynek, Richard de Trevaga, Thomas de Curtur, John Penfran, Nicholas de Bere, Thomas de la Doune, John de Trelauny, that the bishops of Exeter during a vacancy of Launceston priory had no revenue by prescriptive right save what they had for one man guarding the gate of the said priory at the expense of the prior and convent. Sealed with the seals of the jurors. Dated Launceston, 4 July 1273.

MS.: Cartulary, f.14r.

**21.** Grant and confirmation by Richard, count of Poitou and earl of Cornwall, in pure and perpetual alms of 5s. 10d. of rent for the light (before the image of) Blessed Mary. The rent was to come from his burgesses of Dunheved which they paid him twice yearly at Michaelmas and Easter. Clauses of warranty of Earl Richard and for his seal. Witd. the lord Andrew de Cardinan, William de Boterell, Andrew de Cancell(is), Richard de Turre, Walter de Treverbin then sheriff of Cornwall, his son Odo de Treverbin, Robert son of William, Roger de Trelosk, Henry Her' and others. Not dated. [c.1227–42. See no. 15. Modified by death of William (IV) de Botreaux (=Boterell), Maclean, *Trigg Minor* i, 640–1.]

MS.: Cartulary, f.14r.–f.14v.

**22.** Notice that when a controversy arose between Prior Richard and the convent of Launceston on the one side and the parish of Launceston (i.e. the free tenants through their homage) on the other about mortuaries and other customs affecting the church of St Stephen, it was eventually settled by a friendly composition. The prior and convent granted for themselves and their successors that their parishioners and free tenants by homage might have peacefully all free customs reasonable and consonant with law which they justly were accustomed to have in the past. Thus they were quit of the exigency of the sub-prior's habit and best beast when they died. The parishioners were to have whatever was left voluntarily for the work of the church (i.e. legacies by parishioners and not otherwise) by view of the guardian of the said church. Whatever was given or bequeathed for the stock or work of the church (other than of their parish) should be given for the use of the fabric of the church of 'La Forde' forever. The parishioners for themselves and their heirs faithfully promised that they would introduce no unjust or contrary custom to the common right.

Alternative sealing clause for chirograph. Dated Launceston, 31 May 1271.

MS.: Cartulary, ff.14v.–15r.

**23.** Agreement between the prior and convent of Launceston and the parishioners of the parish church of Blessed Stephen of Launceston. All the stock given or left for the fabric of the parish church of St Stephen Launceston should by proctors of the prior and the parishioners especially assigned be immediately and faithfully taken over for the use of the parish church and of the conventual church of Blessed Stephen. As often as it was necessary the prior and parishioners should meet to view the defects of the church of Blessed Stephen and to elect two worthy men through whom sale of the stock should be made faithfully by which the defects might be put right. If any new or old work needed repair in the conventual church of Blessed Stephen which could not be done without heavy expense of the stock it should receive a subvention; neither should the competent sustenance of the parochial church of St Stephen make for the destruction of the stock. Altar dues of the said church at the feast of St Stephen or on other feast days and all other oblations must go to the use of the prior and convent without any claim on the part of the parishioners. The prior's proctor was to swear not to diminish the fabric store of the church and the proctors of the parishioners were to swear not to carry off or diminish the offerings. It was further agreed that everything given for the lights of the church of St Stephen should be kept by two persons elected to look after the lights. The parishioners were to collect money for wax used as well by day as by night and they were to find sufficient money for the wax to suffice. If the wax failed it should be supplied by the view of the prior and the parishioners from the stock. The parishioners undertook to bear all dangers of defects both of the chancel and of the body of the church and of the lights there and to sustain them from the store or from their common fund by the view and advice of the prior. The prior remitted the tithes of each store to the parishioners as a subsidy. The parishioners were to continue to bear the burden of maintaining all books, vestments and other necessaries. Alternate sealing clause for chirograph. Dated Wednesday, 22 May 1280.

MS.: Cartulary, f.15r.–f.15v.

**24.** Pleas of the sworn and assizes *de quo warranto* before John de Berewyk and his colleagues, the itinerant justices at Launceston.

The prior of Launceston claimed prescriptive right in his manor of Launceston Land for gallows, view of frankpledge with hue and cry, fines for the assize of bread and ale broken in the same manor and a moiety of the fines of assize of bread and ale in the vill of Newport (*Neuport*). John de Mutford who followed for the king said that the prior in the time of King John had all the same liberties which he now claimed and afterwards he gave these liberties to Reginald de Morteyn,[a] formerly earl of Cornwall. The same Reginald granted these liberties and divided them with his burgesses of Dunheved for sixty-five shillings and ten pence to be paid yearly to the prior and his successors. The burgesses had seisin of these liberties to the last coming of the justices to Cornwall when the prior assumed these liberties of his own authority and appropriated them to himself.

The jurors on oath said that the prior and all his predecessors had the same liberties from the time which memory did not run to the contrary and used them without interruption to the present day.[b] Not dated [1302].

[a] *sic.* [b] marginal note (f.16r.) *Md. quod exemplum istarum libertatum scribitur in 100 folio a capite istius registri.*

MS.: Cartulary, ff.15v.–16r. Printed: *Placita de Quo Warranto* (Record Commission 1818), 110.

**25.** Writ of King Edward III sent to Hugh de Berewyk, steward of the duke of Cornwall, not to molest the prior of Launceston about his liberties in the manor of Launceston Land (*Launceuelond*): gallows, view of frankpledge with hue and cry, fines for assizes of bread and ale and a moiety of fines for assizes of bread and ale in the vill of Newport, which the prior claimed by prescriptive right and which were granted to him by writ of *quo warranto* by King Edward I by John de Berewyk and his justices as could be seen from the certificate in chancery. Adam, prior of Launceston, was not to be molested in these privileges. Dated Kennington, 16 October 1342.

MS.: f.16r.–f.16v.

**26.** Grant and confirmation by King Henry II to the church of St Stephen of Launceston and the canons of the part of Hamelin, the priest of the chapel of Launceston, as the charter of Earl Reginald, his uncle, witnessed. (See no. 27). Date May–July 1175. [See Delisle, *Recueil*, Introductory volume, 75 for Henry's absence in France 8 August 1174 to 8 or 9 May 1175 and see *Complete Peerage* (2nd. ed., lii, 429), for Earl Reginald's death on 1 July 1175.]

MS.: Cartulary, f.16v.

*Carta Henrici regis Anglie de medietate capelle castelli*
Henricus dei gracia rex Anglie et dux Normannie et Aquitannie et comes Andegavie archiepiscopis episcopis abbatibus comitibus baronibus justiciarijs vicecomitibus et omnibus ministris et fidelibus suis tocius Anglie salutem. Sciatis me concessisse et presenti carta confirmasse ecclesie Sancti Stephani de Lanstavetona et canonicis ibidem Deo servientibus partem Amelini presbiteri de capella de Lanst(avetona) cum omnibus libertatibus et rebus parti illi pertinentibus sicut eis racionabiliter concessa est et sicut carta comitis

Raginaldi avunculi mei quam inde habent testatur. Quare volo et firmiter precipio quod predicta ecclesia et canonici in ea Deo servientes partem illam habeant et teneant bene et in pace libere et quiete integre et plenarie et honorifice cum omnibus pertinenciis et libertatibus et liberis consuetudinibus suis. Testibus R(icardo) Winton(iensi), G(alfrido) El(iensi), B(artholomeo) Exon(iensi) episcopis; Ricardo de Lucy, Ricardo de Humeto, constabulario; Willelmo filio Ald(elini), dapifero; Seer de Quincy; Willelmo de Lanval(eio); Radulfo filio Stephani, camerario; Willelmo de Benden(gis). Apud Westmonasterium.

**27.** Charter of Reginald, the king's son and earl of Cornwall, that he has given in alms to the church of St Stephen the part of Hamelin the priest of the chapel of Launceston. The church was to hold it as well and freely as Hamelin or anyone else held it in the time of King Henry his father. Not dated. [*c.*1154–6 or a little later, cf. no. 11.]

MS.: Cartulary, ff.16v.–17r.

*Carta Raginaldi regis filij de medietate predicta prefate capelle castri.*
Raginaldus regis filius comes Cornubie vicecomitibus et omnibus ministris suis Francis Anglis et Walensibus salutem. Sciatis me concessisse et in elemosinam: dedisse ecclesie Sancti Stephani de Lanst(avetona) partem Amelini presbiteri de capella mea de Lanst(avetona) cum omnibus libertatibus et rebus parti illius pertinentibus. Quare volo et firmiter precipio quod ecclesia predicta Sancti Stephani partem illam ita bene et libere et honorifice teneat sicut Amelinus vel aliquis alius eam melius et liberius tenuit tempore Henrici regis patris mei. Testibus Radulfo de Boscoroham, Roberto filio Aschetill, Hugone de Dunstanvilla, Osberto Pincerna, Roberto de Cantelu, Raginaldo Norresio.

**28.** Notification by King Henry I to Richard fitz Baldwin, sheriff of Devon and Cornwall, and his ministers that he had given to the canons regular of St Stephen Launceston the portion and alms of his chapel in the castle there which Bernard and Hamelin the priest held. The canons were to serve the chapel with one priest as Hamelin did. Not dated. [The editors of *Regesta* ii, no. 1486 suggest a date of 1127, ?22 May, Winchester.]

MS.: Cartulary, f.17r. Calendared: *Regesta* ii, no. 1486 from the Cartulary.

*Carta Henrici regis iij$^a$ de medietate capelle castelli viz. Magd(alene).*
Henricus rex Anglie Ricardo filio Bald(uini) et ministris suis salutem. Sciatis me dedisse concessisse ecclesie Sancti Stephani de Lanstavatona et canonicis regularibus illam partem et elemosinam de capella mea de castello Landstevaton cum terris et decimis et beneficijs eidem capelle pertinentibus quas Bern(ardus) presbiter

[et] Hamelinus[b] tenuerunt. Et canonici faciant servire ecclesie per j presbiterum sicut Hamelinus solebat. Et ideo precipio quod inde sint saiseti[c] et in pace et honorifice teneant. Testibus episcopo Sar(esberiensi) cancellario[d] et Roberto de Ver constabulario. Apud Winton(iam).

[a]*sic* for Henry I. [b]*sic*. Probably *et* should be supplied after *presbiter*. [c]*sic*. [d]omitted in *Regesta* ii, no. 1486.

**29.**   Grant and confirmation by King Stephen addressed to the bishop of Exeter and the sheriff, justices and barons of Cornwall to the church of St Stephen, Launceston and the canons regular giving them in alms that part of his chapel of the castle of Launceston, with the lands and tithes and benefices pertaining, which Bernard the priest and Hamelin held, just as the charter of King Henry attested. The canons were to serve the chapel with one priest and to hold it freely and in peace. Witd. Algar, bishop of Coutances, and H. canon and John Mar(escallus). Not dated. [Woodstock, 1136–9. See *Regesta* iii, no. 435.]

MS.: Cartulary, f.17r. Printed: *Regesta* iii, no. 435 from the Cartulary.

**30.**   Notification by Jordan, abbot of Tavistock and T., abbot of Hartland, to Simon, bishop of Exeter, that they had received a mandate from Pope Innocent III reciting the oppression by R. and certain others of certain chapels belonging to the mother church of Launceston. By the Pope's command they were to be made to cease such oppression and to make competent satisfaction for the injuries sustained. Master G. de Insula had been cited to appear before Pope Innocent III to reply about the moiety of the chapel of Launceston. He had made himself disobedient by neither appearing in person nor by proctor nor providing an excuse. The Pope had commanded the abbots to put the canons of Launceston in corporeal possession of the moiety of the said chapel. Not dated. [Between 5 October 1214 and 16 July 1216. Determined by the consecration of Simon of Apulia, bishop of Exeter, and the death of Pope Innocent III.]

MS.: Cartulary, f.17v.

**31.**   The reply of Robert de Cardinan, sheriff of Cornwall, to John, king of England, on the collation and right of the moiety of the chapel of the castle. The King had asked him to ascertain if he had a right in the collation of the moiety of the castle of Launceston on the day when the King gave the moiety to his clerk, master Godfrey de Insula, or if the collation belonged to the canons of the said vill. After inquisition by legal men Robert replied that the King had no right to confer the said moiety as the right of collation belonged to the canons. The moiety of the chapel was of the prebend of the dean of the secular canons and was worth four marks yearly, including the maintenance of the said chapel. Not dated. [Between Michaelmas 1214 and Michaelmas 1216. See list of sheriffs in *P.R.O. Lists* *and Indexes* no. 9. Robert de C. was also sheriff from 10 July to 8 September 1220, *CPR* (Hen. III) i, 241, 248.]

MS.: Cartulary, ff.17v.–18r.

**32.** Another reply by William de Botrell, sheriff of Cornwall, to John, king of England, about the right and collation of the chapel of the castle. He had made inquisition according to the king's mandate and by letters patent signified that the lands and rents belonged to the dean of the secular canons of the church of Launceston. Roger the chaplain who last held the moiety and his predecessors had it of the gift of the canons of St Stephens. The moiety of the chapel was worth four marks of silver, except for the service of the chaplain of the chapel. Not dated. [Michaelmas 1203 – Michaelmas 1204. Shrievalty of Wm. (III) de Botreaux. P.R.O. *Lists and Indexes* no. 9.]

MS.: Cartulary, f.18r.–f.18v.

**33.** Grant by King John to the prior and canons of Launceston of the advowson of the moiety of the castle of Launceston, which belonged to Roger, a former chaplain. The advowson was granted to the canons notwithstanding that Godfrey de Insula held the moiety of the King's gift. Dated Wareham, 22 August 1215.

MS.: Cartulary, f.18v.

**34.** Settlement of a dispute between the canons of Launceston and the canons of St Germans and the vicar of South Petherwin (*Sudpyderwyne*), John the clerk, son of Andrew, concerning the visitation of the sick and the burial of the dead of Dunheved, i.e. of Hay (*la Heye*), of Hurdon (*Herdynge*), of Badash (*Bodessa*) and of Pennygillam (*Pennegynner*). The sick were to be visited by the chaplain of the castle and the chaplain of St Patern of (South) Petherwin (*Sancti Paterni de Piderwyne*). The latter was to bury the bodies of the dead who were to lie in the cemetery of Launceston. Whatever was given for the soul(s) of the deceased person(s) should go to the church of Launceston, except the offering of the altar, part of which was to go to the church of Launceston and the remaining part to the church of St Patern of South Petherwin. Similarly, for those who were buried in the cemetery of South Petherwin (*Sudpyderwyne*) whatever was given for the soul(s) of the deceased person(s) was to go to the church of St Patern, though the offering of the altar was to be divided between St Patern and the church of Launceston. Those who died after living within the walls of the castle, the 'master mansion', for a year and a day were to be taken to the church of St Stephen like other burgesses. Alternate sealing clause (seals of Launceston and St Germans). Witd. Richard, priest of Trewen; Master Henry the priest; William the clerk, son of Rolland, Guy the clerk, Ralph the clerk, custodian of the church, William the white clerk,[a] Fula the porter, Hervey de Sellario and many others. Not dated. [Before no. 36 which is dated 16 July 1293.]

[a]*clerico albo.*

MS.: Cartulary, ff.18v.–19r.

**35.** Settlement of a dispute between the prior and convent of Launceston and the prior and convent of St Germans about the third part of all tithes from the vills and lands of Dunheved, the Hideland (*la Hidlond*), Scarne (*Scardon*), Hurdon, *Colyngton*, Pennygillam (*Penagynfa*) and from other vills and certain lands within the bounds of the chapel of Blessed Mary Magdalene of the castle, dependent on the church of St Stephens which belonged to the prior and convent of Launceston. The prior and convent of St Germans said that this third part belonged to them and they asserted that they were in possession of it. The dispute was settled by the intervention of friends on both sides. The prior and convent of St Germans surrendered and quitclaimed their right to all kinds of tithes of sheaves and other crops within the true and ancient limits of the parish of the said chapel, reserving only the ordination or composition made between the two convents and the perpetual vicar of South Petherwin touching his vicarage. In settlement of this dispute the prior and convent of Launceston promised the annual payment of one mark of silver at the feast of St Michael at Launceston priory to the prior and convent of St Germans. Launceston priory was bound to make this payment by coercion of the bishop of Exeter or his official or the lord archdeacon of Cornwall. Both parties pledged their faith and swore a corporal oath to observe this agreement. Alternate sealing clause (chirograph). Witd. the lord Robert de Champyans, abbot of Tavistock; Thomas de Canc', Andrew de Trelosk, John de Valle torta, John de Haysleg, Stephen de Haccombe, William Cola, knights; Masters Hamond Parleben, Richard de Plymstoke, Thomas de Botton, Peter de Doneslond, John de Berkhamested, Walter de Bodm(in), clerks; Robert de Stokhay, John de Hallesworth, Thomas le Chaunceler. Dated Launceston Castle, Saturday 25 August, 1291.

MS.: Cartulary, ff.19r.–20r.

**36.** Confirmation by Thomas Bitton, bishop of Exeter, of no. 34. On 16 July 1293 there appeared before him Walter de Bodminia, proctor for Richard, prior of Launceston and Roger Spiria, chaplain, proctor for Henry, prior of St Germans. Forms of agreement were ratified by both parties and the sentence of the Bishop who decreed the parties were bound by apostolic censure. Dated Thursday, 16 July 1293.

MS.: Cartulary, f.20r.–f.20v.

**37.** Notarial instrument on the agreement of the prior and convent of

Launceston and of H. Fox, mayor, and the burgesses of Dunheved on the repair of the chancel, books and vestments of the chapel of the castle. The agreement was made by Prior Stephen and David Treludek, sub-prior, his fellow canon Roger Combrygge and their brethren with the full consent of the chapter on the one hand; on the other by Henry Fox, mayor of Dunheved, John Page, John Colyn, William Tunyow and John Cory, burgesses, with the full consent of the commonalty of the borough. They agreed about the repair and maintenance of the chancel of the chapel of Blessed Mary Magdalene situated in the high street of the said borough. The prior and convent and their successors were to repair and maintain the chancel in walls and timber as well as glass and the roof always and they were to make good any defects in these. John Cokeworthy of his free will gave in honour of Blessed Mary Magdalene for the use of the chapel one antiphonary containing also an invitatory which he was to make available before the following feast of St John the Baptist. The mayor and burgesses were to keep, repair and maintain the other ornaments and books of the chapel. Witd. John Cokeworthi, Thomas Paderda, Benedict Dounhevde. (Followed by the certificate of William Hamownd, clerk and notary public of the diocese of Exeter.) Dated Launceston priory, 14 May 1395.

MS.: Cartulary, ff.20v.–21v.

**38.** Final concord between Stephen, prior of Launceston, and the convent and Richard Cobbethorn, mayor of the borough of Dunheved, and the commonalty of the borough after a dispute about the liberties of the same borough. The mayor and commonalty were to enjoy the liberty of the borough (from the eastern side of Harper's lake (*Harparys Doune lake*) going down by the same lake as it used to run through the garden of the prior as far as Sextonshaye (*Sextayneshay*) and thence to the west of the fulling mill and thus to the water of Kensey at the west of the chapel of St James) without any interference of the prior and convent, saving the Water Fair which they were accustomed to have with profits as of old without the molestation of the mayor and commonalty. The mayor and commonalty ratified and confirmed the state of the prior and convent's steps, porches and stairs erected within the liberty of 'Bastehay' and in all rents, lands and services belonging to the prior and convent and their successors of John Tregorrek and certain others in the same liberty which were held of the mayor and commonalty, except the services due of old to the said mayor and commonalty. The latter were not to have or claim to have the way or path through Sextonshaye to the church of St Thomas next to the priory, but released this in perpetuity to the prior and convent. Alternate sealing clause. Witd. Thomas Kelly, Thomas Polsa, Stephen Bant, Richard Resprynne, John Treludek. Dated Launceston, 4 September 1400.

MS.: Cartulary, f.21v.–22r. Original chirograph in box 2, no. 7, borough of Launceston muniments, Cornwall County Record Office.

**39.** Letter of John, bishop of Exeter, to Edward III, king of England, about a corrody unjustly sought by the same king at Launceston. A certain Nicholas Dyneham had falsely asserted that King Edward I had granted a certain corrody to Richard Peke deceased. The prior declared that Nicholas rendered a service by getting the king to remit a debt of £40 and in recompense of this and at the special instance of the king received the assignment of the corrody. The bishop entreated the king to revoke his writs lest the priory and its protector, the see of Exeter, be prejudiced. Dated Exeter, 30 June 1337.

MS.: Cartulary, f.22r.–f.22v.

**40.** Grant by letters patent of a pardon by King Edward III for certain lands and tenements acquired after the statute of mortmain for a fine paid by the prior. The lands were acquired from Henry Mustard and Roger Prodhome: 4 messuages, one toft, one ferling, one carrucate and 1½ acres of land in Bradridge (*Braderygg*), 'Trelouthet', Overtruscott (*Overtroscote*), 'La Hille' near Launceston, Halswille (lost in St Gennys?), Treworgie (*Treworgy*) and Dunheved for the sustenance of a certain chaplain to celebrate divine service every day in the chapel of Blessed Mary Magdalene for the souls of King Edward I and King Edward II and all the faithful departed forever. A licence had not been obtained from King Edward III nor from his father, King Edward II. Dated Nottingham, 7 October 1327.

MS.: Cartulary, ff.22v.–23r.

**41.** Grant by letters patent of a licence by King Edward III to the prior and convent of Launceston to acquire lands, rents and tenements to the value of £20 yearly as well of their own fee as of others, except the lands which they held of the King in chief, the statute of mortmain notwithstanding. The returns of lands etc. were to be made to Chancery. Dated Westminster, 7 February 1363.

MS.: Cartulary, f.23r.–f.23v.

**42.** Memorandum that the prior and convent acquired land and tenements to the value of 40 shillings as part of the sum of no. 41. Dated 12 December 1377.

MS.: Cartulary, f.23v.

**43.** Memorandum that the prior and convent acquired lands, rents and tenements to the value of £12 yearly as part of the sum of no. 41. Dated 24 September 1392.

MS.: Cartulary, f.23v.

**44.** Grant by Edward, prince of Wales, duke of Cornwall and earl of Chester, to the prior and convent to acquire 100s. worth of land and rents within his fee by due and customary services, notwithstanding the statute of mortmain. Dated Plympton, 20 May 1363.

MS.: Cartulary, ff.23v–24r.

**45.** Confirmation by letters patent by King Richard II of 40s. worth of land yearly acquired by the grant of King Edward III, his grandfather, of £20 worth of land to be acquired by the prior and convent of Launceston. The land (10 messuages and one ferling of land) acquired by Robert Carnek and Stephen Byrordron in Launceston and Newport to the value of 20s. 6d., as was found by the King's escheator, Richard Kendale, and returned into Chancery. The acquisition was notwithstanding the statute etc., and except due and customary service to the chief lords of the fee. Dated Westminster, 12 December 1377.

MS.: Cartulary, f. f.24v.

**46.** Writ by King Edward III to the sheriff of Cornwall to levy 9 marks on the goods of the prior and convent of Launceston owing to Philippa, the queen consort, of a fine of 90 marks for a licence for acquiring lands and tenements to the value of £20 yearly. The money was to be sent to Richard de Ravenser, *receptor auri* at the treasury at Westminster on the morrow of St Hilary (i.e. 14 January) with the king's writ. Witd. William de Skypwith. Dated Westminster, 18 October 1364.

MS.: Cartulary, f. f.24v.

**47.** Writ by King Edward III to the sheriff of Cornwall stating that the prior and convent of Launceston were not to be distrained for the fine of £90 which they had paid into the treasury for a licence for acquiring lands etc. to the value of £20 yearly. Witd. William de Skupwith. Dated Westminster, 20 February 1365.

MS.: Cartulary, ff.24v.–25r.

**48.** Quittance by letters patent of King Richard II of the goods of Sir John Cary, knight. The prior of Launceston received as well 499 marks 6s. 8d. as 297 marks which were Sir John Cary's, forfeited to the King by virtue of a judgement against him in his last Parliament. The prior paid these sums to Sir John Kentwode and William Horbury, clerk, at various times, and was not to be troubled further. (Note of enrolment in the records of Easter term 1401 in a certain process affecting the prior of Launceston on the part of the king's remembrancer). Dated Westminster, 26 August 1388.

MS.: Cartulary, f.25r.

**49.** Writ by letters patent of King Henry IV to William Brenchesle and John Colepeper, justices of assize in Cornwall. The treasurer and barons of the Exchequer wished the justices to ascertain if Prior Stephen has or had £800 sterling of the goods and chattels of John Cary, knight, formerly a chief baron of King Richard in the eleventh year of his reign, which £800 the prior had when John Cary was adjudged disinherited in the same year of the said king, beyond the sum which he (the prior) paid over to John Kentwode, knight, and William Horbury, clerk, the king's commissioners in Devon and Cornwall deputed for the purpose of receiving the goods and chattels. The justices were to hold an enquiry at Launceston on Tuesday after the feast of St Peter ad Vincula (i.e. Tuesday, 5 August 1404); the inquisition to be sent to the Exchequer in the quindene of Michaelmas. Witd. John Cokayn. (Recorded on memoranda roll, second year of Henry IV, Hilary term.) Dated Westminster, 14 July 1404.

MS.: Cartulary, f.25r.–f.25v.

**50.** Writ of King Henry VI to the escheator of Cornwall. Reciting an inquisition at Lostwithiel, Saturday 14 February 1400, before John Lokyngton, Richard Kays and John Sireston, the escheators of the king's grandfather in Cornwall, on the oaths of William Carrak, John Creyk, William Loveputa, Simon Mey, Richard Foke, John Foke, Clement Hervy, John Serle, Henry Bowedon, Thomas Bake, William Phylipp and William Bithewaite by which it was found that Stephen, late prior of Launceston, received £1000 worth of the goods of John, late earl of Huntingdon, and his aiders and advisers in his treachery. On the day when the late earl at the time of the judgement against him and others in the Parliament of the king's grandfather held in the octave of St Hilary 1401 there was no mention in the aforesaid inquisition how the goods and chattels of the said earl and those of his aiders and advisers came into the hands of Prior Stephen. The escheator was ordered to make further enquiry about this and to send the finding to the barons of the Exchequer at Westminster on the morrow of the close of Easter. Witd. J. Juyn. (From the memoranda roll of 8 Henry IV, Hilary term, roll no. 14 and the memoranda roll of 2 Henry V, Michaelmas term, return of writs, roll no. 11.) Dated Westminster, 18 February 1432.

MS.: Cartulary, ff.25v.–26r.

**51.** Inquisition held at Liskeard before James Chuddelegh, sheriff of Cornwall, by virtue of the king's writ directed to the sheriff on the oaths of Clement Hervy and William Phylipp, jurors named in the writ still surviving, and Richard Trelauny, Stephen Trenewyth, Peter Eggecombe, Edward Coryton, John Mayow, John Talcarn, William Symon of Liskeard, William Baak, Robert Trecarll and Richard Chyket, jurors, in lieu of the other jurors named in the writ who are now dead. They said that they could discover or certify nothing of the matter; the prior never received the goods etc. of the earl of Huntingdon. (Seals of jurors affixed). Dated Liskeard, 10 April 1432.

MS.: Cartulary, f.26r.–f.26v.

**52.** Writ of King Edward III to the sheriff of Cornwall to discover on the oath of good and lawful men of the county what prejudice, if any, might arise to the Crown or others if a royal licence were granted to Henry Mustard to alienate 6 messuages, 2 carrucates, 2 ferlings and one rood of land in 'Trelouthet', Overtruscott, 'Halswille', 'Treworgy', Bradridge, Newton, Bastehay and 'La Hulle', by Launceston to the prior and convent of St Stephen of Launceston. He was to discover how these lands were held and by what service and their annual value; whether Henry retained any lands in his own hands and the value of these, and if these would suffice for the customs and services of the lands granted to the priory. The inquisition was to be sent under the seals of the sheriff and the jurors without delay with the return of the writ. Dated Winchester, 1 May 1360.

MS.: Cartulary, ff.26v.–27r.

**53.** Note of execution of the aforesaid writ with an inquisition held on Monday 15 February 1361 on the oaths of Roger de Tredinek, Richard Trevaga, Roger de Landeu, William de Tregodek, John de Trelenny, Henry de Talcarl, William de Croketon, Walter de Ockbere, Roger de Thorn, John de Seten, Geoffrey de Erth and Ralph de Cury. They said that no one was prejudiced by the purposed royal licence for Henry Mustard's alienation of lands to the priory (as in no. 52). The lands and tenements were held of the prior and convent by the service of 9s. 11d. yearly, and were worth beyond the said service 8s. 1d. Henry reserved to himself 3 messuages in Newport and 8 acres of land in Launceston Land which were worth 20s. and sufficed for the customs and services due. Dated Launceston, 15 February 1361.

MS. : Cartulary, f.27r.–f.27v.

**54.** Writ of King Henry IV to the sheriffs to distrain John, then prior of Launceston, to render account of the issues of certain lands and tenements in the vill of Launceston and Landrends (*Landren*) which Stephen, late prior, acquired in March 1387 for himself and his successors of John Tregorrek, Robert Stonard, Ralph Kerll and John Cokeworthie, i.e. from the said month of March 1387 and afterwards. Also to reply and satisfy the king about £12 for the retraction of the sustenance of one lamp burning before the image of Blessed Mary in the parish church of Liskeard for thirty years. For which sustenance the said prior and his successors took 8s. annually of the manor of Liskeard by the gift of the ancestors of the present king as appears by a certain inquisition before Martin Ferrers, commissioner of the late king, at Liskeard, Thursday, 10 April 1399. Also to hear, do and receive what the King's Council ordered to be done in the premises. By the memoranda roll of 3 Henry IV (1401–2) Trinity (1402), roll 11. By Richard Hukele of the Exchequer and for this cause to have the king's charter of pardon for all causes and claims. Dated Trinity term 1402.

MS.: Cartulary, f.27v.

**55.**   General pardon by King Henry V. He had pardoned John, prior of
Launceston and the convent there on the previous 20 April every sort of
escapes, felons chattels of fugitives, outlaws and felons and all transgressions of the right of vert, hunting, sale of wood within the forests and
outside etc. before 8 December last within the realm of England and parts
of Wales; without which due punishment etc. would have been exacted in
debt or fine or redemption or in other pecuniary penalties or in forfeit of
goods and chattels or imprisonments or amercements of communities of
vills or of single persons, or in burdening of free tenants who never
transgressed, or of heirs, executors, lands of tenants, escheators, sheriffs,
coroners and others of this kind before 8 December last. The king also
pardoned all grants, alienations, perquisites for lands and tenements held
from him or his royal predecessors in chief and grants in mortmain made
without the royal licence and entries into inheritance after the death of
ancestors before the said 8 December with profits etc. in the meantime.
The king also pardoned all fines, amercements, reliefs, scutages, accounts
due and arrears of farms and accounts, or outlawries published relating to
these. He also pardoned all penalties before 8 December made before him
or his council, or the chancellor, treasurer or any of the judges and all
penalties due to the king or to his dear father deceased before 8 December
etc. and securities of peace forfeited before the said 8 December, except
debts due to himself or his liegemen who survived and of those who had
died since his coronation due and recognised in the exchequer or by
assignations or obligations to himself alone or together with other persons:
debts accounted to the exchequer by sheriffs or escheators etc. Witd. John,
duke of Bedford. Dated 20 October 1415.

MS.: Cartulary, f.27v.–f28v.

**56.**   Charter of general pardon by King Henry VI at the request of the
commonalty of the realm of England in the last Parliament with the assent
of the lords spiritual and temporal to William, prior of Launceston, and
the convent there, for all transgressions, misprisions committed before 2
September 1431. Also for treasons, murders, rapes, rebellions, insurrec-
tions, felonies, conspiracies etc. before the same date. Also pardon for
counterfeiting money, escapes, chattels of felons and fugitives, transgressions of the vert, sale of wood within and without forests. Pardon of
penalties for forfeit of goods and chattels or imprisonments, amercements
of vills or of persons, free tenements, executors of heirs, or of lands of
tenants, escheators, sheriffs, coroners etc. Pardon also of lands held in
chief or in mortmain made without royal licence, entries into inheritances
after death of ancestors made before the same second day of September.
Also pardon for fines, amercements, reliefs, scutages, debts, accounts,
arrears of farms and accounts before the King's coronation. Except debts
and accounts owed to the king by power of letters patent or writs of privy
seal or assignments of interest. The king pardoned all actions and
demands, outlawries before his coronation, also penalties incurred before
the king's coronation before the king or council or chancellor and
treasurer. Also invasions of lands of the royal demesne as of fee or as a free
tenement. Reception of apostolic bulls against the form of the statutes was

also pardoned. Marriages of widows of noble state by men without royal licence were excepted from the pardon. The king pardoned all wars, redemption of prisoners etc., profits of war to the death of King Henry the king's father. All jewels of the king's father given to the prior and convent for security of pledges of war for the journies of King Henry's father to Harfleur and parts of France and Normandy were pardoned, unless the jewels had been liberated by King Henry VI before 27 March last past etc., but not for the custody of the castle and town of Calais and the marches etc. Witd. King Henry VI at Westminster. (By the King in Parliament). Dated 6 July 1437.

MS.: Cartulary, ff.28v.–29v.

**57.** Inquisition in full county court on Monday after the feast of the Invention of the Holy Cross (which feast was 3 May) by William Cola, John de Treiagu, Reginald de Buvylle, knights; Jordan de Luffyncote, Robert de Trewynnok, William Wise junior, Nicholas de Ros, Richard de Tregudek, William de Landu, Richard de Trekarl, John de Bayllehelf, Auger de Egloskury, Robert Puddyng, Richard Walleys, John Russell de Talcarn, Hamelin de Trevelle. They stated on oath that the prior and convent of St Stephen of Launceston held their manor of Launceston Land as a free manor from time immemorial with soc and sac, tol and theam and infangentheof, with view of frankpledge, and hue and cry. No man of the manor went to any foreign hundred, sheriff's tourn, nor elsewhere except the court of the prior and convent. Since the time when Stephen Heym, sheriff and steward of Cornwall in the reign of Richard, king of Germany, unjustly distrained tithingmen of the said manor to come to foreign hundreds and the sheriff's tourn to present their hue and cry against their liberties, and since William de Moneketon, sheriff and steward of Cornwall, in the time of Edmund, earl of Cornwall, distrained the men of the manor to go to the sheriff's tourn against the customs of the manor. Sealed by those who made the inquisition (names as above). Not dated. [3 May 1277 or 9 May 1278 or 5 May 1281 or 4 May 1282. See dating clause (above) and P.R.O. *Lists and Indexes* ix, shrievalty of William de Monketon.]

MS.: Cartulary, ff.29v.–30r.

**58.** Grant by Jellinus de Landren with the consent of his heirs to the prior and convent of Launceston of a certain hamlet called 'Polepark' outside the gate of the priory between the land of Robert Ysmaug and the land of Jordan Redebyl where there lay at the west side a large stone from the weir of the mill as far as the river Kensey. To hold freely, quietly and in peace. For this grant the prior and convent released to the grantor and his heirs 6d. of annual rent. Confirmed with grantor's seal. Witd. William Wyse, Roger, the clerk, Robert Rem, Henry Trecarll, John Mannyng, Jordan Redbill, Thomas his son. Not dated. [1232–44. William Wise. See nos. 217, 485, 565. *Cornwall FF.i*, no. 54.]

MS.: Cartulary, f.30r.

**59.** Grant and quitclaim by Jellinus de Landren to the church of St Stephen of Launceston and the canons of a certain part of his land under the weir of the mill of the said canons, up to the great stream opposite the meadow of William Pistor which was between the land of the boundary on the east, and the land of Brunstan and Fromund on the west. To hold and possess forever freely, quietly, without any claim by the grantor or his heirs. The prior and convent released the grantor and his heirs 6d. of his 'gabelle' which he had to pay yearly. Confirmed by the grantor's seal. Witd. William Wyse, Hamundus de Trevell, Robert Rem, Jocelin Brytun, Jordan Redebil. Not dated. [1232–44. See no. 58.]

MS.: Cartulary, f.30r.–f.30v.

**60.** Grant by Jordan Redebile with the assent of his heirs to the prior and convent of Launceston of a certain hamlet under the weir of the mill which Richard Prittel formerly held. To have and to hold freely, quietly and in peace forever. For this grant the prior and convent remitted him 7d. of annual rent. Confirmed by the grantor's seal. Witd. William Wyse, Robert Rem, Roger the clerk, Jellinus, Henry Trevella. Not dated. [1232–44. As no. 59.]

MS.: Cartulary, f.30v.

**61.** Grant by Jordan de Ridcarn to the church of St Stephen by Launceston and the canons for the souls of his father and mother and all his kinsmen of a plot of land adjoining their mill which extended westwards as far as the next ditch which lay in transverse from the weir of the mill above to the great stream below. To hold in free and perpetual alms with all appurtenances and liberties etc. Confirmed by the grantor's seal. Witd. Roger de Trelosk, Jordan de Trevaga, William Wyse, Hamelin de Trevell, Gellinus the clerk, Robert Rem, Richard Probus, John Mannyng, Robert Cocus. Not dated. [1232–44. See no. 60.]

MS.: Cartulary, ff.30v.–31r.

**62.** Chirograph stating that Geoffrey, prior of Launceston, and the whole convent, with their common wish and consent, gave 4d. (from 40d. which Osbert Marker owed the same) for the annual rent of one acre of land in Landrends (*Landren*) in exchange for the land which the same Osbert granted from the said acre to the prior and convent for making a garden bounded with certain bounds. Alternate sealing clause. Witd. Henry Blockiu, William Cola, Master Edward, Thomas Ruffus, Richard de Duncham, Henry Godeman. Not dated. [1159–1181. Pontificate of Pope Alexander III, see no. 6. Prior Geoffrey also occurs in 1171.]

MS.: Cartulary, f.31r.

**63.** Grant and confirmation by Richard, count of Poitou and earl of

Cornwall, to the prior and canons of Launceston of a certain fair at St James by the water of Kensey to be held yearly for two days on the vigil and feast of SS Philip and James (i.e. 30 April and 1 May) in pure and perpetual alms. Sealed by grantor. No list of witnesses. Not dated. [*c*.1227–1243. See no. 15.]

MS.: Cartulary, f.31r.

**64.** Grant and confirmation by Odo de Boiton to the church of St Stephen by Launceston and the canons in free and perpetual alms of all his land in North Beer, i.e. one acre in the same vill which was of his demesne of Boyton with the whole meadow which he was accustomed to retain in his hands in the same vill and also an acre and a half in the same vill with appurtenances, free and quit of all secular service etc. which might fall to him and his heirs, except for royal service when it occurred for the acre and a half in the manor of Boyton. The land was bounded on the east as far as the stream flows between the land of North Beer and the land of Bradridge; on the west as the boundary appeared between the same land and the land of Bennacott (*Buningcote*) and on the south as the bounds showed between North Beer and South Beer (*Suthbere*); on the north as the boundaries lay between North Beer and Darracott (*Doddecote*). Witd. Robert de Dintagel, William and Everwinus, brothers of the same, Thomas de Dunham, Richard de Marisco, William Cola, Richard Venator, Richard de Dunham, Richard de Godman. Not dated. [*c*.1242, see no. 451, Richard Venator.]

MS.: Cartulary, f.31v.

**65.** Grant by Odo de Boiton in everlasting alms to the church of St Stephen of Launceston there of all his land of North Beer to have and to hold forever, i.e. one acre in the vill of his demesne of Boyton free and quit from secular service with the meadow he retained in the same vill and another 1½ acres in the same vill quit of secular service except royal service for the land of 1½ acres in the manor of Boyton. Bounds as in no. 64. The prior and convent gave him 15 marks of silver. Clause of warranty or exchange of land in default. Grantor gave fealty and sealed. Witd. John, sheriff of Cornwall; Simon de Puny, Luke son of Bernard and Geoffrey his brother, Robert de Tintagel and his brothers William and Everwinus, Thomas de Dunham, Henry Godman, David de Gunan, Richard de Cunstan, Henry de Grucy, Walter de Stabulo and Roger his brother, Hamelin and Henry de Treu'll, Durandus Cocus. Not dated. [*c*.1209–14, shrievalty of John who was also sheriff for a short time in 1220 (*CPR*).]

MS.: Cartulary, ff.31v.–32r.

**66.** Grant and confirmation by Alan Cissor de Braderigge to Richard, prior of the church of St Stephen of Launceston and the convent there of one messuage and all his land with appurtenances in Bradridge and 60 perches of land in Newton which lay on the western side of the said land opposite the croft which was formerly held by Robert Bonda in exchange for one acre of land English and 20 perches which the said prior had given him in Newton of the land which was formerly Richard le Wodeward's which lay under the croft of John Fraunceys on the eastern and nearer side. To the prior and convent freely etc. forever. Warranty clause. If the prior and convent could not hold the messuage and land peacefully they were to have the acre and (20) perches of land in Newton. Grantor's sealing clause. Witd. Walter de Burdon, John de Settone, John de Westcote, Richard Beamonde, William Page. Not dated. [Reference to Alan Cissor (see also no. 67) might suggest no. 66 should be dated when Richard de Brykevile was prior, i.e. 1291–1307/8.]

MS.: Cartulary, f.32r.–f.32v.

**67.**   Release and quitclaim by Richard called 'le Wodeward' to Brother Richard de Brykevyle, prior of the church of St Stephen of Launceston, and the convent there and their successors of his right in a piece of meadow in Newton which lay on the southern side of the close of John le Baker and continued southwards to the arable land held by the grantor. This piece of land stretched westwards as far as the meadow of John le Bonda and eastwards to the lake which ran towards the south between the said meadow and the meadow of John le Baker. Together with the service of Alan Cissor and 6d. of annual rent received by the grantor for one house and croft in the vill of Bradridge. Grantor's sealing clause. Witd. Roger Cola, Jordan de Lochyngcote, Walter de Burdon, Richard de Bere, John le Baker. Dated Launceston, Thursday, 24 June 1294.

MS.: Cartulary, f.32v.

**68.**   Grant and confirmation by Prior Richard and the convent to John Franceys and Matilda his wife of 22 acres of land English in Newton (formerly the land of Richard le Wodeward) and half an acre English and 15 perches of the demesne of the prior and convent next to the bounds between this demesne and the land of Newton in exchange for one messuage and one ferling of land which John and Matilda gave the prior and convent in Bradridge. To have and to hold to John and Matilda peacefully in perpetuity, for the yearly rent of 15d. sterling in equal instalments at Easter and Michaelmas for all service except suit of court every three weeks to the priory court of Bradridge with reasonable summons. Warranty by the prior and convent to John and Matilda *contra omnes homines et feminas*. Alternate sealing clause for chirograph. Witd. Richard Beaumont, William de Ber, Nicholas Dove, John le Baker, Robert de Bonda. Not dated. [The reference to Richard le Wodeward would suggest the time of prior Richard de Brykevile, i.e. 1291–1307/8.]

MS.: Cartulary, ff.32v.–33r.

**69.**   Grant and confirmation by Richard le Forester of Bradridge to Prior

Richard and the convent of one messuage and one ferling of land in Bradridge which he had formerly held from them. To have and to hold for ever. Grantor's sealing clause. Witd. Robert de Bodmam, Henry Rem, Richard de Doddecote, Richard Stoterigch, Richard Cade. Dated Launceston, Wednesday, 14 September 1295.

MS.: Cartulary, f.33r.

**70.** Notice that Richard, son of William the steward, gave to the church of St Stephen of Launceston the just boundaries of Tackbeare beyond which his predecessors had unjustly encroached: from the flow of the well by the stream as far as the water and from the same flowing well through the ways to Tatson in the ways which turn to the north to the muddy roads which come from the north. This grant Richard made by the payment of one mark which was owing to the church and he confirmed it with his seal with the assent of his wife and heirs. Witd. William de Tetteburna, Pagan son of Serlo, Hugh Pafard, Roger de Duneham, John de Luching', Osbert the priest (son of Cola), Richard Spaillard, Biricold de Miryfeld, Oliver de Luchaha' Hacheman, William the armour-bearer of the prior and Sampson de Botch' and the men of Tackbeare. Not dated. [c.1140–55. See nos. 71 and 72 (Pagan son of Serlo).]

MS.: Cartulary, f.33r.–f.33v.

**71.** Grant by William de Henemerdune and his son John to the priory of the land of West Peke (*Pec*) in perpetual alms when his sons, Walter and Ralph the clerk, were made canons. Donor's sealing clause. Witd. Robert, bishop of Exeter, Reginald, earl of Cornwall, Bricius and Roger, chaplains of the bishop, Roger de Ferarijs, Robert de Dunstavilla and Richard de Raddona. Not dated. [c.April 1140–28 Mar. 1155, date limited by death of Bishop Robert I of Exeter. Cf. Blake, 183 and Cartulary no. 7.]

MS.: Cartulary, f.33v.

**72.** Confirmation of no. 71 by Walter Gyffard at the petition of William de Henermerdona and his son John, for the love of God, indulgence of his sins, and for the souls of his father and mother and of all his ancestors and successors. Sealing clause. Witd. Richard, canon of Plympton; Matilda wife of Walter Giffard, William de Walvilla, Pagan son of Serlo, Edwin de Whitturch, William de Portaurdi and Haid. Not dated. [Either at the same time as no. 71 or slightly later. Perhaps c.1166, see no. 430 (Walter Giffard.]

MS.: Cartulary, ff.33v.–34r.

**73.** Grant by Jordan de Lovyngcote of 8s. of annual rent to the prior and convent. If he failed to pay this he could be distrained by them or their bailiffs in the said land of Peke as far as Bradridge or Boyton and no

further. Witd. John de Bello Prato, seneschal of Cornwall; David de
Fenton, Roger de Oggeber(e), Gregory de Dodistoun, John Carbunel. Not
dated. [1268–9, shrievalty of John de Beaupré, P. L. Hull, *Cartulary of St
Michael's Mount* (1962) no. 22.]

MS.: Cartulary, f.34r.

**74.** ᵃGrant by Ralph de Ferers with the consent of his heir Roger to the
priory of Hornicott (*Horniaĉhot*) and Ditchen (*Twychenys, Twichinas*). The
land of Hornicott had been given to the priory by Roger de Mandavilla
and surrounded a chapel enclosed by three ways: i.e. the way from
Bradridge to Tamerton and from the chapel to Sutton (*Secun'*) and from
'Alindec' to Sutton (*Sectun'*). Also Ralph granted the land of Wuluric de
Spitel and his successors. Prior Geoffrey gave the grantor half a mark of
silver. Witd. Bernard the clerk, Sprachelieius, Jordan and Edward the
reeves, Briccello Ioas and his son Brittvullus de Braderig', Ailricus de
Brad', Hamelin Ruffus de Brad', Wluricus de Spitel, Osbert Cola,
Paganus Rem. Not dated. [*c.*1162, cf. no. 75.]

ᵃMarginal note, right hand margin: *Mᵈ quod placita de Twichen scribuntur in primo folio quinti
quarterni istius regestri et in sequent'* (sic) *in 98 folio in capite.*

MS.: Cartulary, f.34r.–f.34v.

**75.** Notification of an oblation of a small part of the land of Hornicott
(*Hornighacote*), i.e. two parts of Ditchen in free alms on the altar of St
Stephen's by Roger de Mannavillaᵃ so that the prior could serve Roger's
chapel and his men of Hornicott as of his parish. Roger's daughter and
heir Sybil gave her consent by the grant of a gold ring as a fine.ᵇ Roger's
hundred of Hornicott also consented. Witd. Renaldus the clerk of St
Martin, William Banzhan, Ralph the hunter, Auger Flamanc, Bernard
the steward, Alwin the smith and his sons Godwin and Alinus, Alinus de
Estcote and Osbert his son, Osbert son of Cola, Ernald the clerk, William
de Westcote and the whole hundred of Hornicott. Dated 1162. [This date
appears in the text.]

ᵃDoubtless the *Roger de Mandavilla* of no. 74. ᵇ*in Kersum* for which should be read *in gersuma.*

MS.: Cartulary, f.34v.

**76.** Agreement between Stephen de Luchiacote and the prior and
canons of Launceston. Stephen who owned the advowson of the chapel of
Luffincott when there was a vacancy was to choose and present a suitable
priest to that chapel. Before this clerk was presented to the bishop, he was
to swear fealty to the church of Launceston and to be bound by oath to
pay 2s. yearly to the prior and canons at Michaelmas for the chapel of
Luffincott. This clerk was to bear the whole cost of the chapel and the
prior and canons were to make no exactions in addition to the said 2s.,
though the bodies of the dead with their possessions were to be taken to
the mother church of Launceston. Alternate sealing clause. Stephen

promised to keep the agreement without fraud. Witd. Ralph de Mora, Ralph de Bray, Gervase his brother, Ralph the clerk, Philip de Trevella, Osbert Fraunceys, Wydo the clerk, William the baker, William the cook, Alfred Cete. Not dated. [Possibly *c*.1170–86, see no. 285 (Ralph Mora).]

MS.: Cartulary, f.34v.–f.35r.

**77.** Grant and confirmation by Hasent de Solegn' to the church of St Stephen of Launceston of the land of Trebinnick (*Trebegnec*) and of 'Wrkebutor' in free alms, for the soul of his father and mother and all his ancestors, free and quit from all actions forever, except to be held by royal service, as his father had first confirmed it to the same church. Witd. Baudwinus son of Adam, William Grymant, Ralph de Mool, Robert de Capellis (at that time sheriff), Robert de Prydyas, Philip de Trevella, Luke, Ralph, clerks; William Cole, Goscelin son of Robert, Michael the clerk, Giraud the clerk who wrote the charter. Not dated. [If Hasent de Sulleny is Hasculfus, the latter occurs *c*.1199–1212, *Red Book of the Exchequer; Book of Fees, passim*.]

MS.: Cartulary, f.35r.

**78.** Grant and confirmation by Ralph de Sulleny to the church of St Stephen and the canons there in free alms, for the souls of his parents and ancestors, the land of Trebinnick and the lands of 'Cusin' and 'Wrthebutre', free of all exaction except royal service, just as his father had confirmed it to the said church and canons. He also granted for the salvation of his soul 3 acres of lands in the manor of Fawton (*Fawitun*), i.e. the land which was Bloyho's, the half-acre of Edwin and the half-acre of John and the third acre at the long stone to have in free and perpetual alms. His grandfather, John de Sulleny, had given them to Thomas son of William, and Ascuil his father granted them to the same Thomas and received his homage. These lands the canons then had and held as a gift of the same Thomas, son of William, just as the charters of Thomas, son[a] of William, and of John de Sulleny, his grandfather, and of Ascuil, his father witnessed. Ralph confirmed with as much royal service as pertained to the 3 acres according to a lawful composition of other acres of the said manor of Fawton. Grantor's sealing clause. Witd. Robert de Cardinan, Andrew his son, John son of Richard, Robert le Brytune, Auger de Tregrella, Michael the dean, Robert son of William. Not dated. [*c*.1228–9, cf. no. 499. Ralph de Sulleny occurs 1228 to his death in March 1244, *Book of Fees*, index.]

[a]Note in left margin, *M.ᵈ qᵈ ad peticionem Johel Dawbene domini de Faweton de terra de Trebennek videlicet consilio prioris et conventus qᵈ tenetur in pura et perpetua elemosina extra feodum predicti domini Johel.*

MS.: Cartulary, f.35r.–f.35v.

**79.** Notification[a] by Thomas, son of William, that for his redemption he had given to the church of St Stephen the land which John de Sullini had given him, i.e. 3 acres of land in the manor of Fawton, the land which was Blohio's and the half-acre (?of) 'Lowena' and the half-acre of John's and the third acre at the longstone in pure alms. To possess free and quit from all exaction except the royal service which pertains to 3 acres. Sealing clause. Witd. Walter and Robert, the armbearers of the grantor, William the clerk, Ralph the clerk, William the cook, Fula the porter, Roger Crassus, William the baker, Walter of the stable. Not dated. [Before no. 78 where Thomas son of William's gift is mentioned.]

[a]Note in the left margin, *Quantum ad peticionem domini de Faweton de terra de la Neuhous in mora non tenetur facere homagium ut patet per cartam Radulfi de Sulney.*

MS.: Cartulary, f.35v.

**80.** Gift in perpetuity by John de Sullineio, with the consent of his wife and heir, to the church of St Stephen of the lands of 'Buthor's' with the black servant[a] who holds it and the land of 'Cusin' with William son of Judenual, who holds it for the land of Bloihou with Lewinus, son of Sicca, and with Robert his brother who hold it and for the land which was Osulwy Cancar's. For this exchange Prior Osbert gave in recognition a mark of silver and five silver spoons to the grantor's wife. Witd. William the monk, Jordan the dean, Serlo the chaplain, Luke de Melendy, Alwaldus the reeve and Robert his son, Serlo the merchant, Adam, the lord's brother, William the clerk, Osbert Cola, Thomas son of Wlwardus. Not dated. [?1171–83. There was a prior called Geoffrey, 1159–71, and Prior Osbert occurs c.1180–3, Morcy, 152, 158.]

[a]*cum nigro garcifero.*

MS.: Cartulary, f.35v.–f.36r.

**81.** Notice that in the year 1149 Wandreg(esilus) de Curcellis gave to the church of St Stephen of Launceston of his manor of Fawton (*Foitune*) the land which Osulf, son of Eduinus, customarily held from him. To hold for ever in free alms and quit from all secular service for the redemption of his soul and the souls of his father and mother and also of his wife and all their parents, by an offering on the altar of St Stephen with a knife. As well also of his moors by the ford of 'Ridchar' and between the profitable land of Alphegi Herrio as far as near the house of Cola and also of his grove and pastures, as much as was needed to maintain and stock the said land. At a later time he added to this gift the land of Cola de Trebennuc and the land of Blochiu, and he granted with this gift the land which Robert, son of Ailwin, gave to God and St Stephen, i.e. the land of one furlong. (And if mast was in his wood the pigs of the canons might be with his without pannage). The grant was made in the presence of, and with the consent of Reginald, earl of Cornwall, and also in the hearing and sight of Prior Richard and of all the convent on the day when they received him with all his benefits as a brother and all those whom Wandregesilus wished to send. Witd. Robert formerly prior of Bodmin, Richard the priest of

Werrington, Pagan the deacon, Roger *secretarius*, John son of Ailsius the priest, Roger de Valletorta and his brother Ralph, Roger the knight of Wandregesilus, Warin de Penpol, Robert son of Ailwin, Adam son of Baldwin, Alwoldus the reeve of Fawton, Ailward son of Serich', Cola de Bulapit and all the hundred of Fawton (*Fauitune*). Not dated. [1149. After 24 June 1149, see *Heads of Religious Houses*, 169.]

MS.: Cartulary, f.36r.

**82.** Grant and confirmation by Ralph de Suleny, lord of Fawton, to God and the church of Blessed Stephen of Launceston and the canons there of all his land in Fowey moor (*Fawymora*) which lay between these bounds: from the feet of 'Hunghille' as far as the dry tinwork (*siccum stagnarium*) to 'Wluecumbe' and thus by the length of 'Wluecumbe' to the foot of 'Creistume' and thence about Pinnocks Hill (*collem de Pinnochesburge*) to the western head of Dozmary (*Thosmery*) and by certain bounds to the Fowey river and thus coming up the length of the Fowey to the feet of 'Hungerhille'. To hold in perpetuity, freely and quietly, in ways and paths, meadows, pasture, turbary and tinworks belonging to the land. Rendering yearly at the Assumption of Blessed Mary (15 August) for all services etc. Warranty. Donor's sealing clause. Witd. Andrew de Cancellis, then seneschal of Cornwall; Robert son of William, Walter son of William, Roger de Trelosk, Ralph de Trewrta, H. de Trevella, John Mannyng, Henry Kint. Not dated. [*c*.1221–March 1244. See nos. 185, 78.]

MS.: Cartulary, f.36r.–f.36v.

**83.** Grant by Ralph de Bevile, lord of Tredaule, to the church of Blessed Stephen of Launceston and the canons of his moor on Fowey Moor within these bounds: from the ford of 'Ridmerky' ascending through the valley as far as 'Cundos' and again from 'Cundos' to the east in length to the land of Robert Yuning and next to the land of the said Robert Yuning descending through the bounds of the land of the said Robert as far as the water of 'Ridmerky' and thus along the said water as far as the ford of 'Ridmerky'. To have and to hold of him and his successors freely and quietly etc. Rendering for this yearly to him and his heirs a pair of gloves at Michaelmas for all service, plaint and exaction which belonged to him and his heirs for ever. Donor's sealing clause. Witd. William Wise, Ralph de Trewrda, William Le Walleys, Thomas de Lyner, Thomas de Trevaga. Not dated. [*c*.1232–44 (William Wise), see no. 58.]

MS.: Cartulary, f.36v.

**84.** Quitclaim by Reginald de Byvyle for his soul, the soul of Alice his wife and for the souls of his father and mother and ancestors, for himself, his heirs and assigns, to the priory church of St Stephen of Launceston and the convent there of one pennyworth of rent and whatever other service he sought from them or claimed of the land, moor or meadow which they held from him in 'Tredauwel' of the gift of his ancestors. He retained or reclaimed nothing for himself nor for his heirs and assigns. The prior and convent and their successors were to have and to hold the whole land, moor or meadow freely and quietly etc. in free, pure and perpetual alms, quit of all rent, fealties or other services and exactions. Donor's sealing clause, Witd. John de Penfran, Henry Wastepray, Roger de Landu, Hugh Crock*es*, Robert de Bodmam. Dated Launceston, Monday, 26 October 1276.

MS.: Cartulary, f.36v.–f.37r.

**85.** Record of a plea. William Best of St Clether (*Cleder*) was attached to reply to the plaint of the prior of Launceston that William with force and arms dug turves of the turbary of the priory of Newhouse (*Newhous in the more*) next to Dozmary Pool (*Dosmerypoule*) to the value of £20 and to the loss of the priory.

The prior complained by his attorney Pasco Polreden that the said William on Monday before the feast of the Apostles Philip and James (1 May) in the fourth year of the present king with swords, bows and arrows in a separate turbary of the priory at Newhouse in the Moor dug up turves and took 300 cartloads and continued this transgression to the feast of Michaelmas in the eighth year of the present king. The priory had suffered a loss to the value of £40.

William Best by his attorney, Simon Lowys, denied that he was to blame and both parties placed themselves *super patriam*. William maintained that where he dug the turves was on his own free tenement.

The prior maintained it was the land of the priory and not William's land. Again both parties submitted themselves to the local jury. The sheriff was asked to bring the parties to court again in the quindene of Michaelmas etc. Not dated. [Just possibly, Monday, 27 April 1220 from the regnal year given in the text, though it could also be from the same evidence, Monday, 27 April 1276.]

MS.: Cartulary, f.37r.–f.37v.

**86.** Agreement following a papal mandate to the abbot of Sherborne (*Sireburn*) and the prior of Milton (*Middelton*) relating to a case between the prior and convent of Montacute and the prior and convent of Launceston about the tithes arising from the demesne of Fawton (*Fawiton*) and the tithes of Fowey Moor and about the chapel erected on the same moor. It was agreed that the prior and convent of Launceston should take two parts of the tithes arising from Fawton as they did formerly. As for the newly cultivated land within or outside the moor, both priories were to receive each a moiety of the tithes, saving to the prior and convent of Launceston the tithes of one carrucate of land which they cultivated at their own expense and also the small tithes of their own store. A similar privilege was granted to the prior and convent of Montacute for land etc. cultivated at their own cost. The chapel was to be served by shared expenses and the communal profits also shared. The bodies of the dead were to be taken to the church of St Neot until agreement could be reached between the parties tö dedicate a cemetery at the chapel. Both parties swore an oath to bind themselves to keep this form of peace which was ratified by the mandatories and strengthened by the seals of both parties. Followed by a notice of J., prior of Montacute, and by Robert and Alan, canons and proctors of the prior and convent of Launceston, that both parties had sworn to observe this peaceful settlement under a penalty of 20 marks payable on the morrow of the feast of St Peter and St Paul (30 June) or within the octave. Dated Exeter, 17 June 1238.

MS.: Cartulary, ff.37v.–38r.

**87.** Notice by the abbot of Sherborne and the prior of Milton of the diocese of Salisbury reciting a mandate from Pope Gregory IX to them. Complaints had been received by the prior and convent of Montacute of the Cluniac order that the abbot and convent of Muchelney (*Mochelni*) and certain others of the dioceses of Bath, Exeter and Salisbury had injured them over tithes due from their possessions and other matters. They were asked by the pope to hear both parties, doing what was necessary to settle the dispute by ecclesiastical censure etc. The papal mandate was dated Viterbo (*Viterbij*), 2 May 1238. By this authority the prior and convent of Montacute pleaded their cause against the prior and convent of Launceston on all the tithes issuing from the demesne of Fawton and on the tithes of Fowey Moor and about the chapel erected on the same moor. (Settlement follows as in no. 86). The bodies of the dead of the said chapel were to be buried at St Neot until the chapel was dedicated, at the equal costs of both parties. Moreover the chapel was to be served at common charges and all emoluments arising from the same, as well from the living as from the dead, were to be ceded in equal portions for common uses. Both parties swore an oath to keep the settlement under the penalties prescribed by the mandatories. Chirograph sealed by both parties. Dated 29 June 1238.

MS.: Cartulary, f.38r.–f.38v. See also *Two Cartularies of the Augustinian Priory of Bruton and the Cluniac Priory of Montacute* (Somerset Record Society) viii (1894), no. 171.

**88.** Notice of a chirograph setting out the bounds between the prior and convent of Montacute and the prior and convent of Launceston in Fowey Moor within which bounds against the waste they ought to receive all tithes and obventions of the living and the dead and to divide the same by equal portions. From the water of Fowey going up through Smallacoombe (*Smalecombe*)[a] to the way of Browngelly (*Breniegelon*)[b] towards the south and thus by that way as far as 'La Michelworth',[c] and going down through the water as far as 'Halgarsant'[d] and then going up through 'Halgarsant' as the bounds between the lord Ralph de Suleigny and the land of Hammet (*Hamet*) and thus in the length of these bounds to the water of Luny (*Loveny*).[e] And thence by the bounds between the land of Ralph de Sulleigny and the land of Trebinnick (*Trewynnok*)[f] and from there as far as the pools and from thence to the Long Stone and from the Long Stone as far as the bounds between the land of the said Ralph de Suleigny and the land of Bernard and then by the bounds of the said Ralph de Suleigny and the land of Robert de Lutret.[g] Thence by the bounds as far as Deweymeads (*Duy*) and thus in the length of Deweymeads as far as the head of Deweymeads. From there to the bounds of Merrifield (*Miryfeld*)[h] and thus as far as the water of 'Mildardur'[i] and going up by 'Mildardur' as far as the causeway of Temple. Thence by the bounds of the lands of Fawton and the lands of Blisland (*Blyston*)[j] as far as 'Ponteisou'.[k] The prior and convent of Launceston in the future could never exact beyond the tithes of the parish of St Neot anything else except in the demesne of Ralph de Sulleigny. The prior and convent of Launceston were to have the tithes of the land they cultivated on their own moor at their own expense. Similarly the prior and convent of Montacute were to have the tithes they cultivated on their own moor at their own expense. Sealed by both parties. Witd. Nicholas de Bothennek,[l] Robert de Draynes, Robert son of Michael, William de Hamet, Benedict de St Neoto. Dated Sunday, 28 April 1241.

Variant readings from *Two Cartularies . . . of Bruton . . . and the Cluniac Priory of Montacute* (Somerset Record Society) no. 172(=B):— [a]B. *Smalecumbe.* [b]B. *Bremegellon-Way.* [c]B. *La Muchelwrthe.* [d]B. *Halgersant.* [e]B. *Loveyn Water.* [f]*Trebennock.* [g]B. *Lutrot.* [h]B. *Merifeld.* [i]B. *Mindaldur.* [j]B. *Blustone.* [k]B. *Pontyesu.* [l]B. *Botkennoc.*

MS.: Cartulary, f.38v.–f.39r.

**89.** Notice by the official of the bishop of Exeter of a dispute about the possession by the church of Altarnun (*Alternun*) of the tithes arising from the chapel of Drywork (*Dryework*) between the farmer, master Roger le Rus, and the appropriators, the dean and chapter of Exeter, of the one part, and the parishioners of the chapel and the prior and convent of Launceston to whom the aforesaid chapel of St Luke belonged, of the other. The farmer laid his claim upon the ordinance of the late Walter, bishop of Exeter, who decided that until the chapel should be repaired or rebuilt the parishioners of the same should use the church of Altarnun as nearer to them, but not as parochial. The chapel had since been repaired by confession of the adverse party and the official therefore decided that its profits should be yielded as of old to the prior and convent, neither the rector nor the vicar of Altarnun having any right to the same. The parishioners of the chapel before its repair in 1281 used the church of Altarnun and the prior and convent should therefore surrender to the farmer such profits as were lawfully due to him for that year. But for 1282 and ever after the priory should enjoy them. Sealing clause. Dated Exeter, Friday, 25 September 1282.

MS.: Cartulary, f.39r.–f.39v.

**90.** Synodical judgement concerning the portions of the tithes of the manors of Fawton and Bucklawren (*Bokalawern*) before Roger de Otery, canon of the church of Crediton, commissary of Thomas, bishop of Exeter, in an *ex officio* cause promoted by the bishop against the prior and convent of Launceston of the Augustinian order of the same diocese. That the religious received two parts of the greater and lesser tithes of the ancient demesne of Fawton within the limits of an alien parish, St Neot. Also that they did not pay tithe from their demesne of Bucklawren except one fifteenth of the great and small tithes to the mother church of St Martin in the parish of which the demesne is situated, as was discovered by the recent episcopal visitation of the archdeaconry of Cornwall. The priory was represented by Brother William de Penlen, a fellow canon thereof who stated that his house had enjoyed two-thirds of the tithe of Fawton from a time beyond the memory of man, and that the priory of Montacute which held impropriate the church of St Neot had confirmed this arrangement with papal authority. He claimed immemorial prescription as to the immunity claimed at Bucklawren. This proctor was sworn and five witnesses produced and the said instrument of the prior and convent of Montacute. Definitive sentence was given for the priory of Launceston for the possession of the tithes. With the copy of the commission from Thomas Bytton, bishop of Exeter, to Mr Ralph Germeyn, archdeacon of Barnstaple (*Barum*), John de Brineton and Roger de Otery, canons of Crediton, to deal with the business arising from the bishop's late visitation of the archdeaconry of Cornwall. Dated St Germans, 12 October 1303.

MS.: Cartulary, ff.39v.–40v.

**91.** Inspection and confirmation by Thomas Bytton, bishop of Exeter, of no. 90. Dated Clyst, 20 January 1304.

MS.: Cartulary, f.40v.

**92.** Notice by the precentor and succentor of Salisbury of a papal mandate received by him from Pope Gregory IX. Odo, rector of the church of St Breward (*Bruweredus*), had complained that the prior and convent of Launceston, R., knight, and certain other clerks and laymen of the dioceses of Exeter, Salisbury and Bath had injured him. The pope ordered the precentor and succentor to summon the parties and deal with the matter on pain of ecclesiastical censure. (*Agnc'* 28 August 1239). Odo appeared about the tithes of Brown Willy (*Brunwenely*) of the priors and convents of Montacute and Launceston and amicable agreement was reached before the prior delegated 22 November 1239. Odo, rector of St Breward, and his successors were to pay annually to the priors of Montacute and Launceston and their convents 4s. at St Breward by the hands of the chaplain of St Peter of Fowey for the tithes and obventions of Brown Willy. The tithes of Brown Willy within the bounds below were to remain the possession of the church of St Breward for ever, viz. from the water called 'Kip' from the north side of the cliff of Brown Willy as far as the black cliff. Thence to the source of the Fowey (river) and from the source by the great way of waggons as far as 'Stingedelace' and thence as far as 'Polbarth' (and then) the way as far as the water of 'Kip' from the south side of the cliff of Brown Willy. Neither the said Odo nor his successors were to extend the boundaries of the parish of St Breward beyond these bounds. Odo bound himself and his successors in the church to this payment under a penalty of 2s. with the consent and assent of the prior and convent of Tywardreath. The priors and convents and Odo and his successors committed themselves to the jurisdiction and coercion of the prior of Bodmin who was to have powers of compelling their observance of the settlement. Chirograph sealed by the precentor and succentor of Salisbury and the prior of Tywardreath. Dated 22 November 1239.

MS.: Cartulary, ff.40v.–41v.

**93.** Notice by Rannulph de Albo Monasterio that he had done fealty and homage to his lord, Thomas, prior of Launceston, for the whole land of Diptford (*Dupeford*) which he held from him as by right of the church of St Stephen of Launceston and which he and his ancestors had held from the same church for time immemorial. He had attorned and put in his place William de Faunstyston to make suit of court to his lord, the prior of Launceston, every three weeks, which suit he and his ancestors had performed from time immemorial. Sealing clause. Dated Binhamy (*Bename*), Wednesday, 21 May 1348.

MS.: Cartulary, f.41v.

**94.** Notice by John, nephew and heir of the lord Ranulph de Albo Monasterio, that he had done fealty and homage to his lord, Thomas de Burdon, prior of the monastery (*sic*) of Launceston, for the land of Rooke (*Rugog*) which extended to two parts of a knight's fee and for the land of Diptford and appurtenances which he held as of right of the church of St Stephen of Launceston by certain rents and military service just as his ancestors held of the lord prior and his predecessors. Sealing clause. Witd. John Dabernoun, sheriff of Cornwall; John Skirbek, then constable of the castle; the lord John de Haldestowe, rector of the church of St Mabyn (*Mabena*), William de Polglas, Nicholas Wamford. Dated Saturday, 3 July 1361.

MS.: Cartulary, ff.41v.–42r.

**95.** Notice by Richard de Carburra, senior, of his knowledge that the prior of Launceston and the convent had received annually 4s. sterling of rent at Michaelmas in pure and perpetual alms in the manor of Treglasta by the hands of the lord, John de Rypariis, and his ancestors who were lords of the same manor from time immemorial, of which manor John de Ripariis had enfeoffed his tenants freely. Later the said John enfeoffed Walter de Carburra, Richard's father, with all services and rents of the said tenants freely and fully. Walter had enfeoffed Richard with the services and rents and the prior and convent had received the said 4s. annually without interruption or claim from Walter and afterwards from Richard. Richard de Carburra granted that the prior and convent should receive the said 4s. rent for ever. If the said rent was in arrears at Michaelmas the prior and convent might make distraint for it by their bailiffs through all the manor of Treglasta until they had made full satisfaction. Alternate sealing clause. Witd. William de Ferariis, John Treiagu, John de Chalons, knights; John de Burdon, Richard Beamond. Dated Launceston, Monday, 2 February 1321.

MS.: Cartulary, f.42r.–f.42v.

**96.** Notice by Richard, lord of Trelask, of all his right in the advowson of the church of Lewannick (*Lanwanac*) to the canons of Launceston so that they might have free possession of the same by law. Sealing clause. Witd. Walter, archdeacon of Cornwall, Robert, vice-archdeacon; Arlmar the dean, John Walensis, Luke son of Bernard, Gervase de Horningacote, Stephen de Pundestoke, Walter de Vacy, Ralph the clerk, William the cook, William the baker, Richard son of Gilbert, Roger Lirant, Eustace the clerk, Geoffrey of the church. Not dated. [1180–1195, determined by archdeacon Walter (Morey, 127) and date of confirmation by Bishop Henry, see no. 99.]

MS.: Cartulary, f.42v.

**97.** Notice by Richard de Trelosk of his grant to the canons of Launceston of the common pasture of his land of Trelask and his men at Lewannick (*Lanwanoc*). To have quietly for his life and the lives of his heirs for ever. The prior and canons gave him in recognition of this grant 20s. sterling. If the convent was unjustly molested over their possession of the advowson of the church of Lewannick (*Lanwanoc*) by his doing he would again release the advowson to them. He confirmed the oath he had taken in the chapter of the canons of Launceston touching the sacred gospels in the presence of many. Sealing clause of grantor. Witd. Roger chaplain, Adam chaplain, Warin Linar, Robert his brother, Robert Sprakel, Roger Foliot, Ralph the clerk, Auger de Lanwitatune, Osbert Fraunceys, William the baker, Geoffrey of the church (of) Tiraunus. Not dated. [Approximately the same period as no. 96, after the grant of the advowson.]

MS.: Cartulary, f.43r.

**98.** Notice of inspection by William, bishop of Exeter, of the confirmation of his predecessor, Bishop Henry, to the priory of the church of Lewannick (*Lanwennoch*) and the chapel of Egloskerry and the chapel of Boyton (*Boithun*) for quiet possession. (Mentions Luke, vicar of Lewannick, Ralph de Egloskery, and Parisius de Boitona.) Dated Crediton, 7 March 1225.

MS.: Cartulary, f.43r.–f.43v.

**99.** Confirmation of Henry, bishop of Exeter, to the priory of the church of Lewannick and the chapel of Egloskerry. Witd. Master Benedict, Master Milon, Philip[a] the chaplain. Dated Pawton (*Polton*), 9 March

1195. [But the text of Bishop Henry's charter in no. 98 is dated 9 May (*vij idus Maij*), 1195, so possibly 9 May is to be preferred to 9 March.]

ᵃPhilibert in the text of no. 99 recited in no. 98. The text of 98 adds to the witnesses: Gilbert the clerk, Almarius the dean, Adam the dean, Bendict de Cumba, clerk.

MS.: Cartulary, f.43v.–f.44r.

**100.** Notice of a dispute between Launceston priory and the dean and chapter of Exeter about Mount 'Oddedoune' between the parish of Lewannick and the parish of Altarnun.

The dean and chapter of Exeter had the church of Altarnun to their own uses as the prior and convent of Launceston had the church of Lewannick. Disputes arose on the right of possession of the greater and lesser tithes of the mount called 'Oddedoune' which lay between the water called Inny (*Eny*) on the north side of the mount which ran towards the east, and a long ditch which lay between the land of 'Blakadoune' on the southern side of the mount. Both parties sent representatives to view the mount so an amicable settlement of the dispute might be made: viz. Adam Murymouth, precentor, and the lord Thomas de Stapeldon, canons of Exeter, and for the prior of Launceston two canons of his house and Richard de London. Senior and trustworthy neighbours testified truly to the premises and when information was received from them the parties agreed as follows:

All the tithes of the moiety of the mount towards the west were to belong to the church of Altarnun. The tithes of the mount towards the east were to belong perpetually to the church of Lewannick. The mount was to be divided by bounds with the consent of the lord, using stones or brushwood. The bounds were to begin by the said water and to extend southerly to the ditch. If the lord of the mountain would not allow such bounds, they should be measured by the two parties, with Altarnun having the tithes of the western half and the church of Lewannick those of the eastern half. Sealing clause of both parties (chirograph). Dated Exeter, Sunday, 24 July 1328.

MS.: Cartulary, f.44r.–f.44v.

**101.** Notice of an action before the official of the peculiar jurisdiction of the venerable father and lord, the lord John by the grace of God, bishop of Exeter, and his general commissary in the parish church of South Petherwin (*Southpiderwyne*) on Wednesday, 21 July 1333, between the prior and convent of Launceston by their proctor John Godman, clerk, for the one party, and Thomas, perpetual vicar of the church of Lewannick, the accused, of the other party. The official had heard by a letter of the dean of East Wivelshire (*Estwevelschir*) that the proctor aforesaid in the name of his lords and his monasteryᵃ of Launceston (who had obtained the church of Lewannick for their own uses) had justly sought 40s. sterling in the official's presence for the lords of whom he was tenant at the time of costs and expenses about the rebuilding and construction of the church[b] of Lewannick for the rate of the portion of his vicarage. The said vicar acknowledged he owed the said religious men the 40s. for this cause. The official and commissary gave a sentence for the payment to be made by the condemned vicar of Lewannick. Dated South Petherwin, Wednesday, 21 July 1333.

[a]*sic.* [b]The title includes, *ad construccionem cancelli ecclesie de Lawannek.*

MS.: Cartulary, f.44v.–45r.

**102.** Bond by John Mulys of Trelask to the lord Stephen, prior of Launceston, in £20 sterling. To be paid to Stephen or his certain attorney in the conventual church of Launceston at the following Easter by himself, his executors, and heirs. He also bound his goods for the payment. Sealing clause of John Mulys. Dated Launceston, Wednesday, 9 March 1390.

MS.: Cartulary, f.45r.

**103.** Agreement concerning a dispute between Stephen, prior of Launceston, and the convent, and John Mulys, lord of Trelask. Richard, formerly lord of Trelask, granted by charter to the canons of Launceston and their successors in perpetual and free alms common pasture over all his land of Trelask in his pasture and in other advantages of his land and his men at Lewannick. Afterwards a controversy arose over the common pasture between Prior Stephen and the convent of Launceston and John Mulys, lord of Trelask. Later, at the bidding of the lord William de Botreaux, the said parties elected two arbitrators and agreed to abide by their arbitration. If the arbitrators could not agree, the parties chose John Herle, lord of 'Trewelowen'. The arbitrators ordered that John Mulys was to give and grant for himself and his heirs forever to the said prior and convent common pasture in all his land in White Down (*Whitedoune*) with free access for the priory's animals and tenants in Lewannick. Neither John nor his heirs were to cultivate the said land to the detriment of the common pasture. John Herle ordered (because of the disturbance made to Prior Stephen in his common pasture in Trelask) that the prior was to receive from the said John for his expenses £10 sterling which the lord prior received from him when these presents were made. John Herle ordained as well that the said prior and convent could not henceforth claim the said common pasture except only in White Down. If the prior and convent or their successors or tenants in Lewannick were disturbed or impeded in White Down that thenceforward it would be lawful to the said prior and convent and their successors to occupy the common pasture through the whole land of Trelask according to the ancient charter John Mulys granted and confirmed in free alms to the prior and convent and their successors for ever common pasture in all his land of White Down with access for their beasts and those of their tenants in Lewannick. Warranty by John Mulys and his heirs of the common pasture and access. Alternate sealing clause (seals of John Mulys and John Herle). Witd.

Nicholas Wampforde, Richard Kendale, William Trelowny, Warin Dawnant, Robert Tregodek, Robert Pyk, Benedict Dounhevde. Dated Launceston, Friday, 11 March 1390.

MS.: Cartulary, ff.45v.–46r.


**104.** Notice by Thomas Uppeton of his bond to John Selman of 'Nywenham' in £40 sterling. To be paid to John or his attorney at the following Michaelmas by John or his heirs and executors. The condition was that Thomas Uppeton and Joan his wife, Margaret who was the wife of John Uppeton, Sir John Trelauny, knight, Roger Menwynnek and Stephen Trenewith were to abide by the judgement and arbitration of William Wynard in their dispute with John, prior of Launceston, and his tenants of Lewannick, Lemalla (*Lamalla*), Canonhall and Trewanta (*Trewhante*) the day before the present date. Dated 8 May 1422.

MS.: Cartulary, f.46r.–f.46v.


**105.** Notice of no. 104. John Solman (*sic*) and the others named in no. 104 and the tenants of the prior of Launceston in Lewannick, Lemalla, Canonhall and Trewanta were to abide by William Wynard's award. The prior had brought before the justices of assize the question of his common pasture of Trelask which belonged to his free tenement in Lewannick, Lemalla, Canonhall and Trewanta against the persons cited above. On 13 May 1422 William Wynard in the presence of all parties gave his final judgement and award that the prior should prosecute his assize for taking again his common pasture in Trelask which belonged to his free tenants in Lewannick, Lemalla, Canonhall and Trelask. All parties were to appear and then the said prior was to claim that he had been disseised of 1000 acres (more or less) in White Down. The jury were to admit his right of common belonging to his free tenement in Lewannick, Lemalla and Canonhall but not in Trewanta. After this judgement the prior was (out of court) to execute a release to Thomas and the rest for all actions for trespass. They were to take no action against this. Dated 13 May 1422.

MS.: Cartulary, ff.46v.–47v.


**106.** Pleas of assize at Launceston before William Cheyne, Thomas Broune, William Wynard and John Martyn, justices of the lord king, at the assizes in the county of Cornwall on Monday, 10 August 1422.

The assize came to recognise if Thomas Uppeton of Trelask and Joan his wife, and Margaret who was the wife of John Uppeton, Sir John Trelouny, knight, Roger Menwynnek and Stephen Trenewith unjustly disseised Prior John of Launceston of his common of pasture which belonged to his free tenement in Lewannick, Lemalla, Canonhall and Trewanta, viz. 40 acres of land, 40 acres of pasture in the vill of Trelask called White Down with every kind of beast belonging to the free tenement of 9 messuages, one toft and 4 acres of land Cornish in the vills of Lewannick, Lemalla, Canonhall and Trewanta.

Thomas, John Trelouny, Roger and Stephen in their own persons, and Joan and Margaret by John Trelouny junior, their attorney, acknowledged on oath that the said prior was seised of common in 40 acres of land and 40 acres of pasture belonging to 7 messuages, one toft and 3½ acres of land Cornish in the vills of Lewannick, Lemalla and Canonhall which Thomas, Joan and Margaret unjustly disseised to the prior's loss of £20. They said Sir John Trelouny, Roger and Stephen were not present at the disseisin. Two messuages and half an acre Cornish were in the vill of Trewanta and the said Thomas, Joan, Margaret, John, Roger and Stephen said they did not disseise the prior of these lands in Trewanta. Richard, late prior of Launceston, was seised in the right of his church of St Stephen of Launceston of the common of pasture etc. in the time of King Henry III since which time his successors had held it by prescriptive right. The jurors said there was no collusion between the parties contrary to the statute of mortmain. The judgement was that the prior was to recover seisin of his common pasture belonging to his tenements in Lewannick, Lemalla and Canonhall, and he was to recover damages of £20. Thomas, Joan and Margaret were in mercy. Sir John Trelouny, knight, Roger and Stephen were acquitted of the disseisin etc. Dated Launceston, Monday, 10 August 1422.

MS.: Cartulary, ff.47v.–48r.

**107.** Notice by Prior John of Launceston of the receipt from Thomas Uppeton and Joan his wife and from Margaret who was the wife of John Uppeton of £20 adjudged to him by the disseisin of his common pasture in Trelask by the assize lately held at Launceston before William Cheyne and his colleagues. He released and quitclaimed to Thomas, Joan and Margaret all personal actions for the transgression which he suffered before this acquittance. Sealing clause of Prior John to the indenture. Dated Launceston, 12 August 1422.

MS.: Cartulary, f.48v.

**108.** Grant and quitclaim in perpetuity by Isabel de Hyolalond in her independent widowhood to Richard, prior of Launceston, and the convent, and to their successors that they could join to her land of 'Hyolalond' one weir at the use of the mill of the said prior called 'Combreggesmyll'. To have and to hold the said weir adjoining the said land freely quietly and peacefully for ever with free licence to maintain the said weir touching her land. Clause of warranty *contra omnes mortales*. Sealing clause. Witd. Henry Rem, Robert de Bodmam, Henry Mustard, William de Tregodek and John Walso. Not dated. [*c*.1302. See no. 109.]

MS.: Cartulary, ff.48v.–49r.

**109.** Notice of Isabel de la Holdelond that in her widowhood she had granted and confirmed to the prior and convent of St Stephen, Launceston the joining of their mill of Lewannick to her land of 'La Holdelond' with free power of digging turves at the said weir for ever in free and perpetual alms. The prior and convent gave her 40s. for her charter and confirmation. Sealing clause of grantor. Witd. Robert de Bodmam, Henry Rem, Henry Mustard, Robert Tripelot, John Le Walys. Dated at the grange of the prior and convent of Launceston, 6 November 1302.

MS.: Cartulary, f.49r.

**110.** Notice by Thomas de Duneham that he had granted in pure and perpetual alms for the salvation of his soul and the souls of his ancestors and successors that the canons of St Stephen Launceston might make a sluice of a pond on his land of Polyphant (*Polafant*), wherever they thought best, to make a mill in their land of Lewannick. The canons might have from his land of Polyphant as much labour as was necessary to make the sluice. Grantor's sealing clause. Witd. Robert de Tintagel, John his brother, David de Tunan, Hamelin de Trevell, Jordan de Trecarl, Walter Rufus, Henry Godman. Not dated. [*c*.1220 (Hamelin de Trevella, see nos. 482 and 484) or before. See also no. 111.]

MS.: Cartulary, f.49r.–f.49v.

**111.** Grant in pure and perpetual alms by Isobel, daughter and heir of Thomas de Dunham, of her legitimate power in her widowhood, to the canons of St Stephen of Launceston of a licence to strengthen the weir of their mill of Lewannick through the whole of her land of Polyphant where they wanted, and to take stones from there for building when and where they wished. Later she granted as well to the canons the common pasture of the whole land of Polyphant in free and perpetual alms for the salvation of her soul and those of her ancestors and successors. Witd. Robert son of William, Walter son of William, William de Duene, Hamelin de Trevell, William Wyse, Richard Probus, Henry Churt, Henry de Trevell, Ralph Fula. Not dated. [*c*.1206–7 (*Cornwall FF*. no. 36, Robert son of William) – 1220 (Hamelin de Trevella). These dates would fit Robert fitz William (II) or his son Robert (III).]

MS.: Cartulary, f.49v.

**112.** Grant by Richard de Trevaga to the prior and convent and their successors to strengthen and make in his land of 'La Yoldelond' a dam leading to their mill of Lewannick where anciently it was customary to strengthen, and to be placed as would be most useful to the prior and convent. To have and to hold freely and to be sustained from his land for ever, free from all service and exaction. Grantor's sealing clause. Witd. Walter de Carnedon, Henry de Trecarl, Richard Beaumond, Walter de Burdon, Henry Rem. Dated Launceston, Saturday, 1 September 1313.

MS.: Cartularly, ff.49v.–50r.

**113.** Grant by John, son of Richard de Trevaga, to the prior and convent and their successors to strengthen and remake in his land of 'La Yoldelonde' a pool in the water leading to the priory mill of Lewannick where anciently it used to be strengthened and channelled, as it would be to the great use of the prior and convent and their successors. The grant was for ever and free from all service and exaction. Grantor's sealing clause. Witd. Walter de Carnedon, Henry de Trecarill, Richard Beaumond, Walter de Burdone, Henry Rem. Dated Launceston, Saturday, 1 September 1313.

MS.: Cartulary, f.50r.

**114.** Notice by charter that Richard de Raddon, then sheriff of Cornwall, with Phillip his son offered on the altar of St Stephen Launceston one virgate of land called Trewanta free and quit from all service except for 15d. which he had to pay at Rillaton (*Ridlehtuna*) for a certain custom called *motilet*. Witd. William Robert, Simon his son, Richard Swem de Mota, Roger son of Lipsus, Walter son of a widow, Godwin son of Mere, Baldwin and his sons. Not dated. [*c.*1146–65, see note to no. 13 (Richard de Raddon).]

MS.: Cartulary, f.50r.

**115.** Grant and confirmation by Reginald, son of the king, earl of Cornwall, of the land called Trewanta given by Richard his sheriff to the regular canons of the church of St Stephen of Launceston. Not dated. [April 1140–1 July 1175, when Reginald was earl of Cornwall; probably towards the end of these limits, perhaps *c.*1174–5, to judge from the royal confirmation, no. 116.]

MS.: Cartulary, f.50v.

*Alia carta de eadem*
Reginaldus regis filius comes Cornubie omnibus baronibus suis salutem. Sciatis me concessisse et confirmasse donacionem terre que nominatur de Trewanta quam Ricardus vicecomes meus dedit canonicis regularibus ecclesie sancti Stephani de Lanstavet(on). Et volo et precipio ut bene et in pace eam teneant. Testibus Johanne capellano et Hamelino presbitero, Roberto de Dunstanvilla, Roberto filio Asketill, Waltero de Botrell et alijs.

**116.** Grant and confirmation by King Henry II to the church and canons of St Stephen of Launceston of all reasonable gifts to them in alms, i.e. of the gift of Richard de Raddona, a virgate of land called Trewanta, free from all service except for 15d. which he owed by custom at Rillaton for a certain payment called *motileth*. And of the gift of Robert son of Asketill, with the consent of his lord Reginald, of the land called 'Treuthioc'. The canons were to hold freely with all liberties and free customs etc. Not dated. [Between 6 October 1174 and 1 July 1175. Consecration of Richard of Ilchester (for whose title see Delisle, *Recueil des*

*Actes de Henri II,* Introductory vol., 431–4) and Geoffrey Ridel, Powicke and Fryde, *Handbook of British Chronology* (1961), 223; and date of death of Earl Reginald, *Complete Peerage,* (2nd ed.) iii, 429.]

> *Confirmacio regis Henrici de terra de Trewhante*
> Henricus Dei gratia rex Anglorum dux Normannorum et Acquitannorum et comes Andegavorum archiepiscopis episcopis abbatibus comitibus baronibus justiciis vicecomitibus et omnibus ministris et fidelibus suis tocius Anglie salutem. Sciatis me concessisse et presenti carta confirmasse ecclesie sancti Stephani de Lanstaveton et canonicis ibidem Deo servientibus omnia subscripta que eis racionabiliter data sunt in elemosinam scilicet ex dono Ricardi de Raddona unam virgatam terre que nominatur Trewante quietam et liberam ab omni servicio preter xv denarios quos reddere debet ad Ridlethunam de quadam consuetudine que vocatur *motileth.* Ex dono Roberti filij Asketilli concessu comitis Reginaldi domini sui terram que vocatur Treuthioc. Quare volo et concedo et firmiter precipio quod predicta ecclesia et canonici eiusdem ecclesie habeant et teneant hec supradicta cum omnibus pertinencijs suis in bosco et plano in pratis et pasturis in aquis et molendinis in vijs et semitis et in omnibus aliis locis et alijs rebus ad ea pertinentibus bene et in pace libere et quiete plenarie integre et honorifice cum omnibus libertatibus et liberis consuetudinibus suis sicut carte donatorum quas inde habent testantur. Testibus Roberto Wintoniensi,[a] G. Eliensi, B. Exoniensi episcopis etc. Apud Wintoniam.

[a]Probably a mistake for Richard of Ilchester, bishop of Winchester, 1174–88.

MS.: Cartulary, f.50v. Another copy, *Calendar of Patent Rolls 1377–81,* p. 114 (1378).

**117.** Grant and confirmation by Thomas Carhurta to Thomas Bank and John Combe of Polyphant of all his messuages, lands, rents, services and reversions in Lewannick and Treglomb (*Treglomma*). Warranty. Grantor's sealing clause. Witd. Thomas Uppeton, Elias Uppeton, Robert Doune. Dated Lewannick, 20 March 1438.

MS.: Cartulary, f.50v. Another copy, *Calendar of Patent Rolls 1377–81,* p. 114 (1378).

**118.** Notice by Thomas Bank and John Combe of Polyphant of the grant and confirmation to Thomas Carhurta of their messuages, lands, rents, services, reversions in Lewannick and Treglomb (*Treglomma*). To have and to hold to Thomas Carhurta and the right heirs of his body for ever. If Thomas Carhurta died without lawful heirs, the property was to remain with Nicholas Tregoddek of Launceston and his heirs and assigns by due and customary services of right to the chief lords of the fee. Warranty to Thomas Carhurta and Nicholas Tregoddek. Warranty to debar and prohibit grantor and heirs and from putting their tenements at a valuation. Grantor's sealing clause. Witd. Thomas Uppeton, Elyas Uppeton, Robert Doune. Dated 26 March 1438.

MS.: Cartulary, f.51r.–f.51v.

**119.** Memorandum of proceedings at the law court held at 'Bernhay', Saturday 17 Henry VI.[a] The jurors there presented that Thomas Carhurte enfeoffed Thomas Bank and John Combe de Polyphant in fee simple of certain lands and tenements in Lewannick and Treglomb. They also presented that those enfeoffed re-enfeoffed the said Thomas Carhurt of the said tenement and the lawful heirs of his body. In default of lawful issue of Thomas Carhurt the property was on Thomas' death to go to Nicholas Tregoddek of Launceston. They also then presented that the said Nicholas Tregoddek was dead and had been born illegitimate and had died without lawful heirs. Because of this the reversion would go to the prior and convent on the death of Thomas Carhurt and his heirs. They also presented that William Robyn enfeoffed Robert Horn of a fourth part of two parts of one ferling in West Menheniot (*Westmynhynnek*) whence there occurred to the lord for a relief 6½d. Therefore the said Robert should be distrained to make fealty and suit of court to the lord. Not dated. [Between 1 September 1438 and 31 August 1439 on a Saturday.]

[a]*sic* .

MS.: Cartulary, f.51v.

**120.** Release and quitclaim by Alice Yvon, daughter and heir of Richard Yvon of Landrends near Launceston to John Trethewy and Thomas Skydea, chaplains, and Walter Pers and their heirs and assigns for ever of all her right in Landrends and 'Trecaru' by Launceston with the rents and services of all free tenants. She had given these lands to John Ude, as appeared in her charter. Sealing clause of Alice Yvon. Witd. Benedict Dounheved, then free bailiff of Launceston Land; John Ouger of Egloskerry, Stephen de Tredydan, William Mustard, Richard Skaynek, John Landyar. Dated Dounhevd, Friday, 30 January 1388.

MS.: Cartulary, f.52r.

**121.** Quitclaim by William Westcote of Launceston to Prior Stephen and the convent and their successors and assigns of his claim to all messuages and lands in Landrends which formerly belonged to Alice Yvon. Sealing clause. Witd. Jocelin Penros, Stephen Bant, John Godecote, John Treludek, John Lavyngton. Dated London, Friday, 5 February 1389.

MS.: Cartulary, f.52r.–f.52v.

**122.** Release and quitclaim by Walter Whita of the parish of Davidstow (*Dewystowe*), kinsman and heir of Alice Ivon, to John, prior of Launceston, and the convent and their successors and assigns of his rights in lands, tenements, rents, services and reversions with their appurtenances in Landrends and 'Trecaru' within the manor of Launceston Land which formerly belonged to Alice Yvon. Warranty. Sealing clause. Witd.

William Trelauny, Walter Carmynowe, Stephen Cork, Robert Symon de Bodsyny, Robert Cork. Dated Launceston, Saturday, 31 January 1422.

MS.: Cartulary, f.52v.

**123.** Grant and confirmation by Sir Robert de Tresulyan, knight, to John Trethewy, chaplain, Thomas Skudya and Walter Pers etc. of his lands and tenements in the vills of Landrends and 'Trecaru' with the rents and services of William Scherpe, Stephen Tredydan, Stephen Treludek, Magota Batyn, John Page, William Bodyer, John Landyare for the property they hold of him in the aforesaid vills. To hold from the chief lords of the fee by due and customary services. Warranty. Sealing clause. Witd. William Trelouny, Robert Puddyng, Benedict Dounhevd, Richard Skeynok, William Mustard. Dated Launceston, Tuesday, 18 August 1383.

MS.: Cartulary, ff.52v.–53r.

**124.** Letters of attorney of Sir Robert Tresulyan, knight, to John Crese who was to deliver seisin to John Trethewy, chaplain, Thomas Skudya and Walter Peres of lands etc. in Landrends and 'Trecaru'. Dated Launceston, Tuesday, 18 August 1383.

MS.: Cartulary, f.53r.

**125.** Extent of the lands of Sir Robert Tresulyan, knight, in Landrends and Trecaru.

Extent of the free tenants made there by worthy and lawful men: Stephen Tredydan, Stephen Treludek and William Scharpe, coheirs, rendered yearly 12d.
John Page rendered yearly 3d.
Magota Batyn rendered yearly 6d.
William Bodyer rendered yearly 1d.
John Landyar rendered yearly 12d.
Conventionary tenants of the same Robert there:
William Scherpp rendered yearly for a tenement in Landrends 42s. at the usual terms.
William Parkeman rendered for one croft 2s. 2d. and one day's work in the autumn.
Dated Tuesday, 18 August 1383.

MS.: Cartulary, f.53v.

**126.** Inquisition taken at Camelford, Friday, 7 April 1402. Before Stephen Bony, *locum tenens* for Robert Rodyngton, feodary of the lord prince. By the oaths of John Trevesek, Roger Glasta, William Westa, John Hendra, Thomas Mony, Richard Whita, Richard Brebard, William Attewille, William Frankelyng, John Copisden, Stephen Denesell, and

Henry Laverence who said that one messuage and one ferling of land with appurtenances in Landrends and one messuage and one ferling of land with appurtenances in 'Trecarew' and 2s. 10d. of rent in the vill were of the inheritance of Lora, wife of Richard Whita, and were seised in the hand of the lord prince by virtue of a certain office taken before Sir Henry Ilcombe, knight, formerly escheator of Richard II, lately king of England. That it was known by the same inquisition that the prior of Launceston had acquired the messuage, land and rent for himself, his heirs and successors in mortmain without obtaining the licence of the king. And they said that the above mentioned messuage and land were worth yearly in all issues beyond deductions 40s. 4d. and that they were held of the said prior and convent of their manor of Bernhay for the rent of 8d. yearly and suit of court twice a year for all services. And they said that a certain Richard Ivon was seised in demesne as of fee of the said messuage, land and rent and died seised of the same. And he had issue a certain daughter called Alice who entered the same property until a certain Richard Peek of 'Berne' expelled her and took the issues and the profits. Later the said Alice by a certain assize of novel disseisin before Henry Pertehay and his colleagues, justices of the lord king, recovered the said tenement. Later John Ude entered into the said messuage and land and the said Alice about the fortieth year of the lord king Edward III, released her right and claim to these properties to John Ude. And they also said that Sir Robert Tresylyan, knight, afterwards entered into the messuage and land, but by what title they did not know. Recital of no. 123 granted on condition of Sir Robert Tresulyan having land and a tenement of the said priory in the parish of St Eval (*St Uvell*) in exchange. And it was said that the said prior acquired forever from the said John Trethewy, Thomas Skedya, chaplain, and Walter Piers the tenement and rent in Landrends and 'Trecarowe' in the time of King Richard II, but whether or not with licence they did not know. Recital of no. 120. And they said that the said Lora, wife of the said Adam[a] White, daughter of Matilda, sister of the said Richard Ivo, father of the said Alice, was a kinswoman (cousin) of the said Alice Ivo and her nearest heir of the age of 60 years and more. Dated Camelford, Friday, 7 April 1402.

[a]*sic.*

MS.: Cartulary, ff.53v.–54v.

**127.** Notice by Joan, who was the wife of William Mustard de Neuport of her grant and release and perpetual quitclaim to Walter Creke and John Trethewy, chaplains, of her right and claim in all that tenement situated in the free borough of Dunheved in the high street of the said borough, between the tenement of Julian Skoldefynger of the one part and the tenement of Robert Pike on the other. Also notice of her grant and release to Walter and John of her right and claim in two fields at Landrends (once belonging to John Skachard). To them and their heirs and assigns for ever, to hold of the chief lord of that fee by due and customary services. Warranty clause and acquittance. Sealing clause of Joan. Witd. Benedict Dounhevd, bailiff of Launceston Land, William

Godrych, Thomas Raynfrey, Roger Kelyowe. Dated Launceston, Wednesday, 15 October 1393. [Assuming the feast of King Edward the Confessor was the *translatio* of 13 Oct. and not the *depositio* of 5 January. If the latter was intended the date would be Wednesday, 7 January 1394.]

MS.: Cartulary, f.54v.

**128.** Release and quitclaim by Henry Fox of Launceston to Walter Cryke and John Trethewy, chaplains, of his right and claim to the tenement in Ðunheved (as no. 127) and to the two fields in Landrends. Other clauses as in no. 127. Witd. Martin Ferers, Nicholas Wamford, Richard Trevage, John Trelouny, John Podyng. Dated Launceston, Tuesday, 14 October 1393.

MS.: Cartulary, ff.54v.–55r.

**129.** Grant and confirmation by Richard Doty, vicar of St Andrew of Launcells, to Walter Crycke, vicar of Stratton, John Trethewy, chaplain, and John Thomas, clerk, of all his messuages, lands and tenements in the borough of Dunheved as also in the vill of Landrends. To have these and the reversion of the dowry of Joan, widow of John Ronald, in Dunheved and Landrends, when it occurred, freely, in peace, and for ever. To hold of the chief lords of the fees by due and customary services. Warranty of lands and reversion clause. Grantor's sealing clause. Witd. John Colyn, mayor of the borough, Robert Pycke, John Cotell, William Hamond, clerk. Dated borough of Dunheved, Tuesday, 15 October 1392.

MS.: Cartulary, f.55r.–f.55v.

**130.** Quitclaim by Richard Doty, vicar of Launcells, to Walter Crycke, vicar of Stratton, John Trethewy, chaplain and John Thomas, clerk, of his rights in the properties of no. 129. Sealing clause. Dated Launceston, Thursday, 17 October 1392.

MS.: Cartulary, f.55v.

**131.** Notice that Henry Body senior was bound to the lord Stephen, prior of Launceston, in 39s. of rent due before the date of the present document. The lord prior had granted that Henry should pay the said money within the following two years after this bond at the four terms of the year by equal portions until the sum was paid. The lord prior had granted to Henry a certain parcel of land in 'Trecaru' on the west side of the way which ran through the same vill of 'Trecaru', and also granted to Henry three pieces of land in 'Birchdoune' with the meadow (lately Robert Tresulyan's) in exchange for all messuages, lands and tenements of Henry in the vill of Landrends. Henry had to render yearly to the lord prior 5s. as set forth fully in the charters made between them. The lord prior granted also to Henry 2 parks in Landrends, lately Henry's, for a yearly rent of 9s. If this rent was in arrears distraint should be made in the messuages, lands and tenements of Henry in 'Trecaru' and 'Le Byrchdoune' if sufficient distress could not be found in the parks. As for the rents and suits of court to be made to the lord prior for his tenement in Landrends, Henry wished the council of the prior should determine whether these services should be done to the same lord of right or not. Sealing clause of both parties. Dated Wednesday, 18 December 1387.

MS.: Cartulary, ff.55v.–56r.


**132.** Release and quitclaim by Nicholas Cresa and Richard Adam, chaplains, to Henry Body senior of their right in messuages, lands and tenements in Landrends and 'Le Birchdoune' in the manor of Launceston Land. Plural sealing clause. Witd. John Bilney, John Godecote, William Mustard. Dated Launceston, 22 February 1387.

MS.: Cartulary, f.56r.


**133.** Grant and confirmation by Henry Body to John Trethewy, Thomas Skudia, Walter Greek and Reginald Tresker of his land in Landrends with houses, gardens, meadows, pastures etc. with four pieces of land in 'Le Birchedon'. To hold of the chief lord of the fee by due and customary service. Warranty. Grantor's sealing clause. Witd. Nicholas Wampford, Richard Kendale, Benedict Dounhevd, William Mustard, Richard Skaynek. Dated Launceston, Sunday, 10 March 1387.

MS.: Cartulary, f.56v.


**134.** Grant and confirmation by John Trethewy and Thomas Skudya, chaplains, to Henry Body senior of all their land in 'Trecaru' lying between the land formerly of John Vysour on the west and the royal highway which leads from Dunheved towards Landrends on the east, and also of all their meadow in 'Birchdoune'. To Henry and his right heirs for ever for a yearly rent of 2s. 6d. and 18d. for a relief when it happened after the death of any of the tenants. Also by making suit of court to the prior of Launceston at Bernhay twice yearly at the court after the Invention of the Holy Cross (3 May) and the court next after Michaelmas. If it happened the said Henry died without heirs the land would revert to Thomas Bodya and his heirs for the same rent, two suits of court yearly and 18d. for a relief on the death of each tenant. With remainder to William Yeo de Trevsow and his heirs for the same rent and services etc. With remainder to Margaret, wife of Thomas Skynner and the heirs of her body, with the same rent and services. Distraint of goods and chattels could be made for arrears of rent within the manor of Launceston Land. Warranty. Sealing clause of grantors. Witd. Nicholas Wampford, Richard Kendale, Benedict Dounhevd, Richard Skaynek, William Mustard. Dated Launceston, Sunday, 17 March 1387.

MS.: Cartulary, ff.56v.–57r.

**135.** Grant and confirmation by John Trethewy, Thomas Skydya, Walter Greek and Reginald Resker[a] to Henry Body senior of 2 crofts and 4 pieces of land in Landrends in 'Le Birchedoune', lying between their land on the eastern side and the land of John Viser in the west, and royal highways to the north and south. To Henry and his heirs, to hold of the prior of Launceston and the convent there by an annual rent of 9s. at the four principal terms of the year by equal portions, and 6d. for relief after the death of each tenant. Henry was to make suit to the prior of Launceston's court at 'Le Barnehay' twice yearly, i.e. at the court after the feast of the Invention of the Holy Cross (3 May) and the court after Michaelmas. In default of heirs (of Henry Body) to revert to Thomas Body and his heirs for ever, with the same rent, relief and suit of court. With remainder, in default of heirs of Thomas Body, to William Yeo and his heirs on the same terms, and similarly to Margaret, wife of Thomas Skynner. If rent or relief was in arrears it would be lawful for the grantors to make distraint in the manor of Launceston Land. Warranty to Henry, Thomas, William and Margaret. Grantors' seals not known, therefore prior and convent's seal used at grantor's request. Witd. Benedict Dounhevd, then free bailiff of Launceston Land, Richard Skaynek, William Mustard, William Garnek, Stephen Tredydan. Dated Launceston, Monday, 23 September 1387.

[a]*sic.* (cf. no. 133, Tresker).

MS.: Cartulary, ff.57r.–58r.

**136.** Grant and confirmation by Prior Stephen and the convent to Henry Body senior of their land in 'Birchdoune' with its appurtenances and two pieces of land in 'Trecaru'. To Henry and his heirs to hold of the prior and convent and their successors at a yearly rent of 2s. 6d. at the four usual terms by equal portions and 18d. for a relief on the death of each tenant. Suit of court was to be made to the court of the priory in Bernhay twice yearly at the court after the feast of the Invention of the Holy Cross (3 May) and the court after Michaelmas. With remainders in default of heirs to Thomas Body, William Yeo de Trefosou, and Margaret, wife of Thomas Skynner and their heirs. Warranty to Henry, Thomas, William and Margaret. Sealing clause of grantors. Witd. Richard Kendale, Nicholas Wampforde, Benedict Dounhevd, Richard Skaynek, William Mustard. Dated Launceston, Sunday, 10 March 1387.

MS.: Cartulary, f.58r.–f.58v.

**137.** Release and quitclaim[a] by Jordan de Ridkarou to the prior and canons of Launceston, for 20s. received of them, of one acre of land in Landrends which he had held from them for some time. Jordan or his successor could have the land again from the prior and canons by repayment of 20s., provided there was security for the payment of the lawful service for this land, i.e. 40d. for the same acre. Fealty and sealing clause.[b] Witd. Ralph clerk of St Stephens, William Budier, Robert Rem,

Arnold Bern, Tankard and all of the hundred. Not dated. [*c.*1232–44, cf. no. 61.]

<sup>a</sup>Title: charter of the lands of Henry Viser in Landrends. <sup>b</sup>*ut ratum et inconcussum permaneat tam fidei interposicione quam sigilli*, etc.

MS.: Cartulary, f.58v.–f.59r.

**138.** Quitclaim by Jellinus de Castello, son of Geoffrey de Landren, to the church of Blessed Stephen of Launceston and the canons serving God there of all his right in one acre of Landrends which Jellinus the clerk, his uncle, formerly held. The prior and convent gave him 20s. for his quitclaim. Witd. the lord Odo de Treverbyn, then sheriff of Cornwall; William Wise, Ralph de Trewrtha, Adam de Fentune, Wandry de Boytun, Patrick John Maning, Henry de Treull'. Not dated. [*c.*1244–66. (William Wise, no. 565 and Henry de Trevella, no. 462). In *Cornwall FF.* i no. 142 the last occurrence of Odo de Treverbyn is 1253/4.]

MS.: Cartulary, f.59r.

**139.** Release and quitclaim by Margaret, who was the wife of Richard Tolle, to Prior Stephen and the convent and their successors of her right in one messuage and a ferling of land in Landrends. Warranty. Sealing clause. Witd. Stephen Tredidan, Benedict Dounhevd, John Bylney. Dated Launceston, 18 April 1402.

MS.: Cartulary, f.59r.–f.59v.

**140.** Grant and confirmation by Prior Stephen and the convent to Margaret who was the wife of Richard Tolle of 2 closes with their appurtenances which the said Richard formerly held in Dunheved borough. The closes lay in the said borough between the close of John Corke on the west and the closes of John Colyn and John Page on the east. To have and to hold to the said Margaret and the free heirs of her body from the prior and convent and their successors for a rent of 7s. sterling at the feasts of the Invention of the Holy Cross (3 May) and Michaelmas by equal portions and to make one suit to their manor of Bernhay after Michaelmas for all service etc. If the rent was in arrear by one year and there was not sufficient distress, it would be lawful for the grantors to enter and take possession of the closes. If Margaret died without free heirs, the properties were to go to John Corke and his free heirs. If John had no heirs, the 2 closes were to remain to the prior and convent and their successors. Warranty to Margaret and John. Alternate sealing clause: seal of the community of the prior and convent and of Margaret Tolle. Witd. William Twyneo, mayor of Dunheved; Thomas Raynfry and William Bylker, reeves of the same borough; Stephen Tredidan, Benedict Dounhevd. Dated at the chapter house of Launceston priory, 18 April 1402.

MS.: Cartulary, ff.59v.–60r.

**141.** Grant and confirmation by William Mustard to John Trethewy, Thomas Skydea, chaplains, and Walter Cryke of a piece of land lying in Landrends between the garden of the prior and convent of Launceston on the north side and a croft of the same prior and convent to the south. To John, Thomas and Walter and their heirs and assigns for ever. To be held of the chief lords of the fee by due and customary rents and services. Clause of warranty etc. Grantor's sealing clause. Witd. Benedict Dounhevd, then free bailiff of Launceston Land; Stephen de Tredydan, Richard Skaynok, John Landyar, Thomas Raynfry. Dated Launceston, Friday, 15 January 1389.

MS.: Cartulary, f.60r.

**142.** Release and quitclaim by William Mustard of his right in 2 closes in Landrends which he had by the gift of Edmund Jurdan. Sealing clause. Witd. Benedict Dounhevd, John Bylney, Thomas Raynfry. Dated Launceston, 5 January 1395.

MS.: Cartulary, f.60r.–f.60v.

**143.** Bond between Prior Stephen and the convent, and William Sherppe. The prior and convent were bound to the said William in £20 sterling to be paid to the same William in the conventual church of Launceston at the following Michaelmas. On the condition that if the said prior and convent enfeoffed him and his wife Margaret and their lawful heirs with all the lands and tenements in Landrends which John Landyer and Richard Veeke formerly held (which were lately Robert Tresulyan's) and which the said William held by the grant of John Trethewy and Thomas Skudya, they would pay to the prior and convent in the first forty-five years from the date of the bond 42s. yearly at the four terms of the year (Christmas, the Invention of the Holy Cross (3 May), the Nativity of St John the Baptist (24 June) and Michaelmas) by equal portions. At the end of forty-five years they would then pay to the prior and convent £10 sterling yearly at the same terms. If these conditions were observed the bond would be of no effect. Alternate sealing clause. Not witnessed. Dated Launceston, Tuesday, 25 October 1384.

MS.: Cartulary, f.60v.

**144.** Grant from John Trethewy and Thomas Skudya to William Sherpe and Margery his wife of all their messuages, land and tenements in Landrends with a piece of land next to the way which led from Launceston priory towards 'Thornwill', which lands and tenements John Landyare and Richard Veek held and which were lately held by Robert Tresulyan, knight. To hold to William and Margery and their legitimate heirs from the date of the grant for the next forty-five years by an annual rent of a rose to the grantors at the feast of the Nativity of St John the Baptist for all services and demands, and to pay 42s. yearly to the chief lords, the prior and convent of Launceston, by the hands of John and

Thomas at the four usual terms (see no. 143) by equal portions. William and Margaret were to repair the premises at their own expense when it was necessary. They were not to grant or lease any part of the property without the consent of the prior and convent. To hold from the same prior and convent as granted. It was lawful for William and Margery and their heirs to sell the pasture and meadow there, if they wished, without waste and destruction. Right of re-entry to the grantors after the rent was in arrears by one quarter. If there was not sufficient distress John and Thomas had the right to re-enter and retain the premises. Warranty to William and Margery. Alternate sealing clause. Witd. Benedict Dounhevd, Richard Skaynok, Stephen Martyn, John Vysour, William Mustard. Dated Landrends, Tuesday, 4 October 1384.

MS.: Cartularly, ff.60v.–61r.

**145.** Grant and confirmation by John Trethewy and Thomas Skydea, chaplains, to William Sherpa and Margery his wife of their land in Landrends with appurtenances which Richard Vek formerly held together with a piece of land in the same vill between the close of William Mustard on the east and the land called 'Matslade' on the west. To hold to William Sherpa and Margery and the free heirs of their bodies for ever from the grantors and their heirs and assigns, with a rent of 22s. sterling for the first forty-five years by equal portions at the feasts of the Annunciation, the Nativity of St John the Baptist, Michaelmas and Christmas, and two suits of court of the grantors at the next court after Michaelmas wherever it was held within the demesne of Launceston Land for all other services and demands. Re-entry for grantors in default of distress after arrears at any of the yearly terms. After the first forty-five years William and Margery were to pay a rent to the grantors of 100s. yearly at the aforesaid feasts by equal portions. Grantors' clause of warranty. Alternate sealing clause (chirograph). Witd. John Bilney, John Godecot, Stephen Auger, William Mustard, Benedict Dounhevd. Dated Launceston, Monday, 26 December 1384.

MS.: Cartulary, ff.61r.–62r.

**146.** Deed witnessing that Walter Sherpe granted to Prior John and the convent an annual rent of 6d. sterling which he was accustomed to receive at Michaelmas for a certain parcel of land lying in the croft of John Loryng, bastard, in Landrends called 'Batyn ys Crofte'. To have and to hold the said annual rent of 6d. to Prior John and the convent and their successors for a term of 50 years next following. A yearly rent of a rose was to be paid at the feast of St John the Baptist for all services and demands. Warranty by Walter and his heirs to Prior John and the convent. Alternate sealing clause. Witd. Nicholas Trebarthe, Stephen Corke, William Mileton. Dated Landrends, Saturday, 26 June 1428.

MS.: Cartulary, f.62r.

**147.**   Grant and confirmation by Margery, daughter and heir of William Batyn, to John Loryng of all her croft lying between the land of Landrends and Launceston priory, which croft is called 'Batynscrofte'. To be held of her and her heirs by the service of one grain of corn at Michaelmas for all services. Warranty clause. Grantor's sealing clause. Witd. John Landyar, William Mustard, William Godrich. Dated Launceston, Tuesday, 30 November 1378.

MS.: Cartulary, f.62r.–f.62v.

**148.**   Release and quitclaim by Richard Brackyssh and his heirs and executors, to John Loryng and his heirs and assigns of the term which he had by the gift and grant of John Thorn and Cristine Batyn, in the name of her dowry, in a certain croft called 'Battynnyscrofte' near Launceston. Sealing clause. Not witnessed. Dated Launceston, 7 June 1406.

MS.: Cartulary, f.62v.

**149.**   Memorandum that Henry Dowbulday was seised of one tenement in the free borough of Dunheved and a close in Launceston Land. And he had issue Christiana and she married John Batyn. After Henry's death, John and Christiana were seised of the tenement and close. They had issue Margery who married John Loryng, bastard. After the deaths of John and Christiana, John and Margery became seised of the properties. John and Margery had issue Richard Loryng who became seised of the properties but died without heirs. Hawise Dowbulday, sister of Henry Dowbulday, married Stephen Lyon and had issue Joan who married John Champyon. Their issue was Margery and Margery married John Hogge and their issue was Philip.[a] Not dated. [Early 15th-century, after no. 148.]

[a]Note in left margin adds (in Latin), 'who by his charter released all his right therein.'

MS.: Cartulary, ff.62v.–63r.

**150.**   Inquisition taken at Launceston, Wednesday, 15 May 1392, before James de Chedelegh, knight, escheator of the lord king in the county of Cornwall by virtue of a royal writ directed to him. By the oaths of Noel Paderda, Richard Pincerna, Walter Kyngdon, John Vaga de Holewode, Roger Lamaryn, John Josep junior, Richard Doignell, William Stryke, William Broungyft, John Hydon, William Lyegh and William Tre-voseburgh. They stated on oath that it was not to the loss nor prejudice of the king, nor others, that the king should grant to John Trethewy chaplain, Thomas Skydya chaplain, John Spynner chaplain, John Hobba chaplain, John Godecote, William Creke, Reginald Tresker, John Lavyngton, John Treladyk, Walter Piers and Henry King, 7 messuages, 77 acres of land and 12s. worth of rent in Launceston, 'Newelond', Landrends, Liskeard (*Leskerd*), 'Slade' and Stratton that they might give and assign these to the prior and convent. To have and to hold to them and their successors for ever in part satisfaction of £20 worth of lands and rents yearly which the lord Edward, late king of England and grandfather of the present king, by his letters patent permitted them to acquire of their own fee as of another, except lands, tenements and rents which they already held in chief of King Edward III. The jurors stated that 6 of the 7 messuages and 47 acres of the said 77 acres of land (above) were held of the said prior and convent in free socage by the service of 6s. a year in all to be paid to the prior and convent. The jurors said that the 6 messuages and 47 acres were worth in profits, excluding deductions and the said service, 29s. 6d. And they said that the said prior held the 6 messuages and 47 acres of land of the bishop of Exeter with other lands and tenements. And the said bishop held of the lord king in chief. And the jurors stated that one of the 7 messuages and 6 acres of the said 77 acres of land were held of the mayor and commonalty of the borough of Launceston in free burgage as in socage; no yearly rent being paid for them. And the mayor and commonalty held this messuage and land of the lord king as of the duchy of Cornwall; their yearly value in all profits was 5s. And the jurors said that 20 acres of the 77 acres were held of John Wetherdon for a rent of 12d. yearly as in free socage for all services. And John held of the mayor and commonalty of Launceston, and the mayor and commonalty held of the lord king as of the duchy of Cornwall. This land was worth in profits 9s. And the jurors said that 4 acres of land of the 77 acres were held of John Colyn of Launceston for the rent of one pound of cumin as in free socage. The said John held these 4 acres of the mayor and commonalty of the borough and they held them of the king as of the duchy of Cornwall in free socage. They were worth yearly 18d. without deductions. The jurors stated that no land or tenement remained to the said John Trethewy, Thomas Skydya, John Spynner, John Hobbe, chaplains; John Godecote, William Creke, Reginald Tresker, John Lavyngton, John Treludyk, Walter Piers and Henry Kyng, and they did not have before them the aforesaid grant and assignment. And that they were not sufficient to be placed on the jury or assize before the grant and assignment. And they said that the land etc. should not be burdened with a payment more than was customary through the first grant and assignment being their own. Jurors' sealing clause. Dated Launceston, Wednesday, 15 May 1392.

MS.: Cartulary, f.63r.–f.63v.

**151.** Findings of an inquisition taken at St Neot on Monday, 12 May 1399 before Henry Ilcombe, late escheator of the late King Richard in the county of Cornwall, by virtue of his office and a return of the said late king into chancery, that Prior Stephen had acquired of Robert German one messuage, 2 acres of land with appurtenances in Liskeard (*Leskerryd*) for himself and his successors from the eighteenth year of the same king (22 June 1394 – 21 June 1395) without the licence of the said late king. And that the said prior had acquired of William Dobbe a tenement with a close adjoining in Liskeard for himself and his successors in the nineteenth year of the same king (22 June 1395 – 21 June 1396) without such licence. And also that the said prior had acquired for himself and his successors in the thirteenth year of the said late king (22 June 1389 – 21 June 1390) lands and tenements in Launceston and Landrends of John Tregorrek, Robert

Stonard, Ralph Kael and John Cokeworthy without such licence. It was also found out by the said inquisition that the said prior acquired of John Trelouny a tenement in Launceston without such licence. Also that the said prior had of the gift and grant of the progenitors of the lord king for himself and his heirs 8s. annually to be taken of the manor of Liskeard for the maintenance of a lamp burning before the image of Blessed Mary in the parish church of Liskeard. And that Roger Leye, predecessor of the said prior, and the said Prior Stephen withheld the said lamp(-rent) for thirty years past to the serious loss of the late king and parish etc.

After this the said Prior Stephen came in his own person at Westminster before the council of the lord prince of the lord king, viz. on the morrow of the Ascension (Friday, 13 May) 1401 in the hands of which prince the lands, tenements and rents were seised by virtue of the said inquisition as the prior asserted. And he said that to the said messuages there were 2 acres of land which the said Prior Stephen ought to have acquired of the said Robert German without the king's licence for himself and his successors. And one tenement with a garden or close adjoining in Liskeard which the said Prior Stephen ought to have acquired of the said William Dobbe for himself and his successors without royal licence. And certain lands and tenements which the said prior ought to have acquired for himself and his successors in Launceston and Landrends of John Tregorrek (and others as above) without royal licence as is supposed by the said inquisition. He said that a certain John Trethewy, chaplain, Thomas Skydya and John Spynner, chaplains, John Hobbe, chaplain, John Godecote, William Creke, Reginald Tresker, John Lavyngton, John Treludek, Walter Piers and Henry Kyng were seised of the aforesaid lands and tenements and their appurtenances in his demesne as of fee. And the aforesaid lands and tenements were given and granted by a certain charter which Prior Stephen produced in front of the council of the prince, the date of which was Launceston, 28 October 1392, to the prior and convent of Launceston for ever; having first obtained the king's licence for alienation of lands according to the statute of mortmain.[a] King Richard, wishing these letters to take effect, gave and granted for himself and his heirs to John Trethewy (and others as above) that the 7 messuages, 77 acres of land and 38s. worth of rent in Launceston, 'Newlond', Landrends, Liskeard, Slade, Stratton and Exeter not held of King Richard in chief (which were worth 45s. yearly more than the said rent as by the inquisition before James Chudelegh, the king's escheator in Cornwall, was found and returned into chancery) might be given and assigned by them to the same prior and convent who might receive and hold the said messuage, lands and rent from John Trethewy (and others as above) for themselves and their successors as aforesaid.

Prior Stephen had acquired the said land and tenement from the aforesaid Robert German, William Dobbe, John Tregorrek, Robert Stonard, Ralph Kael and John Cokeworthy as is supposed by the said inquisition. All this the present prior was prepared to verify, and he sought judgement and restitution together with profits etc. And for that one tenement which the said Stephen then prior ought to have acquired of John Trelouny in Launceston without the licence of king as supposed, the said Prior Stephen said that a certain Robert Carnek and Stephen

Biroidron of Launceston were seised of the said tenement together with other lands and tenements with their appurtenances in their demesne as of fee, and that tenement together with other lands and tenements by the name of 10 messuages and one ferling of land with their appurtenances in Launceston and Newport by a charter they gave and granted to the prior and his successors through Prior Stephen shown in the council of the said prince, and dated Launceston, 28 January 1378. They gave and granted these to the prior and convent of Launceston, the royal licence having been obtained, just as by the letters patent of the late king of England, which record follows in these words, Richard by the grace of God etc. as appears in the twentieth folio of the first quire of this register.[b]

As for the 8s. annually received from the manor of Liskeard for the keeping of a lamp burning in front of the image of Blessed Mary in the parish church of Liskeard as is supposed by the said inquisition, the said present prior said that he and his predecessors from time immemorial were seised as of right of their church of Launceston of the said 8s. annually received from the said manor in pure and perpetual alms. He sought judgement and restitution with the profits etc.

And after the said Prior Stephen died, the present Prior Roger pretended the verification as before. Therefore thence at the suit of the said Roger there was to be an inquisition and certification in the receipt of the exchequer in the quindene of Easter. Therefore by the advice and counsel of the lord etc., viz. Hugh Huls, John Arundell, Hugh Mortymer and John Wynter, it was considered that the hand of the lord prince should be absolutely removed from the lands and tenements and that the said prior might have liberation of the same together with arrears, saving the rights of the prince etc. Not dated. [Council of the Prince of Wales, duke of Cornwall etc. ? Friday, 13 May 1401. But note the reference to the death of Prior Stephen who died 8 December 1403. His successor Prior Roger does not occur until 1404, see appendix, list of priors. So the date must be between the occurrence of Prior Roger Combrygge, 20 May 1404, and his death 18 June 1410.]

[a]The text of the royal licence dated 24 September 1392 is omitted here. [b]See Cartulary no. 45.

MS.: Cartulary, ff.64r.–65v.

**152.**  Inquisition taken at Launceston on Tuesday, 6 May 1404, before John Darundell, seneschal of the lord prince in Cornwall, by virtue of letters of the lord prince directed to the seneschal together with a record for better information by the oaths of Richard Trevage, Thomas Restarrek, John Pennarth, Robert Hurdewyke, Richard Penvoun, Gilbert Dreynok, Walter Pyper, John Cory, John Giddelegh, John Josepp, John Trevysek and John Calwa, jurors, who recited part of the evidence of no. 151.[a] Moreover the jurors said on oath that Prior Stephen had not acquired of Robert German a messuage and 2 acres in Liskeard, as the inquisition supposed. Neither had Prior Stephen acquired of William Dobbe a tenement with a close adjoining in Liskeard as the inquisition said. Neither had Prior Stephen acquired certain lands and tenements in

Launceston and Landrends of John Tregorrek and others as the inquisition for the late king stated. Also they said that the said Prior Stephen had not acquired from John Trelouny a tenement in Launceston without the licence of the late King Richard. And neither did Prior Stephen receive of the gift and grant of the progenitors of the lord King Richard 8s. of rent annually from the manor of Liskeard for keeping a lamp burning in the parish church of Liskeard as the inquisition for the late king stated. But they said that a certain John Trethewy, Thomas Skydya, John Spynner, John Hobbe, chaplains, John Godecote, William Creek, Reginald Tresker, John Lavyngton, John Treludek, Walter Piers and Henry Kyng were seised of the said lands and tenements and appurtenances together with other lands and tenements and their appurtenances in demesne as of fee as well as the tenement which it was supposed by the inquisition that the said Prior Stephen ought to have acquired from John Trelouny as well as the said 8s. And these said lands and tenements specified in a certain charter they gave and granted to the said Prior Stephen and his successors by the name of the prior and convent and their successors for ever, with the royal licence obtained just as by letters patent of Richard II, late king of England, is specified, and were shown to the jurors. The jurors said as well that a certain Robert Carnek and Stephen Biroidron of Launceston were seised of the said tenement which the said inquisition supposed that the said Prior Stephen ought to have acquired of John Trelouny in Launceston without the licence of the lord king aforesaid, that is, with other lands and tenements and their appurtenances, by the name of 10 messuages and one ferling of land with appurtenances in Launceston and Newport. By the charter specified in the said record they gave and granted to the prior and convent and their successors with the royal licence obtained, just as by the letters patent of the said lord Richard, lately king of England, in the said record is specified and (which) the said jurors were shown in evidence. And further they said that Prior Stephen and his predecessors from time immemorial were seised of the said 8s. as by right of their church of St Stephen of Launceston. To have and to hold annually for themselves and their heirs in pure and perpetual alms for ever. In witness of which the said jurors affixed their seals. Dated Launceston, Tuesday, 6 May 1404.

<sup>a</sup>The substance of the first paragraph of the calendared entry for no. 151.

MS.: Cartulary, ff.65v.–66v.

**153.**   Inquisition of lands and tenements in Launceston and Landrends and of 8s. taken of the manor of Liskeard belonging to the lord duke of Cornwall.

In a memorial of the tenth year of King Henry VI in the records of the term of Holy Trinity of the treasurer's remembrancer. It was known by a certain inquisition taken at Liskeard on Thursday, 10 April 1399, before Martin de Ferers, treasurer in the exchequer of the lord king, by virtue of letters of the same late king directed to the same Martin by the oaths of

John Trelouny, James Forsdon, Edward Beket, John Forsdon, Simon Lawys, Richard Foke, Richard Hendra, William Bethwat', Ralph Wotton, Henry Enys, Ralph Bevell and John Foke, jurors, that Prior Stephen of Launceston and his predecessors had withdrawn the keeping of one lamp burning before the image of Blessed Mary in the parish church of Liskeard. For keeping this lamp the late prior and his predecessors received annually 8s. issuing from the manor of Liskeard of the gift of the ancestors of the lord king. And it was in contempt of the same late king and his prejudice of £12 for withdrawal of the said lamp for thirty years, i.e. for each year 8s. And that the said late Prior Stephen acquired for himself and his successors in the month of March in the tenth year of the late king (1387) without the licence of the said king certain lands and tenements in the vill of Launceston and in Landrends of John Tregorrek, Robert Stonard, Ralph Karll and John Cokworthi (which were then worth nearly £10) in contempt and deception of the said late king, as is contained in the said inquisition enrolled in the remembrances of the third year of King Henry IV (3 September 1401 – 29 September 1402), grandfather of the present king, between the records of the term of Holy Trinity in the twelfth roll by which William Shire then prior of Launceston (Prior Stephen being dead) was summoned in the quindene of Holy Trinity in that term to render to the king an account of the profits of the said lands and tenements in the vills of Launceston and Landrends and to respond to satisfy the king about the £12.

And at the said quindene of Holy Trinity Prior William appeared in his own person. And he said he was not bound to render any account of the issues of other lands or tenements in the said vills to the lord king, nor to render accounts for the said £12. He protested that Prior Stephen never acquired for himself and his successors any lands or tenements in this vill or elsewhere of the said John Tregorrek, Robert Stonard, Ralph Kerll and John Cokworthy nor of them for any plea. He said that Henry, late king of England, father of the present king, by his letters patent (which the said prior brought into the court), the date of which was 25 January in the second year of his reign (1415), pardoned John, late prior of Launceston, predecessor of Prior William and successor of Prior Stephen, between other grants, alienations and perquisites by them (i.e. the prior and convent) held in chief of the said late king or his progenitors, formerly kings of England. And also (he pardoned) grants, alienations etc. in mortmain made without the royal licence together with issues and profits taken in the meantime. And also by the same letters he pardoned and released to the said late prior and convent all fines, judgements, amercements, fines, reliefs, scutages and all debts, accounts, arrears and all actions and demands which the said late king had against him alone or with other persons. Which letters patent follow in these words.

Henry by the grace of God. Witness myself etc., as appears in the last folio of the quire of the pardon of Henry V. Whence it is seen that the present king does not wish to tax the present prior for any account of the profits of any lands or tenements in the said vills of Launceston and Landrends made by the late Prior Stephen or any other prior of Launceston before the said fifth day of January. And as for the said £12 the prior said that he and all his predecessors had the 8s. worth of rent from the manor of Liskeard in their demesne as of the fee and right of the church of St Stephen of Launceston and they and their successors had that rent in free, pure and perpetual alms from time immemorial and for the whole of that time they were accustomed to distrain in the said manor for arrears of rent as often as the rent was not paid until there was full satisfaction. The prior and his predecessors never had it for the keeping of a light in the ecclesiastical parish of Liskeard (*Leskert*). There was no record of this as a gift of the present king or his ancestors, nor were the 8s. from the manor ever paid out in that way. This the prior was prepared to verify. The present king did not wish to force the present prior to reply to the satisfaction of the lord king about the £12. And he sought judgement etc. And because the court wished to deliberate before in the premises etc., a day was given to the present prior from Michaelmas up to fifteen days etc. (i.e. the court adjourned to deliberate). Dated Trinity term 1432.

MS.: Cartulary, ff.67r.–68r.

**154.** Grant and confirmation by John Ude of Pengelly to John Trethewy, John Hobbe, Thomas Frydowe and John Spynner, chaplains, of lands and tenements in Tresmarrow (*Tresmargh*). To have for ever, to hold from the chief lords of the fee. Clause of warranty. Witd. Nicholas Wanford, Serlo Wysa, Robert Tregoddek, Robert Puddyng, Alan Cransy. Dated Launceston, Monday, 23 September 1381.

MS.: Cartulary, f.69r. [f.68v. is blank].

**155.** Grant and confirmation by David de Tresmargh to the lord Gervase Northcote, chaplain, and Walter Keta of 2 acres of land English of his land of Tresmarrow between the aqueduct of the priory and the higher way leading to Trebursy. To Gervase and Walter and their heirs and assigns for ever to hold of the chief lords by the services due and customary for so much land. Warranty. Sealing clause of grantor. Witd. William Mosterd, William Snellard, William Henterdren, John Rem, William Goderich. Dated Tresmarrow, Monday, 8 May 1374.

MS.: Cartulary, f.69r.–f.69v.

**156.** Grant and confirmation by David de Tresmargh in pure and perpetual alms to the church of St Stephen of Launceston and the canons there for the salvation of his soul and the souls of his parents of two acres of land English in the vill of Tresmarrow. One of these lay between the aqueduct of the priory and the way through the close called 'Kytepors' and the other lay from the same way as far as the higher way leading towards the vill of Trebursy. The infirmarer was to have these two acres as a subsidy of his office for ever. To hold of the chief lords etc. Warranty. Sealing clause. Witd. William Mostard, William Snellard, William Henterdren, John Rem, William Godrych. Dated Tresmarrow, Monday, 8 May 1374.

MS.: Cartulary, f.69v.

**157.** Confirmation by Prior Roger and the convent to Thomas, son and heir of John Ude of Pengelly, of the tenure for himself and his heirs of one messuage and one acre of land Cornish[a] with the appurtenances in Tresmarrow, which he held of the prior and convent by fealty and the annual rent of 3s. 1½d. and service to the priory court of Bernhay from three weeks to three weeks. Alternate sealing clause. Witd. William Talbot, knight, John Trelauny, John Lanhergy, Stephen Bant, Thomas Ber. Dated Launceston, 14 October 1404.

[a]i.e. The carucate acre of 64 English acres. See P. L. Hull, *The Caption of Seisin of the Duchy of Cornwall (1337)*, DCRS 1971, lix.

MS.: Cartulary, ff.69v.–70r.

**158.** Pleas of assize of Trebursy.

Pleas of assize at Launceston before Robert Belknapp and his companions, justices of the lord king, taken at the assize in the county of Cornwall on Monday in the third week of Lent in the fourth year of King Richard, king of England and France.

The assize came to recognise if Prior Stephen, Walter Peyrys, Henry Wytefeld and John Nayll', chaplain had unjustly disseised Richard Page of Launceston and Margaret his wife of their free tenement in Trebursy. Whence it was enquired that they disseised them of one messuage and 12 acres of land. And the said prior in his own person came and all the others did not come, but a certain Richard Rous replied for them as well as their bailiffs. He said they had done no injury or disseisin to the said Richard and Margaret.

The prior replied as tenant of the tenement and he said that the assize between them ought not to be because a certain John Wallowe[a] was seised of the said tenements with appurtenances in his demesne as of fee and he held them of Thomas, former prior of Launceston, by fealty and the service of 2s. yearly. And this John Wolfolke was a bastard and died seised of the property without heirs. After his death, Prior Thomas, predecessor of the present prior, entered into the tenements as his escheat and Prior Thomas died seised of the property. After his death the present prior found his church seised of the said property and continued the said seisin. And the said Richard and Margaret claimed that tenement as blood relatives of the said John Wolfolk, i.e. as son of John, son of Richard, brother of John Wolfolk. It was supposed that the said John Wolfolk was legitimate but when he was known to be bastard they intruded themselves into those tenements above the possession of the late prior, and the present prior retained the property and moved there. Whence they sought a hearing if, because of this, the assize ought to cause them to be returned.

And the said Richard and Margaret, not knowing that John Wolfolke was a bastard, nor that the late Prior Thomas was ever seised of the property, said that John Wolfolke enfeoffed a certain John, son of Richard de Hesthendra, father of the said Margaret, to hold to himself and his heirs for ever. By virtue of which gift the said John, son of Richard, was seised of that tenement. And after the said John Wolfolk died the late

Prior Thomas intruded himself into those tenements above the possession of the said John, son of Richard. After being moved away, John, son of Richard, made claim and debate. At his death the said Margaret was of age and claimed these tenements as the daughter and heir of John, son of Richard, when Thomas was prior and during the time of his successor until she married Richard when they both claimed the property as their inheritance, including the time Margaret was under age, and thence they were seised of a free tenement until the present prior unjustly disseised them.

And the present prior said that John Wolfolk died seised of the said tenement but he (the prior) did not enfeoff John, son of Richard, as Richard and Margaret alleged. And he placed himself on the assize, and Richard and Margaret did likewise.

The assize recognised that by the grant of the said parties the property came to Margaret, their heir, to hold to them and their heirs for ever as the said Richard and Margaret allege. And further they said that Richard and Margaret were seised of those tenements as of a free tenement until the said prior and Walter unjustly disseised them, to the loss of 20s. to the said Richard and Margaret. They said that Henry and the others named in the writ were not present at the disseisin. Therefore it was advised that Richard and Margaret were to recover their seisin of the tenement and damages assessed at 20s. And the prior and Walter were at mercy. Richard and Margaret were at mercy for a false claim against Henry and the others acquitted of their disseisin. Dated Launceston, Monday, 18 March 1381.

<sup>a</sup>*sic.*

MS.: Cartulary, ff.70r.–71r.

**159.** Agreement (chirograph) about the exchange of lands and rents between the canons of Launceston and Luke son of Bernard. Luke gave to the canons all his land of Tregadillett and all his land of Trebursy with the estate of 'Challeswich' with all men, woods, gardens, meadows and all other appurtenances. To have and to hold them in demesne for ever, freely and quietly. For these the said Luke son of Bernard, received of the canons in exchange the whole land of Fawton (*Fawinton*), i.e. an acre of land which was Bloiho's and half an acre of Lewinus and half an acre of John and one acre 'ad longam petram' and a ferling of land which was Kiabbel's and one acre of land in 'Tregarros' and half an acre 'ad Rupem' and half an acre in 'Trekynner' which Gilbert held and the land which Martin Augus and Chubba the carpenter hold in the vill of Botternell (*Boturnoll*) except his mill situated in that land which they retained for him with its appurtenances. To have and to hold to them and their heirs with men and their liberties of the same canons freely· and quietly by hereditary right. Rendering as well for the said lands received in exchange as well as the land of Trespearne (*Tresperna*) and the messuages of Launceston half a mark of silver for all service belonging at two terms of the year, i.e. at Easter 40d. and at Michaelmas 40d. The said Luke and his heirs should have twigs for his sheep fold and for his plough of 'Lanwitta' of the wood of Tregadillett or of Trebursy by view of the forester of the canons without waste. And they were held to warrant for ever against all men the said exchanged lands with all the appurtenances to the said canons. And if the latter were not able to give them anything as a competent and reasonable exchange of their heredity elsewhere which the said Luke was holding of them, the said canons would warrant to the said Luke and to his heirs the said lands given in exchange to him or they would give elsewhere in his land another reasonable exchange. Alternate sealing clause for chirograph. Witd. John son of Richard, then sheriff of Cornwall; Simon de Pum, Robert de Tintagel, Gervase Bloiho. Not dated. [*c.*1209–14, shrievalty of John fitz Richard, lord of Connerton.]

MS.: Cartulary, f.71r.–f.71v.

**160.** Grant and quitclaim by Nicholas Batyn, son of William Davy, bailiff of Trebursy, to Richard de Brykevile, prior of Launceston, and the convent all the right he had in one half acre of land Cornish with houses and gardens and all other appurtenances in the vill of Trebursy where William Davy, bailiff, his father, held for some time. Sealing clause. Witd. Robert de Bodmam, Gregory de Doddestone, Walter de Burdon, Henry Rem, Ivo de Landrene. Not dated. [*c.*1301, see no. 161.]

MS.: Cartulary, ff.71v.–72r.

**161.** Release by Nicholas Batyn de Trebursy and Matilda, wife of William Davy of Trebursy to Brother Richard de Brikevyle, prior of Launceston, and the convent and their successors and bailiffs of all actions which they had against the said prior and convent or the bailiffs and their successors of any right they would have had and of all kinds of transgressions suffered by Nicholas and Matilda through them since Tuesday, 31 October 1301. For this the prior gave them 4s. sterling. Witd. Robert de Bodmam, Henry Rem, Henry Mostard, Nicholas de Landren, then bailiff of Launceston Land; Robert Trypelot. Not dated. [Same date as no. 160, on or after 31 October 1301.]

MS.: Cartulary, f.72r.

**162.** Grant and confirmation by John Witefeld to Thomas Lawyer and Margery his wife of his fealty, rent and service of John Gorecota and Agnes his wife of all messuages, lands and tenements which they held of him in Trebursy for the term of the life of the said Agnes with the reversion and appurtenances whenever it fell due. To have to Thomas and Margery and the heirs of Thomas for ever. To hold of the chief lords by service formerly and rightfully due. Warranty to them by John Witefeld. Sealing clause. Witd. Stephen Bant, Nicholas Tregodek, Robert Bartha, Robert Tremayll, Peter Trenydelham. Dated Trebursy, 1 March 1406.

MS.: Cartulary, f.72r.–f.72v.

**163.** Grant and confirmation by Thomas Lawier to the lord John Ayssh, vicar of the parish church of St Martin of Liskeard, of the fealty, rent and service of John Gorecote and Agnes his wife of all messuages, lands and tenements held by them of him in Trebursy for the term of Agnes' life with their reversion when it should fall due and with all the appurtenances, which he had of the gift of John Witefeld. To hold of the chief lords by the customary rights and services by right. Warranty granted by Thomas to John Ayssh. Sealing clause. Witd. Stephen Tredidan, William Trelauny, John Gorecote, Stephen Cok and John Skaynek. Dated Trebursy, Friday, 24 February 1419.

MS.: Cartulary, f.72v.

**164.** Gift and grant in perpetual alms by Bernard the clerk (junior) de Penkyvoc of 2 acres of land which three men held and rendered to St Stephen's 5s. yearly. The land lay under the way near Trebursy, and the grant was free of all service. Witd. etc.[a] Not dated. [Early 13th-cent.; before no. 165.]

[a]*sic.*

MS.: Cartulary, f.72v.

**165.** Grant[a] and confirmation by Geoffrey de Lametin, lord of Poundstock, to the church of St Stephen of Launceston of the land of Pencuke (*Penkyvoc*) with its appurtenances which William, son of Joym, the grandfather of Geoffrey's father gave in pure and perpetual alms, free and quit from all secular service and demands except royal service which is called foreign service.[b] Of this service it often happened that the grantor and his heirs wholly acquitted the church each year by 4s. paid by the prior and canons at Michaelmas whether or not foreign service was called for. And the prior and canons would remain free from this service by payment of the said 4s. Also Geoffrey granted and confirmed to the said prior and canons of Launceston 5s. worth of land and appurtenances in Trebursy under the way which Bernard the clerk gave to the church and canons in free alms. The grantor wished the prior and canons to have and to possess the said land as freely and quietly as the said Bernard gave it to them and confirmed by his charter. Witd. Walter de Treverby(n), then sheriff of Cornwall, Henry, son of William, Walter, son of William, Baldwin de Sancto Genesio. Not dated. [Approximately *c.*1227, see no. 21, or a few years before if Walter Treverbyn was sheriff 1223/4 as Watkin states (ii, 1018).]

[a]Note in right hand corner: (i) *de Penkyvok* et Bysoutheway. (ii) *Mᵈ quod alie carte de Penkyvok scribuntur postea in xiij folio registri ecclesie Sancti Genesii et Treworgy.* [b]*utibannum.*

MS.: Cartulary, f.73r.

**166.** Grant and confirmation by Richard son of Nicholas de Pundestoch to the church of St Stephen of Launceston of the land of Pencuke with all its appurtenances which William Joim his grandfather had first given to the church in pure and perpetual alms free from all secular service. When royal foreign service was called for, Richard and his heirs would freely acquit the said church for 4s. which the prior and canons were held to pay to Richard and his heirs yearly at Michaelmas without any contradiction. Richard also granted and confirmed to the prior and canons of Launceston 5s. worth of land and appurtenances in Trebursy under the way which Bernard the clerk gave to the said church of St Stephen and the canons in free alms. The grantor wished the prior and canons to have and to possess the said land just as the said Bernard gave and confirmed it by his charter. Witd. Ralph the archdeacon, Stephen de Poundestoch, clerk, Everwinus de Whalesbreu. Not dated. [Before no. 165. Two archdeacons of Barnstaple were named Ralph and occur 1209 and 1219. Oliver, *Lives*, 293.]

MS.: Cartulary, f.73r.–f.73v.

**167.** Agreement made between the prior and canons of Launceston of the one part and Stephen de Pundestoch of the other. Stephen granted that the said prior and canons should hold the whole land of lesser Trebursy[a] with all appurtenances (about which there was a controversy between them) which also he had as the gift of Bernard the clerk as the charter of Bernard bore witness. So that the said Stephen or his heirs should in no way molest or vex the said prior and canons or their men in Trebursy for any pact made between the said Stephen and Luke, son of Bernard, or their predecessors about the said land or for any other occasion, or by a distraint or other inquietude. For keeping this grant the said prior and canons gave and granted to the said Stephen all the land of Tregear (*Tregier*) with its appurtenances which they had of the gift of William de Boterell for Stephen and his heirs to hold freely and quietly of the church of Launceston by an annual rent to the prior and canons at Michaelmas of 5s. for all service. Stephen swore on the four Gospels to keep this agreement without deceit. Stephen and William his heir appended their seals to each part of the chirograph; one part of which was to remain with the prior and canons and the other with Stephen and his heirs. Witd. Richard de Trelosk, Philip de Trevella, Ralph de Poundestok. Not dated. [Probably during the last two decades of the twelfth century, see no. 96. Philip de Trevella and Stephen of Poundstock occur in the eyre of 1201.]

[a] *de minori Trebursy.*

MS.: Cartulary, ff.73v.–74r.

**168.** Bond by John Doune of South Petherwin and his son, Thomas Doune, to Prior John and the convent in £40 sterling to be paid to the prior or his successors at the next feast of Michaelmas. John and Thomas also bound their heirs and executors. Sealing clause. Dated Saturday, 26 July 1404.

A dispute had arisen between Prior John and the convent and John Downe of South Petherwin about the right and title of divers services for the lands and tenements of Tregadillett held by John Downe of the prior and convent. John Doune was personally to obtain the verdict of twelve free and lawful men by taking their oaths through the seneschal of the prior and convent in their court at Bernhay before the feast of All Saints. Twelve men of twenty-two should be sworn in the court: i.e. from Stephen Tredidan, William Aunger, Henry Bodygode, Nicholas Tregodek junior, William Roos, Richard Gibbe, John Cargintel, Robert Henterdren, Walter Piers, Richard Skeynok, John Robyn atte Forde, Richard Downyend, Thomas Raynfry, William Stoterych, William Carnok, William Willyam, Stephen Dodeston, Richard Robyn de Attel, John Rem, John Frenssh de Neweton, Henry Viser and Henry Gobyn. These twelve men were to give the verdict. And if, after the verdict, as the rent was sent in advance, the said John Doune should do such services for the said prior and convent as were due and should make satisfaction for arrears, then the bond would be void. But if John Doune was not able to make satisfaction before the feast of All Saints because of the absence or default of the jurors that then the said John should render and restore a young bullock and a gelding in the park of the said prior at Bernhay. Dated Saturday, 26 July 1404.

MS.: Cartulary, f.74r.–f.74v.

**169.** Notice by indenture that John Doune of the parish of South Petherwin held of Prior John and the convent 3½ ferlings of land and their appurtenances in Tregadillett by fealty and a reñ of 3s. 8d. sterling to be paid by equal portions at the feasts of Easter and Michaelmas by the service of reaping the prior and convent's corn each year for one day in the autumn and ploughing each year the land of the prior and convent for one day when required and for the service of being bailiff of the manor of Launceston Land when chosen. Also by the service of suit to the court of the prior and convent within the said manor from three weeks to three weeks, as was found by a certain inquisition held on Saturday, 28 August 1417. John Doune agreed he had paid and would pay this rent and services for ever to the prior and convent and their successors. Sealing clause. Dated Saturday, 28 August 1417.

MS.: Cartulary, ff.74v.–75r.

**170.** Confirmation by Brother Richard de Brykvyle, prior of Launceston, and the convent to Cecilia, daughter of Adam de Algerstoune, the feoffment of half an acre of land with appurtenances in the vill of Kestle which Luke, son of Roger, formerly bought of Stephen Le Duc, chaplain, son of Peter Le Duc, together with the feoffment of one acre of land with its appurtenances. Three ferlings of this acre of land lay on the mount of Kestle, and a ferling of land which Peter, son of Warin, formerly held. This acre of land lay between the land which was formerly Mansipa's and the land of La Thorne as the royal way went towards Bodmin. The said

Luke bought the acre of Prior Robert and the convent, as appeared by a charter. The said Cecilia and her heirs and assigns should have and hold the said acre and a half of land with appurtenances from the prior and convent and their successors as fully and freely as the said Luke held them from the prior and convent at another time by the rent and services which were contained in the main charters and were customary. The prior and convent and their successors would warrant the land to Cecilia and her heirs and assigns. Clause for seals placed on letters patent. Witd. Robert de Bodmam', Henry Rem, Walter de Burdon. Dated Launceston, Friday, 4 June 1294.

MS.: Cartulary, f.75r.–f.75v.


**171.** Release and quitclaim by Richard Tancr(edesmyll) to the church of St Stephen of Launceston for himself and his heir forever of the land under the grove which was his father's and which he (Richard) held by consent of the prior and convent. Sealing clause. Witd. Robert de Tyntagel, Thomas de Dunham, Henry Godman. Not dated. [*c.*1220, see charter of Thomas de Duneham, no. 110. Henry Godman is one of the witnesses.]

MS.: Cartulary, f.75v.


**172.** [a]Quitclaim by Ralph son of Geoffrey Ruffus de La Casteldich, for himself and his heirs for ever to the church of Blessed Stephen of Launceston of his right in 4½ acres at 'La Casteldich' with two closes and all other appurtenances. For this quitclaim, Canon Geoffrey, then sacristan of the church, gave Ralph 20s. of which he acquitted him of usury.[b] The sacristan would pay yearly to the seneschal of the priory 8d. at Easter. Sealing clause, Witd. Ralph Trewitha, Wandry, John Mannyng, Henry de Trevell, Robert Rem, Gregory, Paganus Longus. Not dated. [*c.*1221–44, perhaps in the 1230s.]

[a]Title: *Regestrum cartarum et munimentorum de terris et tenementis in villa Sancti Stephani et Newport.* [b]*de iudaismo.*

MS.: Cartulary, f.76r.


**173.** Grant and confirmation by William Cory and Margery his wife to Robert Carnek, chaplain, of their messuage and close which lay in the vill of Launceston between the tenement formerly of William Pynta and the royal way which leads from Newport (*Neuport*) towards 'Hoghiscrosse'. To hold of the chief lord of the fee by due and customary services. Warranty, acquittal and defence. Sealing clause. Witd. John Page, William Mustard, John Stoterigg senior, John Stoterigg junior. Dated Launceston, Friday, 4 June 1378.

MS.: Cartulary, f.76.

**174.** Grant and confirmation by William Mustard to Robert Carnok, chaplain, of his messuage and close which he had in the vill of Launceston between the tenement of William Cory on the one side and the tenement of John Reche on the other side. To Robert and his heirs for ever to hold from the chief lord etc. Warranty, acquittal and defence. Sealing clause. Witd. John Page, John Stoterigg senior, John Stoterigg junior. Dated Launceston, Friday, 4 June 1378.

MS.: Cartulary, f.76v.

**175.** Gift and confirmation by Robert Carnek, chaplain, to Henry Frund, vicar of Liskeard, of his tenement in Launceston which he had of the gift and feoffment of William Penta and William Cory as it lay in the vill of Launceston between the tenement of John Ryche on the west and the royal highway towards 'Hoggescrosse' on the east. Not dated. [c.1378.]

MS.: Cartulary, f.76v.

**176.** Quitclaim by Richard Hayrun for himself and his heirs to the prior and convent of Launceston of his right in one acre of land in Tredidon, formerly held by Baldwin and Herding. For this the prior and convent granted him ten marks of silver. Sealing clause. Witd. Andrew de Canell', John de Chevertun, then sheriff of Cornwall, Roger de Trelosk. Not dated. [c.1229–42 (Roger de Trelask).]

MS.: Cartulary, f.77r.

**177.** Grant and confirmation by indenture by Prior Stephen and the convent to Stephen Tredydan and his rightful heirs of two messuages and one acre Cornish of land in the vill of Tredidon, i.e. all the land of the prior and convent in the said vill. To Stephen and his right heirs for ever. Rent each year to the prior and convent and their successors: 20s. at Easter, Christmas and Michaelmas by equal portions. Two suits yearly to the court legal of the prior and convent with reasonable summons. With remainder to the prior and convent if Stephen or his heir died. If Stephen or his heirs alienated the messuages and land wholly or partly, after their deaths it would be lawful to the prior and convent and their successors to re-enter and regain possession for ever. Stephen granted for himself and his heirs that if his rent was in arrears distraint could be made in one messuage and in 1½ acres of land Cornish, i.e. in all his other land etc. in Tredidon. If not enough was found there for distraint, the prior and convent could re-enter and have possession, notwithstanding the charter granted to Stephen. Warranty by the prior and convent to Stephen and his heirs for ever. Alternate sealing clause (chirograph). Witd. John Penres, Thomas Paderda, John Bilney, William Hamound, Thomas Raynfry, Benedict Dounhevd, William Godrych. Sealing clause: seal of

John Penres used as grantor's seal unknown to most. Dated at the chapter house of Launceston priory, 29 October, 1394.

MS.: Cartulary, f.77r.–f.77v.


**178.** Manumission by Prior John and the convent. John Hoper de Clompitts junior (alias John Bonney junior) and John and Richard his sons and Joan, Sybil and Margery his daughters were natives in villeinage of stock, by which cause they were subject to servitude and bondage by law. The prior and convent, moved by the intuition of piety and charity, gave manumission to the said John Hoper and to John, Richard, Joan, Sybil and Margery, offspring of John Hoper of Clomputtys junior, and freed them from all yoke of servitude for ever with their future family and household and with their goods and moveable chattels. Alternate sealing clause. Dated at the chapter house of Launceston priory, Wednesday, 19 July 1419.

MS.: Cartulary, f.78r.ᵃ

ᵃHenderson notes, 'this leaf is out of place and ought to come between ff.229–230.' Cf. nos. 179–181 following, and see nos. 584–90 (ff.228v.–230r.).


**179.** Grant by Prior John and the convent to John Hoper de Launceston Clomputtes,ᵃ junior, alias John Bonney junior, (formerly their serf, freed by them) and to Ibot his wife all messuages, lands and tenements which they and their ancestors held of them as of stock. They gave these properties to them and their right heirs forever. To hold of them and their successors by military service and by the annual rent of 3s. 4d. sterling, payable at Michaelmas and Easter by equal portions and they were liable for all rents and due and customary services due to the prior and convent as the chief lords of the fee. The properties were to revert to the prior and convent if John and Ibot Hoper died without legitimate heirs. Alternate sealing clause for chirograph divided between the two parties. Witd. Edward Bornebury, William Trelauny, John Croudecote. Dated at the chapter house of Launceston priory, Wednesday, 2 August 1419.

ᵃsic.

MS.: Cartulary, f.78r.–f.78v.


**180.** Grant by John Hoper de Clomputts, junior, (alias John Bonney) to Prior John and the convent of one annual rent of 13s.4d. to be taken and levied from all lands and messuages in 'Clomputtys' equally at the feasts of Michaelmas and Easter. To have and to hold to the prior and convent and their successors for the term of fifteen years following the next feast of Michaelmas. The prior and convent and their successors were to have a right of distraint in all the tenements if the rent were overdue until all arrears were paid. Sealing clause of John Hoper. Witd. William Trelouny,

John Treludek, Stephen Cork. Dated Launceston, 29 August 1419. [*anno regni regis Henrici sexti quinti post conquestum septimo* (sic).]

MS.: Cartulary, f.78v.

**181.** [a]Bond of John Hoper de Clomputts, junior, and of Walter Ludgard for paying to the prior and convent of Launceston one annual rent of 13s. 4d. from the lands and tenements in Clampit (*Clomputtys*) for fifteen years etc.

[a]Heading only. The text is given in no. 588 which is dated 9 September 1419.

MS.: Cartulary, f.78v.

**182.** Confirmation by Roger Prodhomme of his grant to Henry Mustard of half an acre of land Cornish in 'Hille' near Launceston. To hold of the chief lords of the fee (the prior and convent of Launceston) by due and customary services. Warranty to Henry. Sealing clause of grantor. Witd. Robert de Bodmam, Henry Rem, Henry Mustard, then bailiff of Launceston Land. Dated Launceston, Friday, 31 December 1305.

MS.: Cartulary, f.79r.

**183.** Quitclaim by Hamelin le Clouter to the prior and convent of a messuage and half-acre Cornish (separately) in Treludick (*Trelouthet*) which he held in villeinage of the prior and convent. At any time he could claim this property by hereditary succession, but he relinquished all rights to the properties. Sealing clause of Hamelin. Witd. Robert de Bodmam, Henry Rem, Ivo de Landren, Richard Kade, Henry Mustard. Dated Launceston, Friday, 28 May 1294.

MS.: Cartulary, f.79r.

**184.** Confirmation of grant by William Botrell for the salvation of his soul and of the soul of his wife Aubrey and the souls of his children and ancestors, to the canons of St Stephen of Launceston a half-acre of land in East Downend (*La dunende*)[a] which Algar Wada formerly held with common pasture in 'Richadune' in free and perpetual alms. To have and to hold free from secular service for ever. Witd. Thomas, abbot of Hartland; Hugh Peverell, Simon de Pun, Robert de Tintagel, William son of Simon, Ralph Sor. Not dated. [*c.*1224–1242, i.e. death of Robert de Tintagel (Maclean, *Trigg Minor* iii, 158) and death of Wm. (IV) de Botreaux in 1242 (*Trigg Minor* i, 640.).]

[a]Title: *de terra in Estdownend*.

MS.: Cartulary, f.79v.

**185.** Confirmation of a grant by William de Botrell for the souls of his father, William de Botrell, and Sybil his mother and for his own soul and that of Joan his wife and the souls of his children and of all his ancestors and successors, to the canons of Blessed Stephen of Launceston half an acre of land in East Downend which Algar Wada formerly held with common pasture in 'Richadune' outside the meadow and corn, in free and perpetual alms. To hold free from all service and secular demand for ever. Sealing clause. Witd. Andrew de Cancell, Robert son of William, Simon de Brakell'. Not dated. [*c.*1221–42, the dates of William (IV) de Botreaux, see no. 184.]

MS.: Cartulary, f.79v.–f.80r.


**186.** Plea between Richard Brickevile, prior of Launceston, and Philip de Egloskery, before Henry Spigornell and his companions, justices itinerant concerning 2 acres of land in Penheale (*Penhel Reg'*) called 'Lylyrvdehamme' in the thirtieth year of the reign of King Edward. The jurors came to recognise whether 2 acres of land in Penheale (*Penhel Regis*) were in free alms and belonged to the priory or to the lay fee of Philip de Egloskery. The prior said that a certain Richard, parson of the church of Egloskerry, his predecessor in the time of peace in the reign of the lord King Henry, father of the present king, had alienated the said land.

And Philip came and said that he did not hold the land absolutely integrally because Clarice, his mother, held a third part in dowry at the suing out of the writ (4 October 1302). He also said that he and his ancestors were seised of the said land as of lay fee. And with this he placed himself on the jury and also the prior.

The jury said on their oath that the said Clarice held nothing of her dower, nor did she on the day of suing out the writ. The jury also said that the land was of free alms pertaining to the said church of Egloskerry of which the prior was patron and not the lay fee of Philip. Judgement was given for the said prior to recover his seisin against Philip. And Philip was in mercy. Not dated. [On or shortly after 4 October 1302.]

MS.: Cartulary, f.80r.


**187.** Plea between Prior Richard and Henry Boketh of the moiety of one acre of land in Gospenheale (*Causpenhele*) before the said justices in the same year (as no. 186).

Henry Bogeth sought against the prior of Launceston one messuage and the moiety of one acre of land of Gospenheale (*Causpenhele*) of which the said prior disseised Richard Bogeth, father of the said Henry. The prior denied that he disseised the said Richard. The jurors stated on oath that the said prior did not disseise the said Henry of the said tenement. Henry got nothing by his writ but was in mercy for a false claim. Not dated. [During the last three months of 1302.]

MS.: Cartulary, f.80v.

**188.**   Grant and confirmation by Roger Heyron to David de Gunan a half-acre of land in the vill of Laneast (*Lanast*), that is to say, the land which Osward held in the same vill of Laneast and which Roger had given to the said Osward in marriage with his daughter A(upeys). To be held by David and his heirs of Roger and his heirs by hereditary right and freely and quietly etc. By the annual rent of 1d. at Michaelmas for all service, the right of Osward in the said land excepted: i.e. Osward and his heirs of the donor's daughter Aupeys were to hold the land of the said David and his heirs by the free service of 12s. yearly at Michaelmas. Witd. John, son of Robert, Philip de Trevella, Ralph and Robert, clerks, Henry Godman, Nicholas de Lappaford, Hamelin de Trevella, Wandregesilus. Not dated. [*c*.1212–20. Cf. nos. 77 and 110 (Philip and Hamelin de Trevella and Henry Godman).]

MS.: Cartulary, ff.80v.–81r.

**189.**   Grant and confirmation by Ralph de Trewrtha to the church of Blessed Stephen of Launceston and the canons serving God there for the salvation of his soul and the souls of his ancestors and successors of all the right he had in half an acre in Laneast (*Lanast*) which Aupeys, daughter of Roger Heyrun, had held formerly. The grant was in pure and perpetual alms, without anything being retained or reclaimed by Ralph or his heirs, and free from all secular service. Warranty and sealing clauses. Witd. Simon de Brekill, then sheriff of Cornwall, Roger Trelosk, William Wyse. Not dated. [29 October 1225 (*CPR*) or 1232/3 (see no. 217), years in which Simon de Brekill occurs as sheriff.]

MS.: Cartulary, f.81r.

**190.**   Gift, grant and confirmation by Roger Heyron, for the love of God and for the souls of his mother and father and ancestors and successors, to the church of St Stephen of Launceston and the canons there of a place in the vill of Laneast (*Lanayst*) called 'Wrganeswordy' with the houses and appurtenances and all the land under the site as the embankment extended towards the well and his land of 'Rosymdur' and in the mount opposite all his land, that is from the bridge of 'Brus' ' to the old embankment which extended on the one side towards the green way and from the other side as far as the river bank and all his moor within this land and the land of 'Rolyndur' and as well the common pasture of all his land of Laneast. It was granted to the canons in free and perpetual alms, free and quit from all secular services without any retention of the donor, for the prayers (of the canons.) Witd. Philip de Trevella, David de Gunan, Robert Rem, William Dittone, Tancardus etc. Not dated. [Approximately *c*.1220–32 (Philip de Trevella, Robert Rem.).]

MS.: Cartulary, f.81r.–f.81v.

**191.**   Gift, grant and confirmation by Roger Heyrun, for the love of God and for the souls of his father and mother and ancestors, to the church of St Stephen of Launceston and the canons of a certain plot in the vill of Laneast called 'Wurganeswurdy' with the houses and all the land under the plot as the embankment extends towards the well, and all his lay land of 'Rosendur' and in the opposite mount 10 acres (measured by the perch) from the bridge of 'Brun' under the way just as the green path goes as far as the bounds of the said 10 acres and the common pasture of the whole vill of Laneast. To have and to hold in free and perpetual alms freely and quietly and quit of all service and exaction. Witd. Thomas de Merwynchurch, Roger de Teynton, priests, Ralph Drogo. Not dated. [*c*.1220–32, as related to no. 190.]

MS.: Cartulary, f.81v.

**192.** Final concord made between the canons of Launceston and Roger Hayrun by the common mediation of their friends relating to the service of the land of Laneast about which there had been for a short time a controversy between the canons and Roger. He had given to the church of St Stephen and the canons for the service of the said land of Laneast a certain part of the land of Laneast in which the chapel of Laneast, founded by the canons, lay as the division goes down between the land of Laneast and the land of 'Talgarra' as far as the vill of Laneast on the west and on the east as far as the vill of Laneast from the great embankment which was at the end of the said land on the northern side. Except those 2 *crohitas* of land which adjoined the said land and the land of 'Talgarra' as two great embankments from which the said *crohite* were enclosed and were to be possessed quietly for ever and disposed of as they wished. Besides this Roger was to render one penny at Michaelmas from his land of Laneast for all service. Furthermore the said Roger quitclaimed all right and action which he said he had in right of the advowson of the chapel of Laneast to the canons for himself and his heirs. He renounced this to them absolutely and in the presence of many discreet men, faith being corporally pledged, he established that neither he nor his heirs would raise any question about the said chapel or its patronage. The prior and canons gave for this gift and agreement 6s. (which they had exacted from him for the annual service of the land in Laneast) and granted that he and his heirs could hold the land of Laneast freely and quietly in perpetual possession. Sealing clause of both parties. Witd. Luke the son of Bern(ard) the scribe, Peter his brother, and Geoffrey. Not dated. [*c*.1195–1214 (Luke son of Bernard).]

MS.: Cartulary, f.82r.

**193.** Notice by Richard Heyrun that he had given and granted and confirmed to the church of St Stephen of Launceston and the canons there 3 acres of land in Laneast in demesnes, homages, and all services, in ways and paths, meadows and pastures, water and mills, ponds, turbaries, wood and plain, in dry and wet with all other things and liberties

pertaining to the land which he held of the canons by the free service of
one penny a year in exchange for one acre in Tredidon (*Tredidan*) which
the canons gave him and his heirs. To have and to hold of them for the free
service of one penny yearly at the feast of Blessed Michael for all demands.
Neither Richard nor his heirs would claim any right in the land, but was
held to warrant the prior and canons *contra omnes homines et feminas*. Sealing
clause. Witd. the lord Simon, then sheriff of Cornwall; Roger de Trelosk,
Jordan Trevaga, William Wyse. Not dated. [October 1225 or 1232/3, see
dating note to no. 189.]

MS.: Cartulary, f.82r.–f.82v.

**194.** Agreement (chirograph) concerning a dispute between the prior
and William de Lanast about the service for the land of the latter, i.e. of
the land of Laneast and the hundred-bailiwick. The dispute was ended as
follows. When it was proved and William himself recognised that he had
no right in the bailiwick of the hundred and that for several years he had
detained the service of the land of Laneast of 5s. of annual rent, at first he
recognised the arrears of rent unjustly retained by (the gift of) a bay horse,
and, seeking the grace of the prior, he paid the canons. Afterwards he
swore on the altar of St Stephen and on the relics of the saints (in the sight
and hearing of many) about the yearly rent recognised as due to the
church of St Stephen. Then the prior and canons gave to the said William
the hundred-bailiwick of the hundred of Launceston to hold in his
lifetime, giving him for his service 3s. yearly. And this agreement was
presented in the hundred and county (courts). Witd. Pagan de Gunan,
Daviot his son, Roger Foliot. Sealing clause of the prior. 'And Durandus
the sheriff strengthened it by the confirmation of his own seal.' Not dated.
[No. 556 would suggest a date of *c.*1155–1175 (Durand, sheriff).]

MS.: Cartulary, ff.82v.–83r.

**195.** Grant and confirmation by Richard Godek to Robert Carnek,
Roger Combrygge, chaplains, and Stephen Roydron of all his messuage in
the vill of Badgall (*Bodgalla*) with houses, meadows and pasture. He gave
also to the same Robert, Roger and Stephen the rent and services of Alice
Trodya for the land she held of him in the said vill. Also he then gave the
rents and services of William, son and heir of John Coppyng, from the
land held by William of Richard Godek in the same vill. He granted also
the rents and services there of Thomasia, daughter and heir of Robert
Rogger. To hold by Robert, Roger and Stephen and their heirs and
assigns for ever of the chief lords of these fees by due and customary
service. Richard acquitted, defended and gave warranty. Sealing clause.
Witd. William Henterdren, Benedict Dounhevd, Stephen Tredidan,
William Treburtell, John Willyam. Dated Bàdgall, Monday, 5 October
1377.

MS.: Cartulary, f.83r.–f.83v.

**196.** Quitclaim by William de Trelowny, son and heir of William de Trelowny, for himself and his heirs to Prior Stephen and the convent and their successors of all his right in one messuage in Badgall, together with the rents and services of Alice, daughter and heir of Stephen Trodya, also of William, son and heir of John Coppyng and of Thomasia, daughter and heir of Robert Rogger, of the lands and tenements they formerly held of William (Trelowny) in the said vill which William Trelowny had recently given to Richard Godek and his heirs for ever, as appeared in William's charter. William had as well released to the prior and convent his right in a tenement in Newport which lay between the tenement formerly of Henry atte Heye on the one side and the meadow called Grussmede on the other which John Skaynek formerly held there. Sealing clause of donor. Witd. Benedict Dounhevd, then free bailiff of Launceston Land; John Landyar, John Godecote, William Mustard, Stephen Tredidan. Dated Launceston, Monday, 14 September 1388.

MS.: Cartulary, f.83v.

**197.** Quitclaim by John Trelowny to Prior Stephen and the convent and their successors of a messuage and a garden lying in Launceston in the street there called Newport with one messuage and half an acre Cornish in the vill of Badgall which belonged to his father, William de Trelouny. Warranty. Sealing clause. Witd. Richard Trevaga, John Puddyng, Stephen Devyok, Baldwin Roos, Roger Menwynnek. Dated Launceston, Thursday, 18 April 1392.

MS.: Cartulary, ff.83v.–84r.

**198.** Bond of John Trelouny to Stephen, prior of Launceston, in £40 sterling of English money. To be paid to Prior Stephen or his successors on Monday after the feast of the following Easter (14 April) at Launceston without further delay. John bound his heirs and executors and his goods on the same day and place to repay this money. Sealing clause. Dated Launceston, Thursday, 7 March 1392.

MS.: Cartulary, f.84r.

**199.** Indenture made between Prior Stephen and the convent and John Trelouny explaining the condition of no. 198. If the prior and convent and their successors could peacefully have and hold for ever a messuage and garden in the vill of Launceston in a street called Newport and a messuage and half an acre of land Cornish in Badgall which belonged to William, father of John Trelouny, without the impediment or claim of the said John or his heirs. Or that the said John or his heirs when required would follow the writ of the form of the gift in the descent of the property to the custody of the prior and convent and their successors against the said prior or his successors until it was terminated by inquisition or in another way according to the advice of the council of the said prior or his successors.

And that neither John nor his heirs nor anyone in their name would make a claim sworn in the return of the writ nor any evidence to impede the reply of the said prior or to his successors and against the said John or his heirs. And if the jury should go against the prior or his successors and the said John or his heirs should not follow the execution, and that afterwards the said prior and his successors should have and hold for ever the said messuage and land without the charge or impediment of the said John or his heirs that then the bond would be void, otherwise it would remain in force. Dated Launceston, Thursday, 7 March 1392.

MS.: Cartulary, f.84r.–f.84v.

**200.** Memorandum that on Thursday, 25 July 1359, a friendly agreement was made between Prior Thomas and the convent and Walter Penhirgard about several dissensions between themselves about 3 pieces of land in Badgall (*Bodgealla*) which the said prior claimed were his by a certain gift made to a certain John Grym, his native, by a certain David Bal of a rent of 14d. which the said Walter ought to have paid the lord prior for the year when he only paid 10d. yearly for the third part of one acre of land Cornish in Badgall with the said 3 pieces of land. And concerning his taking away the service of the said land, i.e. ploughing for one day and reaping for the other day for the non-payment of 25s. 0¼d. of reliefs for the deaths of John Poddyng senior and John (Poddyng) junior for the lands they held in Crannow. Also for the non-payment of the said rent of the land of Crannow owed to that day after the death of the said John Poddyng junior and amercements of court for the same time, which came to the sum of £8 for subtraction of the service of ploughing for one day and reaping for another for a certain land which the said Walter held of the lord prior in Tresmeer (*Tresmur*). The settlement of the dispute was that the said Walter would pay for the land, the third part of one acre of land in Badgall with the said 3 pieces of land yearly, 14d. as it used to pay, as is known by the oath of six tenants of both parties and should reap for 1 day in the autumn through the year. And for the other day's work of ploughing the parties agreed that enquiry should be made through the court by the oath of twelve sworn men if it were due or not. If it were owed then the same land should be charged with it, and if it were not, it should be quit of all reliefs, rents and amercements from before to that day for the aforesaid lands in Crannow and Badgall (*Bodgealla*). The lord prior gave to the said Walter up to the sum of 40s. so that he might well and faithfully pay to the prior and convent all rents and services due for the same land and all others which he held of them and should make suit through the year for the two work days due of ploughing and reaping for the said land which Walter held in Tresmeer (*Tresmur*), as was known by the oath of 6 tenants and ought to be done before the suit of John Poddyng. Dated Thursday, 25 July 1359.

MS.: Cartulary, f.84v.–f.85r.

**201.** Quitclaim[a] by Sybil, daughter of Michael, to Prior William and the convent of one acre in the vill of Tresmeer (*Trousmur*) which she held of the priory with a messuage in the vill of Launceston between the messuages of William Gissel and William Maynard. Sealing clause. Witd. Robert Rem, Richard Heyrun, Richard de Trewynnok. Not dated. [1232–8, Prior William.]

[a]Note in right hand margin, *m.ᵈ q.ᵈ alie carte de Tresmur scribuntur in 88 folio istius regestri a capite viz. in ix. fo. sequente.*

MS.: Cartulary, f.85r.–f.85v.

**202.** [a]Gift and quitclaim by William, son of Stephen de Puntestok, for the souls of his parents etc. to the priory of all his land of North Tregeare[a] (*Treger*) which he had in exchange for the land of Trebursy and for the service of a pound of cumin. Sealing clause. Witd. Simon, the seneschal of Cornwall; Henry de Bodrygan, then sheriff of Cornwall; Robert, son of William. Not dated. [1226–7, shrievalty of Henry de Bodrugan.]

[a]Heading: *Carta de Northtreger.*

MS.: Cartulary, f.85v.

**203.** Another copy of no. 202 with similar wording. Witd. Henry de Bodrugan; Robert, son of William. Not dated.

MS.: Cartulary, ff.85v.–86r.

**204.** Grant[a] in perpetual alms by Reginald Mareys to the priory for his soul and the soul of his wife, Muriel etc. of land in North Tregeare (*Tregayres*) including one acre held by Warin and Warin's suit for this. Royal service only. Sealing clause. Witd. Nicholas de Penhag; Henry de Marcis; Hugh de Mareys; Ralph, the clerk. Not dated. [*c.*1226–7; Henry de Bodrugan not mentioned as sheriff.]

[a]Heading: *Carta de Tregaria.*

MS.: Cartulary, f.86r.

**205.** Grant and confirmation in alms by Robert de Cardinan to the priory of grants by his ancestors: the land of Goodmansleigh (*Cudmanesle-ga*) granted by William, son of Richard, except the mill, which Robert son of William, Robert de Cardinan's grandfather had granted. Also 20s. worth of land in the manor of Downinney, viz. Castle Milford (*Kestelmyforda*) for 10s. and the land of North Tregear (*Tregarya*) for another 10s., granted by his grandfather, Robert, son of William, in pure and perpetual alms for the soul of Countess Mabel etc. Sealing clause. Witd. Walter son of Robert, Jocelin, then sheriff, Richard son of Gilbert.[a] Not dated. [*c.*1190–1200, see *HMC Report MSS. Var. Coll.* I (1900), 328–9.]

[a]Note in right hand margin, *M.ᵈ quod alie carte de Cudmaneslegh et Lidisgrave myll . . . postea in xiijᵒ folio sequentur.*

MS.: Cartulary, f.86r.–f.86v.

**206.** Quitclaim by William de Bodbran to Prior Richard and his successors of the warranty and acquittance which they claimed to have for one acre in North Tregeare against Michael de . . .ª and Philip de St Wynnoto. He granted for himself and his heirs to be bound to the prior in 100s. if he or they impleaded the prior about this land. Sealing clause. Witd. the lord Richard Hywys; John de Trelouny, clerk; Richard de Trevaga, Nicholas de Ros. Dated Lostwithiel, Monday, 31 May 1294.

ªblank in MS.

MS.: Cartulary, f.86v.

**207.** Plea of wardship and marriage of heirs in (North) Tregeare.

Devon. John Honylond, prior of Launceston, and Thomas Tregarya of (North) Tregeare (*Tregarya*), yeoman, were attached to answer John Boson why they had abducted Joan, daughter and heir of Walter Tregarya, under age whose marriage John Boson claimed, to Bridgerule (*Briggeruwell*) in the time of King Henry, father of the present king. John Boson (by Thomas Douryssh his attorney) claimed the marriage inasmuch as Walter Tregarya held one messuage and 2 ferlings in 'Treglegha' by homage, fealty and scutage at 40s. when it fell due and a rent of 2s. to the said John Boson. John enjoyed these services and on Walter's death took possession of the heiress and held her from September in the eighth year of the late king until 4 September following. John Boson claimed £100 damages. Thomas and Prior John abducted Joan Tregarya at Bridgerule on 24 May.

The Prior and Thomas by John Polryden their attorney at Westminster (by adjournment) denied that Walter held any lands of Boson by military service, but said that he held 2 messuages and one acre Cornish in 'Tregaria' by homage, fealty, and scutage (40s.) and a rent of 6s. 8d. to the priory and doing suit to the court of the priory at Bernhay every three weeks. Walter held these lands by knights' service of the old enfeoffment. Thomas Tregarya accompanied Prior John as his servant when the ward was abducted.

The case was adjourned to the octave of St John the Baptist. Not dated. [*c*.1413–14, see no. 208.]

MS.: Cartulary, ff.87r.–88r.

**208.** Notice by John Boson of receipt from John Honylond, prior of Launceston; Richard Pomeray and Thomasia, his wife; Robert Dune, Nicholas Strange, Nicholas Cotell and John Hoper of 12 marks sterling which by the assize of novel disseisin heard in front of John Colpeper and William Skrene, justices of the lord king at the assize in the county of Devon, were assigned against the said prior, Richard, Thomasia, Robert, Nicholas, Nicholas, John and others at Exeter. This money was given to John Boson and Eleanor his wife, querents in the same assize for losses and expenses. John Boson gave quittance to the prior. Sealing clause. Dated Thursday, 15 March 1414.

MS.: Cartulary, f.88r.

**209.** Release and quitclaim by John Boson to John Honylond, prior of Launceston, and to Thomas Tregarya of all manner of personal actions. Dated Launceston, Thursday 18 August 1429.

MS.: Cartulary, f.88v.

**210.** Gift and grant[a] by G., son of Baldwin of the land of Smallacombe (*Smalcombe*) which lay next to the land of 'Penros' to the priory in free and perpetual alms, free and quit from every custom except prayers. Sealing clause. He also confirmed to the priory all the land of 'Penros'. These lands were bounded from the heap of stones in the way which went from 'Leia' towards the west. Then directly by that way to the western end of a meadow called 'Brademore' and thence by the said meadow towards the south to the stream which was called 'Smalecombe'. Then by this stream towards the west to the ford called 'Alfredesweie' and then towards the north side by the water to the water which divides the same land and the land of 'Wodeford' and then towards the east by the water to the land of 'Laford'; thence towards the south by a stream as far as 'Sherpwille' and then directly to the heap of stones next to a ruined croft which divides the land and the land of 'Leia'. Witd. Brihonius, priest, Robert, priest, Roger, priest, Pagan, priest; Pagan Rem, then dean; Ralph the clerk. Not dated. [*c*.1162, see no. 74 (Pagan Rem).]

[a]Title: *Carte de Penros in Middelond.*

MS.: Cartulary, ff.88v–89r.

**211.** Obligation by Michael de Penros for himself and his heirs to pay 6s. sterling of yearly rent to the priory at Easter and Michaelmas by equal portions for his land of 'Penros' which he and his heirs held by homage as contained in his charter of enfeoffment. He also granted that if he failed to pay this his land of 'Penros' and all his chattels could be distrained and those chattels of his heirs and his men. Any distraints including those of his heirs and men should be taken to the park of Launceston and held there until full satisfaction had been made. Witd. Robert de Raddon, John Karbunell, Gregory de Dudestun. Not dated. [?*c*.1244–6 (Robert de Raddon) see *Cornwall FF.i* nos. 104 and 112.]

MS.: Cartulary, f.89r.

**212.** Grant of homage and fealty by John Wibbery, esquire, to John, prior of Launceston, at the priory in the chapel of the prior at the end of

the room, for the lands and tenements he held of the priory in 'Penros'.
Alternate sealing clause. Dated Launceston priory, 19 March 1415.

MS.: Cartulary, f.89r.–f.89v.

**213.** Obligation by Benedict Reynward not to call the prior of
Launceston nor his successors to warranty by reason of his homage for the
land he held of the priory in the vill of Treglum (_Treglomma_) in the parish
of Tresmeer (_Tresmur_) and he would grant warranty by reason of his
homage _contra omnes homines mortales_. Sealing clause. Dated Launceston,
Thursday, 18 December 1287.

MS.: Cartulary, f.89v.

**214.** Confirmation by John Burgh de Barlandu of the estate of Prior
Roger and the convent in the weir and mill-dam in Kyrse (_Keuros_) which
ran to their mill of Treglum and which they had released to John without
payment. Warranty and sealing clauses. Witd. John Helygan, Stephen
Bodulget, Nicholas Bokelly, Stephen Bant. Dated Launceston, 7 January
1411.

MS.: Cartulary, ff.89v.–90r.

**215.** Release by John Burgh de Barlandu to Prior Roger and the
convent of his right in the mill-dam and weir of Treglum in Kyrse.
Warranty and sealing clauses. Witd. as in no. 214. Dated Launceston, 7
January 1411.

MS.: Cartulary, f.90r.

**216.** ᵃAgreement between William, prior of Launceston, and the
convent and Walter de Keuros before the justices itinerant at Launceston,
William Ebor', William de St Edmundo and R. de Bello Campo and
Jordan Oliver after a dispute in which Walter sought the mount of Kyrse
by writ of novel disseisin. It was divided by the consent of both parties
from the east side of the middle way as the way went from 'Manneford' as
far as the way above 'Langadon' and then by that way as far as the land of
'Treuraca' and thence the division extended as far as the ford of
'Riddello', except for the land which Walter and his heirs had before the
dispute. Walter's land was bounded from 'Taresford' going up the water
of 'Holedich', thence to the ditch above 'Blakemore' and from there to the
way above 'Ketastan' and thus to the ford of 'Ridello'. After the land was
divided both parties would have common pasture. Walter appointed
Richard de Trewynnoc to make partition with the prior on his behalf.
Mutual sealing clause for chirograph. Witd. Robert son of William, Hugh

de Bodrygan, Simon de Brakeleg, R. de Trewrtha, John Mannyng, H. Treullan, Gregory. Not dated. [1232–8, Prior William.]

<sup>a</sup>Title: *Carta de Keurosdoune viz. de medietate.*

MS.: Cartulary, f.90r.–f.90v.

**217.** Final concord between Prior William and the convent of the one part and William de Keuros and his heirs of the other about the former litigation and controversy between them concerning the waste of a certain mount between the ford of Badgall (*Bodgalla*) and Kyrse. That is to say from the western side of the stream which came down from the well called Sweetwells (*Suetewill*) and then as far as the stream which came down from Kyrse. Thence to the stream which came down from the hollow ditch on the eastern part of 'Blakemor' in the stream of Kyrse just as it went above the turbary as far as above the ploughland called 'Serpewns' and from the ditch to the two grey stones and thence to the ford of 'Riddellon'. Both parties granted that the land should be equally divided between them, measured by small acres by the perch by the view of legal men. The prior and convent quitclaimed Walter de Keuros and his heirs of the right he said he had by the king's writ in the vill of Kyrse. They could not exact from Walter and his heirs any right in the vill of Kyrse except suit which he owed to the free manor of Launceston. It was also agreed that the prior and his men had common pasture through the whole waste without any molestation from William or his heirs or his men for ever. Meadow and turbary in the waste was to be equally divided between both parties without contradiction. Sealing clause of both parties. Witd. Symon de Brakel', sheriff of Cornwall; Robert son of William, William de Whalebr', William Wyse, Henry Godman. Not dated. [Between 28 October 1232 and 27 October 1233. Text begins, *Anno coronacionis Henrici regis Anglie filij Johannis xvij°*.]

MS.: Cartulary, ff.90v.–91r.

**218.** Perpetual quitclaim by Geoffrey de Lametyn to the priory of the whole land adjoining the mount of Kyrse as it went from the ford of Badgall above Sweetwells and from a way which crossed to a certain small ditch which led as far as Sweetwells just as the water ran down under Wolleux (*Wlfholca*) to the said ford. The prior and convent gave Geoffrey half a mark of silver. Sealing clause. Witd. Ralph Trewrtha, Richard Trewynnec, John Mannyng. Not dated. [Obviously related to the date of no. 217.]

MS.: Cartulary, f.91r.–f.91v.

**219.** <sup>a</sup>Quitclaim by William de Bruera for the salvation of his soul and the souls of his wife and ancestors and successors of his right in land disputed between him and the priory: i.e. all the land which lay between the great way from the east which divided his land of 'Ros' and the said land as it extended to the west and between the stream at the southern border between this land and the land of Kyrse, to the priory. The prior or his men were not to make any ploughland whence his men would be restrained or burdened. Sealing clause. Witd. William de Leymene, Warin de Kelly, Ralph de Hampton. Not dated. [Warin de Kelly and William de la Bruera occur in the Cornish eyre of 1201.]

<sup>a</sup>Title: *Alia carta de eadem de Strylond.*

MS.: Cartulary, f.91v.

**220.** Quitclaim by William de Esthendre, chaplain, to the priory of his right in the mount and moor of Kyrse Down (*Keurosdone*) which the prior claimed to hold as waste of the precinct of his manor of Launceston Land (*Launceuelond*). Sealing clause. Witd. Robert de Bodmam, Benedict de Moushole, Henry Snellard, Robert Trypelot, Henry Mustard. Dated Launceston, Wednesday 25 October 1312.

MS.: Cartulary, ff.91v.–92r.

**221.** Grant<sup>a</sup> and quitclaim by Cecilia, widow of Godfrey de Henterdren, to Prior Robert and the convent of her right in 5 small English acres of meadow in Hendra Green (*Henterdren*) which she had claimed at the court of King's Bench. Prior Robert gave her 20 shillings sterling. Sealing clause. Witd. the lord Roger de Trelosk, William Le Walleys, Henry Trevella, Thomas le Lugger, Gregory de Duddeston. Not dated. [*c.*1256–12 Sept. 1261 (Prior Robert Fissacre).]

<sup>a</sup>Title: *Carta de quinque acris prati in Henterdren.*

MS.: Cartulary, f.92r.

**222.** Quitclaim by John Botya, chaplain, to Prior Henry and the convent of the lordship and all the services of Robert, son of Luke de Cargyntel, and his heirs and assigns of the half acre of land Cornish in Cargentle (*Cargyntel*) which were formerly held of him, viz. homage, relief and suit of court, and an annual rent of 16d. and all other services of the half acre of land Cornish. Sealing clause. Witd. the lord Richard de Hiwys, William Cola, knights; Gregory de Dodeston, John Carbonel, Richard Stuterich.<sup>a</sup> Not dated. [*c.*1244–6 (Prior Henry) and see no. 211.]

<sup>a</sup>Note in left margin, *quod alia carta . . . Cargyntel viz. de . . . ywode scribitur in . . . folio sequenc' que . . . hoc scriptum testatur.*

MS.: Cartulary, f.92r.–f.92v.

**223.** Grant and confirmation by William de Botrell for the salvation of his soul and the soul of Joan his wife and the souls of his ancestors and successors to the priory of the chapel of Egloskerry and the chapel of Tremaine (*Tremen*) which belonged to the mother church of Launceston and the chapel of Crackington[a] (*Cracumton*) which appertained to the mother church of St Gennys (*Genesius*) with one carrucate of land, viz. Hill (*Hille*) and one mark of rent viz. the land of Tregeare (*Treger*) which was Saget the priest's, one acre of land, and the land Habba and the land Edwy (a fourth part of one acre) in pure and perpetual alms. He also gave to the priory his land of Crannow (*Cranou*) i.e. 3 acres of land which were in the manor of Crackington (*Cracumpton*) and half an acre of land in 'Ladunhevd' which was in the manor of Penheale. Sealing clause. Witd. the lord Andrew de Cancell', then seneschal of Cornwall; Robert son of William, Henry de Bodrygan. Not dated. [*c*.1221–42, see no. 185, note (William (IV) de Botreaux.).]

[a]Spelt *Crakhampton* in the title to the charter.

MS.: Cartulary, f.92v.

**224.** Settlement by Henry, bishop of Exeter, of a controversy between the priory and Adam Trenchem, clerk, about the church of Egloskerry. Adam renounced all right in the said church and the other rents of the priory which he claimed. He promised by oath that he would never molest the canons or their possessions, but would work for the good of the priory as well as he could. The prior and canons received Adam into their house as a brother: they granted him a corrody wherever he lived and when he wished to assume the religious habit, he would be received kindly. If Adam had by necessity to stay at the priory for 8 or 15 days, the canons would look after him as one of their brothers and he would have sustenance for himself and his men and his horse. Episcopal sealing clause. Witd. Guarin Cicestr', canon; William de Swyndon, clerk; Serlo and John de Lungefeir, chaplains. Not dated. [Between 28 March 1194 and 1 November 1206, the episcopate of Henry Marshal, bishop of Exeter.]

MS.: Cartulary, f.93r.

**225.** Memorandum[a] of a judgment by the prior and convent of William de Penros and William Trewllyuerek, executors of the will of Claricia de Trebrutel deceased, before the official of the archdeacon of Cornwall. The parishioners sought the best beast as a mortuary pertaining to them in the name of their church, the chapel of Tresmeer, by the death of the said Claricia, whence a suit began for the verdict of the chapter. At length the dispute was settled thus. Namely that the said executors promised the prior and convent in front of worthy men 4s. for a mortuary for obtaining peace under a double penalty in the hands of the proctor of the prior and convent and by giving security to the said official under the penalty of coercion. There were present the vicar of Stratton and the vicar of St Gennys, Nicholas Kewe, Roger de Treuangar, clerk, John Letye, chaplain, Richard de Boiton, chaplain, who sealed the memorandum with their seals and the dean of Trigg Major added his seal. Dated Launceston, Tuesday, 24 March 1275.

[a]Right hand margin has the note (Henderson), *M.$^d$ q.$^d$ concordia inter nos et monachos de Tywardraith de Smalehill et de med' dec' garb' de Tresmeer habetur in 109 folio et in 110 folio istius regestri*. (See no. 289)

MS.: Cartulary, f.93r.–93v.

**226.** Agreement between Prior Stephen and the convent and the parish church of St Stephen of Launceston, with the chapel of St Nicholas of Tresmeer annexed, of the one part and John William, John Ros, John Colt, John Broda, John Proute, Walter Langeman and the other parishioners of the same chapel of the other. Dissension had arisen between the parties about the repair of the chapel and chancel in a visitation of the archdeacon of Cornwall. A synodal constitution of Exeter declared that repair of chapels and chancels was the responsibility of the parishioners. The parishioners of Tresmeer accepted this and they promised not to vex the priory in judgement. Later Prior Stephen of his own free will gave to the said parishioners 10s. of silver. Both parties pledged their moveable and immoveable goods to observe the agreement and to abide by the coercion of any judge. Sealing clause of both parties and parishioners of Tresmeer not named above used the seal of the official of the peculiar jurisdiction of the lord bishop of Exeter. The whole document was also sealed by the said official at the request of the parishioners of Tresmeer. Dated Launceston, Saturday, 10 June 1385.

MS.: Cartulary, ff.93v.–94r.

**227.** [a]Obligation by Luke, son of Bernard the scribe, that he and his heirs were bound to pay yearly forever 2s. to the priory for the land under the grove which John, Luke's brother, had given to the priory in alms when William, their kinsman, had become a canon of the priory at his petition. The said 2s. was in sum of the annual rent of 17s. 5d.[b] which he ought to have paid yearly for these tenements as Luke's charter showed. Witd. Robert de Capellis, then sheriff; Richard son of Gilbert; Alan Bloihou; Gervase de Horningachote; Roger and his sons William and Thomas de Duneham; Philip de Trevella. Not dated. [c.1195–1214 (Luke son of Bernard).]

[a]Heading: *Carta de duobus solidis pro terra de Nitherwode (Under wode)*.
[b]*Prefati vere duo solidi in summa annui redditus scilicet x et vij solidorum et v denarios quam eis de tenementis meis annuatim solvere debeo.*

MS.: Cartulary, f.94r.

**228.** Lease by Prior Adam and the convent to John de Cargyntell of a certain land called 'Haywoode' near the vill of 'Nitherwode'. To hold for

20 years for the annual rent of 3s. of silver at Michaelmas and Easter by
equal portions for all services except suit of court every three weeks. John
owed suit to the mill of the priory and was to do the due and accustomed
services by all free conventionaries of Launceston Land (*Lanstauelond*).
John and his heirs were to manure and spread sand on the land as well as
burning it. If the said John or his heirs wished to depart from the said land
he or they were to pay 12d. in the name of a farlieve with the rent of that
year fully paid and with the crop up to Michaelmas. Warranty and
alternate sealing clauses. Witd. John Wobiolk, Walter de Hentredren,
Henry Cosyn, William Stoterych, Nicholas Rem.[a] Launceston, Michaelmas, 1335.

[a]Note at foot of document; *Memorandum quod terra contenta in hac carta accidit domino per mortem heredum Nicholai Grova bastardi.*

MS.: Cartulary, f.94v.

**229.** Quitclaim by Ralph Fula to the priory in half an acre of land in
Menheniot (*Melhunoc*) which he formerly held of the prior and convent.
He also gave the priory for the salvation of his soul and the souls of his
ancestors and successors the reversion of his house in the new borough of
Launceston after his death in pure and perpetual alms. Sealing clause.
Witd. William Wyse, H. Trevella, R. Rem Britun, P. Longo. Not dated.
[*c.*1220–32. (William Wyse, plus earlier limits suggested by attestation of
Ralph Fula to no. 111).]

MS.: Cartulary, ff.94v.–95r.

**230.** [a]Quitclaim by Roger Shurreua to the priory of his right in a
messuage and a ferling and a half of land in East Menheniot
(*Estremynhynnek*) which Matthew de Melhuinec formerly held of the priory
there in villeinage. Sealing clause. Witd. Robert de Bodmam, Henry Rem,
Henry de Tregyn. Dated Dutson (*Dodeston*), Friday, 6 September 1297.

[a]Note in right hand margin, *M.$^d$q.$^d$ placita de Estmenhynnek' . . . folio a capite registri viz. xv fo. sequente.*

MS.: Cartulary, f.95r.

**231.** Quitclaim by John Trolker of East Menheniot to Prior Adam of his
right in one messuage and half an acre of land Cornish, i.e. in all his lands
in the vill of East Menheniot (*Estremelhunec*).´ Warranty and sealing
clauses. Witd. John Daldestawe, rector of the church of St Mabyn;
William de Trelouny, Master John Godman, clerk; William Stotrygge;
Henry Snellard, clerk. Dated Launceston, Monday, 16 August 1344.

MS.: Cartulary, f.95r.–95v.

**232.** [a]Grant and confirmation by Walter, son of Mabanus de Boscho, in

free and perpetual alms to God and Blessed Mary and Blessed Stephen of
Launceston and the canons serving God there for the salvation of his soul
and the souls of his ancestors and successors of one ferling of land in
'Wotganer'. Royal service only. Sealing clause. Witd. Roger de Trelosk,
Henry Borez, lord Jordan of Trevaga. Not dated. [c.1232–44: Jordan de
Trevaga, see no. 61.]

[a]Title: *Carta de bosco videlicet Attewode.*

MS.: Cartulary, f.95v.

**233.** Obligation by William, son of Nicholas de Boscho, that he was by
fealty bound to pay the priory at Michaelmas 16d. of the land de Bosco
which Walter son of Maban formerly held. William had no seal so he used
the seal of his father, Nicholas. Witd. Everwinus de Tintagel, Roger de
Hethland, Nicholas de Bosco, Andrew of Oterham. Not dated. [c.1224
(Everwinus de Tintagel). See no. 364.]

MS.: Cartulary, ff.95v.–96r.

**234.** Grant by Agatha de Gatesden, lady of Lifton of her own right, for
the salvation of Eleanor of the realm of England, her lady, and the soul of
William de Gatesden, her lord, for her own soul and the souls of her
ancestors and successors, to the priory of all her land in her demesne of
Lifton, i.e. the land between Gatherley (*Giderleg*) and the bounds of
Turchington (*Thycheneton*) just as the path went from Turchington as far
as the way going towards Huntford (*Huyteneffprd*) and thence as far as the
valley called 'Bidelake', thence in the direction of the embankment of
'Porfordham' and thence along the embankment to 'Porfordham' at the
east and thus upwards to the cliff and upwards leading to 'Horctorre' and
then just as the bounds made between the land of Roger Loch as far as
Huntford (*Huntenefford*). Sealing clause. Witd. Master Geoffrey Lucy,
Masters Robert and Hugh, John de Torthham, Richard de Cockeworth,
Gybuy, Henry de Grucy, Richard Probus de Trevallet, Richard de
Duneham. Not dated. [Before 1243, see Reichel in *Trans. Devon. Assoc.* xlvi
(1914), 216–17. Queen Eleanor granted Lifton to her foster mother, see
M. A. Henning, *England under Henry III*, 49–50.]

MS.: Cartulary, f.96r.

**235.** Grant of the prior and convent of Launceston to William de
Montibus of all the land of Gatherley with all liberties and villeinages for
his life for an annual rent at Michaelmas of 12d. sterling for all services
except suit to the prior's court twice yearly at their next pleas after the
feast of the Holy Cross[a] at Launceston with a reasonable summons of
eight days and saving foreign service of the lord king, as much as
pertained to so much land in the same fee. Warranty clause *contra omnes
homines et feminas*. The property was to revert to the prior and convent

immediately on William's death, but his moveable and immoveable goods to remain for his heirs and executors. Sealing clause of both parties. Witd. the lord Stephen Hayme, at that time seneschal of Cornwall; Master Peter Haym. Not dated [*c.*1262 or 1267, see no. 236.]

ᵃThe feast of the Invention of the Holy Cross, 3 May.

MS.: Cartulary, f.96v.

**236.** Grant by the chapter to William de Monte for life of the corrody of one canon of the priory with pannage, wine and ale, for the land which he had given to the priory forever; also a competent room for the same William. If he wished to serve the canons as any other freeman of the priory, the cost of a horse and servant would be found and he would receive a good robe as one of the esquires of the priory. The prior and convent of Launceston bound themselves to the jurisdiction of the archdeacon of Cornwall under the penalty of half a mark sterling for making distraint to the lord archdeacon if they failed. If William sustained losses or expenses for their failure, the prior and convent bound themselves to give satisfaction. The corrody was to come into force on Friday after the feast of All Saints 1262 for the life of the said William. Sealing clause of both parties. Witd. Stephen Haym, then seneschal of Cornwall; Randulph de Trenethdun, clerk. Not dated [*c.*1262 or 1267, see no. 479.]

MS.: Cartulary, ff.96v.–97r.

**237.** Grant and confirmation by William de Dudyston to Luke Keade for his homage and service all the piece of land which contained 2 acres of land English on the west side of Smallacombe (*Smalekumbe*) which lay between the land of the lord prior of Launceston and the land of Philip de Dudyston. Luke was to pay a yearly rent of 3d. at Michaelmas and Easter. Warranty clause. Luke paid William half a mark of silver. Sealing clause. Witd. Gregory de Dudyston, John Carbonel, Henry Rem, William Marscallus, Vincent de Trevella, Martin de Bosco. Not dated. [?*c.*1244–6, see nos. 211 and 222.]

MS.: Cartulary, f.97r.–f.97v.

**238.** Grant and confirmation by William de Dodeston to Henry Cosyn and his wife Joan of one acre of meadow in his park of Dutson (*Dodeston*) which lay between the meadow which John de Wyfford held on the west and the meadow of Sampson de Dodeston on the east and between the meadow of Stephen de Dodeston on the south and the meadow of Thomas Hoper on the north. And also a piece of land called 'Torffmor' which lay in length between the said meadow and the land of Thomas Hooper and in width between the land of Sampson de Dodeston and the meadow of Thomas Hoper. To Henry, Joan and their right heirs forever. If they had no legitimate heirs at their deaths, 'Torffmore' was to revert to the heirs and assigns of Henry Cosyn by customary service to the chief lord of the fee. Warranty and sealing clause. Witd. Richard Risoun, then bailiff of Launceston Land; John Walfolk, John Martyn de la Woda, Thomas Hooper, Stephen de Dodeston. Dated Dutson, Wednesday, 25 July 1341.

MS.: Cartulary, ff.97v.–98r.

**239.** Quitclaim[a] by Matilda Candele to the priory of her rights (including dower) in 20 perches of land at Athill (*Atawille*) next to the park of Launceston. Sealing clause. Witd. Thomas le Chaunceler, Robert de Bodmam, Henry Rem, Henry Mustard, John Cosyn. Dated Launceston, Sunday, 17 March 1296.

[a]Heading: *Carta de terris in Wylly.*

MS.: Cartulary, f.98r.

**240.** Quitclaim by William, son of Roger de la Wille, to the priory of 20 perches of land at Athill next to the park of Launceston. Sealing clause. Witd. Thomas le Chaunceler, Robert de Bodmam, Henry Rem, Henry Mustard, John Cosyn. Dated Launceston, Sunday, 17 March 1296.

MS.: Cartulary, f.98r.–f.98v.

**241.** Grant[a] by Ailsius and Erneburg, his wife, to the canons of land they held in the vill of Kernick (*Carneth*), viz. one acre of land which belonged formerly to Brictric Cot. Plural sealing clause. Witd. Luke, son of Bern'; Master Edward, Alexander Bacheler, Robert Rem. Not dated. [*c.*1195–1214: Luke son of Bernard.]

[a]Heading: *Carta de terris in Carnek.*

MS.: Cartulary, f.98v.

**242.** Confirmation of grant by Matilda, formerly wife of Rabboc, to the priory of one acre of land which B., her father, held in the vill of Kernick (*Carnech*) from Ailsius and Erneburg, his wife, and also of Matilda's quitclaim of this. Witd. Luke son of Bern', Master Edward, Alexander Bacheler, Robert Rem, Walter Probo. Not dated. [*c.*1195–1214, as no. 241.]

MS.: Cartulary, f.98v.

**243.** [a]Gift by Robert Iricius of the land of Goodmansleigh (*Cudmaneslec*) to the priory. Witd. Osbert, priest of 'Bryg' ': Edward, clerk; Pagan, clerk.

Not dated. [Edward the clerk is mentioned in the Cornish eyre of 1201.]

<sup>a</sup>Heading: *Carta de terris in Cudmaneslega.*

MS.: Cartulary, f.99r.

**244.** Grant by William, son of Richard, and a regrant to the priory of the land of Goodmansleigh with its appurtenances except the mill which he and his father had wrongly held for a short time. He made the grant for the remission of his and his father's sins, praying 'Earl Reginald as my lord and friend and all my friends that they would maintain these alms against all disturbances'. Witd. Robert, bishop of Exeter; Robert, prior of Bodmin; Segarus, canon; Bernard, clerk; Richard, sheriff of Cornwall; Jocelin Sancy, Saget, the physician, and Maunset and Jordan Chaillo and Gurgo, Master Robert, nephew, and Jordan, Osbert and Peter, serfs. Not dated. [*c.*1140–9, see *Heads of Religious Houses*, 152 (Prior Robert of Bodmin).]

MS.: Cartulary. f.99r.

**245.** Grant by Reginald Heriz to the priory for his soul and the souls of Earl Reginald and his father and mother and his wife and sons of one ferling of land in Goodmansleigh which Brand had held. Witd. Osbert, priest of 'Bruge'; William Breton, Geoffrey de Ridletune, Osbert de Treberthe and William, his brother. Robert, his son and heir, granted and confirmed this by his seal which was witnessed by Radulf the clerk; William, clerk; Fule Osbert, nephew of the prior. Not dated. [*c.*1201–12, *Red Book of the Exchequer* i, 161 (Robert Heriz).]

MS.: Cartulary, f.99r.

**246.** Grant by Robert, son of William, with the advice of his lord, Reginald and of William de Boterell, his kinsman, and with the assent of his wife, Agnes, and of his heirs, Robert and William, for 20 marks and a palfrey and two gold coins, of Goodmansleigh (*Codemanneslege).* He acknowledged his and his father's guilt in retaining this. Sealing clause. Witd. Bern' the clerk, Lewardus the clerk, Richard the steward, Oger de Cabulyon. Not dated. [*c.*1140–66 (Agnes Hay). Also William II de Botreaux, *Red Book of the Exchequer* i, 262.]

MS.: Cartulary, f.99v.

**247.** Grant and confirmation by Roger, son of Rainfrid, to the priory of his land in London in the lane which led to the guildhall of the tanners in the parish of St Peter 'de Bradestrete' which was next to the land of the hospitallers of Jerusalem, 40 feet in width by 74 feet in length, in perpetual alms for the souls of himself and his family and his ancestors, in exchange for a moiety of Ridgegrove (*Riddesgrave*) mill.[a] Witd. Nicholas and William, chaplains; Edward and Ralph Briton and Geoffrey and another Geoffrey, clerks; Robert de St Remigius; Osbert, son of William Brito. Not dated. [Before no. 250.]

[a]From the title of the charter: *quam terram fratres hospitales . . . ibidem habent in escambium pro medietate molendini de Riddesgrave myll.* Cf. no. 249.

MS.: Cartulary, f.99v.

**248.** Agreement of the canons relating to a moiety of the mill of Goodmansleigh. The brothers hospitaller of the Temple had granted the canons in that year half the said mill at the petition of Roger, son of Reinfrid, on the condition that if the said Roger would make a secure exchange within that year, then the canons should hold and quietly possess the moiety of the mill for ever, otherwise the said part of the mill would be returned to the brothers with the chirograph after that year. Not dated. [Before dating limits of no. 250.]

MS.: Cartulary, ff.99v.–100r.

**249.** Grant by Roger, son of Reinfrid, to the brothers hospitaller of Jerusalem of an exchange for a moiety of the mill of Goodmansleigh of land before his house in London. He confirmed this moiety to the priory in pure and perpetual alms for his soul and the soul of Alice, his wife, and for the souls of his children and of his father and mother and ancestors. Witd. Gilbert, son of Reinfrid, Thomas de Duneham, Ralph, son of William, William de Botrell, Oliver Chaillo, Nicholas the chaplain, Richard, son of Warin. Not dated. [See no. 250 for approximate date.]

MS.: Cartulary, f.100r.

**250.** Quitclaim by Ralph de Dina,[a] prior of the brothers hospitaller of Jerusalem in England, with the common consent and counsel of the brethren in chapter, of all their rent in the mill of Goodmansleigh to the priory for some land which Roger son of Reinfrid had granted to them in exchange, being 69 feet in length and 40 feet in the front next to the guildhall of the tanners. Witd. Brother Alan, brother Godard, brother Rembald, chaplains; brother Albert, then master of London; brother William Felledean. Not dated. [*c*.1178–81, see similar charter in M. Gervers, *Cartulary of the Knights of St John of Jerusalem in England. Secunda Camera* (1982), no. 219.]

[a]Ralph de Dina is called Ralph de Dynham in King and Luke, *The Knights of St John in the British Realm* (1967), where he is also noted as Grand Prior of England from 1178–1181.

MS.: Cartulary, f.100r.–f.100v.

**251.** Gift by Robert son of William to the priory for the soul of Countess

Mabel and for the souls of his mother and father and their parents, 20s. of rent, i.e. from the land of North Tregeare and from the mill of Castle Milford (*Kestellemylleford*). Sealing clause. Witd. Earl Reginald, Richard, earl of Devon, Roger de Valletorta, Robert de Dunstavilla,[a] William de Botrell. Not dated. [*c.*1155–62, i.e. the lifetime of Richard de Reviers, second earl of Devon.]

[a]*Sic.*

MS.: Cartulary, f.100v.

**252.** Gift by Robert son of William to the priory of rents of 20s. for the soul of his sister, the Countess Mabel, i.e. the land of North Tregeare with Alwin, the forester, and his progeny by his former wife for 10s. and the mill and all the mulcture of the manor of Downinney (*Dounheny*). Witd. Earl Reginald, Earl Richard de Ridvers, Roger de Valletorte, William de Botrell, Walter, abbot of Tavistock (*Tavystoch*), John and Roger, chaplains; Bernard, notary public; William, sheriff; William de Sancto Claro, Richard, the steward. Sealing clause of donor with the assent of his heirs and of his wife. Amen. Not dated. [*c.*1155–62, as no. 251.]

MS.: Cartulary, f.100v.

**253.** Notice by William of 'the mill' that he was bound to the prior and convent yearly in 3s. sterling payable by equal amounts at Easter and Michaelmas for the mill of Castle Milford. He granted that if this payment ceased the steward of the priory should distrain his lands and moveable goods until full satisfaction was made. Except for the privilege of jurisdiction, he renounced all legal remedy, especially the prohibition of the king by which the payment of the said money might be held up. Sealing clause. Not witnessed or dated. [William 'of the mill' occurs in the Cornish eyre of 1201.]

MS.: Cartulary, ff.100v.–101r.

**254.** Grant by Richard Wales[a] of Launceston and his wife, Joan, to John Trethewy, John Lanyaton, chaplain, and William Frengy, clerk, of all their estate in Launceston and the land called 'Peyglond' with the reversion of the dowry of all properties held by Richard and Joan for the term of their lives, except for one tenement with a garden adjoining in Launceston, situated between the land of Nicholas Webba and the tenement of John Ouger which they had of the grant of Sarra Thomas. Plural sealing clause. Witd. John Bynnele, William Goderygh. Not dated. [*c.*1394, see no. 307.]

[a]*Walleys* in title of charter.

MS.: Cartulary, f.101r.

**255.** Grant and quitclaim by Agnes, daughter and heir of John de Fonte (deceased) of half an acre of land in the vill of 'Fonte', i.e. the land which her father John held there for a time of the prior and convent. The prior and convent gave her 24s. Sealing clause. Witd. Roger de Bodmam, Gregory de Dudeston, Richard Redbyll, Henry Rem, Martin de Tregadylet. Not dated. [?c.1244–6, see no. 237.]

MS.: Cartulary, f.101v.

**256.** Release and quitclaim by Alice, relict of John de Fonte, in her widowhood of all her right in the third part of one acre of land in the vill of 'Fonte', which was her dowry, to the priory. Sealing clause. Witd. Roger de Bodmam, Gregory de Dudeston, Richard Redebile, Henry de Rem, Martin de Tregadilet. Not dated. [?c.1224–6.]

MS.: Cartulary, f.101v.

**257.** Grant and confirmation by Robert de Bodmam to the priory of a piece of land in Launceston containing about one acre of land English, formerly Richard Coda's. He acquired this land of Walter Whita, the heir of Richard Cada junior near the house of the said Richard at 'la Wille' on the eastern side of the way from Newport (*Niweport*) to Werrington (*Wolryngton*) in exchange for a piece of land in Launceston next to the way which led from Newport to Werrington which he had of the prior and convent on the eastern side of their park of Launceston; which land contained one acre of land English. Sealing clause. Witd. Henry Rem, Walter Burdon, Richard Beaumond; Henry Snellard, then bailiff of Launceston Land; John le Wales. Dated Launceston, 30 April 1313.

MS.: Cartulary, ff.101v.–102r.

**258.** Release and quitclaim by Agnes, daughter of John Attewille, to the lord Prior Richard de Brykevile and the convent of all her right in 1 half-acre of land Cornish in the vill of Athill near Launceston, which Agnes had sought by royal writ in the king's court against Richard Stoterich who called the prior to warranty. Prior Richard gave her 18s. sterling. Sealing clause. Witd. Robert de Yestecote, Robert Moly, Robert de Bodmam, Richard Stoterych, Thomas le Chaunceler. Dated Launceston, Easter Sunday, 1289.

MS.: Cartulary, f.102r.–f.102v.

**259.** Plea between Roger Carmynow and Prior Richard of the chantry and land of Ditchen (*Twychen*) at York.

Roger de Carmynow was summoned to reply to the prior why he with Adam le Provost de Hornicote, David Wastwy and Henry, son of Henry le

Clerk, on 29 June in the 23rd year of the then king at Ditchen in 'Estfeld' took four heifers and one ox of the prior and drove them as far as Hornacott and detained them there contrary to their pledges. The prior claimed loss worth 100s. The defendant said that the prior held of Roger one messuage, 80 acres of land and 10 acres of woodland in the said vill of Ditchen by the service of finding for the said Roger a chaplain to celebrate Mass in the chapel of 'Taleburgh' each feast day; on the vigil of Christ's birth and at Christmas and the three days following; also on the vigil of Easter and on Easter day with the three following days; and from the first day of Lent for the whole of Lent. A certain Gervase, grandfather of the said Roger, was seised of this chantry by the hands of a former prior, Richard, predecessor of the said prior in the time of peace in the reign of the lord king H., father of the present king, after the first crossing over of King H. into Gascony etc. Roger said he took the cattle into his fee because the said chantry was in arrears for 30 years.

The prior said the seizure was unjust and that he did not hold the properties in Ditchen from the said Roger.

It was judged that the prior should have damages of half a mark, and Roger was in mercy. Not dated. [York, 1296, see no. 260.]

MS.: Cartulary, ff.102v.–103v.

**260.** Another plea related to no. 259.

Roger de Carmynow by his attorney sought to recover against Richard de Twychene one messuage, 80 acres of land and 10 acres of wood in Ditchen adjoining Hornacott by a royal writ of right. Roger said that Prior Richard held of him these properties for the service of finding a chaplain to celebrate in the chapel of St George of Tealeburgh on certain feast days (named in no. 259). From Gervase the right of the chantry descended to Sarra and Cenota. From Cenota the right went to a certain Margery, as his daughter and heir. As Margery died without heirs, the right of the chantry went to Sarra as the sister and heir of Cenota. The right descended to Sarra's son and heir, John, who died without an heir, when the right went to his brother Roger de Carmynow. The latter was summoned on the Morrow of All Souls in the 24th year of the then king to reply to Prior Richard about the taking of 4 heifers and one ox from 'Estfelde' in Ditchen before John de Metyngham and his companions, justices of the King's Bench at Westminster. Roger said it was a just seizure because the chantry was in arrears for thirty years. Roger said that Gervase, his ancestor, was seised of the chantry by Robert, a former prior. The latter denied holding the properties in Ditchen. Richard de Twychene by his attorney, called to warranty the prior of Launceston who came and placed himself on the great assize of the king to decide whether or not he held the properties in right of the priory and not from Roger. The plea was adjourned to the quindene of Martinmas. Not dated. [Westminster, 1296.]

MS.: Cartulary, f.103r.–f.103v.

**261.**  Another plea about the same matter.

After the adjournment both Roger de Carmynow and the prior appeared
and a jury of four knights was elected: William de Botreaux, Richard de
Sergyaux, Thomas de Prydyas and Reginald de Bevyle, together with
William de Chambernon, Henry de Bodrygan, Reginald de Botreaux,
Stephen de Bello Prato, Walter de Cornub(ia) and Herbert de Pyne.
    The jury on oath said that the prior had a greater right to the tenements
in Ditchen as of the right of the priory; the prior did not hold them from
Roger for the services Roger stated, i.e. the chantry.
    It was judged that the prior and his successors should hold the
tenement in Ditchen of the said Roger and his heirs forever. Not dated.
[Westminster 1296.]

MS.: Cartulary, f.103v.


**262.**  Presentation of the jurors of Dunheved (*Dounheved*) of the liberties
of the vill of Launceston before John de Berwyk, William de Bromton,
Henry Spygurnell, John Randolf and Hervey de Staunton, itinerant
justices in the thirtieth year of King Edward I.

The jury of Dunheved presented that Reginald de Mortayn, formerly earl
of Cornwall, had acquired of a former prior of Launceston certain liberties
which the prior and canons of the church of St Stephen of Launceston
had, viz. fines of the assize of bread and ale in the vill of Launceston at
that time. Reginald had given to the prior and convent for these liberties
65s. 10d. to be taken from the farm of the burgesses of Dunheved and from
that time the prior and convent had received full payment. Recently, since
the last eyre, the prior and convent had appropriated to themselves fines
of bread and ale in the vill of Launceston which they then claimed against
the arrangement they had made with Earl Reginald, yet nevertheless they
received the said 65s. 10d. of the burgesses to the loss of the king and
burgesses. The sheriff was asked to cause the prior to appear.
    The prior said the lord king was seised of a moiety of the fines of the
assize of bread and ale, and claimed the other moiety which his
predecessors had before the time of Earl Reginald.
    A former prior of Launceston, one Richard, had established a title in
the presence of the earl to all the liberties which his predecessors had
before, viz. sac and soc, tol and them and infangentheof, with other
liberties. The prior claimed that he and his men were quit of suits of shire
and hundred pleas and of clyfward and all aids and every secular service
excepting only a market on Sundays which they had formerly. The count
of Mortain had taken this market from the vill of Launceston to his
borough of Dunheved and in return the count had assigned to the prior
and convent and their successors 20s. yearly to be paid from the office of
the reeve of the castle of Dunheved. The prior also said that for a certain
tower of the priory which he had pulled down Earl Reginald gave to the
prior and convent in pure and perpetual alms 40s. to be taken yearly from
his farm of the castle of Dunheved, saving to the prior and convent and

their successors the rent of 20s. which they had yearly of the reeveship of the castle for the said market by the charters of Earl Reginald which he produced. The prior also produced a charter of Richard, formerly count of Poitou, and earl of Cornwall, who had given to the prior and canons 5s. 10d. in pure and perpetual alms as a rent for the light of Blessed Mary to be taken yearly from his borough of Dunheved, for payment of which rent Earl Richard had bound himself and his heirs to warranty.

The prior said he had not received the said 65s. 10d. for the remission of the said assize of bread and ale and he sought judgement. It was found that the said burgesses would not pay the rent of 65s.10d. to the prior and canons for these fines, but only (money) for the market moved away and for the rent for the light of Blessed Mary, so from that time the prior and his predecessors had had a moiety of the issues of the fines from the assize of bread and ale. The jury, together with the jurors of the hundred of East (*Est*), in which the said vill of Launceston lay, required the prior to answer all this. Not dated. [Launceston, Michaelmas 1302, cf. P. L. Hull, *Cartulary of St Michael's Mount*, DCRS 1962, no. 10.]

MS.: Cartulary, f.104r.–f.104v.

**263.** *Quo warranto* pleas in the second roll of the royal pleas for that year (1301–2).

The prior of Launceston was summoned to reply to the lord king by what authority he claimed to have in the manor of Launceston Land the gallows, view of frankpledge with hue and cry, fines of the assize of bread and ale in the same manor, and a moiety of the fines of bread and ale in the vill of Newport (*Nyweporth*).

The prior said that he and all his predecessors from time immemorial to the present day had enjoyed these same liberties without interruption. John de Motford, who followed for the king, said that the prior of Launceston in the time of King John had all the liberties now claimed. Later, one of the priors surrendered the same liberties to a certain Reginald de Mortain,[a] formerly earl of Cornwall. Earl Reginald granted the liberties to his burgesses of Dunheved for 65s. 10d. to be paid to the prior and his successors. John de Motford said that the burgesses after this grant were firmly seised of the said liberties until after the last eyre of the justices in Cornwall, when the prior had taken and appropriated these liberties.

The jury said on oath that the said prior and all his predecessors had enjoyed these liberties from time immemorial and from then until the present they had been used without interruption. The prior claimed to have these liberties. Not dated.

[a]*Sic.* The same title is used for Reginald de Dunstanville in no. 262.

MS.: Cartulary, f.104v.–f.105r. Printed, *Placita de Quo Warranto* (Record Commission 1818), 110.

**264.** Exemplification by letters patent of King Edward III of the privileges of the manor of Launceston Land: about gallows, view of frankpledge and the assize of bread and ale there and at Newport.

Recital of inspeximus of certificate in chancery of the King's mandate through the treasurer and chamberlains of the exchequer as follows:
Pleas of rights and assize before John de Berewyke, William de Burneton, Henry Spygurnell, John Randolf and Hervey de Staunton, justices itinerant at Launceston in the octave of St Michael in the thirtieth year of the reign of Edward son of King Henry (1302).
The prior of Launceston was summoned to reply to the same king by what warrant he claimed to have in the manor of Launceston Land gallows, view of frankpledge, hue and cry, fines of the assize of bread and ale in the same manor and a moiety of the assize of bread and ale in the vill of Newport. The prior came and said that he and all his predecessors from time immemorial until then enjoyed these liberties without any interruption.
John de Mutford who followed for the king said that the said prior in the time of King John had all the liberties which he claimed and afterwards he released these liberties to a certain Reginald de Morteyn, a former earl of Cornwall. Earl Reginald granted these liberties to his burgesses of Dunheved for 65s. 10d. to be paid yearly to the prior and his successors. After this grant the burgesses were in seisin of the said liberties until the last eyre of justices in Cornwall when the said prior by his own authority took and appropriated the said liberties.
The jury said on oath that the said prior and all his predecessors had these liberties from time immemorial and had used them without interruption. Recital that exemplification was made at the request of Prior Adam. Witd. Edward, duke of Cornwall and earl of Chester, 'our most dear son, guardian of England'. Dated Eastry, 9 October 1342.

MS.: Cartulary, f.105r.–f.105v.

**265.** Memorandum about differences which arose between the lord Edmund 'of famous memory', son of Richard, king of Germany, and the prior and convent. The lord Earl for the salvation of his soul and of the soul of the lord Edward, king of England, son of King Henry and for the souls of the lord Richard his father and Senchia his mother and the souls of all his predecessors and successors, granted that the men of the prior and convent of Launceston and of Newport might brew and bake in the said vills at his will without impediment and might sell and buy bread, wine, ale, flesh, fish and all other necessary things for food as well by horses as by men, without having a market or tolls, saving to the prior and convent etc. their fairs and liberties. A bailiff of the men of the priory should be elected bound by an oath to the lord earl, who faithfully and honestly would collect fines of bread and ale whenever the assize was broken and should answer for a moiety of them to the earl or his attorney at Michaelmas yearly. The prior and convent or their bailiffs were not to relax these fines without the assent of the steward of Cornwall. Earl Edmund also granted to the prior and canons that they might have and hold all their land of Caradon (*Carnedon*) wholly and peacefully as it was formerly held and just as the charter of Earl Reginald witnessed within the bounds contained in his charter. The earl's tenants of Rillaton were to have their proper allowance of wood for their hearths and sufficient pasture for feeding their animals, but not by gift or sale. The earl also granted to the prior and canons that they should be quit of suit to Climsland (*Clymesland*) and Caradon for ever. All these gifts were in free, pure and perpetual alms. Alternate sealing clause for chirograph. Witd. Henry de Shotobroke, Peter Becard, William le Alemound, Oliver de Dyneham, William de Botreaux, Thomas de Kancia, knights; Roger de Drayton, William de Monketon, then steward of Cornwall; Master Hamundus Parleben. Dated Exeter, 24 May 1284.[a]

[a]For another copy of this charter, see no. 548.

MS.: Cartulary, f.105v.–f.106r.


**266.**   Plea about the mulcture of the burgesses of Dunheved to the mill of the priory under the castle.

Peter son of John, John de Lideford, Jocelin Velynage, John son of John, Edward de Bulepit, Richard Wandry, Robert Russell, Stephen le Duk, Luke le Chepman, David Pronta and Peter Bela were summoned to reply to the prior of Launceston concerning the suit owed by Peter and the others to the mill of the priory in Launceston.

The prior by his attorney said that Peter and the others ought to make suit to the priory mill for all corn to be ground and expended in the messuages which Peter and the others held separately in Dunheved, that is to say to the twentieth measure. The prior was seised of this suit by the hands of the said Peter and of the others as of the fee and right of his church of St Stephen of Launceston. Peter and the others had withdrawn this suit whence the prior had sustained a loss of £100.

Peter and the others appeared by their attorney in defence and said they did not hold their tenements from the prior or of his fee, nor had the prior shown any evidence to this effect.

The prior said that a certain Reginald, earl of Cornwall, son of Henry, formerly king of England, gave to the priory in alms the mill which he had under the castle of Dunheved with the mulcture of the same vill. And he produced a charter of Reginald, formerly earl of Cornwall. And also a charter of King Henry II[a] which confirmed Earl Reginald's gift of the mill.

And Peter and the others said in defence that neither the said prior nor any predecessor of his were ever seised of the said suit unless by the will of the tenants of the tenements and not by right of the church as the prior maintained. And he placed himself on the country and the prior likewise. The sheriff was ordered to cause them to apear in the quindene of Martinmas. Not dated. [The use of the term *proavi domini regis nunc* after the mention of Henry II would suggest this plea belongs to the reign of Edward I, 1272–1307.]

[a]See no. 539.

MS.: Cartulary, f.106r.–f.106v.

**267.** Plea before John de Battesford and Roger de Heygham, justices, about the sustenance of food and raiment of Ralph Bloyow.

The assize came to recognise if the prior of Launceston unjustly disseised Ralph de Bloyowe of his free tenement in Launceston. And what disseisin there was in sustenance of food and raiment for one chaplain which the same Ralph wanted to place in the priory of Launceston to stay there at the will of the said Ralph and to celebrate divine service for the same Ralph and for the souls of his ancestors.

The prior came and said if the said Ralph had anything relating to this sustenance he had nothing special to show for it, nor had he anything else to say except that from time immemorial he and his ancestors were seised of this sustenance. The prior also said that before the making of the statute a remedy was not available through the assize, and there was nothing expressly in the statute to make amends in this case. For Ralph had not shown that the profit came from the tenement and meanwhile he claimed the profit for the convenience of another. The prior claimed judgement whether or not there should be an assize.

Ralph asked if the profit ought not to arise from the tenement, but, as before, the prior said nothing to this.

The case was adjourned to the Saturday on the morrow of St James the Apostle (26 July). Not dated. [?*c.*1228/9–23 April 1241. (Ralph Bloyou, see *Book of Fees* i, 393, who died 23 April 1241, Maclean, *Trigg Minor* iii, 159).]

MS.: Cartulary, ff.106v.–107r.

**268.** The process of pardon of the transgression of lands and tenements appropriated by Prior Adam after the statute of mortmain without the licence of the lord king.

William Trussel, escheator of the lord king on this side of the Trent, commanded Geoffrey de Leyston his subescheator in Cornwall and Devon that by the oaths of worthy and legal men of his bailiwick he was to ascertain diligently if it would be to the king's loss or any other's loss if the prior and convent acquired 4 messuages, one toft, one ferling and 1½ acres of land in Bradridge (*Bradereg*), 'Trelouthet', Truscott (*Overtruscot*), 'La Hille' next to Launceston, 'Halswille', Treworgy and Dunheved for themselves and their successors in the fee of Henry Mostard and Roger Prodome after the publication of the statute of mortmain for which they had not obtained the king's licence. The prior and convent might keep for themselves and their successors for part of the sustenance of a chaplain to celebrate divine service daily in the chapel of Blessed Mary of Launceston for the soul of the Lord E(dward), king, grandfather of the present king, and for the souls of all the faithful departed forever. Enquiry was to be made about the loss to the king in profits etc. and what lands and tenements remained to the said Henry and Roger as well as the lands above and how the lands were held and by what services and what was the annual value. The writ showing these things was to be returned without delay under seal. Witd. King Edward III. Dated York, 20 June 1327.

MS.: Cartulary, f.107r.–f.107v.

**269.** Inquisition by the king's escheator at Launceston according to the royal writ by the oaths of John de Trevage, Walter de Carnedon, Robert de Churleton, William de Pollebou, Adam de Baak, Baldwin de Langedon, Richard de Regree, John Arthur, Richard Beaumond, Robert de Estecote, William de Nywaleghe and Richard de Legh. They said there would be no loss or prejudice to the king if he were to allow the prior and convent to acquire 4 messuages, one toft, one ferling, and one carrucate of land and 1½ acres in Bradridge, 'Trelouthet', Truscott, Hill next to Launceston, 'Alswille', Treworgy and Dunheved in the fee of Henry Mustard and Roger Prodomme for a chaplain to celebrate forever for the souls of King Edward, grandfather of the present king and of all the faithful departed. The jury said these lands were held of the priory for a yearly rent of 11s. 6d. and the lands were worth besides rent 15s. 2d. yearly. The prior and convent held the lands of the bishop of Exeter in pure and perpetual alms of the gift and confirmation of the king's progenitors, and the bishop of the gift of Reginald. The said ferling of land with the appurtenances of Hill and Treworgy were held of William de Ferr(ers) for the fiftieth part of one knight's fee. And the same William de Ferr(ers) (held them) for the same service of Henry Most(ard) of Trematon (*Tremeton*) in the hands of the present king, and the ferling of land was worth 12d. yearly. These were all the lands of the said Henry and Roger. Sealed by the jurors. Dated Launceston, 5 September 1327.

MS.: Cartulary, f.107v.–f.108r.

**270.** Pardon by letters patent of King Edward III to the prior and convent for holding the lands of no. 269.

The prior and convent were to hold the lands for themselves and their successors from the chief lords of the fee for the due and accustomed service in aid of the sustenance of the chaplain without hindrance from the king or his ministers. Dated Nottingham, 7 October 1327.

MS.: Cartulary, f.108r.

**271.** Plea of assize before William de Sharhull and his companions, justices of the lord king in the county of Cornwall, between the prior of Launceston and John de Skewys about having a corrody.

The assize came to recognise if Prior Adam and brother Angerus de Bant, a fellow canon of the said prior, John Godman, clerk and Geoffrey de Doune unjustly disseised John de Skewys of his free tenement in Launceston and of having a corrody in the priory. This corrody entailed his having for himself every day throughout the whole year food and drink at the table of the squires of the aforesaid prior, just like his own squires, and at Christmas a robe just like those of the squires of the said prior worth 20s. and for shoe money at the same feast each year 10s. And to have food and drink for a servant, just as the servants of the prior have in the same priory, and to take each year at the same feast a robe like that of the servants of the prior himself at the price of 6s. 8d. And John de Skewys was to have his accommodation in any room of the priory throughout the year and a place for his horse in the stables of the priory. He was to have each night yearly at his room a half gallon of ale of the best ale of the cellar of the priory and an allowance of two candles of wax, of the room of the said prior there.[a] Also he was to have every night from the feast of All Saints (1 November) to the Invention of the Holy Cross (3 May) a faggot of dry wood for the hearth of his room. And for his horse each night yearly a botel of oats and sufficient hay for the same horse, just as an esquire of the prior has for his horse.

The prior appeared and not others, but a William de Trelouny replied for them as their bailiff and for them he said no injury or disseisin was done to the said John de Skewys. And he placed himself on the assize and John de Skewys likewise. And the prior said that John de Skewys by his plea intended to burden the said church and priory and he sought that John should show the court why the priory should be burdened with the said corrody.

And John said that a long time before memory a certain William de Botreaux[b] was seised of the advowsons of the churches of Egloskerry, Tremaine (*Tremen*) and St Gregory of Hill. William gave these advowsons to the priory in perpetuity on condition that when William or any of his heirs was buried in the priory on the day of the burial there should be an armed man riding before the corpse of the deceased and that the prior should admit the same riding man to the corrody aforesaid for the term of his life. And John said that the said William de Botreaux was buried in the priory church before the time of memory. On the day of William's burial a certain John Chamburleyn rode armed before the body of William, by which a certain Reginald, son and heir of the said William, nominated a certain John Chamburleyn to the prior for the corrody which he obtained for life. After the death of the said Reginald, a certain Roger le Key rode armed before the body of the said Reginald on the day of his burial in the priory church. By which the said Roger was admitted to the corrody for life in the time of King Henry, great grandfather of the present king, at the nomination of William, son and heir of Reginald. Afterwards William, son of Reginald, died and was buried in the church of the same priory in the time of King E(dward), grandfather of the present king. A certain William Wynnolove who rode armed before the body of William, son of Reginald, obtained the corrody for all his life. After the death of the said William, son of William, he was buried at the priory and the said John Skewys rode armed before his body. After this the same John was admitted to the˙ corrody by the present prior at the nomination of Reginald, son and heir of the same William, son of William, and was seised thereof until the said prior and others named in the writ unjustly disseised him. John de Skewys said that all who were nominated to the corrody were seised in the said form and he sought to proceed to the caption of the assize.

The prior did not know that the said advowsons were given to the priory and his predecessor with this reservation of the corrody. The advowsons, he said, were given to the priory and his predecessor in pure and perpetual alms without any reservation. The prior also said that John de Skewys claimed the said corrody by the title of prescription and it was only possible to maintain this in two ways: to allege seisin in fee in any person etc., or to allege prescriptive right. Neither of these cases applied to John de Skewys who sought judgement by an insufficient title.

The case was adjourned before the justices at Westminster on Wednesday after three weeks from Easter. Not dated. [*c.*1328, i.e. before Prior Adam's resignation on 26 June 1346.]

ᵃ*duas candelas de cero que dicuntur parysshcandell de camera predicti prioris.* ᵇ*sic.* MS

MS.: Cartulary, ff.108v.–109v.

**272.** Plea between the prior of Launceston and John Crocker about a ferling of land and a half in East Menheniot (*Estmynhennek*).

John Crocker sought against the prior a ferling and a half of land in East Menheniot (*Estmelhynnek*) which Matthew de Melhynnek gave to Warin Drew in free marriage with Margery, daughter of the same Matthew, and which after the deaths of Warin and Margery should descend to John, son and heir of the said Warin and Margery, by the form of the gift.

John said that Warin and Margery, were seised of the said tenement in demesne as of fee and right in the time of peace when Edward, grandfather of the present king, was king. The right descended to their son and heir, i.e. John himself.

The prior by his attorney, Robert de Trewynian, came and defended his right and denied that Matthew had given the tenement to Warin in free marriage with Margery and placed himself on the country and John likewise.

The sheriff was asked to bring the parties together on the morrow of All Souls. The process continued to the present day, i.e. in the octave of Michaelmas, 1345. Then John appeared by his attorney, John de Bateshill, and the prior by Robert, his attorney.

The prior said that while the plea continued John Crocker of East Menheniot (*Estremelhynnek*) released and quitclaimed in writing to Prior Adam all his right which he had in the tenement, i.e. one messuage and a quarter of a Cornish acre in East Menheniot to have and to hold to the prior and convent etc. in perpetuity. John granted warranty to the prior and convent and their successors. The prior produced John's bond dated Launceston, Monday, 16 August 1344. The prior sought judgement if the said John could have an action against him. John was declared to be in mercy for a false claim. The plea was enrolled on the plea-roll of Trinity term 16 Edward III (1342). Case continued to octave of Michaelmas term, 1345.

MS.: Cartulary, ff.109v.–110r.

**273.** ªThe plea of Bamham (*Bodmam*) within the fee of the prior before the justices of the King's Bench.

Roger, prior of Launceston, and Adam de Knoll were summoned at the suit of Peter de Bodmam concerning the seizure of cattle of Peter by them and their unjust detention.

Against pledges by Richard de Bosvysek, his attorney, Peter complained that the prior and Adam on Monday after Michaelmas in the fifteenth year of the present king in a place called Stourscombe (*Sturescombe*) took two heifers of Peter against pledges with a loss valued at 40s.

The prior by his attorney, Benedict Bray, for himself and Adam upheld the seizure as just because Peter held of him one messuage and carrucate of land in Bamham (*Bodmam*) by the homage, fealty and scutage of the lord king (whenever it was sought) at 45s., and at the least by the service of 12d. yearly and to make court to the prior of Launceston Land every 3 weeks. Of which homage, fealty and services a certain former prior, Richard de Brekvyll, was seised by the hands of a certain Robert de Bodmam, father of Peter. And because a relief of 12s. 6d. to be paid by Peter to Prior Roger was in arrears, the latter took the said cattle etc.

Peter said the seizure was not just as the said place was outside the prior's fee. And he sought an enquiry on the country and likewise the prior and Adam. The sheriff was commanded to cause the parties to appear in the quindene of St Hilary. There was a further adjournment to the quindene of Trinity and again to the morrow of Martinmas.

Peter did not appear and the prior appeared by his attorney. The parties then appeared before John de Bousser and John de Juge. The jury said on oath that the place was in the fee of the prior. It was judged that the prior should have the return of the cattle. Peter should have nothing but was in mercy for a false claim. Not dated. [2 Edward III (25 January 1328–24 January 1329).]

ªNote in right hand margin: *M.ᵈ quod carte de Bodmam scribentur in xviij fol' sequente.*

MS.: Cartulary, f.110r.–f.110v.


**274.** Grantª and quitclaim by Jordan de Ridcaron to the priory in pure and perpetual alms of one small parcel of land which Robert Fot held of Jordan for 2d. yearly, and another small piece of land which Richard Prutell held of Jordan yearly for a halfpenny in the manor of Launceston: i.e. all the land he had above the way which went from the stream called 'Staphanes laca' to the gate of the court of the priory and from the way up as far as the well of St Stephen. He granted these small pieces of land to the priory to hold for the love of God and for the souls of his ancestors, free and quit from mundane service and exaction. Sealing clause. Witd. Robert son of Pagan, Jellinus de Landren, William de Rosmarch, William Bryton, Osbert son of Marker, Tancard Durant son of Philip. Not dated. [?1232–44, see no. 61.]

ªHeading: 'the charter of Kellygryn near the well of St Stephen.'

MS.: Cartulary, ff.110v.–111r.

**275.** Agreement between the church of the apostles Peter and Paul of Plympton (*Plymptonia*) and the church of St Stephen of Launceston. The prior and convent of Plympton were to pay yearly at Michaelmas 40d. to the said church of Launceston for the land of Risdon (*Rysdon*)[a] which they held of the gift of William Talebot out of which Geoffrey de la Ha was bound to pay yearly to the said church of Plympton at Michaelmas half a mark. When it came to his heirs the church of Launceston should take half the relief. For every burden meanwhile on this land the churches of Plympton and Launceston were to pay as much as if it were to happen that Geoffrey ceased from the payment of half a mark and the prior and convent of Plympton ceased from the payment of 40d. Sealing clauses of both priories. Not dated. [*c*.1160–2, cf. no. 440, witnessed by William de Talebote.]

[a]Title: *Composicio inter priorem et conventum Plympton et priorem et conventum Launceston de quadraginta denarijs et dimidia relevij de terra de Risingdon iuxta Lyfton.*

MS.: Cartulary, f.111r.

**276.** Grant by R., prior of St Petroc of Bodmin and the convent of the land of 'Brunyon'[a] which Remfred with his sons gave to the church of St Stephen of Launceston for the soul of his wife, free and quit from all dispute except for service owed to St Petroc of Bodmin. Dated 1141.

[a]Blank in the text, the name is supplied by the heading of the charter. The grantor, mentioned also in the title, was Richard Pincerna.

MS.: Cartulary, f.111r.

**277.** Notification to Bartholomew, bishop of Exeter, by Richard Pincerna of grant of rent of 8s. from Eggeulf's fee of 'Breignun' in perpetual alms and free of all except royal service to the churches of St Stephen of Launceston and St Petroc of Bodmin. In Richard's presence in the church of Bodmin it was decided between the two priors that the prior of Bodmin because it was nearer should take the fealty and the said rent from Eggeulf and his heirs and pay 5s. yearly to the church of St Stephen of Launceston. Witd. Master Osbert, Master Nicholas; Martin de Troelege, clerk; Osmund clerk; Baldwin de Radduna, Garnundus, Ralph Huett, Geoffrey. Not dated [*c*.1177 (Prior Roger of Bodmin) *Heads of Religious Houses*, 152.]

MS.: Cartulary, f.111r.–f.111v.

**278.** Agreement between the prior of Bodmin and the prior of Launceston about 8s. which Richard Pincerna gave in perpetual alms to their churches from 'Brennyon' in the fee of Eggeulf. If the prior of Bodmin carried out the arrangement in no. 277 (paying the rent of 5s. to Launceston yearly at Michaelmas) the said churches should possess this gift of the said fee. Witd. Master Osbert, Master Nicholas; Martin de

Troelege, clerk; Osmund the clerk, Baldwin de Raddona, Garmundus, Ralph Huett, Geoffrey and Nicholas, esquires. Not dated. [Similar to no. 277.]

MS.: Cartulary, f.111v.

**279.** Grant and confirmation by William de Ceresaus, lord of Kylkoyth, for the salvation of his soul and the souls of his ancestors and successors, to the priory of 30d. of annual rent to be received at Michaelmas at Kylquyt each year. If he or his heirs failed in this payment, distraint could be made through all his lands of Kylquyt and through all his chattels, and the distraints could be taken to Launceston and kept until full payment was made. He renounced all legal remedies both canonical and civil with the exception of royal prohibitions. Sealing clause. Witd. the lord Alan Bloyou and the lord Adam de Rentona, knights; Richard Cola, Roger de Ludacota, Gregory de Dodeston, knights. Not dated. [?c.1242–67 (based on attestations).]

MS.: Cartulary, ff.111v.–112r.

**280.** Another[a] copy of no. 95. (The only variants are in the clause of witnesses: *Treagu* for Treiagu; *Beaumond* for Beamond).

[a]Title: *Carta de iiijs. percipiendis annuatim de manerio de Treglasta de terris quas Johannes Wideslade tenet ibidem de iure uxoris sue.*

MS.: Cartulary, f.112r.–f.112v.

**281.** Gift by Roger Anglicus and confirmation to the canons of 13d. in rent[a] for the soul of King Henry II and Roger's ancestors. Roger's wife Alice had granted this gift and they had assigned the gift which Warin de Bradbureghe owed them at Michaelmas. Witd. Richard son of Gilbert, Richard son of Warin, Henry son of William, G. son of William, William Banc, Walter son of Richard, William Talebot. Not dated. [?c.1160–2 (William de Talebote, cf. no. 275). Another possibility is after the death of King Henry II in 1189.]

[a]Title to charter adds, *de manerio de Wadfast.*

MS.: Cartulary, f.112v.

**282.** Grant and confirmation by Robert son of Robert de Langedon, lord of Halford, to the priory for the salvation of his soul and the souls of his ancestors, successors and heirs in free, perpetual and ecclesiastical alms of a messuage, a ferling of land and a close of land in 'La Berne' in the manor of Halford which Richard Lekyng formerly held. Warranty and sealing clauses. Witd. the lord William de Boterell, Guydon de Nonant, Mauger de Sancto Albino, Rainfred de Arundell, Henry Tyrell, Thomas de Teteburn, William Walerand. Not dated. [*c*.1242–1248/9? (Death of Wm. (IV) de Botreaux, Maclean, *Trigg Minor* i, 640. Occurrence of Guy de Nonant, *Book of Fees* ii, 1424).]

MS.: Cartulary, ff.112v.–113r.

**283.** Memorandum[a] by John, prior of Launceston, and the convent that they had granted and released to William Attelake and his wife Christine of their messuage in 'La Bern' ' near Exeter, which messuage William Spycer formerly held there. To have and to hold to William Attelake and Christine for the term of their lives and the longer liver of them. To render yearly 15s. sterling to the prior and convent at Easter and Michaelmas by equal portions. A best beast was payable as a heriot after the death of one of them. William and Christine were to maintain and repair all the houses, gardens and closes at their own costs and to surrender them in a good state at the end of the term. Right of re-entry to the prior and convent in default of distress after arrears of rent of a quarter of a year. Warranty clause. Alternate sealing clause for chirograph. (Seals of the prior and convent and William Attelake). Witd. William Trelouny, John Treludek, Stephen Corke. Dated Launceston, Thursday, 12 October 1419.

[a]Title: *Carta Willelmi Lake et uxoris sue* . . . etc.

MS.: Cartulary, f.113r.–f.113v.

**284.** Gift by Elias Coffyn for the redemption of his soul and the souls of his ancestors to the priory of Lewersland (*Luverdesland*)[a] in pure and perpetual alms with no service except the royal service pertaining to the thirteenth part of half a knight's fee. He had confirmed the gift by this charter and offered the gift on the altar of St Stephen. Witd. Algar, priest of Sela; Walter Tanchard, Osbern son of Philip de Bulaputa, Walter Scota, Brien the cook; Richard Fele, Roger Pautener, Hamund, William de Cudemanneslega, Gwaryn son of Robert Rusell; Richard son of Ailward de Truscota; Edward son of Chane. Not dated. [For Elias Coffyn, lord of the manor of Okehampton, see H. P. R. Finberg, 'Some Early Tavistock Charters', *EHR* lxii, 364, no. xxx, a charter, by the attestation of Robert, archdeacon of Totnes, dated 1170–86.]

[a]Cf. title . . . *de terra de Lawardezlond in parochia de Monkokhampton*.

MS.: Cartulary, f.113v.

**285.** Gift and confirmation by William Cophyn[a] to the priory of all the land which William Frellard held of his father and afterwards of himself by the free service of 12d., for his soul and the souls of his ancestors, in pure alms, quit of all exactions except prayers. Except for the right of

William Frellard in the same land which he held of the canons in hereditary right by payment of 12d. yearly at the feast of Michaelmas. He also granted and confirmed to the canons the land known as Luwardez-land which his father, Helyas Cophyn, gave to the priory, free from all exactions except royal service. Sealing clause of donor. Witd. Hugo Cophyn, Michael Trenchard, Ralph Mora, Warin de Poldresok. Not dated. [After no. 284. But William and Hugh Cophyn (*Devon FF.* i nos. 330, 360) occur 1238/9).]

[a]Heading has *Coffyn.*

MS.: Cartulary, ff.113v.–114r.

**286.**   Grant, release and quitclaim by Walter de Horton to the priory of 12d. of rent formerly held by William Frellard. And of 2s. from Lewersland, as contained in the charter of Elyas Coffyn. He had cancelled the charter to him by the prior concerning these rents. Sealing clause. Witd. Joel Pollard, Robert de Thorne, Adam de Brodnymet, John Beaumond, John de Oggeworthy, John de Burdon and John de la Grave. Dated Launceston, Thursday, 31 December 1321.

MS.: Cartulary, f.114r.

**287.**   Record of the plea of 'Frillardeslond' at Westminster before John de Stonor and his fellow justices of the King's Bench for Michaelmas term in the twenty-seventh year in roll 130.[a]

Devon. Thomas, prior of Launceston, and brother David Hole, his fellow canon, were summoned to reply to John Moys on a plea of why they took John's bullock and unjustly kept it.

John Moys by John Bozoun, his attorney, complained that the said prior and brother David on the Monday after the feast of St Dunstan in the twenty-sixth year of the then king of England at Stonfordbeare in Brixton took John's bullock and detained it, and his loss thereby was valued at 100s.

The prior and brother David by Robert Wile, their attorney, came and defended themselves. They said they took the bullock in the vill of Frellard in a place called 'Tounlond' above a certain William de Frellard, chaplain, who held of the priory a messuage and 2 ferlings of land in the vill of Frellard for fealty and the service of 12d. yearly at Michaelmas, of which services a certain Roger, formerly prior of Launceston, was seised by the hands of William Frelard, brother of the same William Frelard, chaplain, whose heir he was. The seizure was made because the fealty of William de Frellard, chaplain, after the death of the said William his father, and the said rent were in arrears for thirty years. John Moys said the prior could not justly excuse the seizure in 'Tounlond', because he said the place was outside the fee of the prior.

And they placed themselves on the country. The case was adjourned by the sheriff to the octave of St Hilary. Not dated. [Probably 27 Edwd. III, i.e. Michaelmas 1353.]

<sup>a</sup>*sic.*

MS.: Cartulary, f.114r.–f.114v.


**288.** Agreement (chirograph) between Prior Osbert and the brethren of Tywardreath (*Tivardrait*) and Prior Robert and the brethren of Launceston. The church of Launceston was to pay each year 12d. to the church of Tywardreath at Michaelmas. This closed the controversy between the churches regarding the land of 'Smalehill', being brought about by Robert, son of William, lord of the fee. Witd. the lord R(obert) and his wife, Agnes, and Richard, the steward (*dapifero*); Odo son of Walter, Jordan de Lisnestoc, William Hay, William the student.<sup>a</sup> Not dated. [Before 24 June 1149 (death of Prior Robert, *Heads of Religious Houses*, 169). Osbert must have been prior of Tywardreath at this date, cf. *Heads*, 111.]

<sup>a</sup>*gramaticus.*

MS.: Cartulary, f.114v.


**289.** Memorandum of the settlement of a dispute which lasted for a long time about the chapel of Tresmeer (*Treasmur*) between the monks of St Sergius at Tywardreath and the canons of St Stephen of Launceston. The monks of Tywardreath were to have a moiety of the sheaf tithes of the vills of Tresmeer (*Trewasmur*) and Trew (*Treuyf*) and Treglum and 'de La Dune' and of the houses of Roger Cola. The canons of St Stephens were to have the other moiety of the sheaf tithes of these vills and all obventions and oblations of the said chapel and they were to pay 2s. each year to the prior of Tywardreath. Sealing clause (seals of St Sergius and St Andrew of Tywardreath and of St Stephen of Launceston.) This transaction was made in the year 1185 in the presence of the lord Auger, abbot of St Sergius. Witd. Thomas the canon; John son of Bernard, Almer of St David, Roger the chaplain; Geoffrey, prior of St Sergius; Robert Armarius, Ralph son of the chancellor; Oliver de Brueria. The 2s. were to be paid to the prior of Tywardreath yearly at Michaelmas. Dated 1185.

MS.: Cartulary, ff.114v.–115r.


**290.** Plea between the prior of Launceston and Roger de Nonaunt of the lord of Berne by Exeter.

The assize came to recognise if Roger de Nonant and his wife Isabella and Ralph, son of William de la Berne, had disseised the prior of Launceston of his free tenement in Halford. The prior (by Ralph de Oggeworthy, his attorney) complained that they disseised him of one messuage and one ferling of land.

The jury on oath said the said Roger and the others unjustly disseised the prior of the said tenement. The prior said he and his predecessors had the tenement from time immemorial.

It was judged that the prior should recover seisin and damages were assessed at 5 marks. And the said Roger and the others for their disseisin were in mercy. Not dated. [*c.*1314–15?, see *Devon FF*, ii, nos. 1017, 1018 (Roger and Isabella de Nonant).]

MS.: Cartulary, f.115r.–f.115v.

**291.** Chirograph between the monks of Tavistock (*Tavestoch*) and the canons of Launceston about the chapels of St Martin of Werrington (*Woryngton*) and St Giles (in the Heath).

There had been a long dispute between the abbey of Tavistock and the priory of Launceston about the chapels of St Martin and St Giles which were founded on the land of the abbey, but with a part of both benefices belonging to the priory. The dispute was settled by Henry, bishop of Exeter. The priory of Launceston was to have the 2 chapels in the name of the abbey of Tavistock and to pay yearly to the abbey 50s., saving the tithes of the produce of the abbey's demesne throughout the manor of Werrington (*Wlrinton*). The canons were to have the remaining tithes, but nothing of the tithes and obventions belonging to the church of St Paternus. The chaplain of these chapels chosen by the prior and convent of Launceston was to guarantee to the abbot and monks of Tavistock that he would oppress no man of the abbey with undue exactions. Alternate sealing clause for chirograph. Witd. the lord Henry, bishop of Exeter; William de Bokfasta and Baldwin de Herteland, abbots. Not dated. [*c.*1194–9. (Finberg, and last occurrence of William, abbot of Buckfast, *Heads of Religious Houses*, 128).]

MS.: (A) Cartulary, f.116r. (B) 'Russell Cartulary', see H. P. R. Finberg, 'Some Early Tavistock Charters', *EHR* lxii, 373–4, no. L. Finberg gives the full latin text but the variants from the text of the Launceston Cartulary are of no importance, except for *Wolurinton* as a form of Werrington. In the witness list, B inserts the fact (omitted by A) that William of Buckfast and Baldwin of Hartland were abbots.

**292.** Confirmation by H(ubert), archbishop of Canterbury, of the agreement made by Henry, bishop of Exeter, between the monks of Tavistock and the canons of Launceston about the chapels of St Martin and St Giles founded in the territory of the same monks. Archiepiscopal sealing clause. Witd. master Simon de Siwell, treasurer of Lichfield (*Lichesfeld*); Master John de Timen. Not dated. [Cf. no. 291. *c.*1194–13 July 1205, death of Abp. Hubert Walter, *Handbook of British Chronology* (RHS).]

MS.: Cartulary, f.116v.

**293.** Condemnation of the parishioners of Werrington by the official of the lord archdeacon of Cornwall about the construction and repair of the chancel (of St Martin) there.

Acts before the official of the lord archdeacon of Cornwall, visiting the clergy and people of the archdeaconry of Cornwall as commissary general. At the archdeacon's visitation of the chapel of Werrington, a dependency of the priory, more defects were found in the chancel of this chapel and in the matin books. The visitation was held 1 June 1352.

Master John Godman, clerk, proctor for the prior and convent said the repair of these defects by common law and by the constitutions of the lord Peter, a former bishop of Exeter, belonged wholly to the parishioners.

On the contrary it was alleged by Henry Dobill, the attorney of the parishioners, that the repair or construction of the chapel belonged to the prior and canons.

The case was adjourned to Saturday, 9 June in the chapel of Blessed Mary Magdalene of the castle of Launceston. On which day and place the religious men appeared before the official with letters of certification of the dean of Trigg Major, but the parishioners did not appear. After a further adjournment to the following 5 July in the chapel of the same castle, by the kindness of the official, the canons appeared but not the parishioners who were pronounced contumacious and it was judged that they would be compelled to repair the defects on pain of canonical punishment. Sealing clause of the official. Dated at the chapel of Blessed Mary Magdalene in the castle of Launceston, 5 July 1352.

MS.: Cartulary, ff.116v.–117r.

**294.** Sentence of Mr Adam Sparke, official of the peculiar jurisdiction of the bishop of Exeter in Cornwall and of John Lyndewode, clerk, commissaries to the president of the bishop's consistory court, in a cause between the prior and convent, proprietors of the church of St Stephen with the chapel of Werrington as a dependency, and the parishioners of the said chapel, about defects found in the chancel of the chapel of Werrington and service books by the archdeacon of Cornwall on his last visitation, lately argued before the archdeacon's official.

At length William Cotell, Robert Grove, Walter Marschall and the other parishioners of the chapel of Werrington appealed to the bishop's consistory court. They said that the prior and convent drew 20 marks yearly out of the church of Werrington for 60 years and more since the appropriation. The prior and convent had always repaired the chancel until lately when they had indicted the parishioners in the archdeacon's court to their loss of 100s. for five years or more. The parishioners sought freedom from this vexation.

The proctor for the priory said that the chapel of Werrington was not originally a *matrix ecclesia per se* but had been built as a parochial chapel, having distinct parochial limits, though dependent upon the mother church of St Stephen for the favour and convenience of the parishioners, especially in winter time when they could not go to the mother church because of inundations etc. From time immemorial the parishioners of Werrington had been buried in the cemetery adjacent to St Stephen's church and they maintained part of the enclosed cemetery at their own expense as often as there was need. The chapel lay within the deanery of Trigg Major.

The proctor having been heard, the commissaries produced a mandate from the president of the consistory ordering them to deal with a cause brought by William Vela, William Storme, Robert Douneworthy and Robert Dawnt, parishioners of the chapel of St Giles, against the priory. This mandate was dated Exeter, 24 October 1366.

The parties were summoned to appear in the chapel of Blessed Mary Magdalene of the castle of Launceston on the Tuesday before Michaelmas. On 28 September, the tribunal being seated, the parishioners of Werrington appeared by their proctor, Robert Grove, and the prior and convent by their proctor, brother Roger Leye, canon. After due investigation a sentence was given in favour of the prior and convent and costs were assessed at 12 marks. Dated at the chapel of Blessed Mary Magdalene, Launceston, 28 September 1367.

Notarial certificate of William Todeworth(y) of the diocese of Exeter, clerk, follows.

MS.: Cartulary, ff.117r.–119v.

**295.** Indented bond between the prior and convent, possessors of the chapel of the curate of Werrington, by John Honylond, canon, of the one part, and the parishioners of the said chapel of Werrington, by John Cotell, John Boleputte and Richard White, fellow parishioners of the said chapel, of the other, in the presence of the venerable master Edward Daunttesey, archdeacon of Cornwall, in a visitation of the said chapel of 11 September 1405.

A dispute had arisen between the said parties about the provision of books for matins in the chapel. The proctors of both parties compromised and followed the judgement of the archdeacon under a penalty of £40, payable to the archdeacon, and swore their faith by touching the holy gospels and each one entered the bond. The archdeacon promulgated the judgement before the feast of the Translation of Blessed Thomas the Martyr (7 July) in the chapel of Blessed Thomas at Launceston by one week. Sealing clause of the proctors of both parties. Dated at the chapel of St Thomas, 30 June 1406.

MS.: Cartulary, ff.119v.–120r.

**296.** Notice by William Kewa, clerk of the diocese of Exeter, public notary, by a public instrument, that on 27 June 1406 in the chapel of Blessed Thomas the Martyr at Launceston before Edward Dauntesey, archdeacon of Cornwall, that there was a judgement of the dispute between the parishioners of the chapel of Werrington and the proprietors of the chapel, the prior and convent. The dispute was about the finding of

matins books in the chapel of Werrington, and the judgement was that the
onus was on the parishioners to provide these books before the following
Easter. Witd. David Treludek and John Batyn, canons of the priory;
Henry Person, Richard Trelauny; Alan Cutte, notary public. Dated at the
chapel of St Thomas the Martyr, Launceston, 27 June 1406. Notarial
certificate of William Kewa.

MS.: Cartulary, f.120r.–f.120v.

**297.** Agreement between R., prior of Launceston and Richard Cole of
'Tamer'. The prior and convent granted to Richard Cole and his heirs free
faculty forever of celebrating divine service in his chapel of 'Tamer' which
he had built and of having there an honest chaplain at his own cost.
Neither the chapel nor the chaplain was to be any expense of the prior and
convent, and all oblations were to be paid faithfully to the prior and
convent, so that no one could claim his allowance. The chaplain there was
held to be of the jurisdiction and fealty of the prior and convent and to
respect the indemnity of parochial right of the church of Werrington. And
by pretext of the said chapel or service it was not lawful for Richard or his
heirs or their wives to overlook the due and customary suits to the said
church of Werrington in the principal feasts of the year. Alternate sealing
clause for chirograph. Witd. Thomas de St David, Richard son of Ralph,
canons of Launceston; Roger Cole, canon of Exeter; Master Ralph Cole,
Luke de Pudreham and Richard Cole, clerks. Not dated. [?*c.*1228–38.
Richard Cole(s) occurs in *Devon FF.* i, no. 224 on 22 July 1228 and in 1238
in *Cornwall FF.* i, nos 65 and 69.]

MS.: Cartulary, f.121r.

**298.** Settlement of a long controversy between Richard, prior of
Launceston, and the convent of the one part and William de la Torre,
rector of the church of Sydenham Damarel (*Sideham*) of the other about
the sheaf tithes of the demesne of Panson (*Paneston* or *Passem Minor*) and of
the villeinage of Newton (*Niwetone*). An amicable settlement was made at
length by Walter, bishop of Exeter. The priory was to have yearly a
moiety of the sheaf tithes of the demesne of Panson as well as of the
villeinage of Newton. The rector of Sydenham was to have yearly the
other moiety of these tithes. The rector was to have all the small tithes and
oblations and the whole cure of souls in this demesne, as his predecessors
had, and the priory was to have all small tithes and oblations yearly from
the villeinage of Newton. All contradictory right etc. was renounced by
both parties. Chirograph sealed by Walter, bishop of Exeter, and the lord
John de Albamar', patron of the church; the prior and convent of
Launceston, and William, rector of the church of Sydenham. Dated
Launceston, 7 July 1261.

MS.: Cartulary, f.121r.–f.121v.

**299.** Confirmation by William, bishop of Exeter, of the settlement of a dispute between the prior and convent of Launceston of the one part, and W., rector, and Roger, vicar of Sydenham Damarel, of the other, about the sheaf tithes of Panson (*Paneston Passemer*) in demesne as well as in villeinage. The tithes were to be taken yearly in moieties by both parties. The rectors of Sydenham were to pay the prior and convent yearly at Michaelmas 12d. for the good of peace. Sealing clause of Bishop William. Exeter, Wednesday, 8 October 1236.

MS.: Cartulary, ff.121v.–122r.

**300.** [a]Mandate by the official of the bishop of Exeter to the official of the lord archdeacon of Cornwall to warn Robert de Radeford, Stephen de Wormyslond and Walter Cary and the parishioners of the prior and convent of Launceston to implement speedily the agreement between the prior and convent and the said parishioners about the tithe of hay and taking of a mortuary fee (at St Giles in the Heath). If they disregarded this they should be cited to appear before the official or his commissary in the conventual church of St Petroc of Bodmin on Friday after Michaelmas. Dated Exeter, Friday, 26 July 1202.

[a]Heading: *De mortuario sancti Egidij.*

MS.: Cartulary, f.122r.

**301.** The process of the chapel of St Giles about the repair of the chancel and finding matin books there, carried out before the official of the lord archdeacon of Cornwall. The archdeacon at his late visitation had found defects in the chapel of St Giles appropriated to the priory.

On 1 June 1352 the priory by its proctor, Master John Godman, clerk, claimed that according to the constitutions of Bishop Peter of Exeter the parishioners of St Giles were wholly responsible for the upkeep of the chancel.

For the parishioners it was urged by their proctor, John Bate, that the prior and convent were responsible for the same.

The case was adjourned until Saturday, 9 June, in the chapel of Blessed Mary Magdalene of Launceston Castle, when the prior and convent came with letters of certification of the dean of Trigg Major, but the parishioners did not appear. A further adjournment was made to 5 July in the same chapel but again the parishioners did not appear and they were declared contumacious and ordered to repair their chancel immediately under pain of canonical censure. Dated at the chapel of the Blessed Mary Magdalene, Launceston, 5 July 1352. (Cf. no. 293.)

MS.: Cartulary, f.122r.–f.122v.

**302.** Writ of King Richard II to Richard Kendale, escheator in

Cornwall, to hold an inquest *ad quod damnum* concerning the acquisition from Robert Carnek and Stephen Byroydron of Launceston of 10 messuages and one ferling of land in Launceston and Newport by the prior and convent of Launceston in part satisfaction of £20 worth of lands etc. which King Edward, the king's grandfather, permitted them to acquire in spite of the statute of mortmain. Dated Westminster, 7 November, 1377.

MS.: Cartulary, f.123r.–f.123v.

**303.** Gift, grant and confirmation by Thomas Smyth of Newport (*Neuport*) to John Trethewy, chaplain, of all his messuages, land and tenements in the vills of Launceston and Newport and the rents and services of William Sutton and Alice, his wife, and the reversions of the lands they held from him. Warranty and sealing clauses. Witd. William Mustard, Roger Kelyowe, William Snellard. Dated Launceston, Monday, 26 November 1380.

MS.: Cartulary, f.123v.

**304.** Quitclaim by Thomas Smyth to John Trethewy, chaplain, of his right in the properties of no. 303 which he had given to the said John and enfeoffed him. Sealing clause. Witd. William Mustard, Roger Kelyowe, William Snellard. Dated Newport, Monday, 26 November 1380.

MS.: Cartulary, ff.123v.–124r.

**305.** Lease by John, prior of Launceston, and the convent to John Gune of a tenement and garden adjoining in the vill of St Stephen of Launceston, together with 2 closes, formerly held at will by Nicholas and John Gune. For the term of 40 years and for the rent of 27s. 2d. at Easter, the Nativity of St John the Baptist and Christmas by equal payments. The lessee was to do two suits yearly and two days work in the autumn yearly at Newhouse (*Neuhous*). John Gune was to keep the tenement in repair at his own cost and to leave it in a reasonable state. The prior and convent could re-enter the tenement after arrears of one month.

Joan, the mother of John Gune, was to have a moiety of the tenement and garden and great close (which she and Nicholas had formerly held for twenty years) as long as she lived and stayed there, with no assignment to anyone. She was to pay a moiety of the rent of 20s. (*sic*) to the priory and a moiety of one day's work in the autumn and to maintain a moiety of the tenement, garden and park, if she lived so long. Warranty to John and Joan. Alternate sealing clause (chirograph). Witd. William Trelauny, William Miloton, Stephen Corke. Dated at the chapter house of the priory, Saturday, 16 February 1426.

MS.: Cartulary, f.124r.–f.124v.

**306.** Quitclaim by John Cook of Launceston (alias John Byforth) to William, prior of Launceston, and the convent of the messuages, lands and tenements which formerly belonged to Peter Bodmam in the vills of Launceston, Newport and Wilhous within the manor of Launceston Land. Sealing clause. Witd. Thomas Bank, clerk, Thomas Oterham, Thomas Wokysbrugge. Dated Launceston, Saturday, 24 March 1436.

MS.: Cartulary, ff.124v.–125r.

**307.** Grant by Richard Wales[a] of Launceston and Joan, his wife, of their estate to John Trethewy, John Lavyngton, chaplain, and William Frengy, clerk, in messuages, lands and tenements in the vill of Launceston and of the land called 'Peyglond' ['b] with the reversion of the dowry of these properties held by Richard and Joan for the term of Joan's life (except for a tenement with a garden adjoining in Launceston between the tenement of Nicholas Webba and the tenement of John Honger) which they had of the grant of Sarra Thomas. To have and to hold as fully as the charter between Richard and Joan and Sarra indicated. Sealing clause of parties. Witd. John Bynneley, William Goderygh, Thomas Raynfry. Dated Launceston, 11 June 1394.

[a]Title: *Walleys.* [b]Title: *Peggelond apud Sanctum Stephanum.*

MS.: Cartulary, f.125r. For a similar charter, see no. 254.

**308.** Grant and confirmation by Stephen Pownstok[a] to Ralph, his son, for his homage and service the land of Bamham (*Bodmam*) as he bought it. To hold of Stephen and his heirs by hereditary right and rent for the land yearly at Michaelmas 12d. and 2d. which Stephen rendered yearly to the reeve of the castle of Dunheved. Ralph gave Stephen in recognition 10 marks of silver. Witd. Alan, son of Richard; Renbald de Sancto Neoto; Richard, son of Stephen; Richard de Trelosk. Not dated. [Stephen de Pounstock occurs in the Cornish eyre of 1201 as also does Renbald de St Neot. Richard de Trelosk (I) occurs *c.*1180–95, see no. 96.]

[a]Title: *Powntystok.*

MS.: Cartulary, f.125v.

**309.** Grant and confirmation by William, son of Stephen de Pondestok to Ralph, his brother, for the service of their kinship, of the land of Bamham which Stephen, his father, gave to the same Ralph for his homage and service by hereditary right and by a charter. William had taken his homage and confirmed his father's charter. Ralph gave for recognition to William 2 marks of silver and the saddle of a warhorse. Warranty to Ralph. William granted the service of the land with homage and relief, at the petition of and with the assent of Ralph, to the almoner of the church of St Stephen of Launceston, and confirmed it by his charter for the salvation of his soul and the souls of his ancestors and successors. Witd. Gervase de Horniacote, Rembald de St Neoto, Alan son of Richard; Richard de Trelosk. Not dated. [?*c*.1201–1207. In the latter year Gervase de Hornacott died, Maclean, *Trigg Minor*, iii, 158.]

MS.: Cartulary, ff.125v.–126r.

**310.** Another version of no. 309. Witd. Richard, prior of Launceston, Jordan de Trecarell, William Wise, Hamelin and Henry de Trevella, Richard Probus.[a] Not dated. [The dating limits are *c*.1220–44 (William Wise).]

[a]right margin: *m.$^d$ q.$^d$ placit(a) de Bodmam scribuntur in xviij fo. pre'.*

MS.: Cartulary, f.126r.

**311.** Grant and confirmation by William de Pundestok, at the wish and petition of Ralph de Bodmam, his brother, and for the salvation of his soul and the souls of all his ancestors and successors, to the almoner of the church of St Stephen of Launceston of the service Ralph and his heirs should do yearly to the almoner for the land of Bamham, i.e. 12d. yearly at Michaelmas for all service, to be distributed for the uses of the poor and together with homage and relief. The almoner gave to William 15s. in recognition. Witd. Jordan de Trevagga, William Wise, Hamelin de Trevell' and Henry. Not dated. [*c*.1220–44.]

MS.: Cartulary, f.126r.–f.126v.

**312.** Inquisition taken before the king's escheator at the priory 7 May 1314 of the lands and tenements which Robert de Bodmam held in chief of the king on the day of his death and their services and values and the next heir and the heir's age. By the oaths of William Vacy, John de Sotton, Richard Conceyll, Thomas de Witeston, Philip de Filadone, Richard Beaumond, John Walsa, Henry Snellard, Richard de Tregarya, William Stanwen, Geoffrey David and Henry Castelwike. They stated on oath that the said Robert de Bodmam held no lands of the king in chief on the day he died, but they said that he held the hamlet of Bamham (*Bodmam*) of the prior and convent of Launceston by military service and 12d. rent yearly at Michaelmas. And there was a certain chief messuage with a small garden adjoining which were worth yearly 2 shillings. And there were there 20 acres of arable land worth yearly 3s. 4d. (2d. per acre). And there were three acres of meadow (4d. per acre) worth 12d. yearly. Peter, the son of Robert, was the next heir and was 21 years of age. Sealing clause (jurors' seals), including the seal of the sub-escheator, Martin de Fysshacre. Dated at Launceston priory, 7 May 1314.

MS.: Cartulary, f.126v.

**313.** Notice by Martin de Fisshacre, royal sub-escheator in Devon and Cornwall, of his receipt of the king's writ to deliver to the prior of Launceston the lands and tenements which were formerly Robert de Bodmam's and held by military service of the prior, as appeared by the inquisition (no. 312, above) returned into chancery. He would deliver the lands and tenements to the said prior as the chief lord. Sealing clause of sub-escheator. Dated Exeter, 3 September 1314.

MS.: Cartulary, f.127r.

**314.** Notice by Peter, son and heir of Robert de Bodmam that he had made homage and fealty to the lord Roger de Horton, prior of Launceston, for all his land of Bamham (*Bodmam*) and other lands Peter held of the prior in the manor of Launceston Land. Sealing clause. Witd. Benedict de Bastard, Thomas le Chaunceler, John de Wolfwolk, Richard Beaumond, Walter de Burdon, Henry Rem, William Stoterych. Dated Launceston, Friday, 27 September 1314.

MS.: Cartulary, f.127r.

**315.** Grant and confirmation by John Whitefeld to Andrew Anstis, William vicar of Linkinhorne (*Lankynhorn*) and Robert Aysshe, chaplain, of 2d. of yearly rent which he used to receive yearly at Michaelmas for a certain tenement within the borough of Newport at St Stephen, between the tenement of the heirs of Margaret Tolle and the tenement which Thomas Person had of John Whitefeld's gift and feoffment, which tenement Walter (also called Mason) had of John's gift and feoffment. Andrew and Robert were granted the reversion of the tenement. Warranty and sealing clauses. Witd. John Roos, Stephen Cork, John Broun.[a] Dated Saturday, 27 November 1423.

[a]left margin: *deficit hic relaxacio Jo. Mason de eodem tenemento.*

MS.: Cartulary, f.127v.

**316.** Grant and confirmation by Stephen, prior of Launceston, and the convent to William Mustard of a croft and garden adjoining at Launceston between the land of William Helier and the land of Felicia Hendra. To William and his right heirs from the prior and convent and their successors forever. For a yearly rent to the prior and convent of a penny at Michaelmas for all services. Warranty clause. Alternate sealing clause of both parties for the chirograph. Witd. Benedict Dounhevd, then free bailiff of Launceston Land; Richard Skaynok, Stephen Tredidan.[a] Dated Launceston, Friday, 15 January 1389.

[a]On f.128r. heading in right margin, De villa Sancti Stephani et *Neuport.*

MS.: Cartulary, f.127v.–f.128r.

**317.**  Grant and confirmation by Stephen Dogh, vicar of Lewannick (*Lawanek*) to Henry Frend, chaplain, of his tenement with croft and garden adjoining in the vill of Newport between the tenement of John Graunt and the tenement of John Gile. Warranty and sealing clauses. Witd. Laurence Nosger, Gervase of Stratton, Reginald Kyvener. Dated Lewannick, Thursday, 15 January 1360.

MS.: Cartulary, f.128r.


**318.**  Grant and confirmation by Joan, wife of Henry Cosyn, to John Scacherd and Roger Dorset, chaplains, of her messuages, lands and tenements in the vills of Newport, Launceston, 'Wilhous' and Dutson, together with the rents and services of John Visour for messuages held of her in the said vill and the rents and services of John Trisez for the messuages he held of her in the said vill. John and Roger to hold with homage and fealty. Sealing clause. Witd. William Robyn, then bailiff of Launceston Land; John Skaynek, William Mustard. Dated Launceston, Saturday, 1 February 1365.

MS.: Cartulary, f.128v.


**319.**  Grant and confirmation by John Scachard, parson of the church of Marhamchurch to Robert Carnok and Roger Combrugge, chaplains, and Stephen Roydron of messuages, land and tenements in the vills of Newport, Launceston, 'Wilhous' and Dutson with the rents and services of Adam Cola, John Viser and John Trytez, for all the messuages they held of John Scachard in the same vill of Newport which John had of the gift and feoffment of John Cosyn. Warranty and sealing clauses. Witd. John Stoterigg, William Snellard, Thomas Smyth. Dated Launceston, Monday, 5 October 1377.

MS.: Cartulary, ff.128v.–129r.


**320.**  Letter of attorney by John Scachard, parson of the church of Marhamchurch, appointing John de Godecote to give full and peaceful seisin to Robert Carnok, Roger Combrugge, chaplains, and Stephen Roydron of the lands, rents and services of no. 319. Sealing clause. Dated Launceston, Monday, 5 October 1377.

MS.: Cartulary, f.129r.


**321.**  Quitclaim by Dudemannus, clerk, to the church and canons of St Stephen of Launceston in pure and perpetual alms of a shop and garden which his uncle, Gilbert Dudemannus, left him in the vill of Launceston.

Sealing clause. Witd. John Mannyng, William de Doneham, Henry de Trevella. Not dated. [The attestations suggest dating limits of *c*.1221–44.]

MS.: Cartulary, f.129v.

**322.** Quitclaim[a] by Ralph Dudeman of his right in a certain messuage in the new street of Launceston which was between the house of William de Bracino and the house of John Stukeman. This messuage was formerly of his uncle Gilbert, which he formerly held of the house of St Stephen and which he recovered from Walter Cresa before the justiciar. To the church of St Stephen of Launceston, to hold in pure and perpetual alms. Sealing clause. Witd. Richard de Trevylla, Wandri de Boyton, Hamondus Bodier. Not dated. [Approximately the same dating limits as no. 321, *c*.1221–44.]

[a]Title: *Alia quieta clamancia Radulphi Dudeman ecclesie sancti Stephani Lanceston de uno messuagio in Neuport.*

MS.: Cartulary, f.129v.

**323.** Quitclaim by Walter Crese, son of Gilbert Dudeman, to the priory for alms of his right in the whole tenement he had in the new street of Launceston[a] with houses and gardens, situated between the house of William de Bracino and the house of John Stukeman. For this quitclaim the priory gave him 4 marks of silver. Witd. Andrew de Canell', John Wise, Ralph Dudeman. Not dated. [Only wide dating limits, *c*.1221–44, are supported by the attestations.]

[a]The heading to no. 323 again shows that Newport was the 'new street' of Launceston.

MS.: Cartulary, f.130r.

**324.** Grant by Ralph, son of Dudeman, to his kinsman Walter, son of Gilbert, for his homage and service, of the house he held of the prior of Launceston in the new vill of the manor of Launceston, which house his uncle, Gilbert, held. Walter was to pay Ralph 15d. yearly at Easter for all services. Sealing clause. Witd. Robert Rem, Jollinus de Landren, Jordan Ricraron, Richard Priez de Trenalt. Not dated. [*c*.1232–44, see nos. 61 and 274, Jordan de Ridcaron.]

MS.: Cartulary, f.130r.

**325.** Grant and confirmation by David Tresmargh to John Trethewy, chaplain and Walter Crike of his tenement in Newport which lay between the tenements of Thomas Dyron and of John Hendra. Warranty and sealing clauses. Witd. William Goderigg, Thomas Landyare, Thomas

Smyth, Benedict Donnyend, John Godecote. Dated Launceston, Wednesday, 16 January 1387.

MS.: Cartulary, ff.130r.–130v.

**326.** Quitclaim by David Tresmargh of the tenement of no. 325. Sealing clause. Witd. William Godryg, John Landyare, Benedict Donnyend. Dated Launceston, Sunday, 27 January 1387.

MS.: Cartulary, f.130v.

**327.** Quitclaim by John Whitefeld to Stephen, prior of Launceston, and the convent of his right in a messuage and garden in Launceston in the street called Newport, between the tenement of Nicholas Godek to the north and the tenement formerly of Thomas Dyron to the south. Warranty and sealing clauses. Witd. Nicholas Tregodek, senior; William Treforsburgh, Ralph Treforsburgh, Stephen Tredidan, Roger Menwynnek. Launceston, Sunday, 1 April 1403.

MS.: Cartulary, ff.130v.–131r.

**328.** Grant and confirmation by Prior William and the convent to Thomas Spugernell, tailor, and Joan his wife and their lawful heirs of their tenement in Newport with the bakehouse, oven and garden adjoining, situated between the tenement of the heirs of Thomas Diron, deceased, on the south and the close or garden of Margaret Tregodek on the north. They were to pay the prior and convent in the first forty years 7s. yearly at the Nativity of St John the Baptist, Michaelmas, Christmas and Easter by equal portions. The relief payable on the deaths of Thomas and his heirs was 6s. sterling. Thomas and Joan and their heirs were to perform two suits of court at the prior's court of his borough of Newport and also at his court of the manor of Launceston Land like other tenants. They were to perform one suit of reaping in autumn. At the end of fifty years they were to pay a rent of 10s., relief as before and also suits of court and a day's work in the autumn. Thomas and Joan and their heirs were to repair and maintain the tenement with the bakehouse and oven at their own costs, the prior and convent providing timber when necessary. After arrears of rent of one quarter or non-repair (provided they were given notice by the steward of the priory in the presence of two worthy witnesses), or if they alienated their estate, or went to live outside the manor of Launceston Land without licence, then the prior and convent could enter the tenement and take it into their possession. Thomas recognised the right of the prior and convent to distrain his chattels and goods to the value of twice the rent for non-repair. Thomas and Joan could grant anyone leave to reside in the tenement. Warranty and alternate sealing clauses. Witd. David Treludek, Thomas Bank, clerk; William Loman. Dated at the chapter house of Launceston priory, 3 March 1441.

MS.: Cartulary, ff.131r.–132r. (The rest of f.132r. is blank.)

**329.** Copy of a writ of King Richard II to the prior and convent of Launceston asking them to admit John Elys, for his service to the lord Edward, king of England, King Richard's grandfather, and to give him sustenance at the priory as Ralph Peek formerly had and to make return of this to the king by letters patent. Witd.: King Richard. Dated Westminster, 24 January 1392.

MS.: Cartulary, f.132v.

**330.** Plea in the King's Bench, Hilary term 1392 (roll 38).

Cornwall. The prior of Launceston was attached to reply to the lord king and John Elys as to why he had not made a return to the king's writ to grant John Elys a corrody at the priory.
John Elys by T. Crowe, his attorney for the lord king and for himself, complained that the king's writ delivered at Launceston 26 July 1387 asked for John Elys to have a corrody at the priory like the late Ralph Peek's, viz. a room, a stable for 2 horses within the priory, 4 loaves of bread daily for life, 2 gallons of the best beer and wine on Sundays and feast days as the other canons of the priory received, 2 dishes of cooked food (on days when flesh could be eaten), and 2 dishes of fish (when fish was eaten), also 2 pittances of cooked food and fish. Also every year 4 cartloads of fuel and 40 pounds of candles for his room and 6 cartloads of hay, 3 cartloads of straw, 13 quarters of oats, and lodging for 2 greyhounds and reasonable food for them. And every year a robe of hair for esquires of the same priory or 20s. in lieu and 2 marks for other clothing and necessities. Another writ was sent to the prior in the first week of Lent 1392 and a third writ on Monday in the third week of Lent (1392). The prior had made no returns to these writs to the loss of £100.
The prior appeared by his attorney, Stephen de Fall, and defended his contempt. He denied that there had been more than one writ. And he placed himself on the country and John Elys likewise. The prior further said that Ralph Peek had never been admitted to a corrody within the priory. John (Elys) asked for inquiry to be made *per patriam*. The case was adjourned to the quindene of Easter. Hilary term 1393.

MS.: Cartulary, ff.132v.–133v. (f.134r. is blank.)

**331.** Grant by Richard de Raddona for the salvation of his soul and the souls of his ancestors (as far as pertained to him as the lord of the estate) gave to the priory the church of St Gennys (*Genesius*) with chapels and lands, namely the lands of Heggam, Godric and John, priests. He had taken these lands away from St Gennys, but recognizing his fault and seeking the grace of God, he restored them to the church and gave them to the priory in perpetual alms, free from all service except royal service. Witd. Philip, Thomas, Walter, canons; Stephen de Raddona, knight; William son of Gilbert; Nicholas, baker[a]; Robert, nephew of Richard. Not dated. [*c.*1154–65, see *Red Book of the Exchequer* i, 258; ii, 652, 677 and dating note to no. 13.]

ªPistor. Before the heading of this charter appear the words, *Incipit regestrum de ecclesia matrice sancti Genesij cum capellis Sancte Julitte et Sancti Gregorij de Hill ac eciam de Treworgy cum suis pertinencijs.*

MS.: Cartulary, f.135r.

**332.** Grant and confirmation by Baldwin de Raddona for the salvation of his soul and the souls of his ancestors of the church of St Gennys and the other lands of Eggam, Godric and John, priests, to the priory, just as his father had granted by his charter. (no. 331). The grant was in free alms and free from all service except royal service. Witd. William Dacus, sheriff of Cornwall; William brother of the earl; Stephen de Raddona, Richard de Tregrilla, Anger de Lanwitta, Richard. Not dated. [?*c.*1180–1212 (William Dacus occurs in 1212, *Book of Fees* i, 79). See also note to no. 435.]

MS.: Cartulary, f.135r.–f.135v.

**333.** Grant and confirmation by Baldwin, son of Baldwin de Raddona, of the lands of nos. 331–2 free from all service except royal service which was applicable to the fourth part of a knight's fee. And furthermore as much as fell on half an acre where 13 acres made a knight's fee. The brethren of the priory could serve the church of St Gennys at their will by their canons or by a secular chaplain. The canons were to have the tithes and oblations of the church. Sealing clause. Witd. Hugh, prior of Bodmin; Richard son of Gilbert; Hervey,ª his brother; Roger son of Robert. Not dated. [*c.*1242–4 (Baldwin de Raddon (II) *Book of Fees* ii, 761, 775, 793; *Devon FF. i,* nos. 382, 387).]

ªHervic'.

MS.: Cartulary, f.135v.

**334.** Letter from Richard de Raddona to Bartholomew, bishop of Exeter, asking him to confirm Richard's charter to the priory granting the church of St Gennys. Not dated. [*c.*1161–5 (Richard de Raddon occurs only to 1165, see no. 13).]

MS.: Cartulary. ff.135v.–136r.

**335.** Confirmation by Bartholomew, bishop of Exeter, of the grant of the church of St Gennys with its chapels of St Juliot (*Julitta*) and of Crackington (*Cracumton*). Sealing clause of the bishop, saving episcopal rights. Witd. Master Robert, archdeacon of Totnes, Roger, archdeacon of Barnstaple, Master Walter, archdeacon of Cornwall; Peter Picot. Not dated. [*c.*1180–15 December 1184. The archdeacons who witness provide the dating limits, see Morey, 127; the date of the death of Bishop Bartholomew sets the terminus, see Morey, 43.]

MS.: Cartulary, f.136r.

**336.** Agreement between the prior and convent and the vicar of St Gennys.

Whereas there had been recent disputes and discord between the prior and convent of Launceston, rectors of the church of St Gennys and the chapel of St Juliot of the one part, and Master William de Middelwoda, perpetual vicar of the church of St Gennys of the other, about the repair of the chancel of the said church, and also about the possession and taking of a moiety of the mortuary from the parish of the same chapel for each deceased person and 2d. for the burial of parishioners which the said vicar and his predecessors took by ancient custom. At length both parties submitted themselves to the judgement of Thomas de Okham, rector of the church of 'Wike', and of John, perpetual vicar of the church of Altarnun (*Alternon*). They ordered that the prior and convent take two parts and the said vicar a third part of the burden of the repair of the said chancel, and that the prior and convent should give the vicar a moiety of the said mortuary and 2d. in the name of an oblation for the burial of every parishioner of the said chapel. The vicar should take the moiety of the mortuary and the 2d. for an oblation without any contradiction. The oblation money payable to the vicar before the time of the settlement should be taken from the vicar and used by the prior and convent in the repair of the chancel. Alternate sealing clause (chirograph): seal of the priory for the vicar's part and seal of the official of the archdeacon of Cornwall for the priory's part.[a] Dated Launceston, Saturday, 26 January 1320.

[a]Title, *Composicio inter nos et vicarium sancti Genesij de reparacione tercie partis cancelli ibidem sub sigillo archidiaconi Cornub(ie).*

MS.: Cartulary, f.136v.

**337.** Public instrument whereby it appeared that in 1380[a] in the fourth indiction and in the third year of Pope Urban VI on 9 February in the hall of the priory (in the presence of a notary) Sir Robert Moka, perpetual vicar of the parish church of St Gennys, which was appropriated to the priory saving the vicar's portion in the same, made a final concord with the prior and convent to end a long controversy about the repair of the chancel of the church of St Gennys. The vicar acknowledged that he and his predecessors had been bound to bear a third of the burden. In recompense for his past neglect he handed to the prior a portable breviary.[b] The breviary was to remain in the church of St Gennys for the divine offices in the name of the prior and convent for ever. Robert was to have the book as long as he remained vicar. He also promised to give one noble for his past neglect and promised to support his share of the burden for the future. Witd. Thomas Bevyll, rector of Poundstock; Richard de Penlen, rector of Jacobstow; Robert Kernek and Thomas Bray, chaplains. (Followed by certificate of John Boscofelek, notary public.) Dated Launceston priory, 9 February 1381.

[a] new style 1381. [b] *portiforium.*

MS.: Cartulary, ff.136v.–137r.

**338.** Recognition by Baldwin de Raddona for himself and his heirs forever that the lands in the parish of St Gennys, which the prior of Launceston claimed against him in court of the lord king before the justices itinerant at Launceston by writ of *novel disseisin*, were the right of the prior and convent. That is to say, all the land called 'Stummecat' as far as the stream below it and all the land called 'Candur', saving to him and his heirs the weir of his mill of St Gennys and also saving to him and his heirs the half acre of land which lay by the perch under the perch as far as the water.[a] Furthermore Baldwin granted to the priory for himself and his heirs to the prior and his successors the land which Robert Tutford held to the east of the way to Crackington as far as the stream which flowed to Tremayna as far as the source of the well, and just as the great street went as far as his meadow of St Gennys and thence just as the stalls go for the length of the meadow.[b] He also granted to the prior all the land held from the farmers of the priory under the coast of Pencannow (*Penkener*) towards the south, saving to himself and his heirs for the said prior and his successors and heirs of St Gennys common pasture through all his land of St Gennys for all manner of cattle, driven and redriven without any impediment by himself or his heirs. On behalf of the prior it was granted to Baldwin and his men that they might have common pasture throughout his land of St Gennys without any conditions. Sealing clause of Baldwin. Witd. William de Ralege, Henry de Tracy, Acla, son of William; William de Insula. Not dated. [The attestations of William de Raleghe and William de Insula indicate approximate dating limits of *c.*1228–44; in this case, Baldwin de Raddona and Henry de Tracy were both third of their name (Watkin, vol ii, 1117.).]

[a] *qui iacet per perticam subtus perticam que se extendit usque ad aquam.* [b] *et inde sicut seudos pretenditur in longum prati.*

MS.: Cartulary, f.137r.–f.137v.

**339.** Gift and grant by Baldwin de Raddone to the prior and convent and their men of a way to the sea to take sand over his land of St Gennys. When they could not reach the sea, they were to take the sand from Baldwin's land as others did without let or hindrance of Baldwin or his heirs. For the annual rent of 1d. at Michaelmas for all service etc. For this grant the prior and convent gave Baldwin 3s. Sealing clause. Witd. Ralph Trewisia, W. Duneham, R. Rem. Not dated. [*c.*1220–1244 are the limits supported by the two final attestations, so this is a charter of Baldwin (II) de Raddon.]

MS.: Cartulary, f.137v.

**340.**  Quitclaim by Simon Gynes to Prior Stephen and the convent and their successors of all and every kind of actions and demands which he had in a certain corrody which he had had of the prior and convent. Sealing clause. Witd. Henry Yvelcombe, knight; John Wevyle, Thomas Polsagh, Robert Dens, Robert Poddyng, Benedict Dounyend, then bailiff of Launceston Land. Seal of the mayor and commonalty of the borough of Dunheved used as the donor's seal was not known. Dated Launceston, Monday, 8 March 1389.

MS.: Cartulary, f.138r.

**341.**  Grant by the prior and convent to Simon Gynes and his heirs forever of all their land in the vill of St Gennys (*Genys*), i.e. a fourth part of the vill as it was anciently bounded. Simon was to pay 14s. sterling at Easter and Michaelmas by equal portions. If the rent was in arrears at these terms the prior and his successors could distrain. If the rent was in arrears for one year and there was not sufficient for distraint, the prior or his servants could re-enter the land and take possession of it. Always saving to the prior and his successors 2s. worth of rent issuing from 'Tyrellyslond' in St Gennys (*St Gynes*) held by military service from the prior. Alternate sealing clause; Simon used the seal of the mayor and commonalty of the borough of Dunheved. Witd. John Bevyle, Robert Puddyng, Richard Kendale, William Trelouny, John Godecote, Benedict Dounyend, Stephen Martyn. Dated Launceston, Tuesday, 9 March 1389.

MS.: Cartulary, f.138r.–f.138v.

**342.**  Quitclaim by R(oger) de St Neoto, lord of Hennet (*Hethnand*), of his right in the advowson of the chapel of St Juliot, which rightly belonged to the church of St Gennys, to the priory for his soul and the souls of his mother and father and ancestors and the souls of his wife and children. The canons were to have this chapel with the half acre of land which his father had given to the chapel in free alms forever. He made this grant *quantum dominus fundi potest concedere*. Sealing clause. Witd. G., archdeacon of Cornwall; A. of St David, dean; R. de Lesniewth, and G., chaplains. Not dated. [Possibly G. stands for Galterus or Walter who was archdeacon of Cornwall *c*.1180–1216, Morey, 127.]

MS.: Cartulary, f.138v.

**343.**  Quitclaim by Stephen, chaplain of St Juliot, in full chapter, to the prior and canons of Launceston of his right in the chapel of St Juliot. Sealing clause. Witd. Master John, official of Cornwall; Ralph de Boyton, dean; Master W. de Treneglos, W. de Wynter. Not dated. [Probably at the time or soon after no. 342.]

MS.: Cartulary, ff.138v.–139r.

**344.** Letter from the dean[a] and chapter of Launceston to W(illiam), bishop of Exeter, about the inquisition made at the bishop's mandate about the true patron of the chapel of St Juliot. The prior and convent of Launceston had possessed the church of St Gennys with its chapels of St Juliot and Crackington for some sixty years. There had been various farmers of the chapel of St Juliot. In the time of Walter, archdeacon of Cornwall, Rembaldus, lord of Hennet (*Hethnand*), presented J. Gervans, clerk, to the chapel of St Juliot. Rembaldus had publicly renounced his right in the chapel of St Juliot in full chapter at Egloskerry. In the course of time Roger de Hethnand had raised the question of this chapel with the prior and convent. At the mandate of the bishop an inquisition was held and Roger renounced his rights to the chapel in full chapter. Many of the men of the priory were at this inquisition and renunciation. Stephen, farmer of the said chapel on account of an annual order, and the prior and convent of Launceston by the authority of their letters directed to the official of Cornwall, resumed their possession of the chapel, though Richard, lord of Hennet, obtruded himself into the chapter and said he was patron and that there ought not to have been an inquisition and he appealed against it. Nevertheless the prior and convent executed the bishop's mandate and attached their witness to it. Not dated. [Between 1224–44, episcopate of William Briwere.]

[a]*sic.*

MS.: Cartulary, f.139r.

**345.** Final concord made in the king's court at Launceston before William of York, Robert de Bello Campo, William de St Edmundo and Jordan Olyver, justices itinerant. Between Richard Cole, querent, and William, prior of Launceston, deforciant, of the advowson of the chapel of St Juliot by the assize of *darrein presentment*. Richard quitclaimed for himself and his heirs to the prior of Launceston and his successors his right in this advowson. For this the prior gave Richard 12 marks of silver. Launceston, Wednesday, 2 June 1238.

MS.: Cartulary, f.139r.–f.139v. Printed: *Cornwall FF. i,* no. 69.

**346.** Notice by William de Briwere, bishop of Exeter, that Richard Cole as patron of the chapel of St Juliot had presented Ralph Cole to it. The prior and convent disputed his possession for a time, but he in the royal court and in the presence of the bishop fully recognised the right of the prior and convent. The bishop relaxed the sequestration he had made on the presentation and judged the right of the advowson of the church to belong to the mother church of St Gennys, just as former bishops had confirmed this to the prior and convent. Dated Exeter, Tuesday, 13 April 1238.

MS.: Cartulary, f.139v.

**347.**   Mandate by John de Middelton, commissary of Thomas, bishop of
Exeter, to the dean of Trigg Major. The bishop had heard on visitation
that William Middelwode, vicar of St Gennys, had obtained from the
prior and convent of Launceston the chapel of St Juliot and the glebe there
for the term of eight years without diocesan licence and against canonical
sanctions. The dean was to compel them to desist. Otherwise he was to
cause the prior and convent and William to appear before the commissary
in the church of Blessed Mary Magdalene Major at Exeter on the Monday
before 28 October that he might adjudge the penalty canonically. The
dean was to certify what he had done in this case by letters patent. He was
to warn the vicar not to disfigure the relics in the sacred vessels at
Launceston priory and to make satisfaction for his transgression,
otherwise the vicar was to appear before the commissary on this charge
also. Dated Exeter, Tuesday, 13 October 1293.

MS.: Cartulary, ff.139v.–140r.

**348.**   Gift in pure and perpetual alms by Robert de Tyntagel of the land
of Treworgie (*Treworgy*) to the church of St Stephen of Launceston.
Sealing clause. Witd. by Thomas de Dunham, Henry Abbate;[a] William
Persona. Not dated. [*c*.1207–24, Robert de Tintagel, see Maclean, *Trigg
Minor* iii, 158.]

[a] *tunc clerico comitatus Cornubie.*

MS.: Cartulary, f.140r.

**349.**   Grant and confirmation by William Duneham, for the salvation of
his soul and the souls of his mother and father and wife and his ancestors
and successors, to the priory and the canons there all his land of
Treworgie, i.e. whatever he had in demesne there in free or villein
tenements and in homages, with all rents and escheats of freemen and
villeins etc. The grant was in pure and perpetual alms with no service
except prayers, saving scutage when it arose, i.e. as much as fell due for
three parts of one knight's fee of the honour of Mortain and saving a pair
of white gloves to be paid to his heirs. Warranty and sealing clauses. Witd.
the lord Gervase de Hornigkote, Baldwin de Raddone, William Wyse,
Henry de Trevelle, Roger de Luttecote. Not dated. [The attestations
support dating limits of *c*.1235–44, in which case Gervase of Hornacott
and Baldwin of Raddon were both second of their name.]

MS.: Cartulary, f.140r.–f.140v.

**350.**   Quitclaim by Paulinus de Lammetyn to Prior Henry and the
convent and their successors all his right in Treworgie with wardships,
reliefs, homages, suits of court and all other services and all the liberties
pertaining to the land contained in charters from the first founders.
Sealing clause. Witd. John Carbonell, Henry Rem, Roger de Bodmam,

Gregory de Duddeston, Laurence de Worlyngton. Dated Friday, 28 February 1277.

MS.: Cartulary, f.140v.

**351.** Grant by William de Ferariis, knight. When Prior Adam of Launceston held of him (as his predecessors did of him and his ancestors) all the lands and tenements of Treworgie and Pencuke (*Penkyvok*) for 20s. for a scutage Mortain[a] when it occurred for all secular services, William granted for himself and his heirs that the said prior and his successors should hold all his lands and tenements in the said vills by rendering to him and his heirs 20s. for a scutage Mortain whenever the scutage occurred. Neither he nor his heirs would in future exact homage, fealty, relief, rent or suit of court etc. William's wish was that neither the prior nor his successors nor any canon, nor anyone of the prior's or canons' households, nor free tenants, nor conventionaries, nor any of their successors would be distrained in any real or personal action at the suit of his heirs or of anyone else to reply in his court of Saltash (*Saltesse*) or of Trematon (*Tremeton*) nor in any courts of him and his heirs. Nor would they be distrained to be in his courts in any inquisition etc. William also granted that in future neither the prior nor his successors nor any of their tenants (conventionary or villein) should be distrained or pay anything when his firstborn son was made a knight or his eldest daughter was married. Warranty and sealing clauses of donor. Witd. William de Botriaux, John de Treiagu, knights; John de Trevaignoun, John Billoun, Serlo Wisa, John Cola. Dated at Launceston priory, Monday, 20 January 1332.

[a]For the small fee Mortain and scutage, see P. L. Hull. *The Caption of Seisin of the Duchy of Cornwall (1337)*, DCRS, 1971, xxii.

MS.: Cartulary, f.141r.

**352.** Quitclaim by William de la Mare and confirmation to the prior[a] and convent of a meadow in a spot called 'Smalecote' adjoining Treworgie in pure and perpetual alms. Warranty and sealing clauses. Witd. the lord Richard Hywis, knight, then steward of Launceston priory; John de Sancto Genes, William de Molendino, John Puddyng, Onger de Eglosk(erry). Not dated. [*c*.1244–78. See no. 222 and the index under 'Hewis'.]

[a]note in left margin: *M.ᵈ quod inquisicio de . . .ficone terre de . . . Treworgy et Halswyll patet . . . te in Landren . . . quod dampnum iacet in pixide de Treworgy.*

MS.: Cartulary, f.141r.–f.141v.

**353.** Letter from Richard de Hewyssh and his companions, collectors of the twentieth for the king in the county of Cornwall, to the sub-collectors for the parish of St Gennys. On the part of the king he ordered them that from the properties and chattels of the prior and convent of Launceston in their manor of Treworgie (taxed by them to the twentieth, which had been granted to be taxed to the tenth granted by the clergy) that they should not cease to collect as they had been ordered. They were to relax the distraint which they were to make on this occasion without delay. Written on Tuesday on the morrow of St Peter *in Cathedra* (22 February). No further date. [*c.*1244–78.]

MS.: Cartulary, f.141v.

**354.** Inquisition made before Ralph Carmynow, sheriff of Cornwall, in his tourn held at Lesnewth, to enquire if Prior Stephen of Launceston should pay *akerselvyr* for his lands of Treworgie, by the oaths of Reginald Botreaux, Richard Smyth de Oterham, Robert Puddyng, Thomas Treglasta, Thomas Carneworthy, William Treuartha, Robert Tregu, John Botreaux, Thomas Crom, John Lordeman, Stephen Moles and Thomas Cradek. They said that Prior Stephen and his predecessors were seised of the said land of Treworgie for one hundred and seventy years and that neither Prior Stephen nor his predecessors had been required to pay *akerselvyr* for the said lands. Sealed by the sheriff and the jurors. Dated Lesnewth, Wednesday, 1 June 1379.

MS.: Cartulary, ff.141v.–142r.

**355.** Certified descent by William de Duneham who gave Treworgie to the priory.

Thomas Duneham and Roger Dunham were brothers of a legitimate marriage. Thomas was senior and had the inheritance of his father. Roger had nothing but perquisites. The same Roger had a son William Duneham, father of William Duneham who certified this descent, by a chambress called Frewara (in the chamber of lady Agnes Hay) to whom he pledged his betrothal after which William was born and afterwards Roger left Frewara and married again a certain Eva. And Roger deserted his son William, born of Frewara, caring nothing for him. And afterwards the said Thomas received William his nephew and provided for him. It happened at that time that the said Thomas in the time of King Henry senior had several bailiffs in Normandy and called his nephew William to him and made him his squire and later in process of time he made him a knight and gave him the land of Treworgie. Later Thomas married his only daughter and heiress, Cecilia, to Walter de Bellestan. And the said Walter gave the said land of Treworgie to the said William and confirmed it as appears in a charter. After the death of the said Walter the said Cecilia in her widowhood approved the confirmation. Afterwards the said William held the land of Treworgie for his life and after him his son William Duneham held the land peacefully until he granted it to the prior and convent.

The said William Duneham who enfeoffed the said prior and convent of Launceston made homage to Henry, son of Henry. Afterwards Henry, son of Henry, made homage to Thomas Cophyn. And Thomas Cophyn made homage to Geoffrey de la Mettyn, lord of Poundstock. Of this material Henry (received) the acquittance of the lords of Poundstock, viz. of Paulinus de Lametton. Not dated. [*c.*1243–61 when Geoffrey de Lametton occurs. See *Cornwall FF.* i, nos. 79 and 201.]

MS.: Cartulary, f.142r.

**356.** Gift and confirmation by William Hak and Alice his wife to the prior and convent of the church of St Stephen of Launceston of one messuage and all their land in 'Halswille' which they had of the gift of Walter Tirell, father of the said Alice, in exchange for part of a house and garden in the street of Newport next to the tenement of Robert de Bodmam to the north which Richard Cade and Henry Mostard formerly held at farm. Warranty and sealing clauses. Witd. Robert de Bodmam, Henry Rem, Richard Stoteryg, Henry Mustard, John de Penweren, Thomas Bastard. Not dated. [*c.*1276–91. Based on attestations of Robert de Bodmam and Henry de Rem. See also no. 357.]

MS.: Cartulary, ff.142v.–143r.

**357.** Agreement between Walter Tirell and Richard, prior of Launceston. Walter promised and granted to enfeoff the prior and convent with one messuage and one ferling of land in 'Halswille', except for a house and garden and one acre of land English which William Hak held there. And the said Walter enfeoffed the prior and convent of the rent and service of William Hak for the said tenements. And he would give to the prior and convent full seisin of the said messuage and service on Monday, 10 September 1291 in exchange for one messuage and a ferling of land which Walter *parvus* held at St Gennys of which the prior and convent would enfeoff the said Walter for a rent of 2s. at Easter and Michaelmas and for doing suit and service which he was accustomed to do for the said land of 'Halswille'. Both parties were to be bound to the other in 100s. sterling within a month. Walter gave his faith to the lord Henry, rector of Lesnewth, to keep this agreement. Alternate sealing clause (chirograph). Witd. John de Sancto Genes, Simon de Bosco, William de Hellewithian, Thomas de la Ley. Dated Thursday, 10 May, 1291.

MS.: Cartulary, ff.142v.–143r.

**358.** Grant and confirmation by Walter Tirell, son of Walter Tirell, to the priory of all his land in 'Halswill' and Treworgie, i.e. one messuage and one ferling of land, except one house and garden and one acre English which William Hak and his wife Alice held. With the rent and service of William and Alice for their house and close and acre of land in exchange for one messuage and a ferling of land in the vill of St Gennys which Walter *parvus* formerly held which Walter Tirell then had of the prior and convent. Warranty and sealing clauses. Witd. Henry Rem, Robert de Bodmam, Robert Puddyng, John de Sancto Genesio, William de Helewynyan. Dated Treworgie, Monday after 8 September (Nativity of the B.V.M.) *anno regni regis 12º*. [a] [Very probably 1318.]

[a]*sic.*

MS.: Cartulary, f.143r.

**359.** Release by Thomas de Canfford, of full age, to Thomas, prior of Launceston, and the convent of all actions he had against them by reason of waste in the land, houses and gardens in the vill of Slade in the custody of the said prior and convent during Thomas de Canfford's minority. Sealing clause. Witd. John Godeman, clerk; John Cresa, Constantine Trevisa, Henry Brackyssh. Dated Launceston, Thursday, 26 February, 1355.

MS.: Cartulary, f.143r.–f.143v.

**360.** Notice by William[a] Fitzwater, knight, that he was firmly bound to Stephen, prior of Launceston, and the convent in 24 marks to be paid at the next feast of St John the Baptist. He bound his executors and heirs to this payment. Sealing clause. Dated Launceston, Thursday, 30 March 1385.

[a]Written William in title to charter, see also no. 361. The MS. here reads Walter.

MS.: Cartulary, f.143v.

**361.** Agreement between Stephen, prior of Launceston and William Fitzwater, knight, reciting no. 360. If William enfeoffed and gave a sure estate in fee simple to John Trethewy, Thomas Skudya, chaplain, and John Godecote of one messuage and the moiety of one acre Cornish in Slade with a sufficient clause of warranty and they held it peacefully, then the bond would be cancelled, if not, the bond was to stand. Alternate sealing clause. Dated Launceston, Thursday, 30 March 1385.

MS.: Cartulary, ff.143v.–144r.

**362.** Grant and confirmation by William Fitzwater, knight, to John Trethewy and Thomas Skudya (chaplain) and John Godecote of one messuage and half an acre Cornish in Slade for ever to hold by due and customary services of the chief lord of that fee. Warranty and sealing clauses. Witd. William Trelouny, Stephen Devyok, John Bylney, William Mostard, John Courtes. Dated Launceston, Thursday, 30 March 1385.

MS.: Cartulary, f.144r.

**363.** Letter of attorney of William Fitzwater, knight, to John Bylneye to place John Trethewy, Thomas Skudya and Godecote[a] in full and peaceful seisin of one messuage and the whole land of Slade as contained in his charter. Sealing clause. Dated Launceston, Thursday, 30 March 1385.

[a]*sic.*

MS.: Cartulary, f.144r.


**364.** Grant by the lord Walter de Morton[a] to William Doneham and his heirs that they might grind without toll at his mill of Trencreek (*Trencruk*) when they wished, after the emptying of the measure for the toll of corn and malt and wheat. For this William Doneham and his heirs granted that Walter de Morton could strengthen a certain weir in his land of Treworgie, opposite the head of his wood at the north, and not elsewhere. Walter also granted that if he wished to alienate his mill that the said William might be preferred before all others in the price. He also granted that every miller of the mill (having touched the most holy things) should protect his grove from all malefactors. If the agreement were broken, the water of the weir would be again taken in hand until restitution was made. Witd. Simon de Brach', Walter de Treverby,[b] then sheriff; William son of William, Everwinus de Tyntagell. Not dated. [c.1225–35 (Simon de Brakel.).]

[a]Title to charter adds *dominus de Trencruk.* [b]*sic.* for Treverbyn.

MS.: Cartulary, f.144v.


**365.** Settlement of a controversy between Richard de la Leye and Richard de Brikevyle, prior of the church of St Stephen by Launceston, and the convent on the overburdening of the pasture which Richard would claim he had in the demesne of Treworgie of the said prior and convent from the feast of Michaelmas to the feast of the Invention of the Holy Cross (3 May) except for corn and closes. An agreement was made with the intervention of friends after an assessment. Richard and his heirs and assigns were to have sufficient pasture in the demesne of Treworgie belonging to the prior and convent together with the pasture of his own land for 2 draught animals, 10 animals and 40 sheep from Michaelmas to the Invention of the Holy Cross (3 May) yearly forever. They would also have pasture anywhere outside the land which Walter Tirell once held there but outside the corn of beasts and the closes in which at no time of the year would the said Richard and his heirs have any share and outside the meadows which after the Purification of the Blessed Virgin Mary in no way should be entered. Of which assessment[a] . . . Not dated. [c.1291–1307/8 when Richard de Brykevylle was prior.]

[a]Heading: *Composicio inter nos et Ricardum de La Leye super communi pastura de La Leye.* The *composicio* is not complete nor the document 366 which follows, which lacks the beginning.

MS.: Cartulary, f.144v–f.145r.

**366.** ª . . . there before Richard Neuton and his colleagues of the lord king then at the said term of St Hilary in the eighteenth year of the reign.

Between William, prior of Launceston, querent, and Stephen Gille of the parish of St Neot, tinner, and Edith, his wife, deforciants, and John Gille of the parish of St Neot, servant, about a plea of seizure of custody. It was adjourned to the quindene of Easter, unless the justices of the lord king were to be at the assizes at Launceston by the form of the statute on Monday, 7 March. Dated incompletely. [1233–4. Since William was prior 1232–8, the incomplete regnal year must indicate 18 Henry III.]

ªIncomplete, see note to no. 365.

MS.: Cartulary, f.145r.

**367.** Grant and confirmation by William de Boterell, for the salvation of his soul and the souls of Joan, his wife, and the souls of his ancestors and successors, to the priory of his land of Crannow (*Cranow*) i.e. 3 acres of land in free and perpetual alms, free from all service except prayers. He had laid the burden of distraint for the said land, whenever it was necessary, on the manor of Crackington. Sealing clause. Witd. Andrew Cancell', Henry de Bodrig(an), Ralph le Sore. Not dated. [*c.*1221–42. William (IV) de Botreaux.]

MS.: Cartulary, f.145r.

**368.** Quitclaim by Paulinus, lord of Lametton, to Richard, prior of Launceston, and the convent and their men of a fee of one knight in Treworgie and Pencuke, free from all aids by the king for making his first-born son a knight or marrying his first-born daughter. For the quitclaim the prior and his men gave him 4 marks of silver. Not dated. [1261–13 January 1273. Prior Richard.]

MS.: Cartulary, f.145r.–f.145v.

**369.** Grant and quitclaim by Geoffrey de Lametyn, lord of Poundstock, to the priory of 4s. yearly (which he used to receive from the canons at Michaelmas) of the land of Pencuke in pure and perpetual alms, free from all secular service. So that he was held to acquit all the land of Pencuke of the royal service called *utibannum* whenever it arose and as much as was due from the fourth part of one knight's fee of his land of Poundstock so that the prior and convent for any defect of Geoffrey or of his heirs would not incur any loss for the said royal service. Warranty and sealing clauses. Witd. John, clerk of Lamford, then steward of Cornwall; Roger de Trelosk, William Wyse, Walter the doctor, Henry de Trevella. Not dated. [*c.*1243–62, see no. 355.]

MS.: Cartulary, f.145v.

**370.** Quitclaim by Lucy, who was the wife of Geoffrey de La Metin, in her widowhood of her right in 4s. of annual rent in Pencuke to the church of St Stephen and the canons, which rent they had from her former husband. Sealing clause. Witd. John de Bello Prato, then steward of Cornwall, Alexander de Hokkeston, Ralph de Arundell, John Carbonell. Not dated. [1268–9, John de Beaupré, cf. no. 73.]

MS.: Cartulary, f.145v.–f.146r.

**371.** Extract from the record of a court held at Lostwithiel when Richard de Polhampton was sheriff of Cornwall. Philip de La Metyn was in mercy for a licence for agreement with Roger, prior of Launceston, in a mesne plea. And the pledge and acquittance of 4 messuages and 2 acres of land in Pencuke which the prior held of the same Philip in pure and perpetual alms for the fourth part of a knight's fee and in scutage and other services as appeared in the charter by Geoffrey the ancestor of Philip which the prior produced. Dated Lostwithiel, Monday, 22 September 1281.

MS.: Cartulary, f.146r.

**372.** Extract from the record of a county court at Lostwithiel. Philip de La Metyn was in mercy for licence of concord with Roger de Horton, prior of Launceston, in a mesne plea. Pledges and acquittance of the fourth part of a knight's fee in Pencuke against the lord William de Ferrarijs and others. Sealing clause of John de Treiagu, sheriff and steward of Cornwall. Dated Lostwithiel, Monday, 13 September 1322.

MS.: Cartulary, f.146r.

**373.** Grant by brother Adam de Knolle, prior of Launceston, and the convent (with unanimous assent) to Meliora, who was the wife of Thomas de Canniforda, and her heirs and executors of the custody of all the land in Pencuke and of Alice and Edith, the daughters and heirs of Thomas, until the heirs were of age. Meliora was to have the custody of the said heirs together with their marriage until they came of age. All this was to be held by Meliora of the prior and convent by due and customary rents and services. The prior and convent also granted that Meliora should have the land of the heirs until they were of age and of their marriages when they took place by the same fine which Meliora made with the prior and convent for the custody of the said Alice and Edith. Warranty and sealing clauses. Witd. William de Sancto Genesio, Richard de Penwarn, Richard de la Leye, Robert de Ros, Nicholas de Crannon. Dated Launceston, Sunday, 15 November 1332.

MS.: Cartulary, f.146v.

*Cartulary of Launceston Priory*

**374.** Grant by William, prior of Launceston, to John Mayowe de Smalehill of an annual rent of 10s. from lands in Newham. He also granted to the said John 2s. of annual rent issuing out of certain lands in Pencuke formerly called 'Mounteslond', viz., a rent the prior and his predecessors received from these lands. For John Mayowe to have for the term of his life for good service and counsel. Alternate sealing clause. Dated Launceston, 20 April 1438.

MS.: Cartulary, f.146v.–f.147r.

**375.** Pleas about Treworgie at York before W. Herll and his fellow justices of the King's Bench.

The prior of Launceston by John de Aldestowe, his attorney, was engaged on the fourth day against William de Duneham in a plea that he would acquit himself of the service which William son of Reginald de Ferariis had exacted from him for the free tenement which he held of William de Duneham in Treworgie whence the same William who was mesne tenant ought to acquit him.

William de Duneham did not appear, so the sheriff was ordered to distrain him to the value of 10d. His attendance was ordered at two courts, but he did not appear. Therefore it was judged by the statute that the said William de Duneham should lose the service of the prior. The latter from then should be attentive to the said William (son) of Reginald, his chief lord, for the same service which William customarily gave him. And therefore William de Duneham was in mercy.[a] York, quindene of Michaelmas 1328.

[a] "145" (?number of plea roll.)

MS.: Cartulary, f.147r.

**376.** Pleas of lands in the vill of St Gennys.

The prior of Launceston by John de Aldestowe, his attorney, appeared on the fourth day against Thomas, son of Philip de Lametyn on a plea that he acquitted him of the service which William son of Reginald de Ferarijs exacted from him from the free tenement which he held of the said Thomas whence Thomas who was the mesne tenant ought to acquit him. And he did not appear. And the sheriff was ordered to distrain him. And in two county courts proclamation was made that the said Thomas should be there on a day to answer the prior for the said plea. And the sheriff now commanded that he should distrain his chattels to the value of 10d. and those who gave bail for him viz. Robert de Lametyn and John de Lametyn. Therefore they were in mercy. Proclamation was made in two full courts for Thomas' attendance. It was judged by statute that Thomas should lose the service of the prior and his tenement. And the same prior now owed to the said William, his chief lord, the same services which the said Thomas performed for him and therefore Thomas was in mercy. Roll 145. Not dated [see no. 377, i.e. York, quindene of Michaelmas, 1328.]

MS.: Cartulary, f.147r.–f.147v.

**377.** Pleas of Pencuke at York.

Text as in no. 376, except that those who went bail for Thomas de Lamettyn were Thomas Trewilyas and Richard Trewilyas. The free tenement was named as in Pencuke. The sheriff ordered the distraint of Thomas' chattels to the value of 20d. It was judged that the said Thomas should lose the service of the prior, his tenant, and the mesne tenancy was omitted, he should render the same service as the mesne tenant performed to William the chief lord. Otherwise the text as in no. 376. Roll 118. Dated York, 3 February 1329.

MS.: Cartulary, f.147v.

**378.** Plea of 5s. of annual rent in Trengayor (*Trengeyr*) in the parish of St Gennys in the time of Prior Roger de Horton.

Assize taken at Lostwithiel in the presence of John de Foxle and John de Stonore, justices etc., at the assizes in the county of Cornwall.
The assize came to recognise if Thomas, son of Geoffrey de Trengeyr, Argentela who was the wife of Geoffrey de Trengeyr, William de Sancto Genesio and Warin de Bodulgoyt and Matilda, his wife, unjustly disseised Roger, prior of Launceston, of his free tenement in Trengayor next to Crannow. And it was queried that they disseised him of 5s. of rent with the appurtenances.
   And Thomas and the others did come. And the said Thomas was attached by Gervase Araz and Thomas Bastard. Argentela was attached by William Araz and William Huna. And William was attached by Nicholas Stripa and Richard de Genesio. And Warin de Bodulgoit and Matilda, his wife, were attached by Roger Le Mouner and Walter de Penwaren. Therefore they were in mercy. And the assize was exacted against them by default.
   The jurors said on their oath that the said William de Sancto Genesio held of the said prior a certain tenement in Trengayor by the service of 5s. yearly. They also said that the prior and all his predecessors were seised from time immemorial of the rent by the said William and his ancestors. Because the rent was in arrears, the jurors said, the prior took distraint in the said tenement for arrears, which distraint the said William by the bailiffs of the lord king handed over and thus he unjustly disseised himself.
   And therefore it was judged that the said prior should recover thence his seisin and his losses and arrears to the value of 20s. And the said William was in mercy for disseisin. And the said prior was also in mercy for a false claim. Dated Lostwithiel, Monday, 3 April 1318.

MS.: Cartulary, f.147v.–f.148r.

**379.** The plea of Wooda next to 'Mouthe'. The assize was taken at Launceston in the presence of J. de Foxle and his companion justices.

The assize came to recognise if William de Sancto Genesio and Thomasia, his wife, Robert de Penwaren and Matilda, his wife and William de Leghe and Alice, his wife, unjustly disseised Roger, prior of Launceston, of his free tenement in Wooda next to 'Mouthe'. The said prior by Ralph de Oggeworthi, his attorney, sought that they disseised him of 15d. of rent.

And William de Sancto Genesio and the others did not come. And the same William and Thomasia, his wife, were attached by Richard de Leghe and Thomas Mollyng. And William de Leghe and Alice, his wife were attached by Simon, parson of Otterham, and Stephen Garcoun. Therefore they were in mercy. And the assize went against them by default.

The jurors said on oath that certain of the ancestors of William de Sancto Genesio recently gave and granted to a certain prior of Launceston, predecessor of the present prior, 15d. of rent to be taken yearly from the tenement in pure and perpetual alms. And they said that the present prior and all his ancestors were seised of the rent from time immemorial. They said also that the prior and his predecessors as often as the rent was in arrears made distraint in the said tenement. And because the rent was in arrears the present prior made distraint in the said tenement and because William de Sancto Genesio and the others rescued the distraint they thus disseised the prior unjustly. Therefore it was adjudged that the said prior should recover his seisin and his losses were taxed at half a mark. And the said William was in mercy for the disseisin. And the prior was in mercy for a false claim. Dated Launceston, Monday, 31 July, 1318.

MS.: Cartulary, f.148r.–f.148v.

**380.** Grant by William Duneham for the salvation of his soul and the souls of his ancestors and successors to the priory of all his land at Newham (*Nyweham*), at the western side of the way which came from 'Canesford' and descended as far as the stream of 'Redeford' with one meadow called 'Rugemore' and a third of all his land of Newham at the eastern side of the way, saving to himself and his heirs a meadow called 'Suthmore' and the weir of a mill and his reasonable allowance of turf at his hearth, in pure and perpetual alms, free from all secular exaction and suit of county courts and of hundreds. Sealing clause. Witd. Robert son of William, William son of William, William Wyse. Not dated. [*c.*1221–32 (William Wyse and Robert son of William).]

MS.: Cartulary, f.148v.

**381.** Notice by Thomas de Duneham and his heirs that they were held to pay to the lord of Launceston 10s. for the land of Newham which they gave him (Thomas) for his homage and service, i.e. at the two terms of the year, at Easter and Michaelmas by equal portions. If Thomas and his heirs should cease from the payment of the said 10s., the prior and convent were given leave to distrain in all the land of Newham as far as Pencuke until they had made full payment. Sealing clause. Witd. Robert son of William, Walter son of William, William Wisa, Ralph de Trewurtha, Henry de Trevell, John Manyng and others. Not dated. [*c*.1221–43, cf. no. 82; possibly 1229, see no. 499.]

MS.: Cartulary, f.148v.–f.149r.

**382.** Gift by William de Botrell to the priory of the chapel of Crackington with a carrucate of land, viz. Hill (*Hille*) and one mark of rent; the land of Tregeare (*Treger*)[a] of Saiet the priest, one acre, and the land of Richard Haberha, half an acre, and the land of Hedwy, the fourth part of an acre, and this at the petition of Earl Reginald, on the day of the burial of Aeliz Corbet the wife of William de Botrell for his soul and for the soul of his father and his wife and his own soul.[b] Earl Reginald of Cornwall granted this. Witd. Prior William, Prior Robert, Herv' the clerk; John the chaplain and Drogo de Alternon, clerks.[c] Not dated. [*c*.1140–49 (24 June), i.e. Willam (I) de Botreaux.]

[a]Title: *et de terra de Northtreger.* [b]*sic.* [c]*sic.*

MS.: Cartulary, f.149r.

**383.** Gift in pure and perpetual alms by William de Boterell to the priory of the chapel of Crackington together with a carrucate of land at Hill (*Hille*) and a mark of rent from the land of (North) Tregeare, which was Saget the priest's and one acre in extent, and the land called Harberha, half an acre, and the land of Edwy, the fourth part of one acre. He also granted and quitclaimed all the right he believed he had in the gift of the chapel of Egloskerry in the manor of Penheale (*Penhele*.) The grant and quitclaim were made to the canons at the petition of Earl Reginald on the day of the burial of Aliz, William's wife. Sealing clause. Witd. William, prior of Bodmin; Prior Robert, Bernard, the clerk; John, chaplain; Auger, chaplain. Not dated. [1140–49, i.e. Wm (I) de Botreaux.]

MS.: Cartulary, f.149r.–f.149v.

**384.** Grant and confirmation by William de Botrell[a] for the salvation of his soul and the souls of his father and mother to the priory of the chapel of Crackington with a carrucate of land at Hill and a mark of rent from (North)Tregeare (*Tregier*) (the land of Saiet the priest) one acre in extent and the land of Haberha, half an acre and the land of Edwy, the fourth part of one acre, all which William de Botrell his father, gave to the priory and canons and confirmed by his charter in pure alms at the petition of Earl Reginald on the day of the burial of Aliz Corbet, William's wife. Witd. Robert son of Richard, Thomas Duneham, Richard Boterell. Not dated. [*c.*1158–75, i.e. between the earliest occurrence of William (II) de Botreaux (Watkin, ii, 1039) and the death of Earl Reginald.]

[a]Title: *Confirmacio Willelmi filij Willelmi de Botrell de capella de Cracumton, Hille et Northtreger.*

MS.: Cartulary, f.149v.

**385.**  Gift, grant and confirmation by William Cary to the priory in pure and perpetual alms all his messuages, lands and tenements in Hill in the parish of St Gennys which he had of the gift and feoffment of John Wille, son of Richard Wille. Sealing clause. Witd. Simon Genys, John Courtes, Richard Stede. Dated Launceston, Tuesday, 3 October 1391.

MS.: Cartulary, ff.149v.–150r.

**386.**  Examination of the witnesses of the parishioners of the chapel of Blessed Gregory of Hill (*Hulle*) in the presence of the official of the lord archdeacon of Cornwall on the articles written below.

Sir Symon, rector of the church of Otterham, 40 years old and more said on oath to the first article that Master Philip, vicar of St Gennys had three predecessors of whom he saw Sir John and Master William de Medelwode. The first vicar he knew not, yet he could have seen him in his time and he had not heard that he had had many predecessors. On another article he said that the chapel of St Gregory had a distinct parish and parishioners and he said that this had been so for a hundred years or more. All this he knew from the extent of his memory and before this he knew it from old men and he had never heard or seen anything to the contrary. To the fourth and fifth articles together he said that Master Philip and his predecessors as vicars enjoyed all the fruits and obventions arising from the chapel except the garb tithes and from time immemorial this was so. Also from time immemorial there had been found a chantry until Michaelmas 1335. In the time when there were no vicars, the prior and canons of Launceston enjoyed all the fruits of the church and the chapel and they served the chapel in divine services after the appropriation of the church of St Gennys to the monastery[a] of Launceston. He had heard from older men that there were once rectors of St Gennys who caused the chantry to be kept until Michaelmas 1335. To the sixth article he said that a chaplain in the presence of the parishioners for certain days every year celebrated divine service and at least one mass was sung. He said he knew this to be true for his own time and before that he heard it from older men. To the seventh article he answered that Master Philip and his predecessors found and supported the said chantry. To the eighth article he said that Master Philip for the whole time he was vicar, i.e. for 14 years, undertook to find and maintain the chaplain at his own cost until last Michaelmas. To the ninth article he said that at last Michaelmas Master Philip rashly stopped keeping the chantry to the great loss of the parishioners. To the tenth and eleventh articles he said that the parishioners did not wish to have sustained this loss for 40 shillings but they would rather lose their goods than sustain injury, grievance and loss. To the penultimate article he said that the chantry would in the future be held by the pronouncement of the commissary of the bishop of Exeter by a public instrument to Master Philip's knowledge. To the last article he said that there was a public outcry by the parishioners about this before the present suit.

Thomas Carnek, priest, aged 40 years and more, said on oath that he agreed with the former witness. He added that he knew only one predecessor of the present vicar, i.e. William de Medelton. On all other articles he agreed with the last witness and he said he was present at the proclamation of the pronunciation.

Sir Thomas, priest, aged 30 years and more, agreed with the witness. He knew only one predecessor of the present vicar.

Sir John Hethnant, priest, aged 30 years and more said that Master Philip, the vicar, hired him to serve in the said chapel for one year and he celebrated there at the cost of the vicar.

Robert Nywalegh, priest, aged 60 years and more agreed with the first witness and he also said he saw only one predecessor of the present vicar.

John de Penecrogou, aged 50 years and more, and of free condition, agreed with the first witness.

Walter Attehole, parishioner of the chapel of St Gregory, aged 60 years and more, agreed with the first witness. He said he saw all the predecessors of the present vicar, who let the chantry cease to the loss of the parishioners of 100s.

Thomas Crome, aged 25 and of free condition, agreed with the witness Robert de Newalegh.

William de Hollewyn, aged 50 and of free condition, agreed with the last witness.

Walter Attefenna, aged 35 or more, agreed with the last witness. Dated Hill, 17 July 1336.

ᵃ*sic.*

MS.: Cartulary, ff.150r.–151r.

**387.** Instrument about the celebrationᵃ in the chapel of Hill in the parish of St Gennys by the vicar there on two or three Sundays or at most once weekly.

In the name of God amen. By this present public instrument may it appear evident to all that in the year of our Lord according to the course and computation of the English Church 1402, in the tenth indiction and thirteenth year of the most holy pontificate in Christ, of the father and of the lord Pope Boniface IXth. On the fifth day of January in the parish church of Bodmin in Cornwall in the diocese of Exeter in the (document) written below and in the presence of the underwritten witnesses personally constituted, the discreet men, Masters Benedict Canterbury, William Kelwa and Richard Olyver, clerks of the diocese of Exeter and Sir Adam Thomas, perpetual vicar of the parish church of St Gennys, (came together) for the peaceful settlement of a certain dispute in the consistory of Exeter between the noble lady, the lady Elizabeth Botreaux, relict of the noble man the lord William Botreaux, knight, and the parishioners of the chapel of Hill of the one part and the said lord Adam, the vicar, of the other, about the founding of one chaplain to celebrate in the said chapel continually or on certain days in the week. Master Benedict and Richard appeared on behalf of the lady Elizabeth and the parishioners of the chapel, and Master Kelwa on the part of Adam, the vicar.

At length by the intervention of common friends of the parties a settlement of the dispute was reached. The said Sir Adam should celebrate in the chapel of Hill on two or three days at the most, or cause celebration to be made whilst the chapel was furnished for this.

The said Masters Benedict and Richard granted judgement to the said priest and the parishioners of the said chapel that the said Sir Adam, the vicar, should not be troubled because of his benefice only once a week. Sir Adam should celebrate one ferial day in the same chapel and no more, and the said chapel should be furnished, saving, however, the devotion of the vicar, the said Sir Adam.

These acts were done as written above and recited in the year, indiction, pontificate, month, day and place in the presence of the discreet men, Sir Robert Michell, rector of the church of Helland (*Hellond*), Sir John Hocky, vicar of the parish church of St Breward (*Brueredus*); John Nicoll, reeve of Bodmin and John Danyell and many other witnesses of the said diocese specially called and asked.

And I John Boscofelek, clerk, of Exeter diocese, a notary public by apostolic authority, was present at all and singular the premises and they were done under the year, indiction, pontificate, month, day and place aforesaid and heard them. And occupied from elsewhere by another, I have caused this to be written by another and have reduced it to public form and I have signed it by my accustomed sign and in my own name, asked and required in the faith and testimony of the premises. Dated Bodmin parish church, 5 January 1401.

<sup>a</sup>. . . *super collacione celebracione* etc. (Title).

MS.: Cartulary, f.151r.–f.151v. (f.152r.–f.152v. is blank.)

**388.**   Quitclaim by Richard de Lanwanek to the church of St Stephen of Launceston and the canons of all his land in Eastway (*Byestewey*) in the manor of Milton (*Middelond*). Sealing clause. Witd. the lords Reginald de Boterell, Stephen Heym, Stephen de Podyford. Not dated. [*c*.1242–67 (Reginald de Botreaux, see Maclean, *Trigg Minor* i, 633). For the dating limit of 1267, see P. L. Hull, *Cartulary of St Michael's Mount* (DCRS, 1962) no. 7.]

<sup>a</sup>Title: *Incipit regestrum cartarum manerij Biestwey* . . .

MS.: Cartulary, f.153r.

**389.** Quitclaim by Richard de Lanwanek to the canons of all his land in Eastway. Sealing clause. Witd. as no. 388 and Guy de Nonant. Not dated. [*c.*1242–67, see no. 388.]

MS.: Cartulary, f.153r.–f.153v.

**390.** Grant by Richard de Lawanek, chaplain, to the prior and convent. If by any chance they were to lose judicially the land of Eastway which they had of his grant in the manor of Milton, they should have immediate access to land he held of the prior and convent in Lewannick and possess it peacefully. Also they might remove from him or his sister Olimpiaus the allowance of a prebend of one canon which the said prior and convent gave them together with the tithe of the sheaves of Polyphant (*Polyfont*) which they had given to Richard for a term of five years. Richard renounced all remedies of canon or civil law against the tenor of the present writing. Sealing clause. Witd. the lords Reginald de Boterell, Stephen Heym, Stephen de Podyford, John Baupre, steward of Cornwall; Ralph, the clerk. Dated Launceston, Thursday, 20 January 1267.

MS.: Cartulary, f.153v.

**391.** Agreement between Herbert[a] de Pyn, lord of Milton, of the one part and Richard, prior of Launceston, and the convent of the other. Herbert granted and confirmed to Prior Richard and the convent all the lands and tenements which they held in Cleave (*Clyve*), 'Southerthyscote', 'Northerthyscote', Eastway and elsewhere in the parish of Morwenstow (*Morwynstowe*) in the fee of Milton, in pure, free and perpetual alms. The prior and convent were to pay the amount of scutage which fell on each of the lands in the fee of Milton when scutage was raised. If the prior and convent were impleaded, Herbert and his heirs would in no way place them to warranty. Nor would the prior and convent claim any right in the fees of 'Bere', 'Trethewy', 'Penfentinyou' and 'Westacory' by this grant by which Herbert and his heirs or assigns would be disturbed in their rights in the said fees which they might freely distrain for their rights and make their profit as seemed to them expedient. Alternate sealing clause for chirograph. Witd. the lords Reginald de Bevyle, Stephen de Bello Prato, knights; John de Thorlebear, Thomas le Chanceler, Robert de Bodmam. Dated Launceston, Wednesday, 14 November 1302.[b] Before John de Berwike and his companion justices itinerant.

[a]Text has 'Robert'; title, 'Herbert'. [b]*die mercurij proxima post festum sancti Martini.* The feast of St Martin is assumed to be of the bishop and confessor (11 November).

MS.: Cartulary, ff.153v.–154r.

**392.** Grant and quitclaim by William, son of Walter de Leghe, to the priory of all his right and claim to the whole land of Eastway in the parish of Morwenstow. The prior and convent gave him 40 marks of silver for this. Sealing clause. Witd. the lord Thomas de Kanc(*ia*); John de Bello Prato, John de Aleth, Herbert de Pyn, knights; the lord William de

Monketon, then steward of Cornwall and rector of Morwenstow, and Master Hamundus Parleben. All the above grants were made in the time of the lords Solomon de Roffens', Richard de Boyland, William Braybuf and Robert Foka, justices of the lord king in Cornwall in the twelfth year of Edward, son of King Henry. [i.e. Edward I: 20 Nov. 1283–19 Nov. 1284.]

MS.: Cartulary, f.154r.–f.154v.

**393.** Pleas relating to Eastway before John de Berwyk and his companions, royal justices itinerant, at Launceston in the octave of Michaelmas 1302.

The jurors presented that the prior of Launceston and the canons there held half a knight's fee and one and a half ferlings of land in Milton which were of the fee of Herbert de Pyn who held of the lord king in chief; they did not know by what warrant.

Afterwards the prior came and said that he held the said tenements of the gift of Hamo Parleben in free alms etc. And he said that Edmund, formerly earl of Cornwall, confirmed the grant and he produced the said charter and confirmation which witnessed this. He said that the lord king then granted to the said Hamo licence for him to give the said tenements to the prior and convent notwithstanding the statute. And he produced letters of the king which witnessed this, etc. (Roll 21). Dated Launceston assizes, Michaelmas 1302.

MS.: Cartulary, f.154v.

**394.** Lease between William, prior of Launceston, and the convent and William Hora, Joan his wife and Thomasine their daughter. The prior and convent leased .to William, Joan and Thomasine[a] the messuages, lands and tenements which John Hauk, clerk, lately held of them in Eastway. To William, Joan and Thomasine for the term of their lives and the longest liver of them. They were to pay to the prior and convent and their successors 31s. at the feasts of Easter, the Nativity of St John the Baptist, St Michael the Archangel and the Birth of our Lord by equal portions. They were to render suit of court and mill and were liable to serve as reeve when elected. If William Hora were to die during the term a *farleu*[b] of 31s. was payable and likewise for the deaths of Joan and Thomasine.[a] None of them were to let the land without licence from the prior and convent. They were to keep all houses and buildings and ditches in repair. For arrears of repair or rent for a quarter of a year (without sufficient distress), letting the land without licence, the prior and convent could have re-entry to the land. Warranty and alternate sealing clauses. Witd. Robert Pyne de Hame, Robert Downe, Robert Dene. Dated the chapter house of Launceston priory, 7 January 1436.

[a]*Thomas*, sic. [b]*Farleu*, a word used in Devon and Cornwall for a heriot, see R. E. Latham, *Revised Medieval Latin Word List* (1965).

MS.: Cartulary, f.155r.

**395.** Letters patent of Edward, king of England, lord of Ireland and duke of Aquitaine, reciting that it was not lawful by the common counsel of the realm for religious men to enter into the fee of another, so that without licence it would become mortmain and should be held immediately of the chief lords of the fee. Notice, however, that he had of his grace granted a special licence to Hamo Parleben to assign to the prior and convent of Launceston 2 acres of land in Cleave and Hollygrove (*Holygrove*). To have and to hold from him and his successors for ever. The King also granted licence that the prior and convent might receive that land from Hamo, saving the services due and customary from the chief lords of the fee. Dated Acton Burnell, 20 October 1283.

MS.: Cartulary, f.155v.

**396.** Gift and grant by Master Hamo Parleben, clerk, for the salvation of his soul and the souls of his ancestors and successors, to the priory of all his land in Hollygrove, Cleave and 'Herthyscote' with the mill there in free, pure and perpetual alms with the homage and service of William de Herthyscote and of David de Herthyscote for the land they held of Hamo in the vill of 'Herthyscote' and the homage and service of Alan de Sprutesland for land held of Hamo in Elmsworthy (*Tilmansworthie*) also the homage and service of Robert de Moreton for the land held of him in Lymsworthy (*Lomanesworthie*) and Holacoombe (*Holacombe*) and with the villeins holding villein tenements. Warranty and sealing clauses. Witd. the lords William de Botreaus, Thomas de Kent, John de Bello Prato, John de Treyaggu, Richard de Hywysh. Launceston, Tuesday, in the feast of the translation (7 July) of Blessed Thomas the Martyr in the year (not given) of Edward, son of King Henry. Not dated. [Before no. 398; cf 395 and 402. Possible date, Tuesday 7 July 1282.

MS.: Cartulary, ff.155v.–156r.

**397.** Confirmation by Robert, son of William de Leghe, of Hamo Parleben's grant to the priory church of St Stephen by Launceston of his land in Hollygrove and 'Mideham'. The confirmation was in pure, free and perpetual alms. He also quitclaimed to the prior and convent his right in 2 acres English which his brother, Durandus de Leghe, had in Hollygrove or 'Middeham'. For this confirmation and quitclaim the prior and convent gave him 6 marks of silver. Sealing clause. Witd. Robert de Morton, John de Thurleber, Gervase de Stratton, John de Grymescote, Robert de Bodmam. Not dated. [After 7 July 1282 (no. 396)—18 December 1303 (see no. 468, Robert de Bodmam).]

MS.: Cartulary, f.156r.–f.156v.

**398.** Ratification and confirmation by Edmund, earl of Cornwall, of Hamo Parlebien's grant to the priory of the lands of Hollygrove, Cleave and 'Herthyscote'. Sealing clause. Witd. the venerable father in Christ,

Peter, bishop of Exeter; Roger de Stratton, Walter de la Puille, Richard de Hywys, Ralph Bloyou, Benedict Renward. Dated Exeter, 6 January 1286.

MS.: Cartulary, ff.156v.–157r.

**399.** Pleas of North Cleave (*Northclyve*) between Prior Richard and Joan who was the wife of Richard Podyford, before John Berwyk and his companion justices itinerant in the octave of Michaelmas 1302.

Joan who was the wife of Roger de Podyford sought against the prior of Launceston a third part of 7 messuages, one mill, and 5½ ferlings of land in North Cleave as her dowry. And the prior came and by his licence granted her dowry. Therefore she might have seisin. Dated Launceston assizes, Michaelmas 1302.

MS.: Cartulary, f.157r.

**400.** Lease from Prior William and the convent to William Stanbury of Cleave of all their tenure in Cleave next to Stratton which William and Alice, his wife, formerly held from the prior and convent. The lease was for the term of their lives and the longest liver of them. The yearly rent was 20d. sterling at the feasts of Easter, St John the Baptist, Michaelmas and the Nativity by equal payments. William and Alice were to perform common suit of court of Eastway and to the priory mill in Coombe (*Come*). They were to perform the office of reeve when chosen and make faithful account of their office. If either of them died 20s. would be payable as a *farleu*.[a] They were to keep the houses and ditches in repair at their own costs. If they were to let all or part of the land to another, or if the rent was in arrears by a month at any of the feasts, or if they did not repair for a quarter, the prior and convent could re-enter the land etc. Warranty and alternate sealing clause (chirograph), including seals of both parties. Witd. Robert Doune, Thomas Lannoy, John Lannoy, Thomas Oterham and William Loman. Dated at the chapter house of Launceston priory, 30 December 1439.

[a]see note to no. 394.

MS.: Cartulary, f.157r.–f.157v.

**401.** Gift and confirmation by Thomas, nephew of the earl of Gloucester, and Mabilla, his wife, for the love of God, for their souls and the souls of their fathers and mothers, and for the soul of Richard de Greinvilla, Mabilla's uncle, whose patrimony was all the land of Kilkhampton (*Chilcumtonia*), of land called Heatham (*Heneam*) to the priory free and quit from all service except prayer and the spiritual benefits of the priory. They firmly commanded that no one was to do injury to the prior and convent nor make any claim nor commit any act to their loss. They had also granted the prior and canons common pasture in wood and plain. Witd. Robert, chaplain of Kilkhampton, and Anger the clerk, Reginald, Hericcus[a] and Aylwardus and the whole hundred of Kilkhampton. Not dated. [Presumably after the marriage of Gilbert de Clare, seventh earl of Gloucester to Matilda de Burgh on 29 September 1308, see *Complete Peerage* (2nd. ed.) v, 714.]

[a]*sic.*

MS:. Cartulary, f.157v.–f.158r.

**402.** Confirmation by Richard de Greynvile, lord of Kilkhampton. He had inspected the charter of Master Hamo Parleben which granted to the prior and canons the homage and service of Alan de Spruteslond of the land of Elmsworthy and Spritsland and of the homage and service of Robert de Morton of the land of Lymsworthy. Text[a] of Hamo Parleben's charter given, which shows that his grant was in free and perpetual alms, free from all exaction, homage and fealty and every kind of secular service for ever, except to the chief lords of Kilkhampton 10s. of annual rent from the land of Elmsworthy and Spritsland and 2s. to the lords of the land of Lymsworthy.

All this was confirmed by Richard, in free and perpetual alms, free and quit from secular service, except the rents of 2s. and 10s., saving royal and foreign service whenever it occurred, as much as pertained to so much land in the manor of Kilkhampton. The only distraint Richard or his heirs or assigns would make in these lands against the heirs of Hamo would be only for these rents of 10s. and 2s. and for royal and foreign service when it occurred. The prior gave Richard for this confirmation 40s. In addition the prior and convent added Richard and his ancestors and heirs to their prayers for ever. Alternate sealing clause for bipartite charter. Witd. Robert de Morton, Richard de Yvelcombe, Alan de Spruteslond, William Symond and Thomas le Chauncelere. Dated Bideford, Wednesday, 20 May, 1299.

[a]Cf. no. 396.

MS.: Cartulary, f.158r.–f.158v.

**403.** Memorandum that before the gift of the said Hamo (Parleben) the said Alan de Spruteslond and Robert de Morton held a parcel of the said tenement of the said Hamo and the said Hamo of the ancestors of the said Richard Greynvile. Hamo died without heirs and by his death the whole lordship of Hamo went by escheats to the ancestors of Richard Greynvile, and thus the ancient services of Richard which he or his ancestors had from Hamo and his ancestors were extinct in law. Thus the then prior and his successors were to hold the tenement from the said Richard by the same services which his predecessors made to the said Hamo and not by the services which the said Hamo made to the ancestors of the said Richard Greynvile. Not dated. [*c.*1299, cf. no. 402.]

MS.: Cartulary, f.159r.

**404.** Pleas before R. de Kyngham and his companions, justices of the bench, of the term of Michaelmas 1301.

Thomas de Bernyngcote was present on the fourth day against Robert de Morton to acquit himself on a plea for services which the prior of Launceston exacted from him for his free tenement which he held of the said Robert in Lymsworthy of which the said Robert, who was the mesne tenant between them, ought to acquit.

And Robert did not come. And the sheriff was commanded that he should distrain him through all his lands and bring him to court. Public proclamation was also made in two county courts that the said Robert should come to acquit the said Thomas. But he did not come and the county court ordered Robert should be distrained through his lands and chattels to the value of 2s. And nevertheless Robert Sade and John Pycard went bail for him. Therefore they were in mercy. Further proclamation was made in two county courts for Robert to attend but he did not come. Therefore by the statute it was considered that the said Robert should lose the services of Thomas and henceforth Thomas should make them to the prior. And Robert was in mercy.

MS.: Cartulary, f.159r.–f.159v. The rest of f.159v. is blank.

**405.** [a]Notice by J., abbot of Cleeve (*Clyva*) and the convent of the Cistercian order in the diocese of Bath of their renunciation of their right in the church of St Olaf of Poughill (*Poghwell*) in the diocese of Exeter, having granted the same church to the prior and convent of Launceston to have and possess in pure and perpetual alms. Sealing clause of abbot of Cleeve. Witd. Brother R(ichard), abbot of Dunkeswell, Hugh, monk of the same house, Hervey, prior of Cleeve, Hugh Celler', Walter the sub-prior, William de Treburgo, the seneschal. Not dated. [?c.1228, see *Heads of Religious Houses* 131. (Richard, abbot of Dunkeswell.).]

[a]Title: *Incipit regestrum cartarum ecclesiarum de Stratton et Poghwell.* Subtitle: *Quieta clamancia abbatis et conventus de Clyve ecclesie de Poghwyll.*

MS.: Cartulary, f.160r.

**406.** Grant and confirmation by Brother J. abbot of Cleeve and the convent, of the church of St Olaf of Poughill to the prior and convent of Launceston in pure and perpetual alms. Sealing clause. Dated September 1228.

MS.: Cartulary, f.160r.–f.160v.

**407.** Letter of Abbot J. and the convent of Cleeve to the official of the bishop of Exeter to admit the prior and convent of Launceston to the cure of souls of the church of Poughill. Dated September 1228.

MS.: Cartulary, f.160v.

**408.** Letter of William, bishop of Exeter, to J., official of the archdeacon of Cornwall, or to the dean of East Wivelshire, to place the prior and convent of Launceston in corporal possession of the church of Poughill. Not dated. [*c*.1230, cf. no. 410.]

MS.: Cartulary, ff.160v.–f.161r.

**409.** Notice by Gilbert Potte, former vicar of Poughill, about an annual pension of half a mark due from the vicarage to the prior of Launceston which William, bishop of Exeter, had collated at the presentation of the true patron of Poughill, saving Gilbert's vicarage for the length of his life. Then, after Gilbert had delayed to pay the pension for a little while, he renounced his right to the pension and paid it for one year to Ph(ilip), precentor of Exeter, and W. de Arundell, vicar of the bishop of Exeter, and in their presence he took an oath on the sacrament to pay the pension yearly at Michaelmas. Sealing clause and signatures of the precentor and vicar (W. de Arundell). Witd. Thomas archd. Totnes, Masters J. de Sancto Gorono, R. de Warrewyk. Not dated. [1224–1244, episcopate of William Briwere. Possibly *c*.1233: Philip de Bagetor who witnessed an episcopal charter on 3 August 1233. (Oliver, *Lives*, 278.).]

MS.: Cartulary, f.161r.

**410.** Confirmation by William, bishop of Exeter, with the assent of his chapter, of the grant by the abbot and convent of Cleeve, patrons of the church of Poughill, to the priory of a pension of half a mark in the church of Poughill yearly, saving the perpetual vicarage of Gilbert the clerk, as long as he lived. Sealing clause of Bishop William. Witd. Ralph, archdeacon of Barnstaple, William Gern', clerk, William, *cantor* and Henry, the bishop's chaplain, Alexander, doctor of law, Martin Prodonis, Thomas de Pere. Dated Chudleigh, 31 December 1231.

MS.: Cartulary, f.161r.–f.161v.

**411.** Another confirmation by William, bishop of Exeter, about the entry of the prior and convent of Launceston into the church of Poughill, the pension having ceased on the death of Gilbert Put; saving the rights of the bishop and the archdeacon and a competent vicarage, the taxation of which was reserved to the bishop. Dated Paignton, Monday, 28 March 1244.

MS.: Cartulary, f.161v.

**412.** Letter of John, archbishop of Canterbury, to the archdeacon of Cornwall. At his visitation of the city and diocese of Exeter at the instance of Robert, perpetual vicar of Poughill, proceeding against the dean of Trigg Major, he had ordered an inquisition into the value of the major and minor tithes belonging to the church of Poughill. He ordered the citation of the dean to appear before the archdeacon and the archdeacon of Totnes after the feast of Trinity. Dated 'Ockeburn', 9 April 1282.

MS.: Cartulary, f.162r.

**413.** Commission of John de Esse, archdeacon of Cornwall, to his official, to appear before the archbishop and his commissary at Exeter, reciting Archbishop John Pecham's commission (no. 412). Exeter, 13 April 1282.

MS.: Cartulary, f.162r.–f.162v.

**414.** Inquisition on the value of the vicarage and parsonage of the church of Poughill made by the dean of Trigg Major at the command of Archbishop John Pecham, Crediton, 18 March 1282.

Inquisition made by Sir Robert, vicar of Launcells; Sir Andrew, vicar of Stratton, Nicholas the chaplain called Colman; Roger the priest, called Bele; Thomas de Flexbury, Robert de Newell, Robert de Bosco, Nicholas de Northcote, William de Fonte, Henry Parys and Edward de Nova Domo. They said that the tithe of the sheaves of the church of Poughill is worth in usual years 20 marks. The glebe is worth half a mark of annual rent. The prior and convent of Launceston had then obtained the tithe of the sheaves and the glebe in the name of the parsonage. The portion of the vicarage of the church of Poughill consisted in oblations yearly at Christmas, Easter and the feast of St Olaf, king and martyr (29 July), of 18s.: the tithe of wool yearly at the price of one mark; the tithe of dairy produce 4s.; the tithe of lambs 3s. 9d.; the tithe of honey 6d.; the tithe of pigs 7s.; the tithe of garlic 12d.; the tithe of madder 8s.; the tithe of flax 3s.; the tithe of beans 2s. There belonged to the said vicarage 3 acres of land with a certain close where the houses of the vicarage were built; these were worth 3s. yearly. The total sum of all the above which belonged to the vicarage of Poughill, 63s. 7½d, and the said vicarage sustained all the due and customary burdens.

The dean of Trigg Major had cited the prior and convent of Launceston and the vicar of Poughill to appear before him on the law day after the first Sunday after Easter. Dated Poughill, Wednesday, 1 April 1282.

MS.: Cartulary, f.162v.–f.163v. (The rest of f.163v. and f.164r. are blank.)

**415.** ªGrant and confirmation by Reginald, earl of Cornwall and the king's son, of a gift to the priory of the church of St Andrew of Stratton by William de Acy. To add to these alms William had also given a carrucate of land from the lord of the manor of Stratton next to the other land of the church with an enclosure for making salt at Efford. All this he had confirmed by word of mouth and his writ, saving his dignity of the chapel of the castle of Launceston. Not dated. [*c*.1146–65, Richard de Raddona, see no. 12.]

[a]Title: *Extenta sive regestrum ecclesie sancti Andree de Stratton ac de sanctuario eiusdem cum pertinenciis.*

MS.: Cartulary, f.164v.

*Carta confirmacionis Reginaldi regis filij consulis Cornub' de ecclesia de Stratton.*
Reginaldus regis filius consul Cornubie omnibus fidelibus suis salutem. Sciatis quod Willelmus de Acy donavit ecclesie sancti Stephani de Lanst' ecclesiam sancti Andree de Strattona cum pertinentiis suis. Dedit eciam ipsi ecclesie in augmentum elemosine sue unam carucatam terre de dominio manerij Strattona iuxta alteram terram ecclesie cum quadam area salinarum Ebforde. Et hoc totum concessi ego et confirmavi per os meum atque per breve meum salva capelle dignitate mee de castello Lanst'. Teste Roberto de Dunstanvilla et Ricardo de Redduna vicecomite Cornub' et ipso Willelmo de Acy et Bernardo clerico.

**416.** Confirmation[a] by Bartholomew, son of Peter Turet, lord of Stratton, for the salvation of his soul and the souls of his father and mother, as much as the lord of an estate could grant, to the priory of the gift of the church of St Andrew of Stratton in pure and perpetual alms. Witd. William son of Garinus, Ralph de Mora, Thomas de Dunham, Robert Sprakelin, Reginald Cole. Not dated. [Possibly *c*.1170–86 if the first Thomas de Dunham is intended. See no. 429.]

[a]Title: *Carta Bartholomei de eadem.*

MS.: Cartulary, ff.164v.–165r.

**417.** Quitclaim by Ralph de Albo Monasterio, knight, lord of Stratton, for himself and his heirs and assigns to the church of Blessed Stephen of Launceston and the canons serving God there of all the right of patronage he had in the church of Stratton. Warranty and sealing clauses. Witd. the lord Richard, prior of Bodmin; Walter, prior of St Germans; Stephen Haym then steward of Cornwall; Philip de Cancell(is), Roland de Pudyford, Henry de Bodlek. Not dated. [1262 or 1267, see P. L. Hull, *The Cartulary of St Michael's Mount* (DCRS, 1962), no. 7, though *Cornwall FF*. i, nos. 170 and 185 (R. de Blanchminster) might suggest earlier limits of 1258–62.]

MS.: Cartulary, f.165r.

**418.** Final concord in the king's court at Launceston from the day of St Michael in three weeks in 1262 before Robert de Brywar, Richard de Middelton and William de Staunton, justices itinerant, between Rannulf de Albo Monasterio, querent, and Richard, prior of Launceston, tenant, of the advowson of the church of Stratton. Whence the assize of last presentment was summoned by them in the same court. The same Rannulf recognised the advowson to be the right of the prior and church of St Stephen of Launceston and released the advowson and the church for himself and his heirs to the prior and his successors for ever. The prior received the same Rannulf and his heirs into all the benefits and prayers of their church. Dated Launceston in three weeks of Michaelmas 1262.

MS.: Cartulary, f.165v. Printed: *Cornwall FF.* i, no. 185.

**419.** Quitclaim and acquittance by Robert de Flexbury, steward of the lord Ralph de Albo Monasterio that he had received from the prior of Launceston 15 marks of silver on 2 May in the name of his lord. By this the prior was held to his lord, Ralph de Albo Monasterio, for the agreement after a dispute between them about the church of Stratton by a writ of the king. Dated Stratton 2 May 1262.

MS.: Cartulary, f.165v.

**420.** Release and quitclaim by Gervase, son of Robert, the clerk, of Stratton to the prior and convent and their successors of all the common pasture in the land of the glebe of Stratton in wood and meadow and all other land. The prior and convent gave Gervase 5 marks of silver. Sealing clause. Witd. Robert de Morton, John de Thurlber, Thomas de la Doune, John de Grymescot, Alan de Sprutesland. Dated Stratton, Tuesday, 16 June 1299.

MS.: Cartulary, ff.165v.–166r.

**421.** Record of a dispute between the prior and convent of Launceston and Gervase, son of Robert, the clerk, of Stratton, about a way which Gervase claimed he had beyond the glebe of the prior and convent in Stratton to the land held by Gervase of the prior and convent. A peaceful solution was made in this way: the prior and convent granted to the said Gervase and his heirs a certain way beyond the land of his[a] glebe to the land which Gervase held of them of a width of 18 feet for driving and leading his cattle and his carts at his will. At either side of the said way ditches were to be dug with plants growing in the ditches to ensure that the animals of Gervase did not escape from the way into the corn or pasture of the said prior and convent. But if this did happen through inadequate ditches, Gervase and his heirs were not on account of this to be brought and burdened in the court of the prior and convent. Similarly, Gervase and his heirs were not to be brought to the prior's court if Gervase's cattle strayed before the ditches were dug, unless they were driven or impounded there by the reeve. And if Gervase's animals ate the plants growing in the ditches of the prior and convent, in going or returning, they were not to be interfered with, unless for safe keeping. Alternate sealing clause for chirograph. Witd. Robert de Morton, John de

Thurleber, Thomas de la Doune, John de Grymescot, Alan de Sprutesland. Dated Stratton, Tuesday, 16 June 1299.

<sup>a</sup>*sui.*

MS.: Cartulary, f.166r.–f.166v.

**422.** The taxation of the vicarage of Stratton made by the lord archbishop of Canterbury at his visitation.

Notice by Archbishop John after a visitation of the city and diocese of Exeter. In the deanery of Trigg Major he had learnt that the prior and convent of Launceston had obtained for their own use the church of Stratton. He had also learnt there that Andrew de Kayinges, then vicar of that church, by a taxation or allowance of William of blessed memory, bishop of Exeter, had all the tithes of the sheaves with the glebe, altar dues and all other obventions of the same church both small and great. By this same allowance the vicar had to pay to the prior and convent only 25 marks in cash.

Having considered how this taxation clashed with ancient canons and how he ought to correct its errors, he brought the vicar and the prior before him to hear his judgement. They appeared by a lawful proctor on Monday, 31 March 1281 in the monastery of Hartland. Both parties swore on the Holy Gospels to keep the new allowance. After this a date was given to the prior and convent and the vicar of Stratton viz. Saturday, 5 April 1281 at Crediton, to hear and receive the new allowance.

The prior and convent appeared by proctor and the said vicar in person before Master Alan de Freston, archdeacon of Norfolk, chancellor, and Robert de Lascy, the archbishop's commissaries in the prebendal church of Crediton. The vicar and his successors were to have and take peacefully all the offerings and obventions of the altar and the small tithes belonging to the said church with the manse and the gardens adjoining the manse. The prior and convent and their successors were to have the greater tithes of the said parish together with the whole glebe there for their rectory. The religious each year were to render to the vicar of the church a quarter of wheat in the middle of Lent to make the Host for Easter.

The archbishop confirmed this taxation at Exeter, Monday, 24 March 1281.

MS.: Cartulary, ff.166v.–167v.

**423.** Mandate by John (Pecham), archbishop of Canterbury, to the archdeacon of Cornwall or his official to induct the prior and convent or their lawful proctor in corporeal possession of the greater tithes of Stratton and the whole glebe and to certify that this had been done to both Archbishop John and the prior and convent. Dated Clyst Episcopi, Monday, 24 March 1281.

MS.: Cartulary, ff.167v.–168r.

**424.** <sup>a</sup>Notice by Walter, bishop of Exeter, that Prior Henry and his convent had granted the faculty and goodwill of the vacant vicarage of Stratton to him. This grant was by Prior Henry's kindness and was to be regarded as without prejudice or hurt to the monastery<sup>b</sup> in the future. Dated Fluxton, 15 February 1279. [But note that the 21st year of Bp. Bronescombe's consecration stated in the dating clause started on 7 March 1279.]

<sup>a</sup>Title: *Recognicio Walteri Exoniensis episcopi quod jus prioratus ecclesie de Stratton sibi non spectat.* <sup>b</sup>*sic.*

MS.: Cartulary, f.168r.


**425.** Gift and confirmation by Thomas Graunt of Stratton to William Treludek, vicar of Stratton, John Trethewy and John Hobbe, chaplains, and Thomas Skudya, clerk, of his messuages and tenements in Stratton with the rents and services of Thomas Nordon for all the lands he held of the grantor for the term of his life with their reversion. Warranty and sealing clauses. Witd. Nicholas Wampford, Nicholas Leghe, Thomas Bastard, Richard Symon. Dated Stratton, Wednesday, 10 July 1381.

MS.: Cartulary, f.168r.–f.168v.


**426.** Lease from William Treludek, vicar of Stratton, John Trethewy and John Hobbe, chaplains, Thomas Skudya, clerk, to Thomas Graunt of Stratton of all their messuages and tenements which they had in the vill of Stratton of the gift and feoffment of the said Thomas, for the term of his life by the rent of a red rose at the feast of the Nativity of St John the Baptist, with due and customary services to the chief lord of the fee. Warranty clause. Alternate sealing clause. Witd. Nicholas Leghe, Thomas Bastard, Richard Symon, Robert atte Hele. Dated Stratton, Monday, 9 February 1383.

MS.: Cartulary, f.168v.


**427.** Memorandum that John Trewan, vicar of Stratton, held by charter certain lands and tenements in the glebe there for the term of his life. Rent 24s. 8d., common suit of court, performing office of reeve for two tenures and paying heriot of 20s. for a heriot whenever it occurred. The charter was dated 30 September 1437.

MS.: Cartulary, ff.168v.–169r. (The rest of f.169r. is blank.)


**428.** Grant<sup>a</sup> by Gilbert de Waranda to the priory of the church of Bridgerule (*Bridge*) in pure and perpetual alms for the soul of his father and his ancestors. The same Gilbert made fealty on the day the relics of St Stephen were translated from Launceston to the new church at the ford by the advice and consent of Robert of pious remembrance, bishop of Exeter, who transferred the relics there. Gilbert also gave to the church of St Stephen the vill of the manor of Bridgerule which is called Tatson (*Tottesdon*) quit of all exactions except royal service. Sealing clause of donor. Witd. the lord Robert, bishop of Exeter, Earl Reginald, Alured the archdeacon, Walter de Hermersdon, Robert de Dunstanvile, Richard de Raddona. Not dated. [*c*.1155–56, see note to no. 12. Robert I, bishop of Exeter, died 28 March 1155 after he had transferred the relics to the new priory on 7 February 1155 (Introd. p. xvi and n. 84). But Alured the archdeacon witnesses charters to 1156 (Blake, 169) and the Bishop Robert who witnesses this charter must be Bishop II.]

ªTitle: *Regestrum cartarum ecclesie Sancti Michaelis de Bruggerewall ac terre de Totesdon cum earum pertinenciis.*

MS.: Cartulary, f.169v.

**429.** Grant and confirmation by Thomas Duna, for the salvation of his soul and the souls of his wife and their children, to the church of St Stephen of Launceston, as far as the lord of an estate could grant, of the church of St Michael of Bridgerule (*Brigge*) which anciently was held of the gift of Gilbert de Warenne, then lord of Bridgerule. He also granted to the church of St Stephen and the canons the whole land of Tatson which they held of the gift of Gilbert de Warenne and of the grant of Johel Malneun) and of Serlo, his grandfather, in pure and perpetual alms, quit from all secular service except royal service, as much as could reasonably be assessed on the land of Tatson. Sealing clause. Witd. Ralph de Mora, Thomas de Duneham, Gervase de Bray, Walter de Mora. Not dated. [*c*.1170–86, see note to no. 76.]

MS.: Cartulary, ff.169v.–170r.

**430.** Letter of Walter Gyffard to the bishop of Exeter and the whole chapter. He had granted in perpetual alms (as far as in him lay) the church of Bridgerule to St Stephen of Launceston and the brethren serving God there. Just as if his lord Earl Reginald had granted it and Johel Mauneund (who held the land and church) and Gilbert de Warenna, his uncle, who had given the land of Tatson when he (Gilbert) was received into a canonry. Donor's sealing clause. Witd. Peter, canon of Plympton, Osbert de Brygge and his brother Jordan, Roger the clerk, Roger de Truscote, Roger son of Russell, Richard the clerk, William the armour-bearer of the prior. Not dated. [*c*.1155–66 (Walter Giffard) see Finberg in *EHR* July 1947, p. 357 no. xiv and *Red Book of the Exchequer* i, 207.]

MS.: Cartulary, f.170r.

**431.** Grant and confirmation by Joel Magunnend, for the redemption of his soul, to the priory of the land of Tatson and the church of Bridgerule

which had been formerly granted and confirmed to the priory by
Gylesbert[a] de Warenne in whose ownership they used to be. This gift was
allowed by Serlo, brother of Johel, and the grant on the altar of St Stephen
was witnessed by Osbert, priest of the church of Bridgerule; the chaplain
of the brethren, Almelinus, priest of Boyton, Jordan, priest of Lewannick,
Roger the clerk, son of Lipsus, Pagan de Piderwina. Not dated. [Before
no. 430.]

[a] *sic.*

MS.: Cartulary, f.170v.

**432.**   Grant by William Gyffard, owner of Bridgerule, for the salvation of
his soul and the souls of his wife and children, to the priory of the church
of Bridge in pure and perpetual alms. The church of Bridgerule had been
granted by his ancestors to the priory some time ago. Confirmation of the
grant by the donor, William Gyffard. Witd. Roger, archdeacon of
Barnstaple; Walter, archdeacon of Cornwall; Ralph called Archid';
Osbert de Brigia, William brother of the earl and Reginald his son. Not
dated. [*c.*1180–6 (Roger, archdeacon of Barnstaple, see Morey, 127.)]

MS.: Cartulary, f.170v.

**433.**   Confirmation by Henry, bishop of Exeter, of the grant in perpetual
alms to the priory of the church of Bridgerule, saving his episcopal rights
and those of his successors. Sealing clause. Witd. Hugh de Melewer,
Master H. of Wilton, William de Swyndon. Dated Crediton, 17 April
1204.

MS.: Cartulary, ff.170v.–171r.

**434.**   Grant in pure alms by Thomas de Duna, for the redemption of his
soul, his wife's soul and the souls of his children and of his mother and
father, to the priory of a certain land adjacent to the land of his church of
Bridgerule, which Gregory the clerk had held from him while he lived.
The grant was free from all secular service except royal service, and the
grant was made when Thomas' father was made a canon regular of the
priory. The bounds of the land were on the east a stream running
(*scaturiens*) between the same land and the land of Tatson running down
towards the south; and on the other side a certain ditch in the land of the
glebe of the church of Bridgerule and the said land leading towards the
land of 'Landry' as far as a certain 'Cundos' which is a sufficiently evident
bound on the western side between the said land and the land of 'Landry',
which 'Cundos' also leads towards the south and at last bends towards the
south into the said stream. Sealing clause. Witd. Ralph de Mora, Thomas
de Duneham, Gervase de Bray, Walter de Mora, William Gowyne, Warin
de Lyner, David de Gunam, William the baker. Not dated. [*c.*1170–86, see
no. 429.)

MS.: Cartulary, f.171r.

**435.** Gift and grant from William Gyffard for the redemption of his soul and the souls of his ancestors of his manor of Bridgerule (*Brigia*), consisting of half a knight's fee, to the priory to hold at farm for ever from him and his heirs for 4 marks of annual rent to be paid at the two terms of the Nativity of St John the Baptist and Christmas. Free from all exaction except royal foreign service,[a] and the service of the earl. Witd. William, brother of the earl, and his son, Reginald and William, son of Philip and his brother Osbert, Ralph, the clerk. Not dated. [Before *c.*1200 when William (de Marisco), brother of Earl Reginald, would have been advanced in years. Cf. nos 13, 332 and 442.]

[a]*utibannum*

MS.: Cartulary, f.171v.

**436.** Gift, grant and confirmation by Robert, son of Alard, to the prior and canons of all his land of Crochte with all appurtenances and liberties which he held in the manor of Bridgerule. To hold freely for the rent of 16 shillings yearly to the lords of Bridgerule, for all service except royal service, as much as pertained to so much land in that manor. He resigned his right and all documents to the prior and canons. Witd. the lord Henry Carbones, then dean; Henry Heryz, Walter de Mora, Richard Saer. Not dated. [*c.*1170–86, cf. no. 429 and 434 (Walter de Mora). See also no. 442.]

MS.: Cartulary, f.171v.

**437.** Gift, grant and confirmation by Ralph de Dune, lord of Bridgerule (with the assent of Thomas, his father, and for the salvation of his soul and those of his ancestors and successors) to the priory of a moiety of his mill of Bridge with a moiety of the multure of all his land of Bridgerule in pure and perpetual alms. The yearly rent payable to him and his heirs was 12d. at the feast of Michaelmas. The canons were to find a moiety of all cost to maintain the mill. The donor promised not to erect any other mill in the vicinity to the harm of the mill. If they did erect another mill in a better place it would be at common cost and there would be mutual sharing of the profits. Sealing clause. Witd. Ralph, archdeacon of Barnstaple, Gervase de Uffa. Not dated. [Oliver, *Lives*, 293, lists two archdeacons of Barnstaple called Ralph who occur 30 September 1209 and in 1219.]

MS.: Cartulary, f.172r.

**438.** Memorandum that Stephen, prior of Launceston and the convent of the same place, and Thomas Asseton reached agreement on the tithing and tithingman of Bridgerule who was accustomed to present in the hundred of Black Torrington (*Blaketoryton*). Thomas de Asseton and his heirs were to find one tithingman to present in the said hundred for 2 years beginning at the following Michaelmas for 2 years. And then in the third year the prior and convent and their successors were to find a tithingman to present in the said hundred. This was to continue for ever. The sum of 2s. due yearly should be paid in equal shares to the prior and convent and the said Thomas and his heirs. Witd. Henry Thorne, Richard Felhay, John Gokworthi, John Godecote, Stephen Devyok. Sealing clause of both parties. Dated Launceston, Easter Day, 18 April 1389.

MS.: Cartulary, f.172r.–f.172v.

**439.** Assize at Exeter before John Colpepyr and William Skren, royal justices in the county of Devon.

The assize came to recognise if John, prior of Launceston, Richard Pomeray and Thomasia his wife, Robert Dun, Richard Fogheler and Melior his wife, Nicholas Strange and Joan his wife, Nicholas Cotell and Thomasia his wife, Walter Hamond, John Hoper and John Fordeman had disseised unjustly John Bozon and Eleanor his wife, of their free tenement in Bridgerule. Whence it was pleaded that they had disseised them of 2 acres of land.

Prior John and the others did not come but John Ramisson, their bailiff, replied for them. He said that they had done no injury or disseisin to John Bozon and Eleanor. And about this he placed himself upon the assize. And John Bozon and Eleanor were seised of the said 2 acres as their free tenement. And the said prior, Richard Pomeray and Thomasia, his wife, and Robert, Nicholas, Nicholas and John Hoper had disseised them of it unjustly to the damages of 12 marks. And the said Richard Fogheler, Melior, Thomasia, wife of Nicholas Cotell, Walter and John Fordeman were not present at this disseisin.

Therefore it was adjudged that John Boson and Eleanor should recover seisin of the said two acres; their damages assessed at 12 marks. The prior, Richard Pomeray and Thomasia, Robert, Nicholas, Nicholas and John Hoper were in mercy. John Bozon and Eleanor were in mercy for a false claim against Richard Fogheler and all the other defendants named in the writ who were not present were acquitted of the disseisin and John Bozon and Eleanor paid them damages. Dated Exeter, Saturday, 10 March 1414.

MS.: Cartulary, ff.172v.–173r.

**440.** Grant by Walter Gyffard, his son William and his brother Roger, to the priory of the land of Tatson, part of Bridgerule, which Gilbert de Warenna, his uncle, had given to the same church when he was made a canon. The consideration for the prior and convent was the payment of 4 marks of silver, royal service, and service due to Richard de Ridvers, earl of Devon, Walter's lord. Sealing clause of grantor. Witd. Hugh de Ralege and his brother, Richard, prior of Plympton, and John, his canon; Gelem' de Brivele, William Talebote, Ralph de Langaford. Not dated. [*c*.1160–2. Succession of Richard, prior of Plympton, *Heads of Religious Houses*, 181 and death of Richard, earl of Devon.]

MS.: Cartulary, f.173r.

**441.** Grant and confirmation by William Giffard in pure and perpetual alms of the land of Tatson to the priory for his soul and the souls of his ancestors. It was acquitted of all except royal service: as much as fell due for Tatson as half a knight's fee of Bridgerule, as his ancestors had given it to the priory. Sealing clause. Witd. William, brother of the earl, and his son Reginald; Osbert, priest of Bridge; Johel the deacon, Edward, the donor's clerk; William, clerk of the canons. Not dated. [Late 12th century: William de Marisco, see no. 435.]

MS.: Cartulary, f.173r.–f.173v.

**442.** Grant by Thomas de Dune, lord of the land of Bridgerule, for his health and that of his wife, Constance, and their children and for the souls of his ancestors and successors to the priory of the land of Lodgeworthy (*Lowdeswothe*)[a] which Richard Landry and Roger Dudum held and as much land as he held in demesne, i.e. the whole land, bounded thus:

From the bridge of Riwald (*Ruwold*)[b] as the Tamar descended to the land of Tatson and from thence just as the stream ascended between the same land of Tatson and the said land of Lodgeworthy (*Ludeswothe*) to the land which he had previously given and confirmed by charter in perpetual alms to the canons. From thence just as it was divided it lay between that land (previously given to the canons) and the said land of Lodgeworthy to the land of the glebe of the church of Bridgerule and from thence as the glebe land lay bounding the said land of Lodgeworthy to the highway which went as far as the said bridge of Riwold.

The grant was made in pure and perpetual alms, acquitted from all except royal service: as much as pertained to that quantity of land in the manor of Bridge. Thomas offered the land on the altar of St Stephen with warranty and with an alternative exchange of 10s. worth of land in the manor of Bridgerule. Sealing clause. Witd. Hugh de Mortona, Hugh de Stoddona, Thomas de Duneham, Ralph de Mora, Henry Heriz, Richard de Trecarl. Not dated. [*c*.1170–86. (Ralph de Mora, Thomas de Duneham, Walter de Mora: see nos. 429, 434, 436.).]

[a]Title: *Lowdeshowe*. [b]Bridge of Riwald=Ruald who gave his name to Bridgerule as being the holder in Domesday Book. *EPNS Devon* i, 135.

MS.: Cartulary, ff.173v.–174r.

**443.** Notice by Paschasius, lord of Doune and Bridgerule (*Bruggerewall*) that Adam, prior of the monastery[a] of St Stephen of Launceston, and the convent there had held and then held all the lands in the vills of Tatson and Lodgeworthy with a moiety of the profit and multure of the mill of Bridgerule in free, pure and perpetual alms by the charters of his ancestors. Paschasius confirmed these and excluded prior Adam, the convent, and their successors from homage and fealty and suit of court to his manor of Bridgerule, but they were to provide timber for the mill from the wood of 'Braderygg' '. Warranty clause. Not witnessed or dated. [*c.*1183–1202. See appendix of list of priors for this Prior Adam.]

[a] *sic.*

MS.: Cartulary, f.174r.–f.174v.

**444.** Grant by brother Roger de Horton, prior of Launceston, and the convent to Christine who was the wife of Geoffrey Trote of Lodgeworthy (*Lowdeslouwe*) of the custody of the lands and the marriage of the heirs of the said Geoffrey, formerly their tenant, which Christine might sell or assign up to the full legal age of those heirs. Christine, or the assigns or owners were to pay due and customary services for this. Christine paid 9 marks of silver to the prior and convent. Alternate sealing clause (chirograph). Not witnessed. Dated Launceston, Thursday, 22 February 1313.

MS.: Cartulary, f.174v.

**445.** Inquisition that the prior of Launceston would not be tithingman for Tatson nor any other tenant of his there.

It was presented in the hundred of Black Torrington (*Blaktoryton*) held on Wednesday, 19 October 1356, before Walter de Stepheneston, steward of the lord of the hundred, that the prior of Launceston should be the tithingman of the tithing of Bridgerule, or should find a tithingman from his tenants for the land held by the prior in the vill of Tatson by right of his church of St Stephen of Launceston, or should contribute with the said tithing of Bridgerule to find a tithingman for the tithing or should pay a contribution in the fourth year. The prior was distrained to become tithingman or to pay a contribution or to explain why he had not done this.

The prior appeared in the court of the hundred of Black Torrington on Wednesday, 19 April 1357 by his attorney, John Billoun, who said the presentation was a bad one. Thomas de Doune, once lord of the tithing of Bridgerule, and great-grandfather of a certain Hugh de Doune, the then lord of the tithing, had granted all the land which the previous prior held in Tatson in pure, free and perpetual alms. John Billoun produced the charter of Thomas and sought judgement for the said prior that he should not be burdened contrary to the form of the charter.

The tithingman of the said tithing of Bridgerule said that the prior's predecessors were accustomed to be tithingmen of the tithing every fourth year or to pay a contribution by prescriptive right, so inquiry should be made. And the prior by his attorney sought judgement as above.

The process was adjourned until Wednesday, 26 July 1357, when the hundred court of Black Torrington was held and the prior and tithingman renewed their pleas. The jury (Elyas Bonevylle, Richard Coffyn, Geoffrey atte Clyve, John Broke, Walter Conwyk, Roger Cokeswalle, William Burdon, William atte Trewe, William atte More, Adam Lerkesworthi, Richard Perour and John Gerard) repeated Thomas Doune's charter and said that neither the prior nor his predecessors were tithingmen nor made contributions for tithingmen and that no tenant of the prior and convent from the land of Tatson was tithingman.

Judgement was awarded to the prior. Sealing clause of the jurymen and of John Dabernoun, then sheriff of Devon; Aumary fitz Waryn, Nicholas de Wangford, John Denys of 'Bradeford', Walter Stepheneston, steward of the lord of the hundred. Dated at the hundred court of Black Torrington, Wednesday, 26 July 1357.

MS.: Cartulary, f.175r.–f.175v.

**446.** The[a] tourn of the hundred of Black Torrington held before Aumary fitz Waryn, then sheriff of Devon on Saturday next after the feast of All Saints in the year of King Edward III.[b]

It was presented in the same tourn by the tithingman of the tithing of Werrington (*Worlyngton*) that the bridge of Bullapit (*Boleputte*) in the tithing was broken and that the prior of Launceston was responsible for the repair of the bridge. Wherefore the sheriff commanded the prior's presence at the next county court of Devon.

The prior appeared there and said by his attorney that neither he nor his predecessors had to repair the bridge and he sought an enquiry.

The bailiff of the hundred was commanded to cause to appear before the sheriff at Druxton Bridge (*Durkestonbrugge*) in the same hundred twelve free and legal men on Tuesday, 26 January 1350, to recognise if the prior should or should not repair the bridge. The twelve men who appeared were John de Oskeriswill, Walter Marshell, John de Northdon, William Goweyn, John de Yeldon, Richard Trota, Richard de Sutton, William Cotell, Robert de Grova, Henry de Holadon, Walter Lygha and William atte More. The jury said on oath that neither the prior nor his predecessors had to repair the bridge and this was so from time immemorial. Sealing clause: seals of the twelve jurors and the seal of the sheriff. Dated at the hundred court at Druxton Bridge, Tuesday, 26 January 1350.

[a]Additional title: *Inquisicio capta super decenna de Totesdon in hundredo de Blaktoryton quod prior Lanceston non tenetur invenire decennariu(m) vel reparare pontem de Boleputte nec invenire decennarium pro terra de Hoggyslade.*
[b]regnal year not given, but given the date of the hundred court at Druxton, it is possible that the tourn at Black Torrington was held on Saturday, 7 November 1349.

MS.: Cartulary, f.176r.

**447.** Grant and confirmation by Robert, prior of Launceston, to Roger Lene[a] and Alice, his wife, for their homage and service of half a ferling of land in the priory manor of Bradford which Walter Prikepayne held and the land which Loneman held and a quarter of an acre of the priory demesne of 'Holeburgh', at a rent of 2s. yearly. Except for the land reserved to the priory which Henry Beabrar formerly held, divided as it extended from the land of Beabrar as far as Helisdone and thence to Bradford (*Bradeford*) Lake with the common way as far as the well. Roger and Alice granted the right to grind at the priory mill of Pinkworthy (*Pynkaworth*) in the manor of Bradford without paying toll. Suit of court twice yearly in the prior's court of Bradford. If they were to incur a fine they could acquit themselves by 4 capons for all the pleas of one day. Roger and Alice were held to give warranty for all these lands. Sealing clause. Witd. Alan de Hellys.woth, Robert, his son; Adam de Vacy, knights; Roger de Dyrahill, Alan de Borna. Not dated. [*c.*1256–12 Sept. 1261, when Robert Fissacre was prior.]

[a]*Lene* supplied from title.

MS.: Cartulary, f.176v.


**448.** [a]Gift and confirmation by Henry de Heriz for the salvation of his soul and the soul of Elizabeth, his wife, and the souls of his ancestors to the priory and canons of all his land of Bradford in Devon in free, ecclesiastical and perpetual alms. Free from suits of county and hundred courts and all secular service except for the 10s. which he and his heirs should receive from the prior or reeve on Michaelmas day. Warranty and sealing clauses. Witd. Andrew de Cancell', then steward of Cornwall; John de Cheriton, then sheriff of Cornwall; Roger de Trelōch, William Wise, Hamelin de Stanbury. Not dated. [*c.*1221–44 (Andrew de Chanceux, William Wise).]

[a]Title: *Regestrum cartarum de Bradeforde, Pynkworthy et molendino ibidem . . . Et de maiori Hoggeslade ac de Wynscote.*

MS.: Cartulary, f.177r.


**449.** Notice by William de Hepford,[a] son of Walter, son of William, and Margaret, his wife, that he and his wife were held to warrant and defend all the land of the prior and convent of Launceston in Bradford from all suits and services of court due to the chief lords of the land, which land the prior and convent had by gift of Henry Heriz. William and Margaret granted that the prior and convent should pay the 10s. at Michaelmas to the chief lords of the fee, so that they should suffer no loss for defect of the same payment. If the chief lords should come to their court to distrain, the prior and convent should let them know. And if by chance for defect of certification in the court of the said chief lords, William and Margaret should have a loss, the prior and convent were required to restore that loss by coercion of the sheriff of Cornwall. If the prior and convent had a loss, the sheriff of Cornwall should make just reparation for their loss through all the lands of William and Margaret in Cornwall. Sealing clause of William and Margaret. Witd. the lord Gervase de Hornyncot, the lord Roger de Trelosk, the lord Adam de Fenton, Henry de Trevella, William Dunham. Not dated. [*c*.1242, see no. 451.]

<sup>a</sup>Title has *Hethford* but the 'p' of Hepford could be a thorn.

MS.: Cartulary, f.177v.

**450.** Quitclaim by Roger Venator and Alice, his wife, to the prior and convent of their right in the mill of Bradford with the whole weir of the mill and with the land which Beaubraz formerly held. With bounds which went from the land of the said Beaubraz as far as 'la Hethdich' and thence as far as Bradford Lake with the common way as far as the well. The prior gave 20 marks of silver for the quitclaim. Sealing clause. Witd. Gervase de Hornigcot, Adam de Fenton, Thomas de Estecot, William de Dunham, Henry de Trevella, Henry Chuyt. Not dated. [*c*.1242, see no. 451.]

MS.: Cartulary, ff.177v.–178r.

**451.** Mortgage by Roger Venator and his wife, Alice, and her sister, Sara, to the prior and convent of the mill of Bradford with the weir of the mill and the land which Beaubraz held for which formerly they used to pay one mark yearly. To have and to hold for the term of twenty years for the 20 marks the prior and convent had paid to them. Every year of this term 6d. of the loan should be paid off by the prior and convent. After 20 years they had to pay back to the prior and convent the said money and receive the mill, otherwise the mill would be held by the prior and convent until they made satisfaction for money due and reasonable arrears. Clause for seals. Witd. Henry Heriz, Gervase de Hornigcot, Adam de Fenton, Thomas de Estecote, William de Duneham, Henry Trevella, Henry Chynt. Dated 15 August 1242.

MS.: Cartulary, f.178r.

**452.** Quitclaim by Robert Dogge, son and heir of Roger Venator and his wife, Alice, of the mill of Bradford with the weir and all the land which Beaubraz formerly held. Bounded from the land of Beaubraz as far as 'la Hethdich' and thence to Bradford lake with the common way as far as the well. Warranty *contra omnes mortales*. The prior and convent paid half a mark of silver. Sealing clause. Witd. Adam de Fenton, David de Fenton, William Cola, Gregory de Dodeston, Roger de Luckote. Not dated. [?*c*.1244–6. After no. 451. Cf. nos. 211 and 222.]

MS.: Cartulary, f.178r.–f.178v.

**453.** Grant by William de Hendra to the prior and convent of licence to strengthen the weir of the mill on his land of 'Myryfeld'. The prior and convent were to pay him 18d. at Michaelmas for all service. Warranty and sealing clauses. Witd. Thomas de Estecot, H. Trevella, R. Fula, John Trewynnok.[a] Not dated. [*c.*1220 if H=Hamelin Trevella and R. Fula=Ralph Fula. See no. 229.]

[a]There follows a title: *Carta Henrici Heryz de licencia firmandi badum molendini de Pynkeworthy super terram de Newecote* followed by the words *sciant presentes*. The rest (?a folio) is missing and no. 454 begins on f.179r. immediately afterwards.

MS.: Cartulary, f.178v.

**454.** Notice by Richard Tallan that John Trethewy, vicar of the church of Talland, and all his predecessors held by prescriptive right (as by right of his church of Talland) a certain garden lying on the east side of the churchyard of Talland and on the southern side of the highway leading from Talland cross towards the mill of Talland. This garden Richard quitclaimed to John Trethewy. Richard's seal was unknown to many, therefore he used the seal of Sir John Herle, knight, lord of Trelawne (*Trewelaen*). Witd. Ralph Botreaux, Sir William Talbot, knight; Richard Trevage, John Trelawny, Richard Frankelyn. Dated Talland, Thursday, 12 January 1413.

MS.: Cartulary, f.179r.

**455.** Lease by William, prior of Launceston, and the convent to John Gybbe, perpetual vicar of the priory's church of the parish of Talland, of all the glebe of that church, i.e. one parcel on the eastern side of the manse of the vicar of Talland as far as the manse, and this measured 28 feet in width and 60 feet in length and stretched as far as the royal highway towards the north. The other parcel was on the southern side of the curtilage of the manse of the vicar and went as far as the curtilage, and lay on the north, west and east sides of the land of Hugh Tallan. It measured 15 perches in length, and in width, at the head of the said parcel, 7½ perches; in the middle of the parcel 5 perches in width and, below this, near the end of the parcel, 4¼ perches and, at the very end, was 3 perches in width. With liberty of entry and exit for the vicar and his servants. The advowson was reserved to the prior and convent. The grant was for the life of John Gybbe, as long as he remained vicar. He was to pay an annual rent of 40d. sterling to the priory and the prior and convent had a right of re-entry if the rent was in arrears after one month of Easter. Alternate sealing clause (chirograph). Witd. David Treluddek, Thomas Bank, clerk, John Lannoy. Dated at the chapter house of Launceston Priory, 22 February 1441.

MS.: Cartulary, f.179r.–f.179v.

**456.** Pleas[a] at Westminster before John de Metyngham and his companions, justices of the King's Bench.

John de Tallan sought against the prior of Launceston the advowson of the church of Talland by right. He said his ancestor, Gilbert, was seised of the advowson of the church by fee and right in the time of peace of King John, grandfather of the present king. And he presented a certain John Gervays, his clerk, to the said church who was instituted and admitted at his presentation, taking the greater and lesser tithes. And from Gilbert the right of advowson came to Antony, his son and heir, and thence to Nicholas Petyt, Antony's son and heir.

The prior appeared by attorney and defended his right. He well knew the seisin of Gilbert of his ancestors, but the said Gilbert enfeoffed a certain John Gervays with the advowson of the church, and he enfeoffed a certain prior of Launceston. And the said Antony, son of Gilbert, grandfather of the said John, by whose means the said John Gervays made the grant to the prior and convent, confirmed the grant.

Afterwards the said John de Tallan released and quitclaimed to the prior and convent of Launceston and their successors his right and that of his heirs in the advowson of the church. And he placed himself on the grand assize of the lord king for the matter to be determined by the assize *utrum* etc. Dated quindene of Trinity 1291.

[a]Note on top right corner of MS. *Md. q^d. finis istius placiti est in vij° folio precedente.*

MS.: Cartulary, f.180r.

**457.** Notice of a dispute between the abbot and convent of Glastonbury (*Glaston'*) and the prior and convent of Launceston about the ecclesiastical rights of Glastonbury in its chapel of Lammana (or Looe island). The dispute was settled on Saturday, 27 May 1279.[a]

The prior and convent of Launceston granted all sorts of tithes to the abbot and convent of Glastonbury from the salt sea of Looe (*Lo*) through the highway of 'Porthbyghan' extending as far as the well in the court of the lord of Portlooe (*Porlo*) before its hall and thence by the accustomed way to the sea on the south, except for the tithes of the curtilages and of the men living in the vill of 'Porthbighan'.

For their part, the abbot and convent of Glastonbury granted their right in the tithes to the north of these bounds, except for an ancient pension of 5s. with an increment of 20d. payable at Christmas and the Nativity of St John the Baptist at Lammana, payable to the abbot and convent of Glastonbury. When the sheepfold of the lord of Portlooe was to the south of these bounds the abbot and convent of Glastonbury would benefit from the emoluments, and, similarly, the prior and convent of Launceston when the sheepfold was to the north.

Both parties had taken a corporal oath to observe this settlement. Alternate sealing clause for chirograph. Witd. William de Moneketon, then steward of Cornwall; John de Bello Prato, Thomas de Kent, Hugh de Porlo, William de Campo Arnulphi, knights; Adam Heym, Durand de Pratis, William de Bodrugan, clerks. Dated July 1279.

[a]The date of 27 May 1279 is contained in the text, not in the title of the document.

MS.: Cartulary, ff.180r.–181r.

**458.** Pleas about the advowson of the church of Lammana.

Memorandum that the abbot and convent of Glastonbury held a messuage and a carrucate of land in Lammana and a certain island with a chapel of St Michael on the same island next to Lammana with the greater tithes of the said land of Lammana and the demesne of Portlooe to the south of the royal way which leads from Portlooe to 'Porthbighan' with the oblations and obventions which come from the said chapels which the said abbot and convent held within the limits of the parish of Talland (*Tallan*) which is appropriated to the prior and convent of Launceston, who, through their vicar, have the cure of souls of all the inhabitants of Lammana and maintain ecclesiastical rights. And Ralph Bloyhou bought for the use[a] of Walter de Treverbyn of the abbot and convent of Glastonbury the said lands of Lammana and the island. He bought all the rights of the abbot and convent in Lammana in lands, tithes, oblations and obventions under this formula: one messuage and one carrucate of land with their appurtenances with the advowson of the said chapel of Lammana, and Andrew the chaplain, the rector there, presented by a certain Walter.

And Richard, predecessor of the present prior of Launceston, in the presence of the bishop opposed the said presentation for the right of the church of Launceston and the mother church of Talland in seeking to amalgamate the said chapels to the mother church of Talland, because the vicar of Talland had the cure of souls of men living in the said land of Lammana and ministered to them an ecclesiastical cure, for they were within the limits of the said parish of Talland. Because of this impediment, Walter de Treverbyn brought the royal writ 'quare impedit' against the said prior.

The prior of Launceston was summoned to reply to Walter de Treverbyn about the plea that he should allow him to present a useful parson to the chapel of Lammana which was vacant (and the gift belonged to Walter). A certain John, abbot of Glastonbury, in the time of peace of the present king, held one messuage and one carrucate of land in Lammana to which belonged the advowson of the said chapel. The same John was made parson of the chapel and instituted into the same by the bishop. Afterwards the said John granted these tenements with the advowson of the chapel to the same Walter and resigned the chapel. Thus it was Walter's right to present to the chapel, but the prior prevented him from presenting whence Walter suffered a loss of £40.

The prior appeared by his attorney. He said he should not reply to this writ. Walter said the abbot was parson of the chapel of Lammana and instituted by the bishop to the advowson. Walter ought to have said that anyone having a right in the advowson presented to the said chapel any clerk of his who was admitted and instituted to the same. As Walter had not said that, the said abbot never presented to the said chapel nor any of his feoffees, he sought judgement if he ought to reply. Moreover he said the abbot could not be parson of the chapel, nor admitted to the same, nor instituted by the bishop in that the abbot was chosen by the election of his convent. And he sought judgement. As Walter said the abbot was parson of the chapel as of his own advowson because he held the said tenement in

Lammana. And the said Walter was enfeoffed of the same by the said abbot and convent.

And the said chapel was then vacant through the resignation of the said abbot whence Walter ought to present to the chapel. Walter sought the right of presentation, acknowledging the rights of the prior and convent. He said that the abbot was parson to the feast of St John the Baptist (24 June) 1289. And he said the chapel could not belong to the prior and convent's church of Talland. The prior could show no verification for owning the advowson. There had been a dispute between the abbey and priory for ten years on this matter. The prior and convent had granted tithes pertaining to the chapel of Lammana; he produced the writing. This would suppose the abbot and convent to be in seisin of the same chapel. He sought judgement whether or not the prior could claim the advowson of the chapel.

The prior said this writing did not harm him because before the writing he and the convent were in seisin of the tithes belonging to their church of Talland. And he sought judgement.

And the jurors said the abbot took the tithes as coming from the chapel of Lammana. And therefore it was adjudged that Walter should have the king's writ to the bishop, notwithstanding the prior's claim, to admit a useful parson. Not dated. [After 24 June 1289. See text above. For the sequel of this dispute, see W. M. M. Picken 'Light on Lammana', *D&CN&Q*. October 1985, 281–6.]

[a]*ad opus*

MS.: Cartulary, ff.181r.–182r.

**459.** Notice[a] of obligation of G(eoffrey), prior of Launceston, and the convent (of their own wish) to pay half a mark of silver annually to the prior and convent of Montacute at Michaelmas towards the maintenance of the kitchen of the same house for the quitclaim of the church of Talland and the whole right of the advowson. As soon as they could obtain from the church of Talland a rent of one mark at least, they would pay a whole mark annually to the prior and convent of Montacute at Easter. Witd. the lord Roger, prior of Froncton;[b] Robert, dean of Cornu';[c] Osbert de Stoke,[d] chaplain; Master Samson de Fromton, Robert de Sancto Marcolfo,[e] Robert de Fromton, clerk. Not dated. [*c*.1159–71, i.e. in the time of Prior Geoffrey.]

[a]No. 459 is a separate charter squeezed into the space at the foot of f.182r. in a smaller hand. It may have been inserted into the available space. [b]*Fromton* [c]*Cuinoc* [d]*Stokes* [e]*Marculfo.* Variant readings from *Two Cartularies of the Augustinian Priory of Bruton and the Cluniac Priory of Montacute.* Somerset Record Society, vol. viii (1894), which has a copy of the same charter, no. 173, pp. 188–9.

MS.: Cartulary, f.182r.

**460.** Notice[a] by Otto de Bodrugan that he had appointed as his attorney Roger Kyngk to do suit at the court of the prior of Launceston at

Bucklawren (*Bokkelowarn*) every 3 weeks for the land of 'Bodfus' which Otto held of the prior. Sealing clause. Pendrym, 1 May 1314.

<sup>a</sup>Heading: *Regestrum cartarum manerii de Bockelowarn et molendini eiusdem cum diversis instrumentis de xv parte tam maiorum quam minorum provenientium ibidem rectori Sancti Martini annuatim solvendorum et cartis de ij Treveryys et Benalva cum pertinentiis.*

MS.: Cartulary, f.182v.

**461.** Grant and confirmation by Robert, prior of Launceston and the convent to Henry de Bodrygan for his homage and service of their mill of Bucklawren (*Bokkalawarn*) with its appurtenances, viz. all the course of the water as it flowed with all the land under the weir of the said mill to the north from the millpond as far as the mill. When Henry wished to raise an embankment he and his heirs could do so above the bank of the weir towards the east above the priory's land from the royal way between Pendrym and Bucklawren to the said mill, with the whole flow of water between Bucklawren and Bodigga (*Bodcusuga*) as far as the said mill. With ways and means and reasonable estover in the priory's wood of Bucklawren without waste according to the view of the priory's servant at Bucklawren. To hold to Henry and his heirs with the multure of their manor of Bucklawren, saving the multure owed by the priory's servants at Bucklawren who ought to grind between the multures without toll. All who held part of the pasture or the wood of the priory ought to grind there as before. If any of the men of the priory ground there without Henry's licence or that of his heirs and was convicted, the grain should go to Henry and the priory would be in mercy. Henry was to pay an annual rent of a mark of silver. When Henry and his heirs wanted they could be quit of relief for the payment of 2s. Warranty clause. Sealing clause of both parties. Witd. lord Ralph de Buvyle, lord Ralph de Arundell; the lord Richard Tregoth, the lord Richard Tregrilla, the lord Bernard de Bodbran, William Wise, Robert Crochard, David de Kylmynawith, John Crok. Not dated. [1221–56, i.e. dating limits of Henry de Bodrugan, see W. M. M. Picken in *JRIC* (1981) ns. viii, pt. 4, 351–2.]

MS.: Cartulary, f.182v.–183r.

**462.** Bond of Henry de Bodrygan in one mark of silver to the prior and convent of Launceston for the rent of a certain mill and alder grove at Bucklawren. The rent was a mark of silver and a relief was 2s. The priory's servants were to grind there between the multures, free of toll. If there were arrears, Henry granted that the sheriff or steward of Cornwall could make distraint throughout his land of Pendrym for payment plus a penalty of half a mark to the earl of Cornwall or his bailiffs for making distraint throughout the manor of Pendrym. The distraint could extend to stopping the mill or taking away the ironwork of the mill. Henry had granted that the area or reed-bed under the said mill towards the south, viz. the land under the ford of the water which came from Bodigga (*Bodcusuga*) to the mill, should be common both to the prior and convent and their men and himself and his heirs and men. This meant he could not divert, or stop up, or make any embankment there. Sealing clause. Witd. lord Reginald de Boterell, the lord Gervase de Hornyngcot, the lord Roger de Trelosk, Richard Cola, Richard Trecarll, Henry Trevella. Dated Launceston, Easter 1256.

MS.: Cartulary, ff.183v.–184r.

**463.** Final concord made in the king's court at Launceston in five weeks of Michaelmas 1262 in the presence of Robert Brywes, Richard de Middelton and William de Staunton, justices itinerant. Between Richard, prior of Launceston, querent, and Philip de Bodrugan, deforciant, of the custom of service which the same prior exacted from Philip for his free tenement which he held of the prior in Bucklawren viz., of the 2 acres of alder grove and one mill. The prior exacted that Philip should pay homage and relief to him and rent of one mark of silver. This Philip agreed to do, with relief at 2s. when it occurred. For this concession the prior granted that his men of the manor of Bucklawren and their heirs should pay suit to the mill of Philip at Bucklawren. The prior granted warranty to Philip and his heirs. Dated in the quindene of Michaelmas, 1262.

MS.: Cartulary, f.184r.–f.184v. Printed *Cornwall FF.* i, no. 203 under the date 3 November 1262.

**464.** Agreement between the prior and canons of Launceston and Roger Russell about the stream running between the manor of Bucklawren and Pendrym.[a] Roger Russell, lord of Pendrym,[a] allowed the prior and canons to construct an aqueduct of his mill in the manor of Pendrym to the betterment of the priory. And the prior and canons granted Roger leave to construct a similar aqueduct of his mill in his land of Bucklawren provided it was not to the detriment of the priory. Roger Russell granted the multure of all his men beyond the stream, at the eastern part, to the prior and convent. Both parties granted warranty. Alternate sealing clause for chirograph. Witd. Walter son of Robert, Richard son of Gilbert, Faramus de Walesbreu, Ralph de Rupe. Not dated. [Between 19 October 1196 and 28 April 1214, i.e. occurrences of F. of Whalesborough, *Cornwall FF.* i, nos. 3 and 39.]

[a]These additions are supplied by the title to the charter.

MS.: Cartulary, ff.184v.–185r.

**465.** Quitclaim by Philip de Bodrugan, knight, lord of Pendrym, to the priory of the mill he held of the canons in the manor of Bucklawren with its weir and multure. He had granted free access to his park for repair of the mill. Sealing clause. Witd. John de Bello Prato, steward of Cornwall;

the lord Reginald de Botrell. Not dated. [1268–9 when John de Beaupré was steward of Cornwall.]

MS.: Cartulary, f.185r.

**466.** Grant and confirmation by Roger of Bodrugan, knight, son and heir of Philip de Bodrugan, to the prior and canons of the quitclaim which his father Philip had made to them of the mill with the weir and water to which Philip's charter bore witness. Sealing clause. Witd. John de Bello Prato, then steward of Cornwall; the lords Reginald de Boterell, Guy de Nonnant, Hugh de Treverbyn, Ralph de Bovilla. Not dated. [1268–9, as no. 465.]

MS.: Cartulary, f.185r.–f.185v.

**467.** Copy of instrument by notary public that William Sergeaux, rector of the parish church of St Martin (by Looe), recognised to Roger Leye, prior of Launceston, and his brother canons, David Attehole, William Snowe and William Hilperby, that he received 4s. 8d. in money by tale[a] of the oblations paid to the chapel of St John the Baptist in the manor of Bucklawren within the bounds of the church of St Martin. He agreed that if the oblations by common right belonged from time immemorial to the priory that he would pay them to Prior Roger. After this Mr. William confessed that even if by common law the oblations should seem to be his, if it were proved by the witness of worthy men that the prior and convent had always for time immemorial enjoyed them as their right, they should have the oblations. Accordingly he surrendered them to brother Roger, then prior, and restored them in full. Witd. Henry Frund, perpetual vicar of the church of St Martin of Liskeard; Stephen Devyek, Philip Trethewy, John Sele, Luke Brewys, Robert Germyn, Robert Foryn, William Grega.[b] Dated in the chamber of the prior, 20 July 1370.

[a]For payments by tale rather than *ad pensum*, see R. L. Poole, *The Exchequer in the Twelfth Century* (1912), 31 et. seq. [b]followed by Stephen Cresa's (notary public) certificate of this act.

MS.: Cartulary, ff.185v.–186r.

**468.** Statements of witnesses for the prior and convent of Launceston about the ownership of the greater and lesser tithes of Fawton (*Fawinton*).

Henry Rem, aged 70 and more, said on oath that the prior and convent of Launceston and their predecessors were in peaceful possession of two parts of the greater and lesser tithes arising from the ancient demesne of Fawton for 40 years past and more as well by apostolic authority as by the consent of the prior and convent of Montacute (*Mons Acutus*) who owned the church of St Neot within which parish the manor of Fawton lay. Henry Rem said that he had heard and seen this and the matter was well known in the neighbourhood. The same matter by the authority of judges delegate and the Apostolic See was reduced to a letter of composition indented and sealed by both parties.

John Cosyn, aged 70 and more, said the same.

Alger Payn, aged 60 and more, said the same and added that as a servant of the prior and convent he had sold 2 parts of the said tithes.

Robert de Bodmam, aged 45 and more, said the same. He added that Algar did not sell the tithes but he saw and was present when Henry, prior of Launceston, sold the tithes and received the money.

Robert Tripolet, aged 50 and more, said the same as Robert de Bodmam. Dated Launceston Castle, Wednesday, 18 December 1303.[a]

[a]From title which also states, . . . *super quinta decima parte solvenda in manerio de Bokkalowarn.*

MS.: Cartulary, f.186r.–f.186v. For the tithes of Fawton (and Fowey moor) see also *Two Cartularies . . . of Bruton . . . and Montacute.* Somerset Record Society viii (1894), nos. 171, 172 and 176. 171 is dated 1238, 172 is dated 1241, 176 is not dated.

**469.** Examination of the witnesses of the prior and convent of Launceston, heard before Master Roger Page, doctor of canon law and Thomas Noell, bachelor in law, for arbitration and amicable agreement relating to the greater and lesser tithes and immunities of the manor of Bucklawren (*Boklouwern*) belonging to Launceston priory of the one part and master William Sergeaux of the other part.

Richard Skurell of free condition and of the age of 24 years or more said that there were two parks or fields surrounded with hedges called 'Roketpark' and Pethick park (*Botpedek park*) belonging to the manor of Bucklawren from which the rector of the church of St Martin was accustomed to take the entire tithe of the sheaves by ancient custom. He said that the rector took the whole tithes of the profits of all milch cows, calves and lambs which lay or were depastured in these places. He also said that the rector took the sheaf-tithes from a certain estate of the same manor called 'Cattenepark' (the northern part of which was near 'Boklowwernburgh') which contained 4 acres of land and also from a certain field called 'Loskruc'. The rector of the said church also took a fifteenth part of the sheaf-tithe, and of hay, and of calves, lambs, wool, dairy produce, cheeses, butter, and animals which lay or were depastured. The remaining part went to the prior and convent.

Robert Olyver of free condition of 50 years of age and more said the same as Richard Scurell and added that the parcel of land to the northern part of 'Cattenepark' contained 6 or 7 acres. All the manor of Bucklawren lay within the bounds and limits of the church of St Martin by Looe. Excepting that year when the manor of Bucklawren had been let, the prior and convent of Launceston had kept the manor in their own hands and cultivated it at their cost. The rector took 4d. for the tithe of the toll of grain and no more. Asked if the prior and convent took any tithe of this toll, he said they had not. As for the rent of 15s, the deponent as the reeve took all the rents of the manor every three years and he also took yearly 4d. for the whole tithe of the mill which he paid to the rector.

William Wylsshman of free condition aged 50 agreed with Robert

Olyver. He added he had been reeve for two years of the manor of Bucklawren.

John Damarall of free condition aged 36 agreed entirely with William Wyllschman.

John Pyperell of free condition of the age of 40 and more agreed with Robert Oliver. He did not know the name of 'Roketepark' and said that the parcel of land next to Bucklawrenburgh only contained half an acre of land.

John Lucas of free condition aged 40 or more agreed with Robert Olyver. Dated Bucklawren and Launceston, 24 and 25 August 1384.

MS.: Cartulary, ff.187r.–188r.

**470.** Examination of the witnesses of Master William Sergeaux, rector of the church of St Martin by Looe.

William Kyllyow of free condition aged 55 agreed with Richard Skurell. 'Bocepytpark', 'Roketepark', 'Luskruk' and a parcel of land of 'Cattene park' next to Bucklawrenburgh were of the church of St Martin by Looe and titheable exactly as a fifteenth part cultivated by the labour and at the cost of the prior. If these lands fell in hand he supposed that the fifteenth part would be again restored in lieu of the full tithe. In the time of Thomas, formerly prior of Launceston, there were 9 acres of land, partly in 'Semyslond' and partly in 'Longalond' belonging to the manor of Bucklawren set to laymen who accordingly paid a full tithe to the rector, but formerly when the land had been tilled at the cost of the prior they had paid a fifteenth only. He added to the evidence of Robert Skurell that William the then rector of the church took the whole tithe of hay of the whole manor in that year. Otherwise he agreed with Richard Oliver.

John Godynch of free condition aged 50 or more agreed with William Kyllyowe but he said there were only 4 acres of land where William Kyllyow deposed 9 acres. John himself held 2 acres of these.

Thomas Renald of free condition aged 40 or more agreed with William Kylliowe. Thomas had been a servant of Prior Thomas for seven years.

John Kyll of free condition aged 40 and more agreed with William Kyllyowe. He also said the amount of the tithe of the lands of the priory and of the mill was not recorded. He had been a servant in the manor for nine years, half in the time of the lord Thomas and the rest in the time of Prior Roger Ley.

John Cornyssh of free condition aged 30 or more agreed with the rest.

John Thomas of free condition of the age of 40 years or more agreed with William Kylyowe.[a] Dated in the church of St Martin by Looe, 26 August 1384.

[a]There follows the certificate of Stephen Cresa, notary public.

MS.: Cartulary, f.188r.–f.189r.

**471.** Notarial certificate concerning the prior and convent of Launceston and Mr William Sergeaux, rector of St Martin by Looe, about how the tithes of sheaves of corn, hay, calves, lambs, wool, milch cows, cheese and butter were to be raised from the manor of Bucklawren near Looe belonging to the prior and convent. The prior and convent claimed that the rector had a fifteenth part of the tithe and they had the residue by laudable custom. The rector admitted this but only when the manor was in the actual hands of the prior and convent and tilled at their own cost. When it was let to others it ought to pay the rector the full tithe. To end the dispute Mr Roger Page, Doct. Decret. and Thomas Noell, LL.B., were appointed arbiters. If they failed to come to a decision before the Nativity of the Blessed Virgin Mary (8 September) Mr Ralph Tregow, LL.D. would be added to them as a third arbiter to come to a judgement before Michaelmas 1385. Both parties agreed to be bound by their decision under a penalty of £100 payable by the disobedient party. The arbiters found the time too short for a proper examination of the business and both parties agreed to a prorogation until a week after the feast of St Mary aforesaid.[a] This was done in the presence of Sir Thomas Bray, canon, and Walter Pyers, clerk. There were present at the prorogation of the rector Sir Thomas Couling and John Shevrell, priests, and at the prorogation of the prior Sir John Trethewy, chaplain, and John Tynlegh, clerk. Dated the chapter house of Launceston priory, 23 August 1384. [Prorogation to 7 September 1384 when there were present for the rector Sir Thomas Coulyng and John Shevrell, priests, and for the priory Sir John Trethewy and John Tynlegh, clerk.]

[a]The main instrument is followed by the certificate of Stephen Cresa, notary public.

MS.: Cartulary, ff.189r.–190r.

**472.** Agreement between the prior and convent and Mr William Sergeaux, rector of the parish church of St Martin by Looe. The prior and convent for the life of Mr William were to enjoy all the great and small tithes from the manor of Bucklawren. For this the prior and convent were to pay William yearly 40s. at the Purification and Michaelmas. If the payment was eight days in arrears, the prior and convent were to pay William a further sum of 13s. 4d. Witd. Sir William Kelliou, priest; Stephen Devyok, John Godecote, Walter Cryke, John Lowarn, clerks of the diocese of Exeter. Dated at the chapter house of Launceston priory, 11 June 1389.
Certificate by Nicholas Tresulgan, clerk and notary public.

MS.: Cartulary, f.190v.

**473.** Notice that John Gylys, M.A., rector of St Martin by Looe, in the presence of a notary, made brother Roger Combrych canon of the priory of Launceston, with the consent of his prelate, his lawful proctor to deal on his behalf with the venerable lord Edmund, bishop of Exeter, about a settlement to be made about the tithes of the manor of Bucklawren in St Martin concerning which there had been a dispute between the rector and the priory, who had appropriated the tithes. Witd. Stephen, prior of

Launceston; Henry Person, *litteratus*; John Treludek (all of the diocese of Exeter). Dated in the chapel or oratory within the hospital of Ermyn's Inn in the street which is called Fleet Street (*Flutstret*), London, 17 February 1396.
Certificate by William Hamound, clerk and notary public.

MS.: Cartulary, f.191r.–f.191v.

**474.** Agreement in the presence of Stephen, prior of Launceston, and the brethren David Treludek, Roger Combrigge, Thomas Trethak, John Batyn and Thomas Osborn, canons, and many other canons of the same priory asembled in chapter. Mr John Sergeaux, rector of the parish church of St Martin by Looe appeared to make a settlement of the dispute about the tithes of the manor of Bucklawren in St Martin's parish. It was decided that the prior and convent as formerly should enjoy all the tithes both real and personal during the life of Master John, the rector, and should pay him a pension of 40s. with an addition of 13s. 4d. if the payment were more than eight days in arrear. Witd. John Bilney, Thomas Ude, Walter Fourneys. Dated at the chapter house of Launceston Priory, 1 September 1398. Followed by a certificate by William Hamound, clerk and notary public.

MS.: Cartulary, ff.191v.–192r.

**475.** Agreement of Stephen, prior of Launceston, and the convent to the agreement of no. 474. Same witnesses. Dated at the chapter house of Launceston priory, 1 September 1398. Certificate by William Hamound, clerk and notary public.

MS.: Cartulary, f.192r.–f.192v.

**476.** Ratification by Thomas, bishop of Exeter, of the acts of Mr Roger de Otery his commissary.

The acts were made in the greater church of Exeter before Roger de Otery, canon of Crediton, commissary of Bishop Thomas of Exeter in a cause promoted *ex-officio* by the prior and convent of Launceston, about two-thirds of the great and small tithes of the old demesne of Fawton in the parish of St Neot (*Neothus*) which they claimed. And also about their exemption from paying any tithe but the fifteenth for their demesne of Bucklawren to the mother church of St Martin, as settled in the last episcopal visitation of the archdeaconry of Cornwall. The prior and convent appeared by brother William de Penlen, their canon and proctor, and claimed the tithes of Fawton by prescriptive right, confirmed by a charter of the prior and convent of Montacute, and they also claimed prescriptive right for the exemption for the tithes of Bucklawren. At length the commissary pronounced sentence in favour of the prior and convent of Launceston on both matters in accordance with the powers granted by the bishop in a commission to Ralph Germyn, archdeacon of Barnstaple, and John de Brueton and Roger de Otery, canons of Crediton. Ratification by the Bishop of Exeter at his visitation of the archdeaconry of Cornwall. Dated St Germans, 12 October 1303; confirmation Clyst, 20 January 1304.

MS.: Cartulary, f.193r.–f.193v.

**477.** Grant and quitclaim by Osbert de Treveria to the canons of Launceston of the land of 'Lostruc' with the houses and other appurtenances which he had held for some time by the permission of the canons of their demesne of Bucklawren. He resigned the charter he had had from them. The same Osbert ought to take down the mill which he had unjustly constructed anew in his land of Treveria (*Treverya*) to the harm of the canons' mill in the manor of Bucklawren. The canons promised the same Osbert that he could grind wherever he wished his corn from one acre of land he held of them in the vill of Treveria. In recompense of the expenses sustained by Osbert in the construction of his mill on the land of 'Loscruk', the canons gave Osbert 2 marks of silver. Osbert had taken an oath never to rebuild a mill in the land of Treveria. Alternate sealing clause (chirograph). Witd. Master Gatterus de Sutton, John de Gloucestre, Drogo de Vernun, Jordan de Trevaga, Roger de Kyllys, Roger Tyraunt. Not dated. [*c*.1212–38. (Osbert de Treveria, nos. 478, 482). Jordan de Trevaga occurs 15 June 1238, *Cornwall FF.* i, no. 71 but also as early as *c*.1212.]

MS.: Cartulary, f.194r.

**478.** Grant and confirmation by Lucy Russell, widow and lady of Pendrym (*Pendrim*), for the salvation of her soul and the souls of her ancestors and successors to the priory of a certain place in the south part of the new borough of Looe (*Loo*) in pure and perpetual alms. The place lay between that of Wara and Hamelin Peche and contained a quarter of an acre of land. Sealing clause. Witd. Geoffrey, son of Bernard; Henry de Bodrugan; Robert, parson of the church of St Martin, Thomas Malrew, Edmund de la Haye, Osbert de Treverya, Nicholas de Trecarll. Not dated. [*c*.1220 or a few years later after Lucy Russell's charter to Looe, see Picken in *JRIC* (1981) ns., viii, pt. 4, 352.]

MS.: Cartulary, f.194r.

**479.** Grant and quitclaim by William de Montibus to the conventual church of Blessed Stephen of Launceston and the canons, for the salvation of his soul and the souls of his ancestors and successors, of all his land in lower Treveria in the manor of Bucklawren which he had had for a time of the gift of Robert, formerly prior of Launceston and the convent. William renounced any claim to reclaiming the land which he had formerly of the gift of Bernard de Botuell in the vill of Higher Treveria in either an ecclesiastical or lay court. Sealing clause. Witd. the lord Stephen Heym, then steward of Cornwall; Adam de Fenton, the lord William Wise, knights; Andrew de Trevaga, Roger de Lutecote. Not dated. [Either 1262 or 1267 when Stephen Heym was steward of Cornwall, Hull, *Cartulary of St Michael's Mount* no. 7. See also no. 236.]

MS.: Cartulary, f.194v.


**480.**   Grant and confirmation by William de Montibus to the priory of all his land of Higher Treveria[a] in the manor of Bucklawren in pure, free, quiet and perpetual alms. Clause of warranty *contra omnes mortales* under pain of £40 and submission to the coercion of the sheriffs of Devon and Cornwall by distraint of his lands etc. He who made the distraint of William's lands was to have 20s. sterling for his trouble. The canons gave him the land of Gatherley (*Gyderleghe*) in exchange. Sealing clause. Witd. the lords John de Bello Prato, Richard de Hywys, William de Campo Arnulphi, Bernard de Bodbran, knights; the lord William de Bodrygan. Not dated. [Possibly 1270; certainly after no. 479.]

[a]Title includes, *de superiori Treverya*.

MS.: Cartulary, ff.194v.–195r.


**481.**   Enfeoffment by Andrew de Benalva to his brother Walter of his whole land of Bonyalva which Richard Staneray his father formerly held of the prior of Launceston by homage. To have and to hold to the said Walter and his heirs or assigns of the chief lord of the same vill, the prior of Launceston. The prior should admit Walter as his tenant and exact from him due and customary services as seemed best to him. Sealing clause for letters patent. Launceston, Sunday, 18 May 1292.

MS.: Cartulary, f.195v.


**482.**   Copy of chirograph which attested the agreement made between G(odfrey), prior of the canons of Launceston and Robert, lord of Lydcott (*Luttecote*). The prior and canons had granted to the said Robert, lord of Lydcott, their water which ran between Lydcott and Bonyalva to strengthen the weir to their mill of Lydcott. To hold of the priory by hereditary right for ever, rendering yearly at the feast of Michaelmas to the said canons 6d. for all service. If Robert did not pay the rent at that term, the canons could distrain. Witd. Oliver Foreschu, Robert de Trechinoch, Hamelin de Trevella, Edward de Benavel, Osbert de Treverya. Not dated. [*c.*1220 or a little later (Osbert de Treveria), when Godfrey was probably still prior.]

MS.: Cartulary, f.195v.


**483.**   Grant and gift by Jocelin, lord of Trethew, son of Randulf, to the prior and canons of Launceston to strengthen the weir and water leading from his mill in his land of Bonyalva wherever it seemed best to them through all his land of Trethew (*Tretheu*). They were to render to him yearly 3d. at Michaelmas for all service. Jocelin granted warranty to the prior and canons *contra omnes exactores*. For this grant the prior and canons gave him in recognition half a mark of silver. Sealing clause. Witd. Henry Heryz, Odo de Tregrille, John de Trenode, John de Penchut, Jocelin de Creugalen. Not dated. [*c*.1229–42, Henry Heriz, see nos. 451 and 499.]

MS.: Cartulary, f.196r.

**484.** Grant and quitclaim by Matilda, formerly wife of William Scorch, in her widowhood, for the salvation of her soul and the soul of William her husband and the souls of her mother and father, to the canons of St Stephen 6d. which the said canons used to pay her yearly for the weir which they had strengthened in her wood of Carlean (*Karlechyan*) to their mill of Bonyalva. Warranty and sealing clauses. Witd. Robert de Luthcote, Osbert de Treverya, Hamelin de Trevell', Edward de Benavel. Not dated. [*c*.1220 or a little later, see no. 482.]

MS.: Cartulary, f.196r.

**485.** Agreement between William, prior of Launceston, and the convent and John de Trenoda. John, by an oath of fealty, was to hold of the prior and convent, one ferling of land in 'Roddune',[a] which lay in the fee of Bonyalva, with the whole mill which formerly belonged to the father of John and its appurtenances, i.e. with all the multure of the men of Bonyalva. The prior was not to make any new mill on the land of Bonyalva. John and his heirs were not to construct any corn or fulling mill in the fee of Trenode nor in Bonyalva, except only a corn mill and that on the land of 'Roddun'. John was to pay yearly to the prior and convent 6s. within the octave of Michaelmas and the octave of Easter. The property was to revert to the prior if the rent was in arrears, the prior paying yearly to the said John and his heirs 2s. at Michaelmas and Easter. The prior's men were to have common of pasture over the whole of the ferling in 'Roddune' outside the corn of the said John. Sealing clause (both parties). Witd. Simon de Brak', then sheriff of Cornwall; Roger Trelosk, John de Trevaga, William Wys. Not dated. [*c*.1225–7 (*Rot. Litt. Claus.* ii, 25, 141, 171, 209) when Simon de Brakeli was sheriff, or 1232–3 (no. 217) when he was also sheriff.]

[a]*Rodden'* in heading.

MS.: Cartulary, f.196v.

**486.** Quitclaim by John de Trenoda for himself and his heirs to the prior and convent of the whole right he had in one ferling of land in 'Roddun' and of the site of the mill in the same land of 'Roddun' with the multure of his house and of all the men of his land who wished the prior and convent to strengthen the mill in the same fief wherever it seemed to them most useful. The prior and convent were to pay John and his heirs yearly 6s. for the said land and mill at the terms of Easter and Michaelmas for all service which belonged to John. Neither the latter nor his heirs could erect any other mill in the same fief on the water of Seaton (*Setthul*) to the detriment of the prior and convent. Besides the said John had granted to the prior and canons the said fief and mill to the tenants and to Edward Cock the tenement in which the common pasture of the land was. The prior and canons for their part had granted to John and his heirs and their men the common pasture of the land forever. Alternate sealing clause (chirograph). Witd. Richard de Kygad, Jordan de Trevagg', Anger de Tregeryoc, Roger Devyoc, William, son of Baldwin. Not dated. [See no. 487.]

MS.: Cartulary, ff.196v.–197r.

**487.** Grant, ratification and quitclaim by Alice, formerly wife of Drogo de Trenoda, of the grant which her son and heir John had made to the priory of one ferling of land in 'Roddun' with the site of the mill. She would not make any claim of her dowry dependent on the said land and mill. By fealty and her seal she confirmed her charter. Witd. Richard de Kylgat, Jordan Trevag', Anger de Tregeryoch, Roger de Devyoc, William son of Baldwin. Not dated. [Drogo Trenode died 'in or shortly before October 1212, see *JRIC* viii, pt. 4 (1981), p. 351.]

MS.: Cartulary, f.197r.

**488.** [a]Notice by John Kendale de Bodmalgan concerning a dispute about a certain watercourse between the land of lord Stephen, prior of Launceston, and of the convent in Bonyalva flowing to the mill of the priory and John's land in 'Kylvosowe' and 'Whitelak' and a certain bank pertaining to the said mill. The dispute had continued for some time and John Kendal wished to do away with the controversy and uncertainty. He granted to Prior Stephen that he and the convent might have the course and bank or headweir belonging to the mill of Bonyalva as peacefully as he and his predecessors had held it. The prior and convent could repair the course, bank and head weir with wood, stone and turves from John's land by the watercourse. Sealing clause. Witd. Martin de Feres, Nicholas Wampford, John Bryton of Bodmin, Joceus Alan, John Bynneley. Thursday, 13 October 1390.

[a]Marginal note, *m^d q^d placita de sect' molend' de Benlva scribuntur . . . in fine libr' immediate prius cartas de Tamerton.*

MS.: Cartulary, f.197v.

**489.** Quitclaim by Simon Benalva to the lord Roger Combrygge, prior of Launceston, of his right in the common pasture in the whole land of Bonyalva. Sealing clause. Witd. Noel Paterda, John Cokeworthy, Thomas

Paderda, John Harlysdon, Walter Pyper. St Germans, Tuesday, 20 May 1404.

MS.: Cartulary, ff.197v.–198r.


**490.** Quitclaim by Richard Benalva to John Honylond, prior of Launceston, and the convent of his right in the common pasture in the whole land of West Bonyalva. Sealing clause. Witd. Thomas Paderda, John Trenode, John Talcarn, William Trelauny,[a] John Treludek, Nicholas Tregodek junior, Stephen Cork. Dated Launceston, Thursday, 23 October 1410.

[a]Written *Trelavny*.

MS.: Cartulary, f.198r.


**491.** Inquisition taken for the king at St Ive before Richard Cergeaux, sheriff of Cornwall, in his tourn held on Monday, 25 October 1389. By the oaths of Walter Kyngdon, Robert Benalva, Adam˙Buketon, John Uppaton, Roger Trenalt, Walter Pyper, Thomas Attemore, Thomas Saghier, William Rouald, Reginald Asshlake, John Slade and Thomas Richard. They said that the royal highway at 'Halmurfosse' was bad and muddy. The tithingman and the tithing of Landrake (*Lanrake*) ought to repair this way and had been accustomed to do so for time immemorial. Wherefore it was considered that the said tithingman of Landrake was in mercy for concealment of this road. And it was presented to the bailiff of East that the tithingman and tithing should be distrained to repair this road before the next court. The hundred court was held at St Germans on Monday, 20 December 1389, when the tithingman of Landrake was asked if the said highway of 'Halmurfosse' had been repaired. He said that this road was not in the tithing of Landrake, nor was it accustomed to be repaired by the tithing. And he placed himself on the country.[a] And thus it was commanded to John Harlisdon, bailiff of the hundred there that he was to gather twelve just and legal men of his bailiwick of the better sort by which the truth of the matter could be better known and the truth told to the following hundred. The next hundred was held at Callington (*Calyngton*) before Thomas Peverell, then sheriff, on Thursday, 20 January 1390. And the bailiff returned Walter Kyngdon, Dalvoy*n*,[b] John Dreynek, John Hamme, William Treskelly, John Milhay, John Slade, William Boyelond, William Rest, Peter Helygan, Stephen Attecombe, Roger Cargyntell to make a jury. The jurors said the royal way at 'Halmurfosse' was in the deanery of Landrake and the tithing of Landrake had had to repair it from time immemorial. Thus it was decided by the court that the tithingman and tithing of Landrake should be distrained to repair the highway before the next hundred court under a penalty of 40s. Sealed by the jurors. Dated Callington, Thursday, 20 January 1390.

[a]*super patriam.* [b]*sic.*

MS.: Cartulary, f.198r.–f.198v.

**492.** The bounds of 'Werelond' in the manor of Bonyalva in the thirtieth year of the reign of King Henry VI (1 September 1451–31 August 1452.)

The homage presented the bounds in the holding of 'Werelond', viz. from 'Myllond' and the water of Seaton (*Saythen*) which lay on the western side, as far as the ditch made by William Benalva which lay on the eastern side; the land of John Gayche which he held of the lord prior of Launceston on the other side;[a] and the land of the said William Benalva with 'Hennwade' in the north side and the land of North Bake on the southern side. And further the homage presented within the said ditch a parcel of land in 'Croft' of the said William Benalva under 'Le Rewe' in the said 'Croft' on the western and northern sides. And the land of North Bake lay on the southern side. And by the well called 'Thornewill' lying on the east as measured and bounded by the said homage. 1451–2 (see title).

[a]"This document has been written in later by the same careless 15th-cent. hand which wrote the document' on f.176v. See Henderson's transcript of the Cartulary, 265.

MS.: Cartulary, f.198v.


**493.** Gift of Reginald, son of the king, earl of Cornwall, to the church of St Stephens of Launceston, of the churches of Liskeard and Linkinhorne, for the increase of the church of St Stephen on the day of the translation of the relics and canons of the same church to the ford. Not dated. [7 February 1155, see Introduction, p. xvi and note 84.]

MS.: Cartulary, f.199r.

Reginaldus regis filius consul Cornub' omnibus ministris suis salutem. Sciatis me dedisse ecclesie sancti Stephani de Lanstavaton in incrementum eiusdem ecclesie ecclesiam de Leskeret et ecclesiam de Lankynhorn die translacionis reliquiarum et canonicorum ipsius ecclesie de villa Lanstavaton ad vadum. Habendas et tenendas cum omnibus pertinenciis suis in liberam elemosinam imperpetuum quam cito vacantes exstiterint. Teste Radulfo de Boscoroham, Rob(erto) filio Asketill, Hugone de Dunstanvill etc.


**494.** Gift, grant and confirmation by H., son of the earl[a] of Cornwall, lord of Liskeard (*Lyscharet*), for the souls of his mother and father, to the church of St Stephen of Launceston and the canons there, the church of Liskeard (*Lescharet*) with all its appurtenances which also Roger,[b] his father gave to the church of Launceston on the day of the translation of the relics and canons of the vill of Launceston at the ford. To have and possess wholly and peacefully in pure and perpetual alms forever. Sealing clause. Witd. Robert de Tyntagell, Jocelin de Monte, Hugo de Albo Monasterio, Henry Heriz. Not dated. [*c.*1194–1220. See Round, *Ancient Charters* (PRS.1888) no. 62 and *CPR* (Hen III) i, 241. For Jocelin de Monte, alias Pomeray, see P. L. Hull, *Cartulary of St Michael's Mount* (Devon and Cornwall Record Society, 1962), xxvii.

[a]MS. has *filius Regis Comitis* (for *filius Reginaldi Comitis*). [b]*Sic*, for Reginald: see no. 495.

MS.: Cartulary, f.199r.

**495.** Grant and confirmation by Henry, son of Reginald, earl of Cornwall, of the church of Liskeard (*Leskyred*) to the church and canons of St Stephen of Launceston. His father Reginald had formerly given the church of Liskeard to the canons on the day of their translation, with the relics, to the ford. Sealing clause. Witd. Henry de Pom',[a] Henry de Tracy, Jocelin de Monte, John, son of Richard. Not dated. [1194–1220, see no. 494.]

[a]?Pomeray.

MS.: Cartulary, f.199r.–f.199v.


**496.** Letter by Henry, son of Reginald, earl of Cornwall, to Simon, bishop of Exeter, confirming Henry's confirmation of the gift of his father Reginald, earl of Cornwall, of the church of Liskeard to the church of St Stephen of Launceston. He asked Bishop Simon to admit the grant. Not dated. [5 October 1214–9 September 1223, episcopate of Simon of Apulia, bishop of Exeter. This limit can be shortened to 1214–20 in the light of no. 494.]

MS.: Cartulary, f.199v.


**497.** Grant and confirmation by Simon, bishop of Exeter, of the gift by Henry, son of the earl, to the prior and canons of Launceston, of the church of Liskeard (*Leskereth*) with the sheaf tithes; saving a competent vicarage for a useful vicar whom the prior and convent were to present to him (the vicar would bear all episcopal burdens), and saving the rights of the church and bishops of Exeter. Sealing clause. Witd. Richard and William, chaplains; H., the official of Cornwall, Benjamin the clerk, Master Adam. Not dated. [1214–1220 as no. 496.]

MS.: Cartulary, ff.199v.–200r.


**498.** Grant[a] and confirmation by Earl Baldwin, son of Earl Richard, to the canons in free and perpetual alms of the land of Caradon (*Carnedon*) with the churches of Liskeard and Linkinhorne, just as his grandfather Reginald had granted them as his charters attested. Moreover he granted to them the land and tenement about which he had disagreed with the canons, i.e. 2 acres of land at Sutton and one acre at Addicroft (*Odecrofte*) with the wood, the wood of 'Kingbeara', the wood of 'Attek', the wood of Measham (*Mennesham*) and the land of Notter (*Nottetorre*) which Warin, son of Senara, held. The bounds were from 'Brochole' as far as Notter and thence as far as the green way and from there as far as 'Readesbisen' and thence to 'Bradewey'. He also granted to them common pasture with his men of Rillaton. He was held to warranty to this for the canons in relation to his mother and all exactions forever. Sealing clause. Witd. William Giffard, William de Argentein. Not dated. [1185–8; Baldwin, third earl of Devon.]

ᵃHenderson notes another copy of this charter, ff.214v.–215r., see no. 544, which has the additional witnesses of Phillip de Atrio and Peter de Chaelons.

MS.: Cartulary, f.200r. Another copy, *Calendar of Patent Rolls* 1377–81, p. 115 (1378).


**499.**   Inquisition made at Bodmin before the barons and divers knights, about the churches of Liskeard and Linkinhorne.

In the year 1229, Richard, earl of Cornwall, brother of Henry, king of England, came into Cornwall on 15 August. When he came to Bodmin (*Bodminia*) an inquisition was held about the churches of Liskeard and Linkinhorne before Reginald de Valle torta, Andrew de Cardynan, John son of Richard, Robert son of William, Walter de Treverbyn, Roger de Trelosk, Henry Heryz, Geoffrey son of Bernard, Nicolas de Hiampton, Hugh de Bello Campo, Robert le Bryton and Walter son of William in a full county court.

The inquisition about the church of Liskeard was thus. Earl Reginald, the lord, gave it to Luke son of Bernard. After the death of Earl Reginald, Denise, the countess, gave it to Jocelin Marescall when Luke son of Bernard was in Ireland. When Luke son of Bernard came back to Cornwall, he claimed it from Jocelin and recovered it except for 2s. remaining to the said Jocelin who paid Luke yearly this sum. After the death of Luke son of Bernard the church reverted to Jocelin and after Jocelin's death it came to belong to the priory, confirmed by Simon, bishop of Exeter, in the time of Henry, son of the earl, who was lord of Liskeard because that manor was the inheritance of Henry fitz Count by gift of King Richard. Dated Bodmin, 15 August 1229.

MS.: Cartulary, f.200v.


**500.**   Inquisition concerning the church of Linkinhorne. Earl Reginald, the lord, gave 3 marks from the same church to John, son of Bernard. The rest of the church remained to the father of John de Lankynhorn. After the death of John's father the church went to John his son by gift of Denise, the countess, with 3 marks paid yearly to John, son of Bernard. After the latter's death the countess of Meulan gave to Master Hamon the said 3 marks. On the death of John de Lankynhorn the church went to Master Hamon. Afterwards the prior of Launceston claimed it by papal letters and the priory had the 3 marks yearly and the whole church. The priory also had the charter of the earl from the king,ᵃ the charter of Baldwin de Ryvers, the charter of the countess of Meulan and the confirmation by the lord William, bishop of Exeter, and the chapter. Not dated. [Presumably 15 August 1229 as the title to no. 499 mentions both the church of Liskeard and the church of Linkinhorne.]

ᵃ*cartam com' regis.*

MS.: Cartulary, f.200v. [For another copy of this inquisition, see below, no. 534.]

**501.** Final concord between the prior and canons of Launceston and the canons of Torre about the church of Liskeard (*Leskird*).

The prior and canons of Launceston were to pay to the abbot and canons of Torre 4 marks of silver at Easter and Michaelmas, a payment which was to cease after the death of Master William de Linguire, clerk. The abbot and canons of Torre promised not to molest the church of Liskeard. Seals of both parties and the priors of Plympton and Totnes. Witd. Master Henry, official of Cornwall; Hamon Eustach', Serlo de Peynton. Not dated. [After nos. 494–5. Perhaps when Robert was fourth abbot of Torre, D. Seymour, *Torre Abbey* (1977), 31.]

MS.: Cartulary, f.201r.

**502.** Taxation by the official of the bishop of Exeter of a pension of 100s. paid yearly to the prior and convent of Launceston from the church of Liskeard.

Notice by the official of the bishop of Exeter that by an inquisition made with the assent of the prior and convent of Launceston and Martin Pipard, vicar of Liskeard, it became evident that the fruits and obventions of the church of Liskeard, except the tithe of sheaves and a rent of assize of 32s. 2d., exceeded the value of £15.15s. yearly. Having considered the minimum amount of previous taxations, with the bishop's authority, and at the request of all concerned, he ordained that the vicar was to pay yearly 100s. to the prior and convent at Easter and Michaelmas and was to bear the ordinary burdens of his church, saving the sheaf-tithe and the rent of assize. Sealing clause. Dated Exeter, Saturday, 9 May 1265.

MS.: Cartulary, f.201r.–f.201v.

**503.** Definitive letter of Walter, bishop of Exeter, when he was holding a visitation in the archdeaconry of Cornwall. When Bishop Walter visited the deanery of West he learnt from the complaint of the proctor of the prior and convent of Launceston (who had appropriated the church of Liskeard to their own uses) that John, the then perpetual vicar in that church, from the time of his induction had refused to pay the old and accustomed pension of 100s. due to the prior and convent. The bishop summoned the vicar to appear on Saturday, 2 March 1309 at Bodmin priory to answer Brother William de Penlen, proctor for the priory. Both parties appeared on that day and the vicar confessed his liability and promised to pay the pension for the future. The bishop ordered him to do so and to make good the arrears of £4. 5s. The prior and convent forgave him £2. 5s. of these arrears, provided that he paid the residue by 24 June. Dated Bodmin priory, Saturday, 2 March 1309. [The text gives the wrong year (1409), confusing Bishop Edmund Stafford with Bishop Walter Stapledon.]

MS.: Cartulary, ff.201v–202r.

**504.**   Royal plea about the presentation of the vicar of Liskeard and that the king had not the right of presentation there. Term of St Hilary, first year of King Henry (IV).

Stephen, prior of Launceston, was summoned to answer the king for hindering him from presenting a fit person to the church of Liskeard, the living of which was vacant and in the king's gift. William Ludyngton was attorney for the king and Paschasius Pehuden for the prior. Judgement was given for the prior by default of any declaration of the royal title to the advowson. Dated Hilary term, 1400.

MS.: Cartulary, f.202r.–f.202v.

**505.**   Copy of letters patent of King Henry IV which stated that in a parliament of his grandfather, King Edward, it was enacted that the king should make due enquiry about his title before presenting a clerk to a benefice. The prior and convent of Launceston held the church of Liskeard by appropriation long before the statute of mortmain. King Henry presented Simon Gaunstede who said the church was vacant. The prior and convent were put to great vexation and expense contrary to the form of the statute. The king had ordered the sheriff of Cornwall to bring Simon into chancery to inform the king and his council of the king's title, but on his appearance he produced no satisfactory evidence, whereupon the king with the advice of his judges, serjeants and other counsellors ordered the revocation of the king's presentation. Dated Westminster, 6 February 1400.

MS.: Cartulary, ff.202v.–203r.

**506.**   Grant made by Thomas, formerly prior of Launceston, to the parishioners of Liskeard of 12 feet in length of the chancel in augmentation to the nave of Liskeard.

This indenture made between Thomas, prior of Launceston of the one part, and Roger de Fursedon, Nicholas Lovepitta junior, Richard Noel senior, Simon Dene, Luke Serle, Adam Pouna, John Wanga, Nicholas Wada, John Pouna, Robert Garrek, Roger de Penquite, Richard Bata, Roger de Lanreythow and Roger de Trewithelane, of the other, witnessed that the said Roger de Forsedon.[a]

[a]This deed finishes abruptly here and on f.203v., no. 507, a completely different deed continues, without any sign of any break. (Prior Thomas is Thomas de Burdon, prior from 14 July 1346 to c.1361.)

MS.: Cartulary, f.203r.

**507.**   Charter about the construction of the south choir aisle of the church of Liskeard.

This indenture made between John, prior of Launceston, and the convent of the same place of the one part, and the mayor and commonalty of Liskeard and also the parishioners of the parish church of Saint Martin of Liskeard of the other, witnessed that as the prior and convent were rectors and proprietors of the parish church of Liskeard, they granted to the same mayor and commonalty and to the parishioners and gave licence for the erection and new construction of a certain chapel contiguous to the chancel of the parish church of Liskeard and to join, strengthen and annex this chapel to the same chancel laterally on the south side and to break the wall of the same chancel and to reconstruct the wall in a better manner and form with arches and with timber imposed on and above the wall and to join and strengthen the same. The mayor and commonalty and the parishioners granted that they and their heirs and successors would reconstruct the broken wall well and competently as aforesaid and they would build that chapel and roof and covering of the chapel both in timber and stone and would repair them at their cost. And they would make gutters to preserve the wall and roof of the chancel. Their heirs would maintain these buildings for ever at the cost of the mayor and commonalty and the parishioners. The prior and convent sealed one part of the indenture remaining with the mayor and commonalty, and the mayor and commonalty sealed the part remaining with the prior and convent. Witd. Master William Filham, then archdeacon of Cornwall; Ralph Botreaux, John Herll. Dated at the chapter house of Launceston priory (also Liskeard), 31 March 1430.[a]

[a]The original charter (Liskeard borough MS. no. 79) adds the names of John Herle and John Arundell, knights, Robert Bray, mayor of the borough, John Fursdon and Reginald Toker. For a similar charter between the same parties for the construction of the north choir aisle of Liskeard church (31 March 1477), see below, no. 600.

MS.: Cartulary, ff.203v.–204r. Original, Liskeard borough MS. no. 79, Cornwall County Record Office. For a charter of 4 July 1402 for a south choir aisle, see Liskeard borough MS. no. 78.

MS.: Cartulary, ff.203v.–204r.

**508.** Agreement before a notary public dated 23 June 1403, at Launceston priory, between Prior Stephen and John Waryn, vicar of the parish church of Liskeard, after a long disagreement between them about the vicarage of Liskeard. John Waryn sought the grace of the prior for forgiveness for the disagreement which the prior granted him. He also promised in good faith to produce yearly a pipe of wine for the use of the prior and convent in the refectory of the priory. John Waryn promised the prior that he would pay £15 due to the prior for arrears of a certain pension of 100s. due to Launceston priory yearly; which pension he promised to pay again at the following Michaelmas. Witd. brothers David Treludek, Roger Combrigge, John Honyland, Thomas Tredayk, canons of the priory; the lord William Gidele, deacon, and John Croudecote of the diocese of Exeter. Dated Launceston priory, in the garden next to the infirmary, 23 June 1403. (Certificate of William Kelwa, notary public, after the witnesses.)

MS.: Cartulary, ff.204r.–204v.

**509.** Inquisition taken at Liskeard before John Dabernoun, sheriff and seneschal of Cornwall, concerning the assize of bread and ale of people living in Hagland (*Halgelond*) within the glebe of Liskeard (1353–4ª).

The reeve of the manor of Liskeard was commanded to levy 6d. each from Roger Mornek, Nicholas Mork and Gilbert de Trembras for the assize of ale broken in Hagland, by John Dabernoun, sheriff and seneschal of Cornwall.

After this Thomas, prior of Launceston, went to the manor court of Liskeard held at Liskeard on Thursday, 9 May 1353 before the said John Dabernoun, sheriff. Prior Thomas said Roger, Nicholas and Williamᵇ were tenants of the prior in Hagland. And he said that all his predecessors from time immemorial had fines and amercements from all his tenants in Hagland for the breaking of the assize of bread and ale in the same vill and, he, as prior, was seised with the same right. The prior's tenants of Hagland by law were not answerable to the sheriff and John Dabernoun seneschal, for transgression of the same assize. Prior Thomas sought that enquiry should be made by the oath of just and worthy men of the tenants of the duke of Cornwall of his manor of Liskeard. John Dabernoun commanded the reeve of the manor to nominate such a body of 12 men. They were Robert Crochard, Simon Dena, Walter Hassek, Simon Lansatthen, Walter Hathermore, Robert Treyer, Henry Tredenek, Thomas Bonnok, Henry Penaunt, Walter Wada and Roger Bromboit. On their oaths they said that the prior of Launceston and his predecessors from time immemorial had received fines and amercements for assizes of bread and ale broken from the tenants of Hagland, but these tenants were never fined or punished by the sheriff of Cornwall. Wherefore it was considered that the fines levied should not be paid. Seals of John Dabernoun, sheriff and seneschal of Cornwall and of the 12 jurors. Dated Liskeard, Thursday, 9 May 1353.

ª27 Edwd. III (25 January 1353—24 January 1354). ᵇ*sic* for Gilbert.

MS.: Cartulary, ff.204v.–205r.

**510.** Inquisition at Liskeard, Saturday, 22 August 1377 before Martin de Ferrers and Robert Tresulyan, seneschals of the princess in Cornwall by a mandate from Princess Joan dated Berkhamstead, 5 May 1377.ª The jurors were Vincent Lotte, John Ludcombe, Richard Code, Simon Lanseithen, Roger Bromboite, Roger Serle, Richard Cartuther, Richard Willewerie, William Michell, Walter Wada, William Bonnock and David Kempe. They said that Prior Stephen, the prior at that time, was seised with the punishment of all tenants and people who broke the assize of bread and ale in Liskeard within the demesne of the said prior, and that all his predecessors had the same right as rectors of the church of Liskeard. The present prior and his predecessors had their courts of Hagland every three weeks and they punished for infringements of the assize of bread and ale. No other lord than the prior had this jurisdiction; neither the prince nor princess of Wales, nor any of their predecessors had it. William de Cranewell, late seneschal of the lord prince, amerced the tenants and people of Hagland, but nothing was levied for infringement of the assize of bread and ale. Sealed by the jurors. Dated Liskeard, Saturday, 22 August 1377.

ªCommission recited in full in French is not included here.

MS.: Cartulary, ff.205v.–206r.


**511.**   Grant and confirmation by Robert German of Liskeard (*Leskird*) to Henry Frend, vicar of Liskeard, of a tenement and garden adjoining in the vill of Liskeard situated in the glebe land of the church of Liskeard between the royal way on the one side and a garden of the heirs of John Mory on the other. He also confirmed his grant to Henry of all his croft (which he had acquired of John Atteyete) situated between the croft of John Blake on the east part and the croft of John Shomp on the west part. Warranty and sealing clauses. Witd. William Baak, Simon Attedene, Roger Moyn, John Blake. Dated Liskeard, Sunday, 20 November 1373.

MS.: Cartulary, f.206r.


**512.**   Surrender by John Moile to Stephen, prior of Launceston, and the convent of his estate in messuages, lands and tenements in Liskeard and in the glebe land called Hagland near Liskeard which he had of the grant of the prior and convent for the term of his life. Sealing clause. Dated Launceston, 5 November 1400.

MS.: Cartulary, f.206r.–f.206v.


**513.**   Surrender by Robert Girmanª and Edith his wife, to Roger, prior of Launceston, and the convent, of their estate in a messuage and a garden adjoining and in one croft in the glebe land of Liskeard. The messuage and garden were situated in the glebe land between the garden of a certain John Mory and the way towards the church of Liskeard (*Leskirred*). The croft was between the croft of John Blake on the east side and John Champ on the west. Plural sealing clause. Witd. Richard Trelauny, John Treludek, Thomas Oterham. Dated Launceston, Thursday, 10 May 1408.

ª*Gorman* in heading.

MS.: Cartulary, f.206v.


**514.**   Surrender by Edith, who was the wife of Robert German, to John, prior of Launceston, and the convent, of the estate she had for the term of her life by the indented charter of Roger, formerly prior of Launceston, and the convent in a messuage with garden adjoining and a croft in the glebe land of Liskeard between the garden of Thomas Mory and the road to the church of Liskeard. The croft was also in the glebe land between the close of John Blake on the east and the croft of John Champ on the west.

Sealing clause. Witd. John, vicar of Linkinhorne, William Trelauny, John Treludek. Dated Linkinhorne, Sunday, 24 April 1418.

MS.: Cartulary, ff.206v.–207r.

**515.** Quitclaim by Vincent Gyrman[a] son and heir of Robert Gyrman, to John, prior of Launceston, and the convent, of his right in a messuage with garden adjoining and in a croft in the glebe land of Liskeard. (The croft bounded as in no. 514). Warranty clause. Witd. William Trelauny, John Treludek, Stephen Cork. Dated Launceston, Monday, 27 April 1405.

[a]*German* in title.

MS.: Cartulary, f.207r.

**516.** Grant and confirmation by John Blake of Liskeard (*Leskyrd*), son and heir of John Blake, to Henry Frend, vicar of Liskeard, Peter Treglestek and John Lavyngton, chaplains, of the rents, services, fealties and reliefs of all his tenants in the glebe land of Liskeard: Thomas Bake, Cecilia Bolda, Richard Dagill, Roger Moyn, Richard Attehille, Roger Dreynek, William Dene, John Treworgy, Joan Douna, Thomas Payne, John Kret, John Scoutte and Alice Krenton and their heirs of all the lands they each held separately of him in the glebe land of Liskeard. To hold with all fines, pleas and perquisites of his court forever. Warranty and sealing clauses. Witd. John Kret, mayor of Liskeard; John Bonnek, William Lopyta. Liskeard, Friday, 14 June 1398.

MS.: Cartulary, f.207r.–f.207v.

**517.** Quitclaim by Stephen Heym to Richard, prior of Launceston, and the convent, for his soul and the souls of his predecessors, of a messuage in the vill of Liskeard (*Leskered*) which formerly belonged to William, vicar of the same vill. Witd. the lord John de Bello Prato, knight; Baldewin de Bere, Stephen de Trewynt, Roger, son of Durand etc. Not dated. [Perhaps 1265–9 when Stephen Heym occurs, *Cornwall FF.* i, no. 215, but not in 1267, see Hull, *Cartulary St M. Mount*, no. 7.]

MS.: Cartulary, f.207v.

**518.** Quitclaim by Joan, daughter and heir of Reginald de Northwode, junior, in her widowhood to Brother Roger de Horton, prior of the church of St Stephen of Launceston, and the convent, of her right in one messuage in the vill of Liskeard which formerly belonged to William, vicar of the same vill, with a garden adjoining. Sealing clause using the seal of the official of the peculiar jurisdiction of the bishop, as her own seal was unknown to many. Witd. William de Punchardoune, John de Burlone,

Henry de Trecarll. Dated Launceston, Wednesday, 29 October 1320.
[Roger de Horton was prior 1308–28, so the dating clause must refer to
King Edward II.]

MS.: Cartulary, f.208r.


**519.** Quitclaim by Sibyl who was the wife of Reginald de Northewode,
junior, to the prior and convent, of her right in a third part of one
messuage in Liskeard which she had claimed as a dowry against the said
prior and of her right in all the messuages and tenements held by the same
prior in the vill of Liskeard. The prior gave her a mark of silver. Sealing
clause. Witd. Nicholas de Audener, mayor of Liskeard; John Carpunter,
William Coppyng. Liskeard, Friday, 26 September 1306.

MS.: Cartulary f.208r.


**520.** Quitclaim by Robert Gotta and Joan his wife to Brother Richard,
prior of Launceston and the convent, of a messuage with gardens and
other appurtenances in Liskeard which Reginald de Northwode had from
the prior and convent for a certain sum of money which they then had
satisfied. Plural sealing clause. Witd. Richard de Hywys, Thomas de
Crytur, Richard Lovepita. Dated Launceston, Saturday, 14 January 1296.

MS.: Cartulary, f.208v.


**521.** Quitclaim by Warin Hayron to Prior Richard and the convent of
his right in a messuage and a garden in the vill of Liskeard which Warin
had claimed against Robert Gotta and Joan his wife by writ of mort
d'ancestor before the justices at the assize in the county of Cornwall. The
prior and convent gave Warin 10s. sterling. Sealing clause. Witd.
Nicholas de Audener, Richard Lovepyta, Peter de Trewandra. Liskeard,
Thursday, 5 July 1296.

MS.: Cartulary, f.208v.


**522.** Grant and confirmation by William Dobyn of Liskeard to Henry
Frund,[a] vicar of Liskeard, and to John Trethewy and John Lavyngton,
chaplains, of the rent and service of Richard Walky alias Hoper of all the
messuages, lands and tenements which he held of William for the term of
his life and the reversion, situated between the tenement of John
Kyngesmylle and that of the prior and convent of Launceston. Sealing
and warranty clauses. Witd. John Fouk, mayor of the borough of
Liskeard, Richard Kyngdon and William Bake, reeves there. Dated
Liskeard, Friday, 19 March 1395.

[a]*Frend* in title.

MS.: Cartulary, f.209r.

**523.** Grant and confirmation by John Bonnok, mayor of Liskeard, with the assent of the commonalty, to Prior Stephen and the convent of all manner of easement to be built to the priory's tenement in Liskeard between the tenements of Richard Hoper and Walter Ware, to enlarge their tenement and to make steps there[a] which were guaranteed forever to Prior Stephen and his successors. Sealing clause: seal of the borough of Liskeard. Witd. William Lopita, Richard Gode, William Carrek, Serlo Treverbyn. Dated Liskeard, Friday, 14 January 1390.

[a]Title: *de gradibus domorum in vico.*

MS.: Cartulary, f.209r.

**524.** Manor[a] of Liskeard (*Leskert*)
In the account of Robert Trewythelan the reeve there in the year finished at the feast of Michaelmas 1350 among other entries was found:- In a rent resolute to the priory of Launceston for sustaining one lamp before the image of Blessed Mary in the church of Launceston, 8s. at the feast of Michaelmas.[b] [Between Michaelmas 1349 and Michaelmas 1350.]

[a]In a later hand. [b]the rest of f.209v. is blank.

MS.: Cartulary, f.209v.

**525.** [a]Gift by Reginald, the king's son, earl of Cornwall, to the church of St Stephen of Launceston of the churches of Liskeard and Linkinhorne on the day of the translation of the relics and of the canons of the vill of Launceston to the ford. To have and to hold in free alms for ever as soon as vacant. Not dated. [7 February 1155, see Introduction, p. xvi and note 84.]

[a]Title: *Regestrum cartarum ecclesie parochie de Lankynhorn et pensionis eiusdem. Ac de terris et tenementis in manerijs de Carnedon et Clymeslond cum pertinencijs suis.*

MS.: Cartulary, f.210r. See also no. 493, to which the text below is similar.

*Carta Reginaldi comitis de ecclesia de Lankynhorn.*
Reginaldus regis filius consul Cornub' omnibus ministris suis salutem. Sciatis me dedisse ecclesie sancti Stephani de Lanstavaton in incrementum eiusdem ecclesie ecclesiam de Leskerd et ecclesiam de Lankynhorn in die translacionis reliquiarum et canonicorum ipsius ecclesie de villa Lanstavaton ad vadum. Habendas et tenendas cum omnibus pertinencijs suis in liberam elemosinam imperpetuum quam cito vacantes exstiterint. Testibus Radulfo de Boscoroham, Robert Asketill etc.

**526.** Grant and confirmation by Matilda, countess of Meulan, for the salvation of her soul and the souls of Reginald her father and the Countess her mother to the canons of Launceston the church of Linkinhorne as her father Earl Reginald had granted it to the church of Launceston. To have and to hold forever in pure and perpetual alms. Sealing clause. Witd. Master Hamon de Bodminia, John de St David, Herwinus. Not dated. [*c*.1165–87. After Matilda's marriage to Robert, count of Meulan, and possibly after the death of Earl Reginald in 1175, see P. L. Hull, *Cartulary of St Michael's Mount* (Devon and Cornwall Record Society, 1962.), no. 89. See Round, *CDF.* nos. 347–8 for charters of Count Robert of Meulan dated 1166–87.]

MS.: Cartulary, f.210r.–f.210v.

**527.** Confirmation by William, bishop of Exeter, of the grant to the priory by Reginald, earl of Cornwall, of the church of Linkinhorne of which he (Reginald) was patron. To the canons to have for their own uses, saving a perpetual vicar to celebrate divine service and saving the authority and dignity of himself and his successors in the see of Exeter. Sealing clause. Witd. Dom. Stephen,[a] dean, A. treasurer, A. precentor, H. chancellor, B. archdeacon of Exeter. Dated Exeter 14 April 1227.

[a]Stephen, dean, is a mistake for Serlo, the first dean of Exeter cathedral (Oliver, *Lives*, 274, 278, 280, 283); see no. 528.

MS.: Cartulary, f.210v.

**528.** Confirmation by Serlo, dean of Exeter, and the chapter, of the collation of the church of Linkinhorne to Launceston priory and the canons made by Bishop William, saving a perpetual vicar there to minister divine service and saving the dignity of the church of Exeter. Sealing clause. No witnesses. Not dated. [Shortly after no. 527, i.e. *c*.1227. (Serlo was the first dean of Exeter from 1225 to 1231, Oliver, *Lives*, 274).]

MS.: Cartulary, f.210v.–f.211r.

**529.** Quitclaim by Alan the steward of his right in the advowson of the church of Linkinhorne to William, prior of Launceston, and the canons for ever. Warranty and sealing clauses. Witd. Simon de Brackeley, Roger de Treloch, William Wise. Not dated. [*c*.1232–8, (Prior William).]

MS.: Cartulary, f.211r.

**530.** Final concord between John Le Boteler, querent, and William, prior of Launceston, deforciant, of a moiety of the advowson of the church of Linkinhorne. John recognised this moiety to belong to the priory and quitclaimed it to the prior forever. Prior William received the said John and his heirs into the benefit of the prayers of his church forever. Not witnessed. Dated Huntingdon (*Huntedon*), octave of St John the Baptist (1 July) 1235.

MS.: Cartulary, f.211r. Printed *Cornwall FF.* i no. 59.

**531.** Mandate by King Henry III to William, bishop of Exeter. The prior of Launceston had been summoned before justices itinerant at Cambridge to reply to John le Butiller why he did not permit him to present a suitable person to a moiety of the church of Linkinhorne as it was vacant. The same John in court recognised the advowson of a moiety of the said church to belong to the priory, and he released and quitclaimed his right to the prior and his successors. Notwithstanding this the king commanded the bishop to admit a suitable person. Witd. R. de Lexinton. Dated Huntingdon, 27 June 1235.

MS.: Cartulary, f.211v.

**532.** Notice by Philip, precentor of Exeter and William de Arundell, vicar of the bishop of Exeter that John Pincerna and A., steward, had claimed from the prior and convent of Launceston in the king's court the church of Linkinhorne at the time when Hamo entered into religion. At length the prior in their presence proved that the presentation to the church of Linkinhorne had been collated to the use of the prior and convent by episcopal authority. This had been confirmed by the chapter of Blessed Peter of Exeter and enjoyed peacefully by the priory for a long time. This they had pronounced in full consistory with episcopal authority. Not dated. [1233–42, see list of precentors in Oliver, *Lives*, 278.]

MS.: Cartulary, f.211v.

**533.** Record of the priors J. of Bodmin, T(heobald) of Tywardreath (*Tiwardraid*) and A. of St Germans, delegated in 1225 by Pope Honorius III to settle a dispute about the advowson and pension of the church of Linkinhorne, collated to Launceston priory by Bishop B. of good memory. This priory had been injured by H. a clerk of the diocese of Exeter and other clerks of the same diocese with regard to tithes, possessions and pensions. The dispute was settled by the intervention of the lord W., bishop of Exeter. Master H. was to hold the church of Linkinhorne in the name of the prior and convent and was to pay yearly 3 marks of silver from the same church. He was to bear the ordinary and extraordinary burdens of the church. Sealing clause of the priors. No witnesses. Not dated. [Probably in 1225, or not very much later. Bishop B. must be Bartholomew, bishop of Exeter (1161–1184) and W. bishop of Exeter must be William Briwere (1224–1244).]

MS.: Cartulary, f.212r.

**534.** Another copy of no. 500. Not dated. [15 August 1229.]

MS.: Cartulary, f.212v.

**535.** Letter from the dean and chapter of East Wivelshire to W(illiam), bishop of Exeter. The dean and chapter had made inquisition whether the church of Linkinhorne was vacant or not and who was the true patron and when was it vacant. For thirty years or more Hamo de Bomoñ was parson of the said church; they knew not by what title. The prior and convent of Launceston were in possession of the church; they did not know how, except that they showed Bishop W(illiam's) letters about the oblation of the church and confirmation by the chapter of Exeter and by the pope. They did not know, however, by whom Hamo was presented. Henry the clerk had been presented in the chapter by Alan the steward who had appealed for his right. Plural sealing clause. Not dated. [*c.*1225–7. If the pope was Honorius III this letter would be later than 533. Pope Honorius III died 18 March 1227.]

MS.: Cartulary, f.212v.

**536.** Record of a hearing before the official of the archdeacon of Cornwall in a tribunal held in the chapel of Blessed Mary of Callington.

John Godeman, clerk, was proctor for the prior and convent. Richard, vicar of the church of Linkinhorne, appeared in person. Richard said his vicarage was for an annual pension to the prior and convent of 2 marks of silver. The official judged that Richard should pay this sum in future to the priory. Dated the chapel of St Mary of Callington, Friday, 8 January 1233.

MS.: Cartulary, f.213r.

**537.** Gift and grant in pure and perpetual alms by Reginald, earl of Cornwall, son of King Henry, for the salvation of his soul and the soul of his father and the souls of Matilda the Empress, and of her son King Henry and his children and for the souls of his and his wife's children and of his ancestors and successors to the canons of St Stephen of Launceston the land of Caradon (*Carduna*), part of the manor of Rillaton (*Rilletuna*), so that the canons should have 100s. worth of land and should hold it peacefully (as he did) for ever. Witd. Bartholomew, bishop of Exeter, Roger, bishop of Worcester, Nicholas, son of Earl Reginald. Not dated. [1165–1175, i.e. between the enthronement of Bishop Roger on 2 February 1165 and the death of Earl Reginald on 1 July 1175.]

MS.: Cartulary, f.213r.

*Carta comitis Reginaldi de Carnedon*
Reginaldus comes Cornub' H(enrici) regis filius omnibus hominibus suis Francis et Anglis salutem. Sciatis me pro salute anime mee et patris mee regis Henrici et Matillis imperatricis et filij eius regis Henrici et liberorum suorum et uxoris mee et liberorum meorum et omnium antecessorum et successorum meorum concessisse et in puram et perpetuam elemosinam dedisse Deo et ecclesie sancti Stephani de Lanstavetona et canonicis ibidem Deo servientibus

terram de Carduna que est membrum manerij de Rilletuna ita quidem ut de reliqua parte ipsius manerij de Rilletuna proficiatur eis tantum quod bene et plenarie habeant centum solidatas terre. Quare volo et precipio quod predicti canonici predictam terram liberam et quietam ab omni seculari servicio bene et in pace habeant et adeo libere et quiete perpetuo teneant sicut ego umquam melius et liberius eam tenui. Hijs testibus Bartholomeo episcopo Exon', Rogero episcopo Wigorn', Nicholao filio meo etc.

**538.**   Grant by Earl Reginald of Caradon (*Carnedune*), part of the manor of Rillaton, to the canons of St Stephen of Launceston. Bounds: from 'Gunnecumbe' along the ditch as far as the great street which came from Botternell (*Boturnell*) and then went on to 'Redderise'. And from 'Redderise' to the small wood and along the ditch as far as Notter (*Nottetorre*). And thence as far as 'Stanrewe' to 'Morewey' and from 'Morewey' along the ditch and as far as the conduit of Blackham (*Blakkombe*) as far as the source, and from the source to the three hills. Thence as far as 'Horsewelle' and from there to Witheybrook (*Withy broke*) and the length of the water to 'Fundespole'; then along the water to the river Lynher (*Lyner*) and the stone bridge. Free and quit from all secular service. Not dated. [*c.*1155–65 (Richard de Raddon, see nos. 12 and 13.).]

MS.: Cartulary, f.213v. Partly translated in Charles Henderson, *Essays in Cornish History* (Oxford, 1935), 125–6. Another copy, *Calendar of Patent Rolls 1377–81*, p. 116 (1378).

*Alia carta Reginaldi comitis de Carnedon ac metis et divisis eiusdem*
Reginaldus comes Cornubie omnibus hominibus suis salutem. Sciatis me pro salute anime mee et patris mei regis Henrici et Matildis imperatricis et filij eius regis Henrici et liberorum suorum et uxoris mee et liberorum meorum et omnium antecessorum et successorum meorum concessisse et in puram et perpetuam elemosinam dedisse Deo et ecclesie Sancti Stephani de Launstavaton et canonicis ibidem Deo servientibus terram de Carnedune que est membrum manerij de Rillatune. Habendam et tenendam cum omnibus pertinenciis suis in pratis et pascuis in vijs et semitis in aquis stagnis et molendinis in moris turbarijs et stagnarijs et omnibus alijs rebus et libertatibus suis integre pacifice sicut hijs metis est divisa et distincta. Scilicet de Gunnecombe in longum fossati usque ad magnam stratam que venit de Boturnell et inde protendit usque Redderise et de ipsa Redderise usque ad parvum boscum. De bosco itaque in longum fossati usque Nottetorre. Et ex inde usque Star Stanrewe et de eadem Stanrewe usque Morewey et de Morewey in longum fossati usque ad ductum de Blackombe et ex inde in longum ducti de Blakkombe usque ad sursam et de dicta sursa usque ad tres colles et de ipso loco usque Horsewelle et de Horsewell usque Withy Broke et in longum ipsius aque usque Fundespole et de Fundespole in longum aque usque Lyner fluvium et pontem lapideum. Quare volo et firmiter precipio quod predicti canonici de Lanstavaton predictam terram liberam et quietam ab omni seculari servicio bene et in pace habeant et adeo libere et quiete perpetuo teneant sicut ego umquam liberius eam

tenui. Hijs testibus Roberto de Dunstanvile, Ricardo de Raddon, Bernard(o) vicecomite Cornub' etc.

**539.** Confirmation by King Henry II to St Stephens of Launceston of the gift of Caradon, part of the manor of Rillaton, by his uncle, Earl Reginald, and of the mill which the earl had under the castle of Dunheved and of the 40s. which the Earl also gave of the farm of the castle for the tower of the church which he had destroyed. Not dated. [1174–6. Consecration of Richard de Ilchester, bishop of Winchester and Geoffrey Ridel, bishop of Ely on 6 October 1174. The upper dating limit of 1176 depends on Richard de Humeto, constable. See Delisle, *Recueil*, introductory vol., 430–1.]

MS.: Cartulary, ff.213v.–214r.

*Confirmacio Henrici regis de Carnedon et de molendino subtus castellum cum quadraginta solidis solutis per prepositos de Dounheved.*
Henricus dei gracia rex Anglie et dux Normannie et Aquitanie et comes Andegavie archiepiscopis episcopis abbatibus comitibus baronibus justicijs vicecomitibus et omnibus ministris et fidelibus suis tocius Anglie salutem. Sciatis me concessisse et presenti carta confirmasse ecclesie Sancti Stephani de Lanstavatona et canonicis ibidem Deo servientibus donaciones quas comes Reginaldus Cornub' avunculus meus eis fecit scilicet de terra de Carneduna que est membrum manerij de Rillatona sicut carta eiusdem comitis testatur et de molendino quod ipse comes habebat subtus castellum de Dounheved et de quadraginta solidis quos iam dictus comes eis dedit de firma sua de castello de Dunheved pro turre predicte ecclesie quam prostravit. Quare volo et firmiter precipio quod ecclesia Beati Stephani de Lanstavatona et canonici eiusdem ecclesie habeant et teneant hec supradicta cum omnibus pertinenciis suis in bosco et plano in pratis et pasturis in aquis in molendinis in vivarijs et piscarijs in vijs et semitis et in omnibus alijs locis et alijs rebus ad ea pertinentibus bene et in pace libere et quiete integre et honorifice cum omnibus libertatibus et liberis consuetudinibus suis sicut carte Reginaldi Cornub' quas inde habent testantur. Teste R. Winton., E.[a] Elyens., B. Exon. episcopis, Ricardo de Lucy, Ricardo de Hum(et) etc.

[a]*sic* for Geoffrey.

**540.** Confirmation by King Henry II to the priory of 100s. worth of land in Caradon which his uncle, earl Reginald, gave in alms. No one was to do injury to this and there could be no plea about this land except before himself or his chief justice. Not dated. [?1174–5 (Randulf de Glanville first occurs in 1174 and Earl R. died 1 July 1175).]

MS.: Cartulary, f.214r.

*Carta Henrici regis de centum solidatis terre in Carnedon.*
Henricus Dei gracia rex Anglie et dux Normanie et Acquiet(anie) et
comes Andegavie justicijs vicecomitibus et omnibus ministris Cornub' salutem. Precipio quod canonici de Lancaveto teneant bene et
in pace integre et iuste centum solidatas terre quas comes Reginaldus
avunculus meus dedit eis in elemosinam ubicumque sint in ballivis
vestris. Ita quod nullam eis iniuriam vel contumeliam faciatis nec
fieri permittatis.ᵃ Et non ponantur in inplacitumᵃ nisi coram me vel
coram capitali justic' meo. Teste Randulpho de Glanvyll'.

ᵃ*sic.*

**541.** Notice by King Henry II commanding that the canons hold the
land of Caradon quietly which Earl Reginald, his uncle, gave them in free
alms. Not dated. [1173–1 July 1175 (adoption of *Dei gratia* in Henry II's
style and death of Earl Reginald).]

MS.: Cartulary, f.214r.

*Alia carta Henrici regis de terra de Carnedon.*
Henricus Dei gratia rex Anglie et dux Normannie et Aquitanie et
comes Andegavie vicecomiti et ballivis suis Cornub' salutem.
Precipio quod canonici de Sancto Stephano teneant bene et in pace et
integre terram de Carnedona quam comes Reginaldus avunculus
meus dedit eis in liberam elemosinam et carta sua confirmavit et
quam ego concessi eis et carta mea confirmavi liberam et quietam ab
omni laico servicio et exaccione. Teste Bernardoᵃ episcopo Exon. et
Roberto filio Bernardi.

ᵃa mistake for Bartholomew.

**542.** Mandate by King Henry II to his Cornish bailiffs. The canons of
Launceston were to hold Caradon in peace, with estovers and woods as
Earl Reginald granted, without injury or violence. Not dated. [6 October
1174–1 July 1175 (see no. 539 and date of Earl Reginald's death).]

MS.: Cartulary, f.214r–f.214v.

*Carta H(enrici) regis de rectitudinibus et pertinenciis in estoveria bosco etc. in
terra de Carnedon.*
Henricus Dei gracia rex Anglie et dux Normanie et Aquitanie et
comes Andegavie ballivis suis Cornub' salutem. Precipio quod
canonici de Lanstaveton habeant et teneant bene et in pace et integre
terram de Carnedona quam comes Reginaldus eis dedit cum
omnibus rectitudinibus et pertinenciis et libertatibus suis in estauveria
et in bosco et in omnibus aliis locis et alijs rebus sicut idem comes eis
 dedit. Ita quod nichil inde amittant quod habere debeant. Et nullam
eis inde super hoc iniuriam vel violenciam faciatis nec fieri
permittatis. Teste R. episcopo Winton. apud Westmonasterium.

**543.** Writ of King Henry II to Bernard the Scribe. He was to see that the canons of Launceston had their 100s. worth of land in Caradon etc. The bishop of Exeter would do this if Bernard did not. Not dated. [6 Oct. 1174–1 July 1175, as no. 542.]

MS.: Cartulary, f.214v.

*Breve H(enrici) regis de centum solidatis terre.*
Henricus Dei gratia rex Anglie et dux Normanie et Acquitanie et comes Andegavie Bernardo scribo salutem. Precipio tibi quod sine dilacione facias habere integre et plenarie canonicis Sancti Stephani de Lanstavaton centum solidatas terre quas comes Raginaldus avunculus meus eis divisit. Et facias illas habere in illo manerio in quo ipse divisit in bosco et plano et alijs locis et alijs rebus. Et nisi feceritis episcopus Exon' faciat. Teste Ricardo Winton' episcopo apud Winton'.

**544.** Another copy of no. 498. The only differences are slight changes in spelling: the mention of canons regular at Launceston; a croft at Addicroft. Two witnesses are added: Philip de Atrio and Peter de Chaelons. Not dated. [c.1185–88, see no. 498.]

MS.: Cartulary, ff.214v.–215r.

**545.** Grant and confirmation by John, count of Mortain, to the priory, for the soul of King Henry his father and the souls of his ancestors and successors, of certain possessions of the priory in Launceston, Lewannick, Linkinhorne (including the manor of Rillaton) and Stoke Climsland etc. Not dated. [1189–99 when John was count of Mortain, before he became king on 27 May 1199.]

MS.: Cartulary, f.215r.–f.215v.

*Carta Johannis comitis Moriton' de viginti solidatis et viginti nummatis terre in Clymeslond ac confirmacio eiusdem de Trewhanta, Trenchiek, capelle[a] de castello. Et de quadraginta solid(is) de firma eiusdem castelli ac de ecclesia de Stratton molendinique sub castello de Douneheved ac terra de Carnedon etc.*
Johannes comes Moret' omnibus hominibus et amicis suis Francie et Anglie[b] presentibus et futuris salutem. Sciatis me dedisse et hac mea carta confirmasse Deo et ecclesie Sancti Stephani de Lanstavaton et canonicis ibidem Deo servientibus pro salute anime mee et pro anima regis Henrici patris mei et pro animabus omnium antecessorum et successorum meorum viginti solidatas terre in manerio meo de Clymmeston. Et preterea viginti nummatas terre in eodem manerio scilicet dimidiam acram quam Eggerus de Holrode tenet. Hee autem sunt mete illarum terrarum, scilicet a termino terre Radulphi Pilteman sicut rivus descendit in magnam aquam de Eny et usque ad terminum terre predicti Eggeri de Holrode ex parte orientis et meridei. Item ex parte occidentis et septentrionis a Witestlade sicut

rivus currit et descendit in magnam aquam de Eny inter terram de
Clymeston et terram de Treveris et preter hoc dimidiam acram terre
in Norton quam Warinus tenet. Confirmavi eciam eisdem canonicis
omnia subscripta sicut eis racionabiliter data sunt. Scilicet ex dono
Ricardi de Raddon unam virgatam terre que vocatur Trewanta
quietam et liberam ab omni servicio preter quindecim denarios quos
reddere debet ad Ridlatonam de quadam consuetudine que vocatur
*motiled*. Et ex dono Roberti filij Aschetilli concessu comitis Reginaldi
domini sui terram que vocatur Trenchioc. Et ex dono comitis
Reginaldi partem Hamelini presbiteri de capella de castello cum
omnibus libertatibus et rebus parti illi pertinentibus. Et quadraginta
solidos per annum de firma de castello de Dunheved. Et ecclesiam
Sancti Andree de Stratton cum pertinencijs suis. Et unam carrucatam
terre de dominico manerij de Stratton iuxta alteram terram eiusdem
ecclesie cum quadam area zalinarum Ebfordie, salva dignitate
capelle mee de castello de Landstaveton. Et molendinum quod est
sub castello de Dunheved cum eisdem pertinenciis et consuetudinibus
quas habebat dum erat in manu comitis Reginaldi. Et terram de
Carnedon que est membrum de Ridlatton. Ita quidem quod de
reliqua parte ipsius manerij de Ridlatton perficiatur eis tantum quod
bene et plenarie habeant centum solidatas terre sicut comes
Baldewinus de Reavers eis concessit et assignavit et carta sua
confirmavit. Et ex dono Oseberti de Bicheleia viginti solidatas terre
de manerio de Treverys scilicet villam que vocatur Tregoff et terram
que fuit Luffe et terram Warini iuxta pontem et unam acram in villa
que vocatur Carsbrok cum hominibus et omnibus que ad prefatas
terras pertinent. Et partem nemoris apud orientem sicut via dividit
usque ad aquam. Et ex dono Bernardi clerici duas acras terre quas
tres homines tenent et reddunt Deo et ecclesie Sancti Stephani inde
quinque solidos annuatim que sunt subtus viam de Trebursy. Et ex
dono Willelmi de Henemerdon totam terram de Pech. Hec omnia eis
confirmavi cum omnibus alijs possessionibus suis sicut ea racionabiliter possident et sicut carte donatorum suorum testantur. Testibus
Stephano Rid cancell(ario) meo, Simone de Mariscis, Ricardo de
Vern etc.

<sup>a</sup>*sic.* <sup>b</sup>*sic.*

**546.** Confirmation by King John of the possessions of Launceston
Priory which he had granted as earl of Mortain. As no. 545.<sup>a</sup> Witd. by
E(ustace), bishop of Ely; W(illiam), bishop of Lisieux, William Marescall,
earl of Pembroke. By the hand of H(ubert), archbishop of Canterbury, the
king's chancellor. Dated Aumale 28 June 1199.

<sup>a</sup>The variant readings are of no importance except that *Redvers* is in place of *Reavers; Bikeleya*
for *Bicheleia*.

MS.: Cartulary, f.216r.–f.216v.

**547.** Confirmation by King Henry III (after *inspeximus*) of the charter of
King John his father to Launceston priory. King Henry III also granted

and confirmed to the canons the gift made to them by Reginald, earl of Cornwall, of the churches of Liskeard and Linkinhorne on the day of the translation of the relics and of the canons of the church from the vill of Launceston to the ford, as the charter of Reginald, the king's son, bore witness. Witd. Hubert de Burgo, earl of Kent, justiciar of England; Philip D'Aubigny,[a] Thomas Basset. By the hand of R(alph),[b] bishop of Chichester, the king's chancellor. Dated Merleburg, 20 March 1229.

[a]*De Albiniaco.* [b]See M. A. Hennings, *England under Henry· III* (1932), 158.

MS.: Cartulary, f.216v. Another copy, *Calendar of Patent Rolls 1377–81*, p. 114 (1378).

**548.** Another copy of no. 265,[a] adding that the earl granted to the canons twenty years of rent of his gift which they formerly paid to him about the said moor of Caradon. Dated Exeter, 24 June 1284.

[a]The variant readings are of no importance, except that in the text no. 548 has *Menchia* for *Senchia*, the correct reading, given in no. 265. In no. 548 the list of witnesses ceases with William le Alemaund, cf. no. 265. 265 is dated 24 May 1284.

MS.: Cartulary, ff.216v.–217r.

**549.** Notice of a grant by Bartholomew, bishop of Exeter, of a grant by Reginald, earl of Cornwall, in pure and perpetual alms to the priory of Caradon which was part of the manor of Rillaton, so that the canons might have 100s. worth of land from the remaining part of the manor of Rillaton. Earl Reginald's grant was for the salvation of his soul and the soul of his father, King Henry, and Matilda, the empress, and her son King Henry and his children; and the souls of his ancestors and successors. Witd. Roger, bishop of Worcester, Nicholas, son of the earl; Bernard the clerk, Paganus and Roger, chaplains of the earl. Not dated. [2 February, 1165–1 July 1175 or 9 August 1179. For the enthronement of Roger, bishop of Worcester, see Delisle, *Recueil* i, 453. For Earl Reginald's death, 1 July 1175, see *Complete Peerage* (2nd. ed.) iii, 429. If not in Earl Reginald's lifetime, the grant might be dated after his death in July 1175 with an upper limit of date of 9 August 1179 when Bishop Roger of Worcester died at Tours, Delisle, loc. cit.]

MS.: Cartulary, f.217r.–f.217v.

**550.** Similar notice to no. 549 by Roger, bishop of Worcester, of Earl Reginald's gift of Caradon, part of the manor of Rillaton. Witd. Bartholomew, bishop of Exeter; Nicholas, son of the earl; Bernard the clerk. Not dated. [1165–1175, or 1175–1179, as no. 549.]

MS.: Cartulary, f.217v.

**551.** Promise and grant by Davit Cana[a] for himself and his heirs that they would not call to warranty the prior of Launceston by reason of the homage which the prior paid him for half an acre of land in Mollow Down (*Moletdon*)[b] which he had of Thomas de Tresalet. If there was a plea about this land, or his heirs called the prior to warranty, the said prior should have of David's goods £10 for his labour and expense. And the sheriff should have 20s. worth of David's goods for distraint for the work of the said prior to whom the £10 was payable before the quindene when the prior was called to warranty. He made himself and his heirs and their goods a security for this. Witd. Henry Rem, Robert de Bodmam, Henry Mustard. Dated Launceston, Sunday, 23 March 1292.

[a]Title: *clamancia Warini David Cana* [b]Title: *infra manerium de Clymeslond.*

MS.: Cartulary, ff.217v.–218r.

**552.** Obligation by Thomas de Tresalak to save harmless his lord, the prior of Launceston and his successors, against all lay and ecclesiastical persons forever. He would not call them into warranty by reason of his homage for half an acre of Mollow Down in the hundred of Climsland (*Clymeslaund*) which his father Richard formerly held there. In case he or his heirs ever called the prior and convent to warranty in any court, he bound himself and his heirs to the said prior and convent in 20 marks of silver. He bound all his moveable and immoveable goods for the distraint of his lord the prior and his bailiffs so that the 20 marks would be paid by the distraint of the sheriff of Cornwall if the prior and convent were impleaded for warranty. Sealing clause. Dated Launceston, 26 March 1291.

MS.: Cartulary, f.218r.–f.218v.

**553.** Bond of Richard de Tresalak in 20d. of annual rent to the prior and convent of Launceston for half an acre of land in Stoke Climsland which he held of the prior and convent. If he or his heirs failed to pay this rent, he granted that the prior or his steward or their servants could distrain by taking pledges throughout his land of Tresallack (*Tresalac*). He renounced all legal remedy by canon or civil law which might aid him but might be injurious to the prior and convent. Sealing clause. Witd. Dom. Richard, chaplain of the bishop of Exeter; Henry de Trevella, John Carbonel. Dated Launceston, Monday, 7 June 1260.

MS.: Cartulary, f.218v.

**554.** Notice by King Richard II to Robert de Tresulian, the steward of Cornwall. It had been shown to him on the part of the prior and convent of Launceston that his predecessor, King John, had given to the canons certain lands within his manor of Climsland. The canons and their yearly tenants, by reason of the view of frankpledge in the same manor, were obliged to find tithing men when they were elected at the view of frankpledge and to make a contribution with the tithing and to bear all other burdens pertaining to the tithing contrary to the force and effect of the charter of King John. The prior and convent had suffered distraint and loss and asked that they might be exonerated from these burdens. The king ordered the steward that the tenants and farmers (other than the serfs) of the lands of the priory granted by King John, whatever their estate, were not to be distrained or burdened with duties relating to the tithing, though they were to attend the leets of the manor aforesaid. Witd. the King himself at Westminster, 21 February 1378.[a]

[a]The charter ends with these words written underneath: *per peticionem de consilio Faryngton.*

MS.: Cartulary, f.219r.

**555.** Final concord between Prior Stephen and the convent of the one part, and John Bile of the other. There had been a dispute by the tenants of the priory within the manor of Climsland whether multure was due for a term of years or at will at the mill of John Bile within the manor. The parties reached agreement in this way. The prior and convent granted for themselves and their successors for ever that the said John and his heirs should have and hold the multure of the tenants of the priory. If any of the tenants or their heirs did not render this service, John and his heirs could exact the multure in the court of the lord of Climsland by a plea. The prior and convent were to have an annual rent of 12d. from the messuages, lands and tenements which they claimed they had had from ancient times in Beals Mill bridge (*Bilisbrigge*) and in the lands and tenements of John Bile. For arrears of rent of one month the prior and convent could distrain in the lands of John Bile.

John granted for himself and his heirs that the tenants of the prior could grind their corn and malt at his mill for a reasonable toll just as the other tenants of the manor did. Alternate sealing clause for chirograph. Witd. Serlo Wise, Noel de Paderda, John de Langdon. Dated Launceston, Tuesday, 13 January 1389.

MS.: Cartulary, f.219r.–f.219v.

**556.** Gift by Osbert de Bikelega,[a] for the salvation of the king of England and his heirs and of his lord, Earl Reginald, and for the redemption of his soul and the souls of his parents and friends, to the canons of Launceston of 20s. worth of land of the manor of Trefrize (*Trevris*), i.e. the land which was called Tregoiffe, the land of Luffa and the land of Warin by the bridge just as the stream descended into the great water of Inny. Also he gave one acre called Kersbrook (*Carsbroke*), with their men and appurtenances and the part of the grove at the east, just as the way divided, as far as the water in free and quiet alms forever. Witd. Durand the clerk, then sheriff; Pagan de Gunam and Roger his son; Nicholas brother of Osbert. Not dated. [Possibly *c.*1155–65 (Osbert de Bichaliga, see no. 13) and probably before Earl Reginald's death on 1 July 1175.]

[a]Heading: *Carta Osberti Bicheley de Tregoff et nemore de Treveris.*

MS.: Cartulary, ff.219v.–220r.

**557.**   Process of the hundred of East that none of the tenants of the prior of Launceston at Trelabe, Tregoiffe and Kersbrook would be the tithingman of Trefrize.

The bailiff of East warned that John de Trelaba was elected to the office of tithingman in the tithing of Trefrize, just as the tithingman presented others before Robert de Bilkeman, sheriff of Cornwall, at his tourn of East in the term of Easter 1273.

And the prior of Launceston (whose native the said John was) came and said that John was a native of the prior and convent and the land which he held from them in Trelabe was villein land pertaining to the priory which they had had of the gift of a certain Osbert de Bikelegh, formerly lord of Trefrize, which he gave to the canons in free, pure and perpetual alms free and quit of all secular service. Osbert's charter had been ratified and confirmed by the lord King John of good memory and the prior produced the charters which showed this. And he also produced the king's writ of which land he said was exonerated from such service and the lord king and the earls of Cornwall had long abandoned the idea that any of the tenants of the aforesaid prior and convent in Trelabe, Tregoiffe and Kersbrook (part of the manor of Trefrize) performed the office of tithingman from the time of Osbert's gift to the present time.[a] The prior sought judgement by view of the twelve men.

And the said tithingman of Trefrize came that day and maintained his suit. John declined to do the service and similarly sought enquiry through the tourn of the twelve jurymen.    Inquisition was made by the jury on Monday, 7 May 1274 at St Ive. The jury declared John was quit of the service and the tithingman was in mercy for a false presentment. Dated St Ive, Monday, 7 May 1274.

[a]The text continues *secundum formam magne carte.*

MS.: Cartulary, f.220r.–f.220v.

**558.**   Cornwall. Assize of novel disseisin to recognise if Ralph Botreaux and Reginald Pleute had unjustly disseised the prior of his free tenement in Trefrize (*Trevrys*) and of 2 acres of meadow and 10 acres of wood.
The said Ralph and Reginald did not appear, but a certain Thomas Polsagh replied for them as their bailiff. Thomas said the jury was summoned by Pascasius Polryden, undersheriff of Cornwall, who was of the counsel of the said prior. It was found out, however, by Vivian Penros and John Trevarthian (sworn triers of the jurors) that the jury was well and competently summoned by John Colshull, sheriff of Cornwall, without the nomination of the prior or any of his counsel and Pascasius had not interfered. And the assize was adjourned until Thursday after the feast of St James the Apostle (25 July) next to come etc. (i.e. Thursday, 1 August 1398). Not dated. [1398 cf. nos. 559, 560.]

MS.: Cartulary, f.221r.

**559.**   The assize taken between the lord John Honylond, prior of

Launceston, and Ralph Botreaux, knight, and Reginald Pleute about the wood of Trefrize.

Writ of the king to the sheriff of Cornwall to empanel a jury of 12 men and by pledges to arrange the attendance of Ralph and Reginald in a suit of the prior of Launceston that Reginald and Ralph had unjustly disseised him of his free tenement of Trefrize. Dated Shrewsbury, 28 January 1398.

MS.: Cartulary, f.221r.

**560.** Writ from King Richard II to William Rikehill and William Brenchesle appointing them and their companions justices at the assize of novel disseisin which the prior of Launceston had summoned before them versus Ralph Botreaux and Reginald Pleute about a tenement in Trefrize. They were to take the assize at the place and time appointed according to the law and custom of the realm of England, saving the amercements which would arise for the king himself. Witd. the King. Dated Shrewsbury, 28 January 1398.

MS.: Cartulary, f.221v.

**561.** The panel of jurors returned in the said assize.
John Greynefeld, knight; John Arundell; Thomas Peverell, William Talbot, Oliver Wise, Richard Trevage, John Chaynat, John Bevile, James Fursedon, John Moill, Nicholas Bokelly, Richard Tirell of St Columb, Ralph Sore, John Penarthe, Edmund Beket, Odo Resgerens, John Petyt, William Langedon, Robert Bommam, Richard Tredynnek, Richard Frankelyn, Henry Tresulgan, Thomas Trikell, John Cryke of Liskeard (*Leskerd*). Not dated. [1398].

MS.: Cartulary, f.221v.

**562.** Mainpernors:   Reginald Pleute for carrying peace[a]
                    100 marks[b]

  M' Reginald Pleute for conserving the peace
  £20[b] ⎤
  David Recan ⎬     of the county of Cornwall
  £20[b]
  Michael Recan ⎦
  Stephen, prior of Launceston by plea of the lord King
  £20[b] ⎤
  John Denys ⎬     of the county of Devon
  £20[b]
  Geoffrey Giffard ⎦
Not dated. [1398, cf. nos. 559–60.]

[a] *de pace portand'* [b] interlined

MS.: Cartulary, f.221v.

**563.** Release and quitclaim by Bernard de Bodbrant[a] to the canons of St Stephen of all his right in half an acre Cornish in Botternell (*Boturnell*) and in 3 acres of land in Notter and in all other lands and tenements which the prior and convent possessed there from his ancestors. He also ratified and confirmed all previous donations by his ancestors to the priory. Sealing clause. Witd. the lord John de Bello Prato, Richard de Hiwis, William Wise, knights. Dated Launceston, Sunday, 24 April 1278.

[a]Heading has *de Bodbran*.

MS.: Cartulary, f.222r.


**564.** Final concord made in the court of the lord king at Launceston from Easter day in one month 1244. Before Henry de Tracy, Gilbert de Preston, Robert de Haya, justices itinerant, between Bernard son of Roger, petitioner, and Henry, prior of Launceston, tenant, of one acre of land in Botternell, and the question of the tenure of the holding of one acre of land in 'Trekenever'. Whence the assize of mort d'ancestor was summoned between them in the same court. The same Bernard released and quitclaimed to the prior and convent and their successors all his right in these lands forever. The prior gave Bernard 4 marks of silver. Dated Easter term, 1244.

MS.: Cartulary, f.222r.–f222v. Printed *Cornwall FF.*, i no. 87.


**565.** Quitclaim by Bernard, son of Roger, to the prior and convent of his right in the land of Botternell or in the land of 'Trekynnever' (which he was seeking by assize of mort d'ancestor) and in all other lands which had been given to the priory by his father or in lands which had been exchanged between the priory and his father. The prior gave Bernard 4 marks of silver. Sealing clause. Witd. Randulf de Trewint, William Wise, Roger de Treloske. Not dated. [*c.*1244, see no. 564.]

MS.: Cartulary, f.222v.


**566.** Notice by Luke, son of Bernard, that for the salvation of his soul and the souls of his mother and father, he had been moved by charity to give and grant in pure and perpetual alms to the priory the land which Martin Augustin and Chubba the carpenter held in the vill of Botternell which Luke formerly held of the priory. To have and to hold in free and perpetual alms, saving his heirs and the rest of the tenements which Luke held of the prior and convent; rendering yearly to the prior and convent 6d. at Michaelmas for all service. Sealing clause. Witd. John, then sheriff of Cornwall; Roger de Lancuch, Ralph de Alton, Gervase Bloyho, Master Haymon, Geoffrey son of Bernard. Not dated. [*c.*1209–14, John, sheriff of Cornwall. He was also sheriff for a brief period in 1220, *CPR* (Hen. 3) i, 274.]

MS.: Cartulary, f.222v.

**567.** Grant and gift by unanimous consent of Robert Snylfoth, Roger and Geoffrey, sons of William Snylfoth, to the prior and canons of Launceston to strengthen their weir in their land of 'Lyner' which is contiguous to the land of the priory, i.e. Botternell to the water flowing down from its mills on whichever site it seemed best and most useful. For which the prior and convent were to pay to Robert Snytfoth[a] and his heirs one pound of cummin at Michaelmas for all service. For this grant the prior and convent gave to Robert, Roger and Geoffrey half a mark between them. Warranty clause of donors. The prior and canons granted to Robert, Roger and Geoffrey the pond of the mill weir for a fishery in their land. Sealing clause of Robert, Roger and Geoffrey. Witd. Jordan de Trecarle, Jordan de Trevagga, Roger de Trelosk, Hamelin de Trevella. Not dated. [*c.*1220–42 by attestations. Possibly earlier, see no. 486.]

[a]*sic.*

MS.: Cartulary, f.223r.


**568.** Release and quitclaim by Robert Friton to John Martyn, his heirs and assigns, of all his right in two parts of one half acre of land Cornish in the vill of Botternell. Sealing clause. Witd. John Baret, Henry Hervy, Walter Hervy. Dated Botternell, Monday, 4 June 1397.

MS.: Cartulary, f.223r.–f.223v.


**569.** Grant and confirmation by John Martyn and Matilda his wife to John Bela and Baldewin Bastard, chaplain, of two parts of one half acre of land Cornish in the vill of Botternell which Robert Fryton lately held of them. They had also given and granted to John and Baldewin the rents and services of Robert Fryton which he held of them in Botternell for the term of his life with the reversion when it fell due. Warranty clause and plural sealing clause. Witd. John Baret, Henry Hervy, Walter Hervy. Dated Botternell, Monday, 25 June 1397.

MS.: Cartulary, f.223v.


**570.** Release and quitclaim by Matilda, formerly wife of John Martyn, in her widowhood and lawful power, to John Bela and John Lavyngton, chaplains, of her right and claim in all messuages, lands and tenements in Botternell in the parish of Linkinhorne. Warranty and sealing clauses. Witd. John Cokeworthie, Robert Trebartha, John Joseph, John Rem, Roger Lamaryn. Dated Botternell, Tuesday, 9 April 1398.

MS.: Cartulary, ff.223v.–224r.


**571.** Grant and lease by John Bela and Baldewin Bastard, chaplains, for 12 years to Robert Fryton and Margery his wife and their lawful heirs, of two parts of one acre of land Cornish in the vill of Botternell which they

had of the gift of John Martyn. They were to pay yearly to John and
Baldewin and their assigns 3s. 8d. for all services, save the best beast if the
said Robert or his heirs died within the said term. Warranty and alternate
sealing clauses. Witd. John Baret, Henry Hervy and John Godecote.
Dated Botternell, Saturday, 30 June 1397.

MS.: Cartulary, f.224r.   .


**572.**   Bond of John Martyn, Richard Martyn and Richard Southcombe
(separately and together) to John Bela and Baldewin Bastard, chaplains,
in £20 of silver or gold of legal money. They were to pay this sum to John
and Baldewin or their attorney in the conventual church of Launceston at
Michaelmas following. Plural sealing clause.[a] Dated Launceston,
Wednesday, 27 June 1397.

[a]Condition in title: peaceful tenure of John and Baldwin of land in Botternell of the gift of
John Martyn.

MS.: Cartulary, f.224v.


**573.**   Quitclaim by Richard Southecombe[a] to John Bela and Baldewin
Bastard, chaplains, to his claim to two parts of one acre of land Cornish in
the vill of Botternell which Robert Fryton lately held there, together with
the rent and service of Robert Fryton, for the term of his life with the
reversion whenever it fell due. Warranty and sealing clauses. Witd.
Benedict Dounhevd, John Landear, John Treludek. Dated Launceston,
Monday, 1 July 1397.

[a]*Seccombe* in heading.

MS.: Cartulary, ff.224v.–225r.          See p. 222 for no. **573 A**.


**574.**   Quitclaim by Roger Pafford and Claricia his wife to Roger, prior of
Launceston, and the convent of his right in messuages, lands and
tenements in Botternell. Warranty and plural sealing clauses. Witd.
Richard Trelauny, Henry Person, John Josep, Roger Lamaron, Stephen
Cork. Dated Launceston, Wednesday, 10 August 1407.

MS.: Cartulary, f.225r.–f.225v.


**575.**   Indented charter of Twelve Mens Moor (*Twelfmanamore*) granted
by Henry, formerly prior of Launceston.

Agreement on Wednesday, 21 February 1285, between Prior Henry and
the convent of the one part and Thomas de Keluystok, David of the same
place, William Foth, Robert Faber, Jordan Cada, Robert Broda, Walter

de la Lak, Robert le Legha, Roger Boglawoda, John Can, William de Trewortha and Nicholas Cada of the other part. Prior Henry and the convent gave and confirmed to Thomas, David, William, Robert, Jordan, Robert, Walter, Robert, Roger, John, William and Nicholas for their homage and service all their land enclosed within these bounds: from Blackham (*Blakcecumbford*) as far as the head of 'Waterrytha' with all the land which pertained to the same as far as Witheybrook (*Withybroke*) and through Witheybrook as far as Trewortha hedge (*la Worthadich*), again in Witheybrook as far as the divisions of the said Thomas de Keluystoke as far as Cloven barrow (*la Clovenaburgh*) in the Shard (*La Sherde*) through the Port way (*la Portewey*) as far as the burrow by the mill way (*Mileweyisburgh*) and then through the divisions of William Cada as far as Sheepstone (*Sypstone*), thence as far as Lidgate (*La Lydhet*) of Roger Boglewode and thus by the ditch of Roger as far as the ditch of Robert Brode, then as far as the ditch of Robert Hegha, thence as far as 'la Frundesdiche' again in Blackham (*Blakecombford*) with the turbary which is called 'Maghmore' and with all the other turbaries and appurtenances within the said bounds in dry and wet. To have and to hold all the land to the said men and their heirs from Prior Henry and the convent and their successors freely and quietly, wholly, peacefully, in fee and heredity, for ever. The yearly rent to Prior Henry and the convent and their successors or attornies was 4s. of silver at Michaelmas for all service. Saving the common pasture above the said land to the farmers and serfs with their draught animals adjoining the manor of Caradon (*Carnedon*) with as many beasts in summer as they held in winter. Each one of them who used the said pasture with his animals was to pay yearly at Michaelmas one penny, to go to the twelve named men and their heirs. The tenants of the earl of Cornwall of the manor of Rillaton were to have for their hearth the first estover (or allowance of wood) and sufficient pasture for feeding their own animals at no cost. And if the twelve men or their heirs together or any of them were in mercy for any transgression they were to be quit of the forfeiture by the view of lawful men, their peers, in the court of the said prior and convent for 6d. for a whole plea of one day. Each heir of the said twelve men was to be quit of relief for 4s. of silver. Warranty *contra omnes homines et feminas* by Prior Henry and the convent. Alternate sealing clause (chirograph) of both parties. Witd. the lords Richard de Hiwys, John de Mules, knights; William de Tregrilla, Richard le Walleys. Dated Wednesday, 21 February 1285.

MS.: Cartulary, f.225v.–f.226r. [See Charles Henderson, 'Twelve Men's Moor' in *Essays in Cornish History* (Oxford 1935), reprinted from *Old Cornwall* (October 1929). The year is 1285, not 1284.]

**576.** Quitclaim by Hamelin Chan, son of Warin Chan, of half an acre of land in the vill of Upton (*Uppeton*) which his father Warin held of the priory. Sealing clause. Witd. the lord Roger de Trelosk, Roger Crabbe, William Brode. Not dated. [*c*.1229–1242, Roger de Trelosk.]

MS.: Cartulary, f.226r.

**577.** Lease from Prior William and the convent to John Hervy and Felicia his wife of their messuages, lands and tenements in Upton within their manor of Caradon (*Carnedon Pryor*) which the same John formerly held there. To have and to hold to John and Felicia and their legitimate heirs from the following feast of Michaelmas for 65 years. They were to pay yearly to the prior and convent a rent of 9s. 11d. by payments at the terms of Christmas, Easter, the Nativity of St John the Baptist and Michaelmas. John and Felicia and their heirs were to make common suit of court to the priory manor and to serve the office of tithingman when chosen by the homage. They were also to carry lime and salt as the other conventionary tenants did. If John and Felicia or any of their heirs died, a best beast was to be paid in the name of a heriot. They were to repair all the houses, buildings, ditches at their own cost. Re-entry in default of distress was permissible after arrears of rent of fifteen days, or if John and Felicia divided the land without permission, or placed it outside the hands of the prior and convent, except for an exchange of herbage through the summer between tenant and tenant, i.e. for the easement of the priory tenants. Warranty and alternate sealing clauses. Witd. Richard Knolle, Richard Cayrowe, Richard Bear. Dated at the chapter house of Launceston priory, Friday, 25 June 1434.

MS.: Cartulary, f.226r.–f.226v.

**578.** Grant and confirmation by Robert, prior of Launceston, and the convent to Roger de Lanhergy for his homage and service of 1½ acres of land in 'Wideslade' which John de Maneton formerly held. The bounds were from 'Pleyngstret' descending through the bounds of Lanhargy as far as the land which Hardyng once held in 'Wideslade' and then ascending as far as 'La Holde Vaunnynghous' and then from 'la Hornemerke' through the landyoke which John Faber of Bunchadon formerly held and thus to the royal highway; then by that way as far as 'Pleyngstret'. To Roger to hold peacefully in fee and inheritance forever. The yearly rent was 20d., payable at Easter and Michaelmas. Roger and his heirs were only to do suit to the prior's court twice yearly and then by reasonable summons unless they were in plea (which would be at the manor court of Climson). If they fell into mercy they would be judged by their peers in the prior's court and for a plea of one day they could aquit themselves of the fine for 3d. Warranty and (plural) sealing clause. Witd. Thomas de Maneton, Roger de Hamet, Benedict Bile. Not dated. [Probably *c*.1256–12 Sept. 1261, if the prior was Robert de Fissacre.]

MS.: Cartulary, f.227r.

**579.** Grant and confirmation by Joan, daughter of Reginald Nywelond, to William Trelowny, Robert Puddyng and John Godecote of the rents and services of Walter Hervy and Thomas Broune of all the lands and tenements which they held of her in the vill of Newland (*Nywelond*) with the reversions when they occurred. Warranty and sealing clauses. Witd. John Baret, John Joseph, Warin Hervy, William Perkyn and Robert Bere.

Dated Newland, Tuesday, 2 July or Tuesday, 16 July 1381. [*die martis proxima ante festum sancte Margarete*. See C. R. Cheney, *Handbook of Dates*, for the two feasts of St Margaret.]

MS.: Cartulary, f.227v.


**580.** Quitclaim by Joan, daughter of Reginald Nywelond, to William Trelouny, Robert Puddyng and John Godecote of her right in the lands and tenements in Newland which they had of the gift and feoffment of Thomas Broune and Alice his wife. Sealing clause. Witd. John Baret, John Joseph, Warin Hervy. Newland, Monday, 5 August 1381..

MS.: Cartulary, f.227v.


**581.** Another quitclaim of Joan, daughter of Reginald Nywelond to the same people. (William Trelawny etc.) of her right in the rents and services of Thos. Browne and Walter Hervy in Newland. As no. 580, but dated Launceston, 20 July 1382.

MS.: Cartulary, ff.227v.–228r.


**582.** Release and quitclaim by Thomas Broune and Walter Hervy to William Trelouny, Robert Puddyng and John Godecote of their right to lands and tenements in Newland. Sealing clause (plural). Witd. John Baret, Warin Hervy, Henry Lanhergy. Dated Linkinhorne (*Lankenhorne*), Tuesday, 23 July 1381.

MS.: Cartulary, f.228r.


**583.** Grant and confirmation by Thomas Broune and Alice his wife to William Trelowny, Robert Puddyng and John Godecote of their messuages, lands and tenements in the vill and fields of Newland. Warranty and sealing clauses (the latter plural). Witd. John Baret, John Joseph, Warin Hervy. Dated Newland, Wednesday, 24 July 1381.

MS.: Cartulary, f.228r.–f.228v.


**584.** General release and quitclaim by John Hooper of Clampit to Stephen, prior of Launceston, and the convent of all actions. Sealing clause. Witd. John Baret, Roger Menwynnek, Walter Crike. Launceston, Tuesday, 27 April 1389.

MS.: Cartulary, f.228v. (See also nos. 179–181.)


**585.** Gift, grant and confirmation by John Hoper of Clampit to Gervase Northcote and John Symon, chaplains, of his tenement in the free borough of Dunheved in the street called 'Bastestret' between the tenement which was William Raynfray's on the south side and the tenement of the mayor and commonalty on the north with the oven and crofts adjoining. He also gave Gervase and John all his garden in the said borough and street between the tenements of John Page and the mayor and commonalty. Also he gave Gervase and John his croft which lay by the cross of Dunheved on the western side and the land of Richard Tolla on the eastern side and the croft formerly of Thomas Miles on the west. He also gave to Gervase and John 9½d. of annual rent which he was owed annually from a certain tenement which Richard Adam, chaplain, held of him in the said borough; a pennyworth of annual rent for a certain tenement which Denise Beauchamp held of him in the said borough, and 9d. of yearly rent which he used to receive from the croft held of him by John Landyare, between the crofts of John Cary and John Page. Warranty and sealing clauses. Witd. John Fernehill, then mayor of the borough; Robert Tregoddek, John Couch, Robert Puddyng, John Page, John Landyare. Dated Dunheved, *die jovis proxima ante festum nativitatis sancti Johannis Baptiste anno regni regis Edwardi tercij post conquestum Anglie quinquagesimo nono.* [*sic*. There were only 51 regnal years in the reign of Edward III. If *uno* was intended the date would be Thursday, 18 June 1377.]

MS.: Cartulary, ff.228v.–229r.

**586.** Pleas of assize at Launceston before William Brynchele, justice of the lord king, Thursday, 1 August 1398.

The assize came to recognise whether Henry Fox, Margaret his wife and Felicia his daughter, John Cokeworthy, Henry Page, William Nottehull, Walter Skynner, John Colyn, John Cork, John Landyare, Thomas Wondry, Oliver Wisa, and Edward, son of Walter Skynner had unjustly disseised John Hoper of his free tenement in Dunheved borough, i.e. of 4 acres of land. Henry and the others did not come, but a certain Richard Reste replied for them as their bailiff. Richard Reste said there was no tenant in the view of the reeve of the said tenement named in the writ, nor was there on the day of the delivery of the said writ of the said John Hoper on 16 June 1398. And judgement was sought on the writ. Richard Reste said no injury had been done by them or disseisin to John Hoper. Both parties placed themselves on the assize.

The jury claimed John Hoper had been disseised by Henry and Margaret, John Cork and Felicia Fox. John Hoper was to recover seisin and his loss assessed at 5s. Henry and Margaret and Felicia Fox and John Cork were in mercy and John Hoper for a false claim versus the said John Cokeworthy and the others named in the writ. Dated Launceston, Thursday, 1 August 1398.

MS.: Cartulary, f.229r.–f.229v.

**587.** Manumission by John, prior of Launceston, of John Hoper of Clampit, senior (alias Bonney), his native of stock, from the yoke of servitude with his goods and moveable chattels. Alternate sealing clause. Dated at the chapter house, Launceston priory, Wednesday, *ante festum sancte Margarete* (8 or 20 July, see C. R. Cheney, *Handbook of Dates*). [i.e. 5 or 19 July, 1419.]

MS.: Cartulary, f.229v. [See also no. 178 and 179–80.]

**588.** Bond[a] of John Hoper of Clampit (*Clomputtys*), junior (alias John Bonney) and Walter Ludgard of the parish of St Pinnock (*Pinnocus*) to John, prior of Launceston, and the convent in £10 to be paid at the following Christmas. Plural sealing clause.

John Hoper of Clampit, junior (alias John Bonney) by his charter had granted to the prior and convent and their successors an annual rent of 13s. 4d. from his lands and tenements for the term of fifteen years after the following Michaelmas. Walter Ludgard or his heirs and successors were to pay any arrears of the rent if John Hoper died before the end of the term. 9 September, 1419.

[a]The heading to this bond is misplaced at no. 181. See no. 180 for the grant of one mark by John Hoper to the priory.

MS.: Cartulary, f.230r.

**589.** The testament of John Bovervale who married Ibota, the widow of John Hoper of Clampit, junior.
   He was sound of mind and left his soul to God and his body to holy burial.
   To Richard his son: 2 cows and 1 heifer and 20 head of sheep; an old brass vessel; an ancient *crof* of brass; 3 best bowls of brass; a basin and ewer; half of 12 pewter vessels; one half of his debts.
   To John his servant: 12 head of sheep and a new brass measure.
   To the store of St Michael of Linkinhorne; 6s. 8d. to endow an obit for his parents and for himself and for his wife Rosea.
   To John his son: his best dagger garnished with silver.
   To Magota, daughter of John Drew, his best silver-plated belt.
   The residue of all his goods and chattels to his executors.
   Executors: his son Richard and his daughter Christiana, wife of John Drew, to distribute the remainder of his goods according to his last will. Dated 1 August 1427.

MS.: Cartulary, f.230r.–f.230v.

**590.** Clampit (*Clomputtys*). Memorandum for rendering legal assistance[a] in the name of William, prior of Launceston, concerning one messuage and one carrucate of land there for 10 marks sterling due in arrears to the prior by reason of a certain rent lately granted to Prior John and the convent by John Hoper of Clampit, junior, i.e. 13s. 4d. a year for ten years passed by, i.e. from Michaelmas 1424. And for 33s. 4d. in arrears for the same time for rent from the said messuage as in the charter. And for homage and fealty.[b] Not dated. [c.1434.]

*advocacionem.* [b]Probably incomplete.

MS.: Cartulary, f.230v.

**591.** Note of settlement of dispute between the prior and convent of Launceston, proprietors of the parochial chapel of Tamerton, and the parishioners of the same chapel about the tithe of hay of the whole parish. The parishioners paid a composition of 5s. 6d. yearly for the tithe of hay. It was settled that the prior and convent should receive 6s. 8d. for the tithe of hay of the whole parish, except the tithe of hay of the vill of Tamerton which was glebe land and of the demesne of the church of St Stephen, Launceston, by consent of the parishioners. The sum of 6s. 8d. was to be paid yearly to the prior and convent or their attorney in the chapel of the parish of Tamerton on the Sunday after 8 September under a double penalty. Witd. Roger Combrugge, prior of Launceston; David Treludek, sub-prior; John Wille, John Honylond, canons, on behalf of the priory. On behalf of the parishioners: William Oggebeare, John Attehole, William Semeston, Walter Vacy with the consent of the parishioners. Dated Launceston, Wednesday, 15 June 1407.

MS.: Cartulary, ff.230v.–231r.

**592.** Plea between the priory and Nicholas de Trenoda about the suit of the mill at Bonyalva, 1301–2.

The prior of Launceston was summoned to reply to Nicholas de Trenoda in a plea which would permit his villeins in West Bonyalva (*Westre Benalva*) to make suit to the mill of the said Nicholas in Trenode bridge (*Trenoda Brigge*) which they should have done. And the said Nicholas said that the villeins were accustomed to make no suit to the said mill for every kind of corn growing in three carrucates of land which was the villein land of the said prior in West Bonyalva and of every sort of corn of the same villeins to the twentieth measure. And the said Nicholas was seised in demesne and fee by right in time of peace of the present lord king to take tolls and multure. But the said prior for the past ten years had withdrawn this suit by not allowing his villeins to make it. Whence Nicholas had a loss of £40.

And the prior appeared and defended his right. And he said that at one time the prior of Launceston and his predecessors had a certain mill at Bonyalva. A former prior, without the assent of his chapter, had alienated the mill to the predecessor of Nicholas for a rent to the prior and his successors of 6s. yearly. And he also said that Nicholas had constructed a new mill at Trenode bridge outside the vill of Bonyalva and outside the fee of the prior. And he sought judgement whether or not the said Nicholas should have the suit at the newly-constructed mill as he had nothing to show for this.

Nicholas said that the villeins of the prior and his predecessors in the time of Nicholas and his ancestors were accustomed to make suit to his mill of Trenode bridge and he sought enquiry. The prior said his villeins never made suit to any mill of Nicholas but only to his mill of Bonyalva and not in Trenode bridge. Both parties placed themselves *super patriam.*

And the jury said on their oath that the villeins of the said prior of West Bonyalva were accustomed to make suit to the mill of the ancestors of Nicholas situated in the fee of the same prior. They said, however, that Nicholas had erected a new mill in Trenode bridge outside the fee of the prior in another fee and on the other side of the flow of water of the old mill (where suit was due) and in another parish. The jury said that the said villeins were never accustomed to make suit to the mill which Nicholas had raised outside the fee of the prior in the time of the ancestors of Nicholas but only to the mill in the fee of the prior. Nicholas was in mercy for making a false claim. Not dated. [1301–2. For an occurrence of Nicholas de Trenode in 1302, see *Cornwall FF.* i, no. 370.] The memorandum (below) was probably not part of the plea.

Memorandum that John de Trenode was not seised in multure of the tenants of Launceston of Bonyalva. Afterwards the said John enfeoffed Nicholas de Benalva his son with all his lands and tenements and with the mill of Bonyalva of which Nicholas was not seised of the said multure. And afterwards the said John disseised the said Nicholas of all the lands and tenements and the said mill. And he gave (them) to John de Kendale in the eighteenth year of Edward III (1344–5).

MS.: Cartulary, f.231r.–f.231v.

**593.** Memorandum of the settlement of a dispute between the prior and convent of Launceston, the rectors of the chapel of Tamerton, of the one part and Luke de Algreston, Warin de Fenton, John de Trehorsta, Walter de Willysworthy, clerk, Walter Whita de eadem, Walter Blakedon, Walter Greya, Roger de la Slo and other parishioners of the same parish, of the other part, about the taking of mortuaries of the goods of the said parishioners when they died. The dispute lasted for some time and was wearisome to both parties with a danger to souls. At length it was settled in this way. For every parishioner of whatever status who held land and died, if he had 5 draught beasts or animals, the rectors or their agents should take and have the fifth best animal in the name of a mortuary, or the rectors could have 4s. for a mortuary instead of a best beast. If a widow was endowed with a free tenement, if she held no other land at farm than her dowry, she would give that as a mortuary. If she held other land than her dowry she would give a mortuary from her goods but not her widow's veil. When a married woman died she would give nothing except her wimple as a mortuary. If any parishioner died without five beasts and the goods were no more than 20s. then the said rectors would have 3s. for a mortuary. Alternate sealing clause for chirograph: the part

sealed by the prior and convent to remain with the parishioners; the part
sealed by the seal of the official of the lord archdeacon of Cornwall to
remain with the prior and convent. Dated Launceston, Friday, 30
November 1319.

MS.: Cartulary, f.232r. [A later and more careless hand begins here and continues to the end
of the cartulary.]

**594.** Gift of Henry de Umfranville to the church of the Blessed
protomartyr Stephen of Launceston and the canons regular of one mark of
silver from the church of Lapford by the hand of the parson of that church
in the name of alms at Michaelmas and Easter, saving Henry's right of
presenting the parson to that church. Sealing clause. Witd. H(enry),
bishop of Exeter, whose seal was appended, Master William Par, Serlo the
chaplain, William Chereburg and Gilbert the bishop's clerks, William the
bishop's butler, William de Hama, Master Ralph of Launceston. Not
dated. [During episcopate of Henry Marshal, bishop of Exeter, *ante* 28
March 1194—1 November 1206.]

MS.: Cartulary, f.232v.

**595.** Pleas between the priory and Nicholas de Treryse, parson of
Lapford, for a pension there by Umfridus Conyngesby. Michaelmas term
1491. (Roll 444).

Recital of evidence from Hilary term 1491 (roll 156): Nicholas Treryse,
parson of the parish church of Lapford, Devon, to reply to William
Hopkyn, prior of Launceston, on a plea that he should pay to William 26
marks in arrears of the annual rent of 13s. 4d. which he owed him.
And the prior by Thomas Glyn, his attorney, said that a certain William
Shere, late prior and his immediate predecessor, was seised by right of the
priory and of the said annual rent by the hands of John Andrewe, then
parson of the said church of Lapford, who was predecessor of the present
parson, by equal portions at the feasts of Easter and Michaelmas. This
pension was paid at Lapford from time immemorial. Prior William and
John Andrewe died, Nicholas the next parson withheld the pension for
twenty-six years before the date of the original writ (12 October 1488) and
went on withholding it and thereby the priory sustained a loss of £10.
    And the said Nicholas appeared by John Kyrton, his attorney. He said
he was parson of Lapford by the presentation of Alexander Arundell and
found his church totally exonerated from the payment. He could not pay it
without the consent of R(ichard), bishop of Exeter, the ordinary, and the
patron, the said Alexander. The sheriff was asked to cause the bishop and
patron to appear in the quindene of Easter (1492) to reply to the prior and
Nicholas.
    On that day the prior and Nicholas appeared by their attornies. The
ordinary and patron made excuses for non-appearance. The day was
postponed to the quindene of Trinity when the attornies of the prior and
Nicholas appeared but not the ordinary. It was judged that Nicholas

alone should reply. Nicholas sought leave to appear in the octave of Michaelmas. This was granted and the prior and Nicholas appeared by their attornies. Nicholas denied that the priors were seised of the pension. Then both parties placed themselves *super patriam*. Then the sheriff was asked to cause the parties to appear in the octave of St Hilary. Dated Michaelmas 1491. [From title: *De termino sancti Michaelis anno regni regis Henrici septimi septimo*.]

MS.: Cartulary, ff.232v.–233v.

**596.** Acknowledgement from Prior William Hopkyn to Nicholas Treryse, rector of the church of All Saints of Lapford, that he had received 35 marks for arrears of the pension of one mark yearly. Alternate sealing clause. Witd. Thomas Corke, senior, Thomas Talcarn, John Corke, William Jane, John Wolgarn, Thomas Uppecot, John Talcarn. Launceston, 23 May 1494.

MS.: Cartulary, f.233v.

**597.** Gift and confirmation in pure and perpetual alms by Robert with his father Alfred by charter to the priory of the church of Ashbury (*Ayssheb'y*) and his land in 'Whytedoune' between the two streams and Little 'Develcumbe', i.e. all the land which Geoffrey le Wyse held there, land which lay between the land of Roger de Langford and the glebe land, together with a part of the wood of Ashbury as bounded with the small meadow under the same wood. This gift was in addition to the land already held there by the prior and convent who were to have free entrance and exit to and from the wood. Witd. Thomas, archdeacon of Totnes; Roger Everard, Philip Poer, Robert de Bonevile and Henry his brother. Not dated. [Perhaps between *c*.3 December 1242 and Easter 1254, two dates when Thomas de Pincerna occurs as archdeacon of Totnes, Oliver, *Lives* 290–1.]

MS.: Cartulary, f.234r.

**598.** Memorandum that in 1393 Stephen, prior of Launceston, granted at the special request of the lord Thomas Sulling, abbot of Tavistock (*Tawistochia*), a tree growing towards the east of the abbey within the precincts of the chapel of St Martin of Werrington (*Woryngton*). The place in which it was planted belonged to the priory of Launceston. These things were enacted at Werrington in the house of William Leyne, chaplain, and of Thomas de Paderda and Simon Traweys, then bailiff of the manor (of Werrington). Dated 1393.

MS.: Cartulary, f.234r. (Folio 234v. is blank.)

**599.** Dispute between William Hopkyn, prior of Launceston, and a certain Nicholas Treryse, rector of Lapford, about an annual pension of one mark from the church of Lapford from time immemorial. Nicholas had withdrawn the annual pension and the said lord William Hopkyn had impleaded Nicholas by writ of the king. The prior stated that the said annual pension was due to him and his successors, and he said that he had seen that his ancestors had been proprietors of the same by the agreement and the deed in the time of Prior Roger under the seal of the said lord prior and convent in the house of Alexander Treryse.

On Tuesday, 26 May 1495 in the presence of John Wolgarn, mayor of the borough of Launceston, John Corke, steward of the lord Prince, Thomas Waryn, John Meryfyld, John Porlate, the said Nicholas Treryse on bended knees sought grace from the lord prior for arrears of the pension. Having obtained this, Nicholas of his own free will confessed that the pension was due to the priory by an oath on the Holy Gospel. Dated 26 May 1495 at Launceston (as above).

MS.: Cartulary, f.235r. (f.235v. is blank.)

**600.** Charter about the construction of the north choir aisle of the church of Liskeard.

Agreement between Robert, prior of Launceston, and the mayor and commonalty of Liskeard and the parishioners of the parish church of Liskeard (*Leskyred*). As rectors and proprietors of the church of Liskeard, the prior and convent granted licence to the mayor and commonalty and parishioners to erect and newly construct a certain chapel, contiguous to and on the north side of the chancel. And they were to break down the wall of the chancel and to build a new wall in a better way, with arches between the two and to place timber on and above the same wall and to join and strengthen the same. The mayor and commonalty and parishioners promised that they and their heirs and successors would do this and protect the wall and roof of the chancel and maintain the same chapel and roof in timber and stone with sufficient guttering. Their heirs would maintain this building at the cost of the mayor and commonalty and the parishioners. The mayor and commonalty and their heirs and successors would indemnify the prior and convent of this responsibility. Alternate sealing clause (priory seal and seal of the burgesses) for chirograph. Witd. Master Roger Keys, Walter Kyngdon, Henry Bodrugan, John Colshull, knights; Nicholas Russell, mayor; Thomas Clemens, John Marke. Dated at the chapter house of Launceston priory and Liskeard, 31 March 1477. (Cf. no. 507, a charter of 1430 for the construction of the south choir aisle.)

MS.: Cartulary, f.236r. Original charter, Liskeard borough MSS. no. 80 at Cornwall County Record Office, Truro.

# APPENDIX

## LIST OF DEANS OF THE SECULAR COLLEGE OF ST STEPHEN LAUNCESTON, PRIORS OF THE CANONS REGULAR OF LAUNCESTON PRIORY, AND CANONS OF THE PRIORY.

Abbreviations are as given in the list of common abbreviations on p. vi. Occ.=occurs. A question mark—?—before a prior indicates an uncertainty and indicates only one reference to an otherwise unknown person whose date(s) are problematical. As in the text of the cartulary and the introduction, 'no.' followed by a number refers to the number of the document in the cartulary. 'HR'=Hingeston-Randolph followed by the name of the bishop's register where the reference occurs. 'Dunstan' refers to Professor G. R. Dunstan's edition of the register of Bishop Edmund Lacy, 5 vols. (1963–1972) published by the Devon and Cornwall Record Society. Only the list of priors goes beyond the period of the cartulary with a list of later priors to the dissolution of the priory. The list of canons has been continued only as far as 1448. It was not thought useful to extend this list as, although the names of a number of canons are known just before and at the time of the dissolution of Launceston priory, unlike the list of priors, there would have been considerable gaps, if the list had been extended.

## DEANS OF THE SECULAR COLLEGE

1 Robert occ. 1076 (no. 3).
2 Ralph Pullo, c.1121–8 (nos. 4, 17).

## PRIORS OF THE AUGUSTINIAN PRIORY OF LAUNCESTON

1 Theoricus, c.1128 (Above, p. viii).
2 Robert. Died 24 June 1149 (*Heads of Religious Houses*, 169).
3 Richard occ. 1149 (no. 81).
4 Geoffrey, c.1159–71 (nos. 62, 459, 74. HR. *Stapeldon*, 229).
5 Osbert, c.1180–3 (no. 80).
6 ?Adam, ? c.1183–before Easter 1202 (no. 443).
7 Godfrey occ. Easter 1202 (HR. *Stapeldon*, 229). He may still have been prior c.1220 (no. 482).
8 ?Richard, ?c.1220+ (no. 310). See also no. 297.
9 William, c.1232–8 (nos. 216–17, 345, 530).
10 Henry, 1244 (no. 564).
11 Robert Fissacre, c.1256 (no. 461) Excommunicated September 1258 but absolved almost immediately (*Mon. Dioc. Exon.*, 22). Resigned 12 September 1261 (HR. *Bronescombe*, 200–2).
12 Richard occ. 7 July 1261 (no. 298), 31 May 1271 (no. 22) Dead by 13 January 1273 (no. 18). R. and O. Peter, *Histories of Launceston and Dunheved*, 78 refer to a Richard de Montisfont as prior at this time.
13 Henry occ. 28 February 1276 (no. 350) and 15 February 1278 (no. 424).
14 Roger occ. 22 September 1281 (no. 371).
15 Henry occ. 21 February 1285 (no. 575).
16 Richard de Brykevyle occ. 10 May 1291 (no. 357). Died 1307–8 (HR. *Stapeldon*, 229).

17 Roger de Horton installed 4 May 1308 (HR. *Stapeldon*, 229). Had gone blind by 29 September 1316 when a co-adjutor, Canon Ralph de Huggeworthi, was appointed (HR. *Stapeldon*, 279). Roger de Horton also occ. 29 October 1320 (no. 518) and possibly also in 1322 (no. 372).

18 ?Roger occ. at some time between 25 January 1328 and 24 January 1329 (no. 273).

19 Adam de Knolle occ. 13 November 1328 (HR. *Grandisson* I, 187). Resigned 26 June 1346 (HR. *Grandisson* II, 1004).

20 Thomas de Burdon. Elected 14 July 1346 (HR. *Grandisson* II, 1007). Occ. 3 July 1361 (no. 94).

21 Roger Leye occ. 20 July 1370 (no. 467).

22 Stephen de Tredidon occ. 1 June 1379 (no. 354). Died 8 December 1403 (HR. *Stafford*, 237).

23 John occ. Trinity 1402 (no. 54) and 26 July 1404 (no. 168) and 27 April 1405 (no. 415).

24 Roger Combrygge occ. 20 May 1404 (no. 489). Died 18 June 1410 (HR. *Stafford*, 237).

25 John Honylond. Elected 28 June 1410 (HR. *Stafford*, 237). Died 28 September 1430 (*Mon. Dioc. Exon.*, 22.).

26 William Shyre 21 August 1431 (*Mon. Dioc. Exon.*, 22). Occ. 5 October 1443 (Dunstan, *Lacy* II, 300).

## LATER PRIORS

27 Robert occ. 1474 (Rental of Launceston priory, f.7) and 1477 (no. 600).

28 William Hopkyn, 1483 (O. B. Peter, *Launceston Priory*, printed lecture 7 January 1889, p. 13). Died 10 August 1507 (*Mon. Dioc. Exon.*, 22).

29 John Carlian elected 10 September 1507 (*Mon. Dioc. Exon.*, 23).

30 John Baker occ. 1 August 1521 (*Mon. Dioc. Exon.*, 23). Resigned 1532 (*recte* 1531) (L. S. Snell, *Suppression of the Religious Foundations of Devon and Cornwall* (1967), 69).

31 John Sheyr succeeded 6 June 1531. Subscribed with eleven canons to the royal supremacy 28 August 1534 (*Mon. Dioc. Exon.*, 23). (Launceston priory dissolved 24 February 1539).

## CANONS OF LAUNCESTON PRIORY

1 Ralph de Henermerdune, *c*.1140–55 (no. 71).
2 Walter de Henermerdune, *c*.1140–55 (no. 71).
3 Philip, *c*.1154–65 (no. 331).
4 Thomas, *c*.1154–65 (no. 331).
5 Walter, *c*.1154–65 (no. 331).
6 Gilbert de Warenna. Before *c*.1160–2. (no. 440).
7 Thomas de Duna, *c*.1170–86 (no. 434).
8 Geoffrey, *c*.1221–44 (no. 172). SACRISTAN.
9 Thomas de St David, *c*.1228–38 (no. 297).

10 Richard son of Ralph, *c.*1228–38 (no. 297).
11 Robert occ. 17 June 1238 (no. 86).
12 Alan occ. 17 June 1238 (no. 86).
13 Henry de Trewvinecke (?Trewinnek). Appointed prior of Canonsleigh 17 December 1260. Living 28 October 1282, see Vera C. M. London, *The Cartulary of Canonsleigh Abbey* (Devon and Cornwall Record Society 1965), 116.
14 Stephen de Altarnun occ. 13 January 1273 (no. 18).
15 Warin de St Germans occ. 13 January 1273 (no. 18).
16 William de Penlen occ. 12 October 1303 (no. 90), 2 March 1308 (no. 503).
17 Commission for admission of John de Sancto Uvelo, 13 December 1308 (HR. *Stapeldon*, 279).
18 Ralph de Huggeworthi (Oggeworthi) occ. 29 December 1316 as co-adjutor of Prior Roger de Horton (HR. *Stapeldon*, 279). Also occ. 31 July 1318 (no. 379).
19 William de Mershe occ. 21 December 1344 (HR. *Grandisson* II, 989) and 9 February 1345 (HR. *Grandisson* II, 991).
20 Richard de Trelouny occ. 21 December 1344 (HR. *Grandisson* II, 989).
21 David Attehole occ. 13 January 1345 (HR. *Grandisson* II, 990) and 20 July 1370 (no. 467).
22 Angerus de Bant occ. 13 January 1345 (HR. *Grandisson* II, 990). Appointed prior of Bodmin 22 March 1349 (HR. *Grandisson* II, 1078).
23 John Goudman (Godman), *c.*1328–22 March 1349 (no. 271) SUB-PRIOR 3 July 1346 (HR. *Grandisson* II, 1004).
24 Richard Prideaux occ. 9 February 1345 (HR. *Grandisson* II, 991).
25 Stephen occ. 9 February 1345 (HR. *Grandisson* II, 991).
26 William de Leye occ. 20 September 1349 (HR. *Grandisson* I, 149).
27 David Hole occ. Michaelmas 1353 (no. 287).
28 Roger Leye occ. 28 September 1367 (no. 294). PRIOR *c.*1370.
29 William Snowe occ. 20 July 1370 (no. 467).
30 William Hilperby occ. 20 July 1370 (no. 467).
31 Thomas Bray occ. 23 August 1384 (no. 471).
32 Roger Combrigge (Combrych) occ. 14 May 1395 (no. 37) and 23 June 1403 (no. 508). PRIOR *c.*1404.
33 David de Treludek occ. 14 May 1395 (no. 37). Appointed SUB-PRIOR 20 June 1410 (HR. *Stafford*, 237).
34 John Batyn occ. 1 September 1398 (no. 474) and 28 June 1410 (HR. *Stafford*, 237).
35 Thomas Osborn occ. 1 September 1398 (no. 474) and 28 December 1430 (HR. *Lacy* i, 133).
36 Thomas Trethak (Tredayk) occ. 1 September 1398 (no. 474) and 28 June 1410 (HR. *Stafford*, 237).
37 John Honylond occ. 23 June 1403 (no. 508). PRIOR 28 June 1410.
38 John William occ. 15 June 1407 (no. 591).
39 John Cleve occ. 28 June 1410 (HR. *Stafford*, 237).
40 William Frengy occ. 28 June 1410 (HR. *Stafford*, 237).
41 Robert Hervy occ. 28 June 1410 (HR. *Stafford*, 237).
42 John Wylkyn occ. 28 June 1410 (HR. *Stafford*, 237).
43 John Thomme occ. 28 June 1410 (HR. *Stafford*, 237).

44 John Lancels alias Wylle occ. 28 June 1410 (HR. *Stafford*, 237) and 28 December 1430 (HR. *Lacy* i, 133).

45 Simon Anstewylle (Anstyswylle) alias Oteram occ. 28 June 1410 (HR. *Stafford*, 237) SUB-PRIOR 28 December 1430 (HR. *Lacy* i, 133).

46 John Cade occ. 28 June 1410 (HR. *Stafford*, 237) and 28 December 1430 (HR. *Lacy* i, 133).

47 Robert Paris occ. 28 December 1430 (HR. *Lacy*, i, 133). CELLARER Michaelmas 1445 (Dunstan, *Lacy* III, 321). Occ. also 23 September 1447 (Dunstan, *Lacy* II, 398). Instituted as vicar of Liskeard 11 November 1457 and on 25 April 1460 he exchanged for Milton Abbot. See John Allen, *History of Liskeard* (1856), 115.

48 Peter Genys (Gyves, Genes) occ. 18 March 1424 (Dunstan, *Lacy* IV, 86) and 28 December 1430 (HR. *Lacy* i, 133) and 28 December 1430 (HR. *Lacy* i, 133).

49 Stephen Kent occ. 18 March 1424 (Dunstan, *Lacy* IV, 86) and 28 December 1430 (HR. *Lacy* i, 133).

50 William Glasier occ. 8 August 1427 (Dunstan *Lacy* IV, 111.) and 22 September 1436 (Dunstan, *Lacy* IV, 162).

51 Robert Toker occ. 18 March 1424 (Dunstan, *Lacy* IV, 86) and 28 December 1430 (HR. *Lacy* i, 133).

52 William Shyre occ. 28 December 1430 (HR. *Lacy* i, 133). PRIOR 21 August 1431.

53 Nicholas Gerecote (Gorecot) occ. 24 September 1429 (Dunstan, *Lacy* IV, 127) and 26 May 1431. (Dunstan, *Lacy* IV, 139).

54 Robert Alan (Alyn) occ. 24 September 1429 (Dunstan, *Lacy* IV, 127) and 19 September 1433. (Dunstan, *Lacy* IV, 150).

55 John Degendon alias Gendelle occ. 28 December 1430 (HR. *Lacy* i, 133).

56 William Laneman (*Lavenian*) occ. 30 December 1428 (HR. *Lacy* i, 133). Occurs as SUB-PRIOR 20 June 1447 (Dunstan, *Lacy* II, 389).

57 Richard Yerle (Yurle) occ. 28 December 1430 (HR. *Lacy*, i, 133) and 5 October 1443. (Dunstan, *Lacy* II, 301).

58 John Denbaude (Denbawde, Denbowde) occ. 18 December 1434 (Dunstan, *Lacy* IV, 153), 21 December 1437 (Dunstan, *Lacy* IV, 164) STEWARD AND RECEIVER Michaelmas 1445 (Dunstan, *Lacy* III, 321).

59 Walter Coll occ. 23 February 1447 (Dunstan, *Lacy* II, 374) and 20 January 1448 (Dunstan, *Lacy* II, 411).

*Addendum*

**573A.** Quitclaim by Joan Shorta, widow, to Roger, prior of Launceston, and the convent, of her right in messuages, etc. in Botternell (*Boturnell*). Warranty and sealing clauses. Witd. Richard Trelauny, Henry Person, John Josep. Dated Launceston, Wednesday, 10 August 1407. MS.: Cartulary, f.225r.

# INDEX I: PERSONS AND PLACES

Roman numerals refer to pages of the introduction, Arabic to documents in the cartulary. Fathers and sons without any surname are indexed under 'sons of'. Place-names are followed by the parish in which the place is located, then by the forms appearing in the text.

## Abbreviations used in the Indexes

Christian names

| | | | |
|---|---|---|---|
| Edward | Edw | Richard | Ric |
| Geoffrey | Geof | Robert | Rob |
| Henry | Hen | Roger | Rog |
| John | Jn | Thomas | Thos |
| Nicholas | Nic | Walter | Wal |
| Philip | Phil | William | Wm |
| Reginald | Reg | | |

Relationships

| | | | |
|---|---|---|---|
| brother | bro. | mother | m. |
| daughter | dau. | son | s. |
| father | f. | grandson | gs. |
| grandfather | gf. | sister | sis. |
| heir | hr | wife | w. |

Ecclesiastics

| | |
|---|---|
| bishop | bp |
| archbishop | abp |
| chaplain | chap. |

Places

| | | | |
|---|---|---|---|
| Launceston | L | Gloucestershire | Glos |
| Cornwall | Corn | Huntingdonshire | Hunts |
| Dorset | Dors | Somersetshire | Som |
| Oxfordshire | Oxon | Staffordshire | Staffs |
| Bedfordshire | Beds | Warwickshire | Warw |
| Berkshire | Berks | | |

Miscellaneous

| | | | |
|---|---|---|---|
| département | dép | note | n. |
| junior | jun | North | N. |
| senior | sen | Saint | St (pl. Sts) |
| knight | kt | South | S. |

A., precentor of Exeter, 527; steward, 532; treasurer of Exeter, 527

Abbate, Hen, clerk, 348

Acton Burnell, Salop, letters dated at, 395

Acy, Wm de, 415

Adam, chap., 97; dean, 99n; master, 497; prior of L, 443; Ric, chap., 132, 585

Adam de Knolle, prior of L, see Knolle

Addicroft in Linkinhorne, Odecrofte, and wood, 498, 544

Adric Ghegia, burgess of L, 3

Agnc', papal mandate dated at, 92

Ailsi, xv, xvi and n, xix, xxii; ss. Bernard, Jordan, Nic, Pagan, xv, xvi and n,

Ailsi—cont.
xix; bro. Brichtric, xvi and n; gs. Peter of Cornwall, see Peter, and Holy Trinity, Aldgate; f. Theodulf, xvi and n; see also Bernard the Scribe

Ailsius and w. Erneburg, 241, 242

Alan, bro. and chap., 250; canon of L priory, 86; steward, 529, 532, 535; Joceus, 488

Alan (III) count of Britanny, earl of Corn, xviii and n, xix and n.

Albamar', lord Jn de, 298

Albert, bro., master of Knights Hospitallers, London, 250

Albineio, see D'Aubigny

St Albino, Mauger de, 282

Albo Monasterio (Blanchminster), Hugh
de, 494; Jn, nephew and hr of
Ranulph, 94; Ralph de, kt, lord of
Stratton, 417, 419; his steward, *see*
Flexbury; Ranulph de, 93, 418
Aldestowe, Jn de, 375-7
Aldgate, *see* Holy Trinity, Aldgate
Alexander, doctor of law, 410
Alexander III, pope, xxiv-xxvii, xxxvi,
xl, 6
Alfredsweie, ford, 210
Alfricus, 1
Algar, bp of Coutances, 9, 29; priest of
Sela, 284
Algerstoune, Cecilia, dau. of Adam de,
170
Algreston, (Allisdon, N. Tamerton), Luke
de, 593
Alindec', 74
Allet in Kenwyn, Aleth, Jn de, kt, 392
Almarius, dean, 99n
Almelinus, priest of Boyton, 431
Altarnun, Alternon, Alternun, xxvi;
church of, 89, 100; tithes of chapel
of St Luke at Drywork, xxxv, 89;
parish of, 100; vicar, *see* John; Drogo
de, clerk, 382; Stephen de, canon, 18
Alton, Ralph de, 566
Alured, archdeacon, 428; prior of St
Germans, 533
Alwaldus, Alwoldus, reeve, 80; reeve of
Fawton, 81
Alwin, forester, 252; *see also* Son of
Andrew, Andrewe, chap., rector of Lam-
mana, 458; Jn, rector of Lapford,
Devon, 595; lord, seneschal of Corn,
223; vicar of Stratton, 414
St Andrew, church of, *see* Stratton
Angers, St Sergius of, abbot Auger, xxxv
n, 289; prior Geof, xxxv n, 289
Anger, clerk, 401. Cf. Auger
Anglicus, *see* Roger
St Anselm, xv
Anstis, Andrew, 315
Apulia, Simon of, bp of Exeter, *see* Simon
Araz, Gervase, 378; Wm, 378
Archer, Wal, 7
Archid', Ralph, 432
Argentein, Wm de, 498, 544
Arlmar, dean, 96
Armarius, Rob, 289
Arthur, Jn, juror, 269
Arundell, Darundell, Alexander, 595; Jn,
151, 561; kt, 507n; seneschal of the
prince, 152; Rainfred de, 282; Ralph
de, 370, 461; Rob, 9; W. de, vicar of
bp of Exeter, 409, 532
Ashburton, Devon, Arsbernatona, manor,
8
Ashbury, Devon, Ayssheb'y, church 597;
glebe and wood, 597
Asketill, *see* Son of
Asseton, Thos, 438
Asshlake, Reg, juror, 491
Athill, St Stephen by L, Atawille, Atte-
wille, Attel, Hattel, La Wille, Wylly,
xxv, 3, 6, 239-40, 257-8; Agnes, dau.
of Jn, 258; Ric Robyn de, 168; Wm,
s. of Rog de, 240

Atrio, Phil de, 498n, 544
Atte, *see also* following word
Attecombe, Stephen, juror, 491
Attedene, Simon, 511
Attefenna, Wal, 386
Attehille, Ric, 516
Attehole, (Trehole in St Gennys), David,
canon, 467; Jn, 591; Wal, 386
Attek, Attec (in Linkinhorne?), wood,
498, 544
Attelake, Wm, and w. Christine, 283
Attel, *see* Athill
Attemore, Thos, juror, 491
Attewille, Wm, juror, 126
Attewode, wood, 232n; cf. Bosco
Atteyete, Jn, 511
Aubigny, *see* D'Aubigny
Audener, Nic de, 521; mayor of Liskeard,
519
Auger, Auco, Augo, chap., 383; Hugh,
archdeacon of Totnes, 7; Stephen,
145; Wm de, archdeacon of Corn, 7,
17. *See also* Anger
Augus, Martin, 159
Augustin, Martin, 566
Aumale, Normandy, *dép* Seine-Inf., Albem-
arla, (aput) Aumarllem, 546
Auners, Thos de, steward of Corn, 16
Aunger, Wm, 168
Ayllesbur', Wal de, lord of, 16
Aylwardus, 401
Ayssh, Jn, vicar of St Martin of Liskeard,
163
Aysshe, Rob, chap., 315


B., archdeacon of Exeter, 527
Bacheler, Alexander, 241-2
Badash, Dunheved, Bodessa, xxii, xxiii,
34
Badgall in Laneast, Bodgall, Bodgalla,
Bod(e)gealla, Bodgeulla, Bodgalle,
Botgallon, xxv, xxxviii, 195-7, 199-
200; ford of, 217-18
Bagetor, Phil de, 409n
Bake in St Germans, N. Bake, Baak, 492;
Adam de, juror, 269; Thos, 516;
juror, 50; Wm, 511, juror, 51; reeve
of Liskeard, 522
Baker, Jn le, 67-8. *See also* Pistor
Bal, David, 200
Baldwin, 176; and his ss., 114
Bamham in Lawhitton, Bodmam,
Bommam, xxv, 272, 308-14; Peter
(de), 273, 306; Peter, s. of Rob de,
312, 314; Ralph de, 308-9, 311; Rob
de, 16, 69, 84, 108-9, 160-1, 170,
182-3, 220, 230, 239-40, 257-8, 272,
312-14, 356, 358, 391, 397, 468, 551,
(juror) 561
Bampton, Oxon, Bentona, church of, 8
Bank, Banc, Thos, possibly scribe of the
cartulary, viii, 117-19; clerk, 306,
328, 455; Wm, 281
Bant, Angerus de, canon, 271; Stephen,
38, 121, 157, 162, 214-15
Banzhan, Wm, 75

Baret, Jn, 568-9, 571, 579-84
Barlendew in Blisland, Barlandu, Jn de, *see* Burgh
Barnstaple, archdeacon of, *see* German, Ralph, Roger
Bartha, Rob, 162
Bartholomew, bp of Exeter, xv n, 26, 116, 277, 334-5, 533, 537, 539, 541, 549-50
Basset, Thos, 547
Bastard, Baldwin, chap., 569, 571-3; Benedict de, 314; Thos, 356, 378, 425-6
Bastehay in St Thomas by L, liberty of, xxxiv, 38, 52; prior and convent's steps, porches and stair in, xxxiv, 38. *See also* Tregorrek
Bastestret in L, 585
Bata, Ric, 506
Bate, Jn, 301
Bateshill, Jn de, 272
Bath and Wells, diocese of, 87, 92, 405
Battesford, Jn de, justice, 267
Batyn, Christine, 148; Jn, canon, 296, 474; Jn, w. Christiana, and dau. Margery, 149; Magota, 123, 125; Margery, dau. of Wm, 147; *see also* Loryng; Nic, de Trebursy, 160-1
Batynscrofte, Battynnyscrofte, Batyn ys Crofte, 'near L', 146-8
Bayllehelf, Jn de, juror, 57
Beabrar (in Bradford, Devon?), 447; Hen, 447
Bealsmill in Stoke Climsland, Bilisbrigge, 555
Bear, Ric, 577
Beatrice, Countess, w. of Reg de Dunstanville, earl of Corn, xvii, 526 Beaubraz, 450-2
Beaumond, Beaumont, Beamond(e), Jn, 286; Ric, 66, 68, 95, 112-13, 257, 280, 314; juror, 269, 312
Beaupre, *see* Bello Prato
Beaworthy, Devon, Becchwrthi, church of, xxvi, 6
Becard, Peter, kt, 265, 548
Bedford, Jn, duke of, 55
Beket, Edmund, juror, 561; Edw, juror, 153
Bela, Jn, (chap.) 569-73; Peter, 266
Bele, Rog, priest, 414
Belknapp, Rob, justice, 158
Bellestan, Wal de, and w. Cecilia, 355
Bello Campo, Beauchamp, Denise, 585; Hugh de, 499; R. de, justice, 216; Rob de, justice, 345
Bello Prato, Beaupre, Jn de, kt, 392, 396, 457, 480, 517, 563, steward of Corn, 73, 370, 390, 465-6; Stephen de, 16; juror, 261; kt, 391
Benden(gis), Wm de, 26
Benedict, master, 99, 387
Benjamin, clerk, 497
Bennacott in Boyton, Biningcott, Bunningcote, 64
Ber, Thos, 157; Wm de, 68
Bere, fee of in Stratton Hundred, 391
Bere, Baldewin de, 517; Nic de, 20; Ric de, 67; Rob, 579

Berewyk, Berewyke, Berwike, Berwyk, Hugh de, steward of duke of Corn, 25; Jn (de), justice, 24-5, 262, 264, 391, 393, 399
Berkhamstead, Herts, Berkhamested, 510; Master Jn de, clerk, 35
Bern, Arnold, 137
Bernard, 17, 88; clerk, de Penkyvoc, 74, 164-7, 244, 246, 383, 415, 545-6, 549-50; notary public, 252; priest, 28, 29; the Scribe, xiv and n, xv, xvi and n, xxi, 543; Jn, s. of the Scribe, xvi n, 227; Luke, s. of the Scribe, xvi n, 192, 227; Peter, s. of the Scribe, xvi n, 192; steward, 75; sheriff of Corn, 11, 538. *See also* Henry I
Berne, *see* Peek and La Berne
Bernhay in Dunheved, Barnhaye, Le Barnehay, xxiii and n, 119, 126, 134; park, 168; priory court, xxiii, xxviii, xxxvii, xxxviii, 135-6, 140, 157, 207; manor court, xxxviii. *See also* Hay
Bernyngcote, Thos de, 404
Best, Wm, of St Clether, 85
Bethwat', Wm, juror, 153
Bevill, Bevell, Bevile, Bevyle, Bevyll, Bovilla, Buvyle, Byvyle, Alice, w. of Reg de, lord of Tredaule, 84; Jn, 341; juror, 561; Ralph, juror, 153; Ralph de, lord, 461, 466; of Tredaule, 83; Reg de, 84; kt, 16, 20, 261, 391, (juror) 57; Thos, rector of Poundstock, 337
Bichalega, Bicheleia, Bicheley, Bikelega, Bikelegh, Bikeleya, Osbert de, lord of Trefrize, 13, 545-6, 556 and n, 557
Bideford, Devon, charter dated at, 402
Bidelake, Devon, 234
Bile, Benedict, 578; Jn, 555
Bilkeman, Rob de, sheriff of Corn, 557
Billoun, Jn, 351, 445
Bilney, Bylney(e), Jn, 132, 139, 142, 145, 177, 362-3, 474
Binhamy in Stratton, Bename, 93
Birchdoune, *see* Le Birchdoune
Birford, 3, 6
Biroidron, *see* Roydron
Biset, Manasser, steward of King Henry II, 10
Bishop's Tawton, Devon, Tawatona, manor, 8
Bishopsteignton, Devon, Teintona, manor, 8
Bithewaite, Wm, juror, 50
Bitton, *see* Bytton
Blackaton in Lewannick, Blakadoune, 100
Black Torrington, Devon, Blaketoryton, Blaktoryton, hundred, xxix, 438, 445-6; steward of lord of the hundred, *see* Stephen(e)ston
Blackham (in Linkinhorne?), Blakecombford, Blakcecumbford, Blakkombe, 538, 575
Blagdon in N. Tamerton, Blakedon, Wal, 593
Blake, Jn, 511, 513-15; Jn, his s., 516
Blakemore, Blakemor, 216-17
Blanchminster, *see* Albo Monasterio

Bletheu, 17
Blisland, Blustone, Blyston, 88
Blois, Henry of, *see* Henry
Bloyou, Blochiu, Blohio, Bloiho(u), Bloihu, Bloy(h)o, Bloyhou, Bloyow(e), land of, 78-81, 159; Alan, 227; kt, 279; Gervase, 159, 566; Hen, 62; Ralph (de), 15, 267, 398, 458
Blund, Ric, bp of Exeter, xiii n.
Blundus, Rob, chanter of Exeter, 7; Rob, writer, 5
Boctholoma, *see* Bucklawren
Bodardle in Lanlivery, honour of, xvii
Bodbrane in Duloe, Bodbran(t), lord Bernard de, 461, 563; kt, 480; Wm de, 206
Bodfus, land of, 460
Bodier, Hamondus, 322
Bodigga in St Martin by Looe, Bodcodigu, Bodcusuga, xiii n, xxvi, 3, 461-2
Bodlek, Hen de, 417
Bodmam, *see* Bamham
Bodmin, Bodminia, borough and parish of, xxxiv, xxxvi, 170, 488; reeve of, *see* Nicoll; church of St Petroc, 2, 8, 14, 277, 300, 387; Augustinian priory of, xv and n, xxxiv; priors, xxxiii, 92, 278, 417, and *see* Hugh, J(ames), R., Robert, William; inquisition at, 499; documents dated at, xviii n, 503; Hamo de, 526, 535; *see also* Hamo and Briton; Master Wal de, clerk, 35-6
Bodrugan in Gorran, Bodrig', Bodrygan, Hen de, 15, 203, 223, 261, 367, 461 and n, 462, 478; kt, 600; sheriff, 202; Hugh de, 216; Otto de, 460; Phil de, 463; kt, lord of Pendrym, 465-6; s. Rog de, kt, 466; Wm de, 480; clerk, 457
Bodulgate in Lanteglos by Camelford, Bodulget, Bodulgoit, Bodulgoyt, Stephen, 214-15; Warin and w. Matilda, 378
Bodway in Menheniot, xvi n.
Body, Bodya, Hen sen, 131-6; Thos, 134-6
Bodyer, Wm, 123, 125
Bodygode, Hen, 168
Bogeth, Boketh, Hen and his f. Ric, 187
Boglawoda, Boglewode, Rog, 575
Bokelly, Nic, 214-15; juror, 561
Bolda, Cecilia, 516
Boleputte, Jn, 295
Bonda, Jn le, 67; Rob (de), 66, 68
Bonevile, Bonevylle, Elyas, juror, 445; Rob de and his bro. Hen, 597
Boniface IX, pope, 387
Bonney, Jn jun, *see* Hoper
Bonno(c)k, Bonnek, Jn, 516; mayor of Liskeard, 523; Thos, juror, 509-10
Bony, Stephen, 126
Bonyalva in St Germans, Banathelva, Benalva, Benavel, Benlva, including West Bonyalva, xiii n, xxvi, xl, 3, 6, 460n, 481-92, 592; common pasture in, xl, 489-90; mill at 483-5, 488, 592; Andrew de and his bro. Wal, ss. of Ric Staneray, 481; Edw de,

Bonyalva in St Germans—*cont.*
482, 484; Ric, 490; Rob, juror, 491; Simon, 489; Wm, 492; Nic de, *see* Trenode
Borez, Hen, 232
Borna, Alan de, 447
Bornebury, Edw, 179
Bosco, Boscho, land of, 233; Martin de, 237; Nic de, seal of, 233; s. Wm, 233; Rob de, 414; Simon de, 357; Wal, s. of Mabanus de, 232-3
Boscofelek, Jn, notary public, 337, 387
Boscoroham, Ralph de, 27, 493, 525
Bosmawgan in St Winnow, Bodmalgan, Jn Kendal(e) de, 488
Boson, Bozo(n), Jn, 207-9, 287, 439; w. Eleanor, 208, 439
Bossiney in Tintagel, Bodsyny, Rob Simon de, 122
Bosvysek, Ric de, 273
Botch', Sampson de, 70
Boterell, Botreaux, Botrell, Botriaux, Jn, juror, 354; Ralph, kt, 454, 507, 558-60; Reg de, 16, 261, (juror) 354, 388-90, 462, 465-6; s. and hr of Wm, 271; Wm, s. and hr of Wm, 271; Ric, 384; Wal de, 115; Wm (1) de, xxviii n, 382-4; w. A(e)liz Corbet, 382-4; Wm (2) xx, xxviii n, 13, 167, 184, 246, 249, 251-2, 384; sheriff, 32; his w. Aubrey, 184; Wm (3), 185; Wm (4), 21, 185, 223, 282, 367; his w. Joan, 185, 223, 367; Sybil, m. of, 185; Wm (5), 16, 396; kt (and juror) 261, 265, 271, 351; Wm (6), 271; Wm (occ. 1390), 103; Lady Elizabeth, relict of Wm, 387
Bothennek, Botkennoc, Nic de, 88
St Botolph, Colchester, Augustinian priory of, xv
Botternell in Linkinhorne, Boturnell, Boturnoll, 538, 563-74; grants dated at, 568-71; mill(s), 159, 567
Botton, Master Thos de, clerk, 35
Botuell, Bernard de, 479
Botya, Jn, chap., 222
Bousser, Jn de, 273
Bovervale, Jn and his ww., Ibota and Rosea, dau. Christiana, ss. Jn and Ric, and servant Jn, 589
Bovilla, *see* Bevill
Bowedon, Hen, juror, 50
Boy(e)lond, Ric de, justice, 392; Wm, juror, 491
Boyton, Boithun, Boiton, Boitona, Boituna, Boytun, xxvi, xxix n, xxxviii, xxxix, 64-5, 73; chapel of, 6, 98; manor of, 64-5; priest of, *see* Almelinus; Odo de, 64-5; Parisius de, 98; Ralph de, dean, 343; Ric de, chap., 225; Wandry de, 138, 322
Bozo(u)n, *see* Boson
Brackeley, Brakeleg, Brekelay, Brekel, Brake(l)l', Brekill, Brach', Brak', Simon de, 15, 185, 364, 529; Simon de, sheriff of Corn, 189, 193, 216-17, 485
Bracino, Wm de, 322-3
Brackyssh, Hen, 359; Ric, 148

Dowbulday, Hen, 149; dau. Christiana, 149; sis. Hawise, w. of Stephen Lyon, 149

Downinney in Warbstow, Dounech', Dounheny, Dunechin, forest of, xxvi, 6; manor, 205, 252; mill of, xxvi, 6

Dozmary Pool in St Neot, Dosmery Poole, Thosmery, xl, 82, 85

Draynes in St Neot, Rob de, 88

Drayton, Rog de, 265; lord, 16

Drew, Jn, w. Christiana, and dau. Magota, 589; Warin and his w. Margery, and Jn, their s., 272

Dreynek, Dreynok, Gilbert, juror, 152; Jn, juror, 491; Rog, 516

Drogo, Ralph, 191

Druxton Bridge in Werrington, Durkeston-brugge, hundred court at, xxix, 446

Drywork in Altarnun, tithes of chapel of, xxxv, 89

Dudeman, Dudemannus, clerk, 321; Gilbert, his uncle, 321; Gilbert's s. Wal, *see* Crese; Ralph, nephew of Gilbert, 322-4

Dudum, Rog, 442

Duene, Wm de, 111

Dumnonia, kings of, xii n.

Dun, Duna, Dune, *see* Doune

Duneham, Duncham, Dunham, Done-ham, Ric de, 62, 64, 234; Rog (de), 70, 227, 355; ws. Eva and Frewara, 355; bro. Thos, 355; Wm, son of Rog, 355; ss. Wm and Thos, 227; Thos (de), 64-5, 110, 171, 249, 348, 381, 384, 416, 429, 434, 442; dau. Cecilia, 355; dau. Isobel, 111; Wm (de), 321, 349, 355, 364, 375, 380, 449-451; W., 339

Dunheved, Donnyend, Douneheved, Dounhevd, Dounheved, Dounhevde, Dounhevedburgh, Dounhevyd, Dou-nyend, Downhevde, xi, xii n, xxii, xxiii, xxxiii, 40; Bastestret in, 585: *see also* Bastehay; borough of, xxxiv, 127, 129-30, 134, 140, 149, 262, 268-9, 340-1, 585-6; burgesses, 21, 24, 34, 37-8, 262-4; mayor and burgesses, xxxiv; mulcture of, 13, 266; burial of the dead and visitation of the sick of, 34; castle, xi, xii n, xviii, xxviii n, xxxiv, 12, 13; farm of, 12, 13, 262, 539, 545-6; fortifications of, xi; mill under, 13, 266, 539, 545-6; new vill of, 11; well of, xiv n; reeves of xi, 11, 13, 308, 586, and *see* Bylker and Raynfry; cross of, 585; high street, xxxiii, 37; jurors of, 262; mayors, *see* Cobbethorn, Colyn, Fernehill, Fox, Miles, and Twyneo; mayor and commonalty of, xxxiii, xxxiv, 585; tithes of, xxxiv n, 35; charters dated at, 120, 129, 585; Benedict, xxiv and n; free bailiff of L Land, 37, 103, 120, 123, 127, 133-6, 139, 140-1, 142, 144, 145, 177, 195-6, 316, 325-6, 340-1, 573; Ric, 168. *See also* Launceston

Dunkeswell, Som, R(ichard), abbot of, 405; Hugh, monk of, 405

Dunstable, St Peter, Beds, Augustinian priory of, xv

Dunstanville, Normandy, *dép* Seine-Inf., Dunstavilla, Dunstanvile, Dunstan-vill, Dunstanvilla, Reg, earl of Corn, xi, xvi-xxii, xxvii, xl, 10-13, 16, 24, 26-7, 71, 81, 115-6, 244-6, 251-2, 262-6, 269, 382-4, 428, 430, 494n, 495-6, 498-500, 525, 526 and n, 527, 534, 537-42, 544-50, 556; and Count of Mortain, 262-3; charters of, xi and n, xix, xxi and n, 12, 13, 16, 27, 115, 415, 493, 525, 537-8; daus. of, *see* Denise and Meulan; m. of, *see* Corbet; w. of, *see* Beatrice; s. Hen, 'Hen fitz Count', lord of Liskeard, 494-7, 499; s. Nic, 537, 549-50; bro. Wm (= Wm de Marisco), 13, 332, 432, 435, 441; Reg, his s., 432, 435, 441; Ric 'his sheriff', 115; Hugh de, 11, 27, 493; Rob de, 11, 12, 13, 71, 115, 251, 415, 428, 538; chaps of Earl Reg, Paganus and Rog, 549

Durand, Durandus, sheriff, 194; clerk, sheriff, 556; Rog, s. of, 517. *See also* son of Philip

Dutson in St Stephen by L, Doddestone, Dodeston, Dodestona, Dodistoun, Duddeston, Duddestuna, Dudeston, Dudestun, Dudyston, x, xxv, 3, 6, 230, 318-19; park of, 238; Gregory de, 73, 160, 211, 221-2, 237, 255-6, 350, 452; kt, 279; Phil de, 237; Sampson de, 238; Stephen (de), 168, 238; Wm de, 237-8

Duy, *see* Deweymeads

Dynham, Dyneham, Nic, 39; Oliver de, kt, 265; Ralph, *see* Dina. *See also* Duneham

Dyrahill, Rog de, 447

EADSINUS, 1

East Downend in Egloskerry, Estdown-end, La dunende, Ladunhende, 184-5

Eastry in Kent, document dated at, 264

Eastway in Morwenstow parish, Biestwey, Byestewey, xxxviii, 388-94; court at, 400

East Wivelshire, Estwevelschir, Est, rural deanery of, xxxi; dean of, 101, 408; and chapter of, 535; hundred of, 262, 557; bailiff of, 491, 557; *see also* Harlisdon; court of, 491

Ebor', Wm, justice, 216

Edeman, burgess of L, 3

Edmund, Earl of Corn, xxviii, 15-16, 57, 265, 393, 398, 548

St Edmundo, Wm de, justice at L, 216, 345

Edward, clerk, 243, 247, 441; master, 62, 241-2; reeve, 74

Edward the Confessor, king of England, ix; diploma of, 1; Edith, his w., Eadgydia, 1; feasts of, 127n

Edward I, king of England, 18-19, 25, 39-40, 262-5, 268-9, 271-2, 392-3, 395, 548

Edward II, 40, 329

Ridel, Geof, bp of Ely, 26, 116, 539
Ridgegrove in St Stephen by L, Riddes-
grave, mill of, xxv, 247; *see also*
Goodmansleigh, mill
Ridmerky, ford of, 83
Rigensona, Cola, burgess of L, 3
Rikehill, Wm, justice, 560
Rillaton, manor in Linkinhorne, Ridla-
tona, Ridlehtuna, Ridlethuna, Ridle-
tune, Rilletuna, Rillatune, Rillatona,
xiii and n, xxvii, 3, 114, 116, 265,
498, 537-9, 544-6, 548-50, 575; Geof
de, 245
Risdon (in Bratton Clovelly, Devon?),
Risduna, Rysdon, xxvi, 6, 275
Risoun, Ric, bailiff of L Land, 238
Riwald, Ruwold, bridge of, in Bridgerule,
Devon, 442
Robert, bp of Exeter, I, xvi n, xviii, xix,
xl, 7-8, 71, 244, 428; his chaps., *see*
Brictius, Roger; his chamberlain, 7;
Rob II, bp of Exeter, 428; count, *see*
Meulan, Mortain; earl of Gloucester,
xvii-xx; master, 234; archdeacon of
Totnes, 284n, 335; parson of St
Martin by Looe, 478; priors of L, I,
11, 288, 382-3; II, 600; *see also*
Fissacre; dean of L college, xiii; vicar
of Launcells, 414; vicar of Poughill,
412; priest, 210; vice-archdeacon of
Cornwall, 96; chap. of Kilkhampton,
401; prior of Bodmin, 81, 224; canon
of L, 86; clerk, 188; arm-bearer, 79;
Rob and his f. Alfred, 597
Robert, Wm, justice, Simon, 114
Robyn, Jn, *see* Forde; Ric, *see* Athill; Wm,
119; Wm, bailiff of L Land, 318
Roddun(e), Rodden (in St Germans?),
485-7; mill, 486-7
Rodyngton, Rob, feodary of the prince,
126
Roffens', lord Solomon de, justice, 392
Roger, Anglicus and w. Alice, 281;
archdeacon of Barnstaple, 335, 432;
chap., 97, 252, 289; chap. of L castle,
32-3; chap. to Earl Reg, 549; chap.
of Rob I, bp of Exeter, 71; clerk, 58,
60, 430, *see also* son of Lipsus; priest,
210; priors of L, I, 371, II, 273, 287,
*see also* Combrygge; secretary, 81;
vicar, 299
Rogger, Thomasia, dau. of Rob, 195-6
Roket(e)park, field in St Martin by Looe,
469-70
Ronald, Jn, Joan, widow of, 129
Rooke in St Kew, Rugog, 94
Roos, Baldwin, 197; Jn, 315; Wm, 168
Roose in Treneglos, Ros, 219
Ros, Jn, of Tresmeer, 226; Nic de, juror,
57; Nic de, 206; Rob de, 373
Rosecraddock in St Cleer, Rethirhaduc,
Rethtraduc, xxvi, 6
Rosendur, Rosymdur, Rolyndur, in Lane-
ast, 190-1
Rosymdur, land of in Laneast, 190
Rosmarch, 6; Wm de, 274
Rouald, Wm, juror, 491
Rous, Ric, 158
Roydron, Byroydron, Byroidron, Byror-

Roydron—*cont.*
dron, Stephen, 45, 151-2, 195, 302,
319-20
Rufus, Wal, 110; Wm, xxiv n.
Ruffus, Ralph, s. of Geof, 172; Hamelin,
de Braderig, 74; Thos, 62
Rugemore, meadow in Otterham, 380
Rugog, *see* Rooke
Rupe, Ralph de, 464
Rupem, land at, 159
Rus(s)ell, Jn, de Talcarn, juror, 57; Lucy,
widow, lady of Pendrym, 478; Nic,
mayor of Liskeard, 600; Rob, 266;
Gwaryn s. of Rob, 284; Rog, lord of
Pendrym, 464
Ryche, Jn, 175

Slade, Rob, 404
Saer, Ric, 436
Saget, Saiet, physician, 244; priest, 223,
382-4
Saghier, Thos, juror, 491
Saint, Sanctus, St, *see* next word
Salisbury, Saresberiensis, bp of, chancel-
lor of King Henry I, 28; diocese
of, 87, 92; precentor and succentor
of, xxxv, 92
Saltash, Saltesse, 351
Sancy, Jocelin, 244
Scachard, Skachard, Scacherd, Jn, 127,
chap., 318, parson of Marhamchurch,
319-20
Scarne, Scardon, in Dunheved/S. Pether-
win, xxii, xxiii, 35, 319-20
Scharpe, S(c)herpe, Scherpp(e), Sherpa,
Wal, 146; Wm, 123, 125, and w.
Margery (Margaret), 143-5
Scorch, Wm and w. Matilda, 484
Scota, Wal, 284
Scoutte, Jn, 516
Screek in St Martin by Looe, Loscruk,
Luskruk, Loskruc, 469-70, 477
Seaton, river, Saythen, Setthul, 486, 492
Seccombe, *see* Southcombe
Segarus, canon, 244
Sela, *see* Algar
Sele, Jn, 467
Sellario, Hervey de, 34
Selman, Solman, Jn de Nywenham, 104-
5
Semeston (Semersdown in N. Tamerton),
Wm, 591
Semyslond in St Martin by Looe, 470
Senchia, w. of Ric, earl of Corn, q.v.
Sergeaux, Sergyaux, Ric de, kt and juror,
261; Ric, sheriff of Corn, 491; Wm,
rector of St Martin by Looe, 467,
469-72; Jn, rector, 474; *see also*
Cergeaux
St Sergius, *see* Angers
Serle, Jn, juror, 50; Luke, 506; Rog,
juror, 510
Serlo, chap., 80, 224, 594; dean of Exeter,
527-8; merchant, 80; *see also* Malneun
Serpewns, ploughland, 217
Seten, Jn de, juror, 53
Settone, Jn de, 66

South Beer in Boyton, Suthbere, 64
South Carne in Altarnun, xvi n.
South(e)combe, Seccombe, Ric, 572-3
Southerthyscote, *see* Harscott
South Petherwin, St Paternus, South
   Piderwyn, Southpiderwyne, Southpy-
   derwyn, xii, xix, xxii and n, xxiv,
   xxv, xxx, xxxi; cemetery of, 34;
   church of, 101; vicars of, xxiii, 35
   *and see* John; custodian of church of,
   *see* Ralph the clerk; tithes of, xxii,
   xxiii. *See also* Doune
Spaillard, Ric, 70
Sparke, Adam, official of bp of Exeter,
   294
Spigornell, Spygurnell, Hen, justice, 186,
   262, 264
Spiria, Rog, chap., 36
Spitel, Wluricus de, 74; land (site of
   hospital of Gillemartin in St Stephen
   by L?), 6
Sprachelieius, 74
Sprakel, Rob, 97
Sprakelin, Mordant, 11; Rob, 416
Spritsland in Kilkhampton, Sprutesland,
   Spruteslond, xxvii n, 402; Alan de,
   396, 402-3, 420-1
Spugernell, Thos, tailor, and w. Joan,
   328
Spycer, Wm, 283
Spynner, Jn, chap., 150-2, 154
Stabulo, Rog de and his bro., Wal de, 65
Stafford, Edmund, bp of Exeter, xx n,
   473, 503n
Stanbury, Hamelin de, 448; Wm and w.
   Alice, of Cleave, 400
Stanrewe (in Linkinhorne?), 538
Stanwen, Wm, juror, 312
Stapeldon, Thos de, canon of Exeter, 100
Staphanes laca, stream, 274
Stapledon, Wal, bp of Exeter, 503
Stoterigg,     Stoterych,     Stoterigch,
   Stotrygge, Jn, 319; Jn sen and jun,
   173-4; Ric, 69, 222, 258, 356; Wm,
   168, 228, 231, 314
Staunton, Hervey de, justice, 262, 264;
   Wm de, justice, 418, 463
Stede, Ric, 385
Stephen, chap. of St Juliot, 343-4; prior
   of L, 37-8, 49-50, 54, 102-3, *see also*
   Tredidon; owner of advowson of
   Luffincott, xxx-xxxi
St Stephen, xvi, xxii
St Stephen by L, ix, xi-xii, xxii, xxiv-
   xxvi, xxx, 14, 23-4, 171, 172n;
   cemetery of, 34; chapels of, 226, 294:
   *see also* Tresmeer; church of, xx-xxi,
   xxxi, 7, 8, 12, 13, 14, 22, 23, 34,
   171, 172n, 226; guardian of church
   of, xxx, 22; parishioners of, xxx, 22-
   3; demesne of, xxxvii, 591; foundation
   charter of college, xiv, 5; granted to
   see of Exeter, 2; lands of, xii, xiv,
   xvi, xxv, xxxvii, 14, 305; market
   and priory of, *see under* Launceston;
   regular canons at, xiv, xvi, xxi, xxx;
   secular canons of, xii, xxi, 3, 4, 9,
   10; dean Ralph, 4, 17; dean Rob, 3;
   sacristan of, *see* Geoffrey; tower of,

St Stephen by L—*cont.*
   xvii, xix, xxi, 12, 13; well of, 274;
   free tenants by homage of priory,
   xxx, xxxvii, 22
St Stephen, Exeter, church of, 2, 8
Stephen, king of England, xi, xvi-xx, 2n;
   charters of, 9, 29
Stephen(e)ston, Wal de, 445
Stingedelace (Codda in Altarnun), 92
Stoddona, Hugh de, 442
Stoke(s), Osbert de, chap., 459
Stoke Climsland, Clymeslaund, xxxvii-
   xxxviii, xl, 553; *see also* Climsland
Stokhay, Rob de, 35
Stonard, Rob, 54, 151, 153
Stonfordbeare in Brixton, Devon, 287;
   Tounland, 287
Stonore, Jn de, justice, 287, 378
Storme, Wm, 294
Stourscombe in Lawhitton, Sturescombe,
   273
Strange, Nic, 208; and w. Joan, 439
Stratton, Stratuna, xxvi; church of St
   Andrew, 6, 405n, 415-19, 422, 424,
   545-6; glebe of, xxxvi, xxxviii, xl,
   420-3, 427; vicars of, 225, *and see*
   Andrew, Creke, Kayinges, Treludek,
   Trewan; vicarage, 422; tithes of,
   xxxv, 422-3; land in, 425-6; rent in,
   150-1; assession at, xxxix; lords of,
   *see* Albo Monasterio, Turet; manor,
   415, 545-6; documents dated at, 419-
   21, 425-6; Gervase de, 317, 397;
   Gervase, clerk, s. of Rob, 420-1; Rog
   de, 398; *see also* Graunt
Stratton hundred, xxix
Strenn, Ailricus, 17
Stripa, Nic, 378
Stryke, Wm, juror, 150
Strylond (in Treneglos?), 219n
Stukeman, Jn, 322-3
Stummecat, land in St Gennys, 338
Subligny, Normandy, *dép* Manche, Sul-
   (l)eigny, Sulleny, Sullineio, Sulney,
   Hascullus, 77; Hasent de, 77; Ralph
   de, lord of Fawton, 78, 79n, 82, 88;
   Ascuil, f. of Ralph, 78; Jn de, gf. of
   Ralph, 78; Jn de, 79-80; Adam, bro.
   of Jn de, 80; Hastutus, s. of Jn de,
   xxxvi and n.
Suffolk, Sudfulc, properties in, 8
Sulling, Thos, abbot of Tavistock, 598
Surrey, Surreia, properties in, 8
Sussex, Sudsexa, properties in, 8
Suthmore, meadow in Otterham, 380
Sutton, Gatterus de, 477; Ric de, juror,
   446; Wm and w. Alice, 303
Sutton in Boyton, Sec(c)un', 74
Sutton in Linkinhorne, 498, 544
Sweetwells in Laneast, Suetewill, 217-18
Swem, Ric, de Mota, 114
Swyndon, Wm de, clerk, 224, 433
Sydenham Damarel, Devon, Sideham,
   rector of, xxxvi, 298-9; vicar of, 299
Symon, Jn, chap., 585; Ric, 425-6; Rob
   de Bodsyny, 122; Wm de´Liskeard,
   juror, 51
Symond, Wm, 402

Trefrize in Linkinhorne—*cont.*
545-6, 556-7; tithing, 557; wood of, 556, 559
Tregadillet in St Thos by L, Tregadilet, Tregadylet, Tregudilet, xxv, xxxviii, 3, 6, 159, 168-9; wood of, 159; Martin de, 255-6
Tregarros, land, 159
Tregarya, Ric de, 312; *see also* North Tregeare
Tregastick in Morval, xvi n
Tregear in Gerrans, Treger, manor, 8
Tregeare in St Gennys, Treger, 223
Tregeare, North, in Tresmeer, *see* North Tregeare
Tregemon, 3
Tregeryoc(h) (Tregarrick in Pelynt), Anger de, 486-7
Treglasta in Davidstow, Treglastan, manor, xiii, xxvi, 3, 95, 280n; Thos, juror, 354
Treglestek, Peter, chap., 516
Treglith in Treneglos, Treglegha, 207
Treglum in Tresmeer, Tregloman, Tre-glomma, Treglumma, xxv, xxxv, 3, 6, 117-19, 213, 289; mill of, xxv, 214
Tregoiffe in Linkinhorne, Tregoff, Tren-gof, 545-6, 556-7
Tregorrek, Jn, xxxiv, 38, 54, 151-3
Tregoth (Tregoad in St Martin by Looe?), lord Ric, 461
Tregow, Ralph, LL.D., 471
Tregrella, Auger de, 78
Tregrilla, Tregrille (Tregrill in Menheniot?), Odo de, 483; Ric de, 332; lord Ric de, 461; Wm de, 575
Tregu, Rob, juror, 354
Treguddick in S. Petherwin, Tregod(d)ek, Tregudek, Margaret, 328; Nic, 118-19, 162; Nic jun, 168, 490; Nic sen, 327; Ric de, juror, 57; Rob, 103, 154, 585; Wm de, 53, 108. Cf. Godek
Tregyn, Hen de, 230
Treheer in Liskeard, Treyer, Rob, juror, 509
Trehole in St Gennys, *see* Attehole
Trehonnudr', 3
Trehorsta, Jn de, 593
Trehummer in Tresmeer, Trehemener, xxv, 6
Treiagu, Treagu, Treyaggu, Jn de, kt, 57 (juror), 95, 280, 351, 396; sheriff and steward of Corn, 372
Trekarl, *see* Trecarrell
Trekee in St Teath, Trenchioc, Trenchiek, 545-6
Trekelland in Lezant, xvi n, 6
Trekeneth (Trekennick in Altarnun?), 6
Trekenner in Laneast, Trekenever, Tre-kynn(ev)er, Tregenner, xxv, 3, 159, 564-5
Trelabe in Linkinhorne, Trelaba, 557; Jn de, 557
Trelaske in Lewannick, Trelask, Trelo-scus, Trelosk(e), Trelonch, common of pasture in, 97, 103, 105, 106; Andrew de, kt, 35; Jn Mulys, lord of, 102-3; Ric de, 96, 97, 103, 167,

Trelaske in Lewannick—*cont.*
308, 309; Rog (de), 21, 61, 82, 176, 189, 193, 221, 232, 369, 448-9, 462, 485, 499, 529, 565, 567, 576
Trelawne in Pelynt, Trewelowen, Trew-elaen, 454; Jn Herle, lord of, 103
Trelawny, Trelauny, Jn (de), 20, 106, 157, 454; Jn jun, 106; Jn, kt, 104-6; Ric, 296, 513, 573a, 574, juror, 51; Wm, 103, 122, 163, 179, 305, 490, 514-15. *See also* Trelouny
Trelay in St Gennys, *see* La Ley
Treleuny, Trelenny, Jn de, 16, juror, 53
Treliever in Mabe, Treliver, manor, 8
Trelouthet, Trelodat, Trelouthat (Trelu-dick in Egloskerry?), xxvi, 3, 40, 52, 183, 268-9
Trelouny, Jn, 128, 151-3; Jn de, clerk, 206; Wm (de), 123, 180, 231, 271, 283, 341, 579-83; Wm, s. of Wm, 196; Jn s. of Wm de, 197-9. *See also* Trelawny
Treludek, Treluddek, Treladyk, David, 328, 455; David, canon, 296, 474, 508; David, sub-prior of L, 37, 591; Jn, 38, 121, 150-2, 180, 283, 473, 490, 513-15, 573; Stephen, 123, 125; Wm, vicar of Stratton, 425-6. *See also* Trelouthet
Tremaine, parish, Tremen, xxi, xxvi; advowson of, 271; chapel of, 223
Trematon in St Stephen by Saltash, Tremeton, 269, 351; castle at, xi; honour of, xx
Tremayll, Rob, 162
Tremayna in St Gennys, 338
Trembraze in Liskeard, Trembras, Gil-bert de, 509
Tremoutha in St Gennys, 379
Tremuer, 6
Trenalt, Rog, juror, 491; *see also* Priez
Trenchard, Michael, 285
Trenchem, Adam, clerk, 224
Trenchioc, Trenchiek, *see* Trekee
Trencreek in St Gennys, Trencruk, mill of, 364
Treneglos, xxiv, xxv; master W. de, 343
Trenethdun, Randulph de, clerk, 236
Trenewith, Trenewyth, Stephen, 104-6, juror, 51
Trengayor in St Gennys, Trengeyr, 378; Geof de, Argentela his w. and Thos his s., 378
Trenode in Morval, Trenoda, 592; bridge, 485, 592; mill at, 592; Drogo de, w. Alice, and s. Jn, 487; Jn (de), 483, 485-6, 490, 592; his s. Nic de, 592 and n
Trenydelham, Peter, 162
Treryse, Alexander, 599; Nic (de), rector of Lapford, Devon, xxxii n, 595-6, 599
Tresallack in Stoke Climsland, Tresalac, Tresalak, Tresalet, 553; Ric de, 552-3; his s. Thos de, 551-2
Treskelly (in St Germans), Wm, juror, 491
Tresker, Treskeer, Resker, Reg, 133, 135, 150-2

# INDEX II: SUBJECTS

The index is intended to show points of interest and is not exhaustive.